the book of the
DOBERMAN
PINSCHER

joan mcdonald brearley

Cover photo:
Ch. Damasyn The Forecast (owned by Carol Selzle) and his daughter, Alisaton Rain Check (owned by Joanne and Gwyn Satalino). Photo by Miceli Studios, Ltd.

Frontispiece:
Beautiful William Brown portrait of Tess Henseler's Ch. Friederun v Ahrtal and Ch. Frederica v Ahrtal. This magnificent pair won Best Working Brace at the Westminster Kennel Club Show in 1953.

Distributed in the U.S.A. by T.F.H. Publications, Inc., 211 West Sylvania Avenue, P.O. Box 27, Neptune City, N.J. 07753; in England by T.F.H. (Gt. Britain) Ltd., 13 Nutley Lane, Reigate, Surrey; in Canada to the book store and library trade by Clarke, Irwin & Company, Clarwin House, 791 St. Clair Avenue West, Toronto 10, Ontario; in Canada to the pet trade by Rolf C. Hagen Ltd., 3225 Sartelon Street, Montreal 382, Quebec; in Southeast Asia by Y.W. Ong, 9 Lorong 36 Geylang, Singapore 14; in Australia and the south Pacific by Pet Imports Pty. Ltd., P.O. Box 149, Brookvale 2100, N.S.W., Australia. Published by T.F.H. Publications Inc. Ltd., The British Crown Colony of Hong Kong.

CONTENTS

Two Dobermans, Damasyn The Shawn and Damasyn The Aurien with Peggy Adamson and a Pan American Airlines Stewardess just before leaving San Francisco for their new home in Bangkok, Siam in 1948. They were purchased for Prince Bhanuband Yukol. Both were sired by Ch. Dictator von Glenhugel; Aurien was shipped in whelp to Damasyn Delegate.

DEDICATION
to
PEGGY ADAMSON

few people in the history of the breed have been more devoted to the Doberman Pinscher, or have served it so well in many capacities. This devotion has made her a legend in her own time.

"...when properly reared, it is a paragon of amiable fidelity."
    Philipp Gruenig, on the Doberman Pinscher.

ACKNOWLEDGMENTS

A book on a breed with such a rich heritage could not be undertaken without the help of many people willing to share their knowledge and the benefits of their years of experience.

First and foremost my sincere appreciation goes to Peggy Adamson for a wealth of valuable research material and rare old photographs and papers given so willingly, and for her enthusiasm over the book. Thanks are due to Mrs. Carl Muser and her daughter, Johanne, for ancient pedigrees, photographs and information from the early bygone era; to Len Carey for the last of his treasured photographs of Storm; to Dr. Howard Cohen for specific necessary information; to Kay Martin for obedience information; to Stephen McDonald for special research; and to Robert Shomer, D.V.M., for expert counsel.

Special thanks are extended to the staffs at the American Kennel Club library, the 42nd Street Library in New York City, and the Museum of Natural History.

I am grateful also for the assistance given by the "foreign correspondents" who supplied information on the Doberman in their countries; R.G. Hodges for reporting on the breed in Great Britain; to J.P. Schlesinger for breed progress in South Africa; to Mrs. Jackie Perry for breed development in Malaysia and Singapore; to Malcolm McDonald for facts from Australia; to Avi Marshak for news on the Doberman in Israel; and to Robin F. Hernandez, my liaison in Mexico.

A very special word of thanks goes to all of the Doberman fanciers all over the world proud enough to send photographs of their dogs to be included in this book devoted to a great breed—sleek, powerful, intelligent and beautiful—created to work with, and for, man.

Joan McDonald Brearley
New York City, 1976

ABOUT THE AUTHOR. . .

JOAN McDONALD BREARLEY

Joan Brearley has loved animals ever since she was old enough to know what they were. Over the years there has been a constant succession of dogs, cats, birds, fish, rabbits, snakes, turtles, alligators, squirrels, lizards, etc., for her own personal menagerie. Through these same years she has owned over thirty different breeds of purebred dogs, as well as countless mixtures, since the door was never closed to a needy or homeless animal.

A graduate of the American Academy of Dramatic Arts, Joan started her career as a writer for movie magazines, actress and dancer. She also studied journalism at Columbia University and has been a radio, television and magazine writer, writing for some of the major New York City agencies. She was also a television producer-director for a major network on such shows as *Nick Carter, Master Detective*, and has written, cast, directed, produced and, on occasion, starred in television film commercials. She has written material for such personalities as Dick Van Dyke, Bill Stern, Herman Hickman, Dione Lucas, Amy Vanderbilt and many others prominent in the entertainment world.

Her accomplishments in the dog fancy include being an American Kennel Club approved judge, breeder-exhibitor of top show dogs, writer for various dog magazines, author or co-author of many breed books including *This is the Afghan Hound, This is the Shih Tzu, This is the St. Bernard, This is the Bichon Frise, This is the Old English Sheepdog, This is the Siberian Husky, This is the Skye Terrier, This is the Alaskan Malamute, This is the Irish Setter,* and many others. For five years she was Executive Vice-President of the Popular Dogs Publishing Company and editor of *Popular Dogs* magazine, the national prestige publication for the dog fancy at that time.

Joan Brearley is just as active in the cat fancy, and in almost all the same capacities. She is editor of the Cat Fanciers Association Annual Yearbook and writes for the various cat magazines as well. Joan speaks at kennel clubs and humane organizations on animal legislation and has received many awards and citations for her work in this field, including an award from the Morris Animal Foundation.

At present Joan lives in a penthouse apartment overlooking all of Manhattan in New York City with three dogs and a dozen or more cats, all of which are Best in Show winners and have been professional models for television and magazines. Joan is proud of the fact that in her first litter of Afghan Hounds she bred a Westminster Kennel Club Group winner, Champion Sahadi (her kennel prefix) Shikari, the top-winning Afghan Hound in the history of the breed for many years.

In addition to her activities in the world of animals, Joan Brearley is a movie buff and spends time at the art and auction galleries, the theatre, creating needlepoint (for which she has also won awards), dancing, the typewriter—and the zoo!

1. THE HISTORY OF THE "MAN-MADE DOG" IN GERMANY

Herr Louis Dobermann, born on February 2, 1823, became a rent and tax collector and served during the evening hours as a police officer in the town of Apolda, in the state of Thuringia, in the south-central part of Germany. In 1880, while also keeper of the local dog pound, he decided to try his hand at breeding the perfect guard dog, the kind of dog he felt would serve as a protector for him as he made his rounds.

The German Pinscher dog existed in great numbers, of course, but Herr Dobermann believed he could produce, with the German Pinscher and the other available dogs in his pound, a new breed of guard dog better than any seen before. The German Pinscher was far from being considered a "handsome" dog but it possessed the alertness and aggressiveness that Herr Dobermann believed would be the essential foundation trait of his ideal dog. Herr Dobermann and two friends, one a grave digger and the other a church bell-ringer, made great strides in their plans during those early years. While no written records were kept on these earliest breedings between the German Pinschers and the various other dogs of unknown ancestry, Herr Dobermann's "ideal dogs" were black, medium-sized, rather massive and came to be known as Dobermann's dogs, then Thuringer Pinschers or Plizeilich Soldatenhunds.

It was also becoming obvious that during those early years of development the Rottweiler had been introduced into the breeding program. Herr Dobermann owned purebred Rottweilers and German Shepherds, and it became evident that it was the Rottweiler that gave the breed the additional size and stature. It was actually to become one of the strongest influences in establishing the strain. It was also the Rottweiler that gave some of the longer, wavier coats that they quickly bred out since they were undesirable according to Herr Dobermann's plan. It is also believed that the German Shorthaired Pointer, the Great Dane and the Weimaraner which introduced the genes for the blue dogs, were all a part of the breeding program. A man named Stegmann also encouraged Herr Dobermann to incorporate some of the blood of his strongest cattle-driving dogs as well. The Manchester Terrier influence cannot be denied either, and it should be recalled that the Manchester Terrier was considerably larger in size at that time. This certainly did not diminish the added size the Rottweiler and the cattle dogs brought into the breeding!

It is interesting to note also that it was the Manchester Terrier which also introduced the black "thumb prints" in the tan area on the Doberman paws. These markings are still required in the Manchester breed today and on occasion are found in Doberman puppies also, but they disappear during the first few months of life. The Manchester certainly added refinement to the dogs of the time, as well as their color and type, and the short, shiny coat which Herr Dobermann had desired in his "master plan" for the breed.

There are also those who hold to the belief that yet another breed of dog was introduced into the line in those early days. The Beauceron was said to have been bred to some of the original dogs used and also contributed a measure of both size and color. Even though the Beauceron was a French breed, they were known to be in the area of Thuringia at the time Herr Dobermann was actively perpetuating his breeding program, and at his disposal.

EARLY REGISTRATIONS

The first entry in a German stud book for a Doberman was in 1893, and the dog was named Bosco. A bitch named Caesi was whelped and registered the following year, and a dog which resulted from a mating of these two was the single entry in the stud book for 1895. He was named Sieger Prinz Matzi v Groenland, though even by the earliest Standard for the breed he was far from the desired representative of the breed. In spite of his lack of perfection, he was awarded the German championship title of "Sieger."

This was of little consequence, however, since Matzi proved to be lacking in prepotency also. Within three generations the stud books failed to show a record of any continuing line bearing his name.

Fortunately for the breed, interest in the continuation of a Doberman dog was burgeoning in Thuringia, which was a considerable distance from the Frankfurt area of Germany, where a dog named Prinz Matzi was enjoying local stud success. However, it was only fitting and proper that Thuringia earned the reputation as the foundation base for the breed since it was actually where it all began.

Dogs named Lux, Schnupp, Landgraf and Rambo, and bitches named Tilly I v Groenland, Helmtrude, Hertha and Elly formed the nucleus of the breed there, and it was these 'Dobermanns' that accounted for the early significant registrations in the 1896 stud book .

A photograph of the Royal Doulton figurine of Ch. Rancho Dobe's Storm, rendered in 1953 at the peak of his popularity and still sold around the world. Photograph courtesy of Royal Doulton.

Herr Otto Goeller, also of Apolda, and eventual successor to the plan and principles of Herr Dobermann in the perfecting of this new breed, owned and bred many fine dogs—at one point in such numbers that there were complaints about the noise from the neighbors and he had to cut down considerably. Among the best of his dogs was Graf Belling v Thueringen. While never attaining the title himself, Graf sired Sieger winners when bred to a bitch named Ullrich's Glocke v Thueringen. Herr Goeller also owned one of the acknowledged great bitches in those early days: Freya v Thueringen, whelped in 1898 and sired by Schnupp x Helmtrude. His brown dog, Junker Hans v d Ronneburg, proved to be a potent stud and a show winner in those days when the browns were competing right along with the blacks.

Other important Dobermans in the 1890's were Jungfer Grete, Ines v Thueringen, Gerhilde v Thueringen, and Winfried v Thueringen, a son of Landgraf and Hertha that became one of the very first Dobermans to be exported to Switzerland. Lady v Ilm-Athen, whose exact pedigree was in doubt because of a reported, and actually quite obvious, Manchester Terrier outcross, produced the legendary Prinz v Ilm-Athen. The popular Prinz was sired by Grief v Groenland and whelped in 1901. Both Lady and her son Prinz did much to intensify the Manchester Terrier refinement and coloration in the breed at that time.

Herr Muenzenberg of Giebichstein whelped a litter of Dobermans in December of 1897, by Rambo x Elly, which produced a dog named Junker Slenz v Thueringen. In the early days dog clubs purchased show dogs in the name of their club, and Junker became famous as the property of the Frankfurt Club that allowed him to be used at stud and was therefore responsible for contributing great improvement to the breed. Descendents of his line, through a successful breeding with a bitch named Leporello v d Nidda, established the breed in Switzerland right after the turn of the century.

In 1898 a bitch named Tilly I v Groenland produced a litter of five which were to make their mark on the breed. Sired by a dog named Lord and out of Schnupine, Tilly I whelped Gelling, Greif, Krone, Lottchen and Tilly II for owner Goswin Tischler. The sire was a dog named Lux, and because of the great quality was thereafter referred to as the "five star litter." Tilly I also whelped a dog named Troll v Groenland whose daughter Flora v Groenland was the dam of the previously mentioned Leporello v d Nidda which launched the Swiss Doberman line.

At any rate, by the end of the 1890's the Doberman was still gaining in popularity, but was also very much the embodiment of a coarse, thick, medium-sized dog, which resembled the Rottweiler more than any other dog credited with having been introduced somewhere along the line during the previous two decades devoted to its development.

In 1899 it officially became known as the Dobermannpinscher, named after its creator, Herr Dobermann, five years after he died. . . It was also the year that Otto Goeller organized the National Dobermannpinscher Club in Germany, approved by the Commission of Delegates, Germany's "highest authority" in the dog world. One year later the Standard for the breed was drawn up and immediately approved and accepted by the German Kennel Club.

With the exception of a few small changes regarding the conformation for Dobermans, the Standard has remained basically the same over the years, though it was said to be at the time one of the most precise and demanding for any breed.

DOBERMANS IN GERMANY FROM THE TURN OF THE CENTURY

1900 was the year that the black and tan Doberman was recognized in Germany, followed by the browns and blues in 1901. It was also at the beginning of this century that Otto Goeller published his pamphlet on the breed entitled, "The Dobermannpinscher in Word and Picture."

At the beginning of the twentieth century in Germany the Doberman had become quite popular and more clearly defined among the dog breeds. To such an extent, as a matter of fact, that in 1904 one of the strongest and most influential stud dogs in the history of the breed came to the fore. His name was Hellegraf v Thueringen. By 1906, the year the first stud book was issued, another prominent dog, known for his good, rich color, came along to further strengthen the type. His name was Sturmfried v Ilm-Athen, and together with Hellegraf and Sturmfried's grandson, Modern v Ilm-Athen (whelped in 1909), we find their names in the pedigrees of almost every Doberman Pinscher in the world today.

The first decade in the 20th century saw the requirement of stud book entries for every breeding animal and the names of dogs and bitches which were to become prominent during this first part of a new era were contained therein. Goswin Tischler's name was being mentioned more and more in praise of his "five star litter" and Prinz v Ilm-Athen became even more renowned as a potent sire. While noted for his desirable color and markings his line was also noted for its sharpness.

Certain kennel names became prominent during the first decade; Groenland and Thueringen continued to be outstanding producers and Ilm-Athen, Isenburg, Aprath, Burgwall, Luetzellinden, Langen, and Elster were breeding Dobermans. A bitch named Lady v Calenberg which was never registered became recognized as a dominant factor in determining the prototype of the Doberman in the years ahead.

Another prominent male of the decade was Hans v Thueringen. Hans was the first widely exhibited "brown" Doberman and for this reason called much attention to color variation in the breed. But in spite of the "newness" of the chocolate coloring, he was a winner at the shows in South Germany. His only predecessor was Gunzo v Thueringen, born in July 1900, who actually has claim to the title of being the first brown Doberman to be exhibited at any show. Gunzo was a Belling x Freya son, but was of such poor "Doberman" quality that he was not widely shown, therefore, Hans took over in the show ring to head the brown category. The bitch Thina v Aprath, whelped in November 1903, whelped two brown Dobermans when bred to Tell v Kirchweyhe which were to do well in the breed—Fedor and Hans v Aprath.

These first ten years of the new century also produced Beda Frischauf in 1905. She was to become famous as the dam of Ch. Lord v Ried. This was also the decade of the scandal which resulted from the owner of a dog called Immo v Isenburg superimposing a picture of Leporello v d Nidda over one of Immo, though it was agreed that Immo was actually the better dog! However, the deed was discovered and the owner barred from membership in the German Verein.

The name Edel v Ilm-Athem became prominent in the breed during this period, as did Lotte v Ilm-Athen, a Sturmfried daughter noted also as the dam of the famous Modern v Ilm-Athen. Another bitch worthy of mention was Jula v d Engelsburg, whelped in 1907; she was a daughter of Benno v Thueringen. Her son Theo v d Funkenburg and a granddaughter, Senta v Jaegerheim, helped to establish the Blankenburg strain. Marko v Luetzellinden, whelped in 1908, was widely acknowledged as one of the greatest brown stud dogs to date. Referred to by Philipp Gruenig as "anatomically and aesthetically well nigh perfect," this dog was descended from Fedor v Aprath and Zilla v Luetzellinden and was one of the first Dobermans referred to as having "elegance." Unfortunately, he was a coward and passed this most regrettable trait on to his get. We must recall that even in the earliest days in the breed the Dobermans were either most aggressive or very cowardly. There were also those of his get that carried on his desirable traits, to be sure, but in the Doberman breed cowardice is most unfortunate. Both the good and the bad about Marko was to be seen in the breed for many, many succeeding generations.

This was also the time of a dog who gained fame as the sire of Prinz Modern. Lux Edelblut v Ilm-Athen never gained success on his own, and as legend has it, he spent the last years of his life as a guard dog chained outside a brewery.

In 1908 a black bitch named Stella appeared on the scene. Her background was unknown, other than that she had been born in Ried,

Hessia; it was concluded after an investigation by the authority Philipp Gruenig that her sire was a black English Greyhound. Since all sorts of breeding experiments were being conducted in the area at the time this is highly likely, according to Mr. Gruenig. It was even more likely since it was reported that her daughter Sybille v Langen was said to be visibly like a Greyhound. In spite of her ancestry Sybille was to become the foundation bitch of the Silberberg kennels, which along with the Blankenburg strain had a marked influence on the breed, especially through Heidi, Hispa and Bayard v Silberberg.

It was also believed at the time that it was this Greyhound blood which brought back to the Doberman breed the desired aggressive personality which had been somewhat "watered down" with the placid Manchester Terrier breeding.

In 1906 the blue Doberman Gunzelin v Altenburg was whelped. He was an excellent dog in conformation and appearance, but one that did not pass on his quality to his progeny. In 1908 another blue of

Champion Modern v Simmenau-Rhinegold, famous European Doberman imported to America by the Rhinegold Kennels in Detroit, Michigan. His pedigree includes the early German doberman Modern v Ilm-Athen.

quality was born. This bitch was almost pure Alm-Athen lines and was named Loni v d Wendenburg. Unfortunately, her line died out before the blues could be firmly established at her kennel.

However, the blues and later the fawns, or Isabellas, were rather rare and never really were appreciated or acceptable in any country. To this day they are not recognized in Germany. It was thought that it was of sufficient concern to try and produce good blacks and browns. Perhaps this was true, since it must be remembered that when we speak of color in those years the blacks were almost a gray color, and most of the dogs bore white patches on their chests. The "tan" as we know it today was more of a "yellow" or parchment color than an actual shade of tan or rust.

In 1909 the second stud book was issued in Germany, and by 1910 other kennels were appearing and registering their best stock. Dogs bearing the names of Roemerschanz, Wendenburg, Haide, Dambachtal, Deutz, Hohen Burg, Hoernsheim, Eckardtstein, Boerde, Hornegg, Frohse and others were creating what Philipp Gruenig referred to as the Golden Age of Dobermans. . . an age which was to peak right up to an abrupt halt with the arrival of World War I. The Dobermans had made such progress during the first decade since its recognition, however, that at the 1910 Cologne Dog Show there was an entry of 105 dogs!

In May, 1912 Assad v Roederberg was whelped. Although listed in the stud book as a "blue," Assad was actually the first fawn, or Isabella, born in Germany.

WORLD WAR I AND THE DOBERMAN IN GERMANY

The year 1916 was a year of famine in Germany, and the Doberman fanciers began to see the beginning of the end of the Golden Age of Dobermans. The devastating malnutrition brought on by the famine, which was ravaging all of Europe, and the hardships of all kinds brought on by the war, made the breeders realize there would be a terrible toll on the canine population as well. In his Doberman book Philipp Gruenig tells of his leaving for the front lines after 18 of the half-grown puppies in his kennel had to be put down with strychnine. He kept two favorites, a bitch named Walhall v Jaegerhoff and a dog, Ebbo v Adalheim. But they too eventually succumbed to malnutrition.

This was the case with many of the breeders in Europe all through the war. Even though it was reported that over 6,000 dogs had been trained for war services, those that remained behind with their owners were always in jeopardy. If they were not exported to foreign countries or sold to foreign soldiers who took them home with them after the Armistice, they risked being devoured by hungry people and having to be put down by their owners.

Fortunately for the breed in Germany, a dog named Burschel v Simmenan was whelped in 1915 and survived the rigors of the war; this dog was largely responsible for getting the Doberman breed started once again. His son, Lux v d Blankenburg, and a daughter, Leddy v d Blankenburg, and a grandson, Alex v d Sinohoele, were used extensively in breeding during the post-war era and got the breed on its feet once again. By way of mention, Lux became one of the greatest sires of all time in Germany and died in the United States in 1931 at a very ripe old age!

But there is no denying that by the time World War I ended the majority of the top quality Dobermans in Europe had been sold to the United States. Lux was exported to the U.S.A., and a dog named Ari v Sigalsburg was sent here but died shortly after his arrival and before producing anything in this country.

In 1916 a dog named Salto v Rottal also survived the conditions in Germany. This brown dog did little in his own country but left a heritage to the breed through his get in Czechoslovakia, especially in the Funkenburg Kennels lines.

1917 produced the famous Troll v d Blankenburg, and at least a half dozen major bloodlines developed from his stud services, including a Russian strain. Troll was sent to California and was important there as a stud in the early days. In spite of the trials of the war, 1917 also produced the black Achim v Langerode and the brown dog Zeus v Parthengrund, which helped keep the breed alive.

Ch. Lux v d Blankenburg, whelped in 1918 and imported by Glenn Staines for his Pontchartrain Kennels in Detroit. This great sire had a strong influence on the breed and died in 1931. This rare and treasured photograph was taken of Lux in his old age and is used through the courtesy of the Thornes.

Ch. Hamlet v Herthasee, born in 1926 in Germany. His sire was Alto v Signalsburg x Comtess v Steyerberg. Philipp Gruenig considered Hamlet the best progenitor of that year. Hamlet's brown mother carried both the Blankenburg and Langerode blood on her paternal side. Ikos v Siegerstor, Bessie v Brandenburg and Alraune v Abendrot bore witness of his quality and power in Germany.

This second decade of the 20th century saw names like Thessa v Ostersee, Senta v Nesselrode, Melitta v Parthengrund, Asta Schirback and Meta v Ostersee carrying on the breed during the tough times, and in 1919 Carlo v d Koningstad came onto the scene and became the most important dog of that period. He was of Dutch breeding, with all the great dogs of the past represented in his pedigree. He was just what the war-depleted Doberman bloodlines needed to pick up again. While he made his mark as was intended, this dog also was sold to America. His son Apollo v Schuetzeneck was left to carry on, before he too was sold abroad.

Bitches were among the survivors also, and Adela v Ostern, Lotte v Stresow, Asta v d Finohoehe, Anita v d Blankenburg, Freya v Rottal and Dora II v d Falkensteinerburg all contributed to the breed.

But the ravages of the war were apparent in the stud books. . . owners and buyers alike neglected to enter papers, and the abandoned and no longer needed war dogs were set free to fend for themselves. Many were appropriated by interested Doberman breeders, of course, but the dogs' parentage was always to be a mystery. Certain considerations were made by the kennel club when applications were made, and Volume VIII of the D.P.Z. contains more than 100 entries of pedigrees which actually can only be guessed at, but the quality of the animal was such that breeding to restore the breed was acceptable though the Standard was revised, for the first time since its original drafting in 1899, in 1920 and again in 1925.

1920 came to be the year that was the most productive up to that time. The occupation troops in Germany were buying dogs and so were foreign countries, and at good prices. Breeding was going full speed ahead and there seemed to be a market for Dobermans all over the continent. The old German breeding was speaking well for itself in other lands and everyone seemed to be wanting more.

It was in this year of 1920 that Alex v d Finohoehe came along. He possessed a remarkable pedigree but was unappreciated and not used to advantage in his native Germany. It was only after his exportation to Czechoslovakia for a nominal fee that he proved his worth in that country through his outstanding progeny.

By 1921 the bitches began to come into their own, with Ilsa v d Koningstad, Cilly v d Spree, Fredegunde v Gernsicht, Dora v Eckardtsburg, Agathe v Roemerwall and Alruna Haeusser, the latter being very valuable to the Schnabenhuck strain.

1921 was also the year the Dutch-bred dog Favorite v d Koningstad was exhibited all over Europe and then exported to the U.S.A. where he was said to be the best sire to arrive in America up to that time.

During these post war years the numbers of registrations grew to such proportions that it is impossible to recall them all here. One year the bitches would excel over the males, the next year it would be the other way around. All during the 1920's the breed continued to prosper and grow in number with the new accent on youth. New blood and new breedings were giving new impetus and a new look to the Doberman. By the mid-twenties the stud book recorded over ten thousand registrations and the consolidated Doberman clubs in Germany boasted a membership of nearly 3,500!

1924 was the year Claus v Sigalsburg excelled, in 1925 it was Figaro v Sigalsburg, and in 1926 Hamlet v Herthasee was the first name which came to mind. 1926 was also the year that the breed seemed to suddenly sink into a spell of disinterest. Their popularity waned in spite of an impressive presentation of both show dogs and quality breeding stock. Good dogs appeared and were shown, but it wasn't until 1929 when a daughter of Lux, Freya v Burgund, was whelped that this brown bitch was of importance to the breed because of her illustrious background.

THE THIRTIES

In 1930 and 1931 Philipp Gruenig considered only two dogs worthy of mention in his book on the breed. They were Kanzler v Sigalsburg, which went back to Alex v d Finohoehe and Troll v d Blankenburg, and in 1931 Kloth v Adalheim-Goldaue, which was a product of scientific breeding at that time based on Jaegerhof and Simmenau bloodlines.

In 1932 there were three dogs of quality bred. Asso v Memmingermau Cherloc v Rauhfelsen, mother of the world famous Jessy v Sonnenhoehe, Gretl v Kiènlesberg (later exported to Italy) and Jockel v Burgund, later exported to the U.S.A. where his "over-size" did not go so much against him. The outstanding bitch in Germany in 1932 was Asta v d Domstadt, and a Siegerin in 1934.

In 1933 it was "Troll's year." He became the outstanding stud dog in Germany from 1935 to 1937, when he was shipped to the U.S. But before he set sail for America he was used extensively on the top brood bitches in Germany; in 1938 about one half of all the dogs and bitches at the Sieger Show were direct descendants of the mighty Troll. This included the black Sieger and Siegerin, and the Second V dog. His daughter was Best of Breed. He also sired Reich Siegerin of 1937, Ossi v Stahlhelm. He was the only male to have won Best Breed at two consecutive Sieger shows, these in 1934 and 1935.

Two other black dogs came to prominence in 1933, Blitz v d Domstadt and Blank v d Domstad. A brown bitch, Alma v Sailerhaus, was outstanding and eventually made her championship in Switzerland; she was purchased for the betterment of the breed in that country.

The year 1934 was not a good year for Dobermans in Germany, but two black daughters of Charloc v Rauhfelsen appeared. Jessy v d

The World Sieger and Tri-International Champion Troll v d Engelsburg, imported in the early days by E. Bronstein of Peoria, Illinois. Troll was one of the most influential of all Dobermans in the U.S. and in the history of the breed. Whelped June 1, 1933, Troll was the outstanding stud in Germany from 1935 through 1937 when he was sent to the United States. The remarkable Sieger and Int. Ch. Muck v Brunia was his sire, his dam Adda v Heek. Troll was twice a German Sieger and a champion in Canada and the U.S. He was recognized also as "the world's greatest sire."

Ch. Kurt v d Rheinperle-Rhinegold, imported from Germany in the 1930's by Mr. John Zimmerman, who owns the Rhinegold Kennels in Detroit, Michigan. The sire was Astor of Westphalia x Anita v Immermannhoehe. Kurt was whelped on December 28, 1931.

Sonnenhoehe was one of them and became the second bitch to have whelped a Sieger and Siegerin (1938) in the same litter. She is the only bitch up to that time to have won Best of Breed at the Sieger shows for two consecutive years. Her show record in the United States was equally impressive. Gretl, her half sister, was a top show bitch also.

German dogs of prominence during 1935 were Moritz v Roedeltal, Carlo v Fasenenheim and Ossi v Stahlhelm. Ossi, a brown bitch, whelped a single litter before her exportation to the United States, with an impressive show career in this country.

1937 was a banner year with the whelping of Ferry v Rauhfelsen. Sired by Troll out of Jessy he was a top sire and an outstanding sire and show dog in America. His litter sister Freya v Rauhfelsen was the Reich Siegerin for 1938.

And such were the thirties in the Doberman's native Germany. It must be remembered that this accounting is by no means complete.

The dogs were too numerous to mention. It is suggested that anyone desiring a more complete listing of individual dogs secure Philipp Gruenig's book, *The Dobermann Pinscher—History and Development of the Breed*, in which he lists many more German dogs with the personal critique of each which he had recorded on a year to year basis. It is truly a must for every Doberman fancier interested in the background of the breed in its native land. The book has just been re-issued.

Ch. Jockel v Burgund, imported to the U.S. in 1935 by Owen West. Owned by James Randle. During his first one and one-half years in the show ring he won 22 all-breed Bests in Show.

It must also be noted that in World War II the importation of dogs from Germany was discontinued and the same hardships befell the dogs in Germany as had during World War I. We can only guess at the progress which could have been made had the war not interrupted these outcrosses to other lands, and yet we need only look around us to see that in spite of everything the war did not cause the Doberman either here or abroad to become extinct, or any less attractive to those of us who love the breed and were determined to carry it on.

A WORD TO THE WISE

We must remember when reading about Doberman history, especially in the earliest days, that litter registrations were kept informally and that individual registrations were highly inaccurate on occasion. We find over and over again that the same dog was registered under different names or suffixes and that there were many dogs with the same name.

For instance, there are no fewer than six Dobermans listed with the name Troll from 1912 to 1928. We find six Freyas, nine Astas,

Ch. Dow's Cassie v Kienlesberg, owned and bred by Bert Dow. This bitch was a winner in the late 1930's.

seven Carlos, five Lords, six Lottes and six Luxes, to mention a few. Therefore, it is important when reading or writing about the dogs to bear in mind the full name in each reference to them. We also find that there may be a deliberate different spelling of the same name to indicate a mother-daughter or father-son relationship, such as the dam with the name spelled Ilisa and the daughter, Ilissa, doubling the letter "s." Not only is it necessary for accuracy to properly identify each dog and its contribution to the breed, but it is necessary to be sure each dog gets proper identification. We have three Rolands in the breed during the first years of this century: Roland v Stahlhelm, Roland v Tale, an excellent sire and show dog, and Roland, later named Roland v d Haide, who did more harm than good to the breed. It would be regrettable indeed to have them confused.

It must also be remembered when recalling the history of the Doberman that in the old days the breed was praised and valued for its aggressiveness. While there are still places in the world where this is highly desired, especially where Dobermans are used for guard work, the accent today is on the temperament of the Doberman; it should be suitable as a companion and family dog and a dog that can be approached and handled without the danger of attack or, on the other extreme, showing evidence of shyness.

When you think of the original Doberman breed remember, too, that the original dogs used by Herr Doberman and Otto Goeller had cropped ears like most working breeds in those early times. And I mean cropped close...almost no ears at all. The theory behind this was that during battle there was little or nothing for their adversaries to "grab on to." Several decades later, more leather was allowed on the head, and the ears were said to have "the long crop."

There was also controversy on the hereditary factors concerning tails. Otto Goeller professed he had seen litters in which every puppy had a bobbed tail, and admitted nearly all of his dogs had one at birth. He claimed it was a result of the German Shepherd being introduced into the line. For awhile the ideal was said to be dogs with natural bob tails rather than those with docked tails. It was believed that breeding bob tail males to bob tail bitches produced bob tail offspring, and this, of course, is not necessarily so. It was soon a matter of fact that breeders could no more expect a natural bob tail anymore than a natural cropped ear.

GERMAN DOG SHOWS

Germany has two major dog show events each year which are comparable to our Westminster and DPCA Convention; the Bundessieger Show held in Berlin and the DV Championship Show. Popular German judges such as Ernst Wilking and Werner Niermann, both of whom have judged in this country as well, draw entries of over one hundred dogs.

Two famous early imports, Ch. Muck v Brunia and Ch. Ella v Graf Zeppelin, imported and owned by Mr. Owen A. West of the Lindenhof Kennels in Lake Forest, Illinois. Muck was a German Sieger and won Working Groups in this country during his show career; Ella was also a German Siegerin. Before leaving Germany, Muck was winner of the Great Wanderpreis in 1932 and of the Beauty Championship diploma; he also won the Bessie Wanderpreis for the best dog with a training degree.

Champion and Sieger Moritz von Rodeltal (whelped September 1, 1935) was sired by Blank v d Domstadt x Bubine v Deutschen-Eck. He was described by Philipp Gruenig as "a large dog with splendid body and excellent substance." However, he had congenitally faulty teeth, though he sired many promising puppies after his arrival in the United States. He was owned here by Sam H. Miller of Youngstown, Ohio.

In the early 1970's a new "test" was inaugurated in Germany for Dobermans, called a Korung. Dogs that pass the test are considered "angekort" and it is written on their papers. This rating may be obtained from the Dobermann Verein for owners who consider breeding their dog, and it is considered highly desirable in a breeding program. By 1973 only 16 Dobermans had passed the test based on the one originated with the German Shepherd Club program.

The test consists of first posing the dog while the judge checks it for conformation, recording his comments in detail. Then the dog is actually measured and this is recorded as well. The test for the dog's "nerves" varies at the judge's discretion but usually involves subjecting the animal to some minor form of psychological pressure while pacing through a group of people. After the "pressure" the dog is gaited and checked for proper movement. Pistol shots are fired while the dog is heeling, seated and in the down position. Any shyness and he is eliminated from further testing.

The dog is then gaited off lead, and a figure springs out totally without warning and attacks the dog. The dog is expected to bite immediately and hold on while receiving two blows across the back, with the attacker constantly and silently advancing on him. Then the dog is taken away and sent after the attacker from a distance of approximately one hundred yards. At the last moment of approach the attacker turns and charges at the dog very hard, and once again, the dog must bite and hold. Many a dog, even those with SchH III titles have been known to crack under this pressure. However, if the dog passes he is deemed angekort for two years and is highly recommended for breeding. The dogs that fail may try once more one year later. In order to take the test an initial test must be passed in order to qualify with a rating of at least "Very Good."

American SSgt. James Nary, a member of the Doberman Pinscher Club of America who is also a marvelous source of information on the German Doberman since he has been stationed there, is the proud owner of one of the 16 Dobes that have passed the test. A bitch that he has used for breeding.

In the early 1970's the membership of the Doberman Verein was over one thousand. Herr Niermann serves as President, and Herr Wilking heads the judging association. The entire Doberman breeding program is under the watchful eyes of Herr Hensel.

NEW WORLD CHAMPION REQUIREMENTS

At the 1973 meeting of the Dobermann Verein it was decided that the World Champion titles bestowed on worthy specimens at the World Championship shows in Dortmund would only be awarded to Dobermans that had a Schutzhund rating or its equal, and that the test must include attack work. This qualification was already in effect for the Bundessieger and the DV Sieger titles.

2. THE DOBERMAN COMES TO AMERICA

The first Doberman Pinschers to reach our shores arrived around 1908, the same year the kennel name of "Doberman" was granted to Theodore F. Jaeger, who established his kennel in Rochester, New York. The following year Mr. Jaeger took on a partner, a man said to be a descendent of the Herr Dobermann who created the breed. He was W. Doberman and he and Mr. Jaeger imported Hertha Hohenstein and Bertel v Hohenstein to start their "Doberman" strain. In those days names could be changed almost as frequently as dogs changed owners, and Hertha Hohenstein became Hertha Doberman on her American registration papers.

Ch. Doberman Dix, a home-bred from this very first kennel, became the first American-bred Doberman in this country to achieve a championship.

Actually it was during World War I that the Doberman breed became popular in this country. As a result of the starvation and famine in war-torn Europe it was painful for the Europeans to contemplate the fate of their beloved dogs. Those that were not chosen for war duty were either put down because of the lack of food or were stolen and frequently eaten by starving neighbors or dognappers. Little wonder they shipped their dogs to America where it meant their survival. Many were sold to American soldiers after peace was declared, or sent on ahead to help establish kennels in this country.

It was this substantial importation of the European dogs that accounted for most of the winning in the show rings from the post-war period through 1927. It was the American-bred Ch. Big Boy of White Gate that broke the European "winning streak" by being awarded Best in Show in 1928, at the Rhode Island Kennel Club show. However, not before such great imports as Ch. Lux v d Blankenburg, so famous and so highly respected in his own land, had made his mark in this country as both show dog and valuable stud. Rappo, his half-brother was also imported from Germany. Another import of note was Dolf v Wiesengrun; though on in years, he was sent to California to be used at stud and died there in 1929. Ajax v Grammont, whelped in 1917, was imported from Holland and contributed widely to our American strains. Carlo v d Koningstad also made a name for himself after his importation to America in 1923, after producing well in both Holland and Belgium. He died in 1931.

Howard K. Mohr imported Angola v Grammont for his White Gate Kennels in Philadelphia. A brood bitch of high value, Mr. Mohr bred her well and she most assuredly passed on her quality and beauty to her progeny. The offspring she had left behind in Holland also did well and proved her value.

Two of Frau Stahr's Dobermans from her Silberberg line, including Sybille Silberberg whelped in 1917, were imported and were behind Mr. Mohr's top stud and Best in Show winner, Ch. Big Boy of White Gate. Big Boy's sire was Claus v d Spree and his dam was Dutch-bred import Elfreida v d Koningstad. Elfrieda was also imported to the U.S. and Big Boy was said to be her best son on either side of the Atlantic.

Ch. Dow's Cassie v Kienlesberg, bred and owned by the late Bert Dow of Davenport, Iowa; Cassie's dam, Ch. Gretl v Kienlesberg, was a half-sister to the famous Jessy von Sonnenhohe through their sire, Cherloc, and was imported by Mr. Dow in the 1930's. In one litter sired by Ch. Kurt v d Rheinperle-Rhinegold, all of the puppies were lost except Cassie and Cora; both became champions and were known for their beautiful heads. Their offspring are behind many of the best American champions.

Benno v Burgholz, a brown dog whelped October 17, 1920, was sent here to enforce the "brown" breeding especially, and did well by the bitches he was bred to during his reign. A black bitch, Hela v Goetteffelson (whelped in 1920) also found her way to this country. Hela was from the Parthengrund lines and when bred with Troll v d Blankenburg started the Goldgrund strain in Germany. Later in

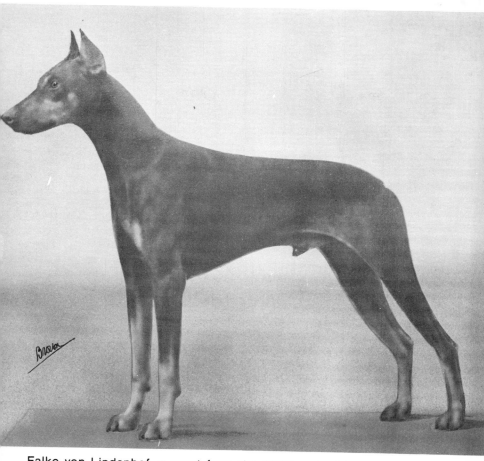

Falko von Lindenhof, a great from the 1930's, sired by Ch. Muck v Brunia x Cora v Ruppersburg.

America she continued to produce good stock. Another top bitch which contributed much to the American kennels, and whelped this same year, was Bella v Stolzenberg. Bella was another Troll daughter that carried through on the quality offspring this line was known for.

In 1921 the brown Dutch-bred "great" Favoriet v d Koningstad was born and was sent to America while still a young dog. Some of his get were left behind in Germany, and others produced here were sent back to Germany and did well also. Favoriet was said to be the best Doberman sire ever to come to America. This was an opinion held by many breeders at the time and for several years after. His sister, Ilisa, also came to this country, and a daughter of hers, Ilissa of Westphalia, was exported to Germany and found more acclaim there than her mother had before she left the country.

A litter of brother and sister, Eido and Freya v Stresow, was imported by one of the kennels in Michigan and improved the breeding in the mid-west to a great degree. And it was this year of 1921 that the Doberman Pinscher Club of America was founded by George H. Earle III, later Governor Earle, at a meeting held during the Westminster Kennel Club show that year. Little did they know at that time what a strong guiding force the DPCA would come to be!

There is a story behind the importation of Moritz v Blankenfeld, whelped in 1922. The acquisition of this dog illustrates the perfect example of how eager Americans were to buy the foreign dogs, and how the opportunists were always there to see that they got them! An American agent purchased Moritz for thirty dollars, then resold the dog to his American client for twelve hundred dollars. Moritz had a Sieger title in his native Germany which he had won on the strength of his good looks. But in spite of his appearance and bloodlines, he produced nothing of value when used at stud here.

A brown dog, whelped in 1922, and also holder of the Sieger title, was Carlo v d Schwanenhoehe. Though watched with many hopes pinned on him he proved to be worthless in the stud department also.

The year 1922 also produced a black bitch named Brangaene v Weingarten. Philipp Gruenig, at the time he owned her said, "There just was no fault which she did not have. Small, ugly, crooked, and unattractive but with a transmitter of good hereditary traits." Mr. Gruenig gave her away while still a young puppy, but nevertheless she became the dam of all the Sinsgut strain with puppies reaching as far as America and all the way to South Africa!

A Troll daughter of Hela v Goetterfelsen was imported to America and used extensively as a brood bitch--which she was to perfection! Bred to Favoriet they produced a litter of five, all of which attained championships. Their most famous offspring was Alli v Rhinegold. And it was in 1922 that the German breeders extended an invitation to Francis F. H. Fleitmann to judge their Sieger show. A neat honor for him.

In 1923 Mia v Stresow was whelped and before long had been given the title of the most beautiful bitch of that year in her native Germany. A top show bitch, it was almost inevitable that she would find her way to America. However, her progeny proved somewhat less than exciting no matter what stud was used on her, and unfortunately no important line was established to carry on her individual beauty.

In 1923 three German judges came to the United States to judge. One was the Doberman expert, Phillip Gruenig, another was Herr

Willi Hirscher, and the third was Peter Umlauff who was invited to judge at our prestigous Westminster Kennel Club. Also, a Norwegian judge, Julius Selikowitz, came over to officiate at one of our shows. It was obvious to these men that the breed's existence in this country had produced two very definite, very *different*, types of Doberman. While Europe was still breeding the solid, aggressive, working-dog type; America had evolved a more refined, more even-tempered type.

1924 saw the first blue Doberman attain championship status in this country, a bitch named Burga v Kumpmuehl. Her sire was Artus v Siegstor.

In 1924 Claus v Sigalsburg was imported. His arrival evoked great hope; but even when bred to the fine Mia v Stresow, he did not sire anything of value. Disappointing to say the least since the pedigree was excellent...his sire was Lux v d Blankenburg and his dam Asta v Stolzenberg.

A brown bitch, Bajadere v Zinsgut, was imported this same year and was to produce some excellent offspring. Through her own excellent bloodlines—carrying Edelblut v Jaegerhof—she certainly passed on the desired quality the breeders were hoping for.

In 1925 another Doberman named Claus also made a name for himself. Already famous as the sire of Ch. Big Boy of White Gate. Claus v d Spree came into his own when he sired yet another litter for the White Gate Kennels out of Elfreida v d Koningstad. This bitch, mentioned earlier also, was a champion in both Holland and the United States and whelped a litter in April of 1925 containing three future champions. They were referred to as the "A" litter and were named Acta, Algarda, and Amerant of White Gate.

This same year Lux v Saumhof was imported to the United States. An impressive dog of good size, he also passed on his good qualities to his get. He combined the Edelblut and the Blankenburg lines and gave his offspring the best of both.

By 1926 there had been enough interest and enough breeding and importing of the Doberman to inspire William Sidney Schmidt to publish a book on the breed entitled *The Doberman Pinscher in America*. This book was thought to be of such value to the fancy that it was re-issued in 1929, 1935 and 1940, but is now out of print.

In 1926 another "Carlo" came along. His name was Carlo of Rhinegold. This Favoriet v d Koningstad x Alli v Goldgrund son was the first Doberman bred in America to win a Best in Show award.

1926 was also the year when the Ponchartrain Kennel owned by Glenn S. Staines, began to make its mark--a mark which was to be reckoned with in the breed for the next several decades. In 1926, on June ninth, Ilisa of Pontchartrain was whelped. She starred as a brood matron at this kennel and three of her get became champions.

In 1927 Mars v Simmenau also came to Detroit to be bred to the

Ch. Carlo von Bassewitz (whelped in June, 1931) was owned by Col. C.P. Dodson, who used him extensively at stud in the New England area. His sire was Boby v Hohenzollernpark and his dam Fifi v Heimfeldt. There was a great deal of Sigalsburg blood behind this dog.

"Lux" lines previously imported. It is said of Mars that he was never in top show condition. It seems he was a "fighter" and was almost always covered with scars incurred in battle. Again we quote Phillipp Gruenig who professed to have known almost all Dobermans since 1900 and declared Mars to be "the sharpest one I ever became acquainted with. A fighter of the greatest heart and courage, he feared no opponent and preferred to go down fighting rather admit defeat."

Gustl v Tannenhaus, whelped in 1927 and a grandson of Alex v d Finohoehe, was imported to be bred with the Blankenburg blood already in this country.

1927 was also the year of the first Morris and Essex Kennel Club show: an entry of 12 Dobermans, representing almost a decade of blending imported bloodlines and bearing the kennel names which were to go down in Doberman history as the foundation of the breed in the United States. It was on March 22 of this year also, that Hesta of Pontchartrain was born. Just as Ilisa proved herself outstanding as a brood bitch, so did Hesta. Another Favoriet daughter, out of Freya v Stresow, Hesta whelped a litter of four: Hertha, Hexie, Hella and Hyde, all of which became American Champions. Unfortunately, the breeding was not repeated, because it was certainly the perfect blending of both the Dutch and German bloodlines imported to this country.

In 1928 the Pontchartrain Kennels produced Adonis. Adonis was sired by Lux v d Blankenburg out of the above-mentioned, home-bred bitch, Hella of Pontchartrain. He was an important sire for this kennel during the following years. It was also the year 1928 that Tinker of Rhinegold came along to earn the title of one of the best American-bred males to date.

The world famous Francis F.H. Fleitmann (owner of the equally famous Westphalia Kennels) in an informal photograph taken by Tauskey many years ago with his show-winning Ch. Duvetyn of Stonecroft.

In 1929 Pontchartrain came along with a trio of beauties, Prince Claus, Princess Flora and Lady Ortry. Claus produced four champions; Princess, five champions; and Lady had to be satisfied with being sired by the famous Lux v d Blankenburg.

A dog named Astor of Westphalia was the Fleitmann entry for outstanding stud dog of the year. His early demise put an end to the hopes pinned on him for improvement in the breed through his stud services. His sire was Helios v Siegestor and the dam Francis Fleitmann's excellent Ilissa of Westphalia.

In 1929 Eike zum Ziel was whelped. Sired by Achill v d Rheinperle x Lotte II v Simmenau, he came to this country at a young age and did well from the very beginning as a stud force. Other imports during these early years that did not necessarily distinguish themselves but

Another of the famous early "greats"—Francis F.H. Fleitmann's Ch. Westphalia's Uranus.

made a contribution to the breed through their bloodlines, were Lord v d Horstburg, Rival v Kranichstein, and three brown dogs named Apollo v Schuetzenek, Baldur v Zinsgut, and Karl v Blankenburg.

A dog and a bitch also whelped in 1929 are worthy of mention: Alto v Torrez, who sired five champions, and a black bitch named Doddy of Rhinegold, who whelped four American champions.

By the end of the "roaring Twenties" there were many celebrated names in Dobermans...Herman Meyer of Philadelphia, another of the early fanciers to import Dobermans, as was Mr. Vucassovitch in Boston and the Marienland Kennels in Baltimore; other names include: Schroth, Milde, Glenwood, Oxbo, Randhof, Rogermidt, Plantation Grove, Silvergate, Damasyn, Millsdod, Coldod, Glenhugel and Jerry Run.

But when speaking of the early years and the twenties, special attention must be given to certain advocates who contributed to the breed in several ways. Such is the case of Francis F. H. Fleitmann, perhaps the first name which comes to mind. He was known for his many Doberman imports from Germany and Holland and did much to popularize the breed in this country by extensive campaigning and a worthy breeding program.

The most famous of his imports was the magnificent Ch. Jessy von der Sonnenhohe. She went on to distinguish herself as both a show dog and as a brood bitch producing top quality offspring. Jessy had whelped a few litters in Germany before coming to Mr. Fleitmann and the progeny she left in Europe did well in the show rings also.

Her reputation for excellence could only be equalled by her son, Ch. Ferry von Rauhfelsen, bred by Wilhelm Rothfess in Germany. He brought additional fame to the Giraldo Kennels of Mrs. Geralda Phelps Dodge of Madison, New Jersey. His greatest achievement was his winning Best in Show at the Westminster Kennel Club Show in

Madison Square Garden, New York City, in 1939. McClure Halley, Mrs. Dodge's handler and manager, piloted Ferry throughout his ring career.

Ferry's sire, Ch. Troll v d Engelsburg, was brought to this country by another of the early Doberman breeders, E. Bornstein of Peoria, Illinois. Ironically, Troll and his son, Ferry, were to meet in the show ring at the 1939 Westminster show and it was only after great deliberation that judge W. H. Moore gave the Best of Breed award to Ferry. Ferry then went on to win the Group under judge G. V. Glebe, and the coveted Best in Show rosette under judge George S. Thomas.

An interesting story regarding Ferry's Garden victory is the quote from the judge stating that the only thing he didn't like about the dog was that he couldn't touch him. It must be remembered that they liked them like this in Germany, which is surely different from today's judging procedures where judges are required to handle the dogs they judge!

During the early 1940's Ferry was listed in the show catalogues as being owned by the Randhof Kennels in San Francisco, California, and handled by Ben Brown.

GLENN STAINES AND THE PONTCHARTRAIN KENNELS

One of the earliest and staunchest supporters of the breed in this country was Glenn Staines who founded the Pontchartrain Kennels in Michigan. Born on November 15, 1887, Mr. Staines helped to compose the first American version of the Doberman Standard and wrote the Articles of Incorporation which established the Doberman Pinscher

Ch. Westphalia's Ursula, bred by Francis Fleitmann and owned by Howard Mohr.

Club of America. He was a devoted fancier, obedience trainer and judge who wrote about the Doberman as well.

Glenn Staines wrote a monthly column for *Dog News* magazine for a long time; he gave freely of his knowledge of the Doberman through his column. He was of tremendous help to those who were just coming into the breed and was very active in promoting the Doberman as a guide dog for the blind.

Many years of active breeding put the name of Pontchartrain champions at the top of the lists along with those of Francis Fleitmann, Carl Muser, Howard Mohr, and other well-known breeders and exhibitors of the day. Glenn Staines died on July 7, 1951, but not his memory, which will live on in the history of the breed as one of its major benefactors.

CARL MUSER AND THE MUSBRO KENNELS

One of the important contributors to the breed for over four decades starting in the 1920's was Carl Muser.

Carl Muser was born in Schopfheim, Germany, on April 5, 1890. As early as 1912 Carl Muser organized one of the largest police-dog training clubs in his native Germany. The club had over 500 members and the training was taken by police officials and prison guards as well as those seeking a well-mannered companion dog. When World War I came along he also trained dogs for the army. In 1916 he was in command of a contingent of dogs he had specially trained for work as messengers, meal carriers, Red Cross work and guard duty in the camps.

After World War I he was chosen to be chief trainer for a large police training club in Leubben, Germany, where he was cited on several occasions for his training dogs for the army and police.

It was in 1922 that Carl Muser came to the United States to live and open a kennel. And, of course, he became interested in dog training in this country as well. However, it wasn't until 1935 that he founded the First Working Dog Club in America, and that was the name given to it. A history of this famous club can be found in our obedience chapter.

Over the years Carl Muser belonged to other clubs as well as those he helped to establish. Among these were the First Dog Training Club of Northern New Jersey, the Penn-Jersey Doberman Pinscher Club, Kennel Club of Northern New Jersey, Northern New Jersey German Shepherd Dog Club and of course the S. V. in Germany. At the time of his death in November 1960, Carl Muser had put in over fifty years as a dog trainer.

Before World War II, however, he inaugurated the Canine College of America, a course of instruction designed for persons wishing to become trainers or professional handlers. There were also courses in pre-veterinary training, the operation and management of canine beauty parlors—the grooming shops, as we call them today—and in later years the college introduced dog obedience and show handling in the curriculum.

Carl Muser was an obedience judge for many years and personally trained dogs for many prominent people including Lou Gehrig, the baseball player; Governor Walter Edge of New Jersey; Howard Barlow, the early TV personality; Floyd Gibbons, the flyer; actor Clifton Webb; Warner Brothers movie mogul, Pohley Myers; and many others.

Although Carl Muser became an American citizen, he also spent time training dogs in foreign countries. His instruction covered 35 countries including Argentina, Cuba, Spain, Venezuela, England, etc.

A fantastic leap over seven chairs during an obedience and training session at Carl Muser's Musbro Kennels training school in West Englewood, New Jersey, several decades ago. The "straight out" position of the body displays the powerful leap which can be achieved by the Doberman when properly trained for such work.

While Carl Muser's primary concern was the obedience field, the Musbro Kennels was also well represented in the show ring. Two of his most famous Dobermans were Ch. Mona von der Rheinperle-Musbro and her brother, Ch. Black Ulan von der Rheinperle-Musbro. Others were Franz von der Rheinperle-Musbro and Helios von der Rheinperle-Musbro, but none ever reached the prominence or place in Carl Muser's heart that the lovely Mona did. The author would also like to add that it was from Carl Muser that she bought her first Dobermans which added so much pleasure to her life for so many years.

THE THIRTIES

Kanzler v Sigalsburg was whelped in January 1930 and was imported to this country to be used with the bloodlines introduced here by Troll v d Blankenburg.

1930 was also the year another Troll was whelped, Troll v d Hoehen, one of the last of Favoriet's sons. Although he produced well as a stud, he was not used to any great extent and achieved most of his praise through a trio of bitches whelped at Mr. Fleitmann's kennel. They were Orama, Orissa and Orsove of Westphalia.

A West coast Kennel registered a dog named Attila of Oxbo in 1930; so by now the breed had reached the Pacific coast. And note

The very beautiful Ch. Mona v d Rheinperle-Musbro and her first litter of puppies, bred by Carl Muser at his Musbro Kennels in West Englewood, New Jersey, in the 1930's.

Mr. M. Reynolds and his Ch. Gust v Bad-Heidelberg photographed in Chicago many years ago.

also that the Pontchartrain Kennel was off to a good start in this decade with Princess Pan of Pontchartrain. She was a Favoriet granddaughter who started her show career in the mid-west before being sold to the West Coast.

In 1931 Erna v Graf Zeppelin and her brown sister Ella were whelped in their native Germany. While Ella was the 1933 red Sieger-in, she and Erna were imported to the United States at an early age and Erna used for breeding with Kanzler v Sigalsburg. This was the year another German Sieger and Siegerin brother and sister were whelped in Germany; later Daisy was sold to American breeders and Desir to a Japanese sportsman who used him at stud extensively in Japan. Desir v Glueckswinkel and Daisy v Glueckswinkel were ranked as the best dog and bitch for the year 1933.

In 1932 Sonai of Westphalia was whelped. Sired by Big Boy of White Gate out of Aurora of Westphalia, she was a top show dog and made a record for herself in the show ring which has not yet been achieved by any other American-bred bitch. A dog named Nicholas of Randhof was also whelped this year. A Favoriet grandson, this large black male was to prove himself as the sire of many champions.

Ch. Muck von Brunia

German Sieger and American Ch. Muck von Brunia was whelped on July 9, 1929. He was of great influence on the breed in this country after being imported in 1933 by Mr. and Mrs. Owen A. West of Chicago. His price was $3,500. One can imagine what that price would be in today's market!! Muck was considered the outstanding Doberman of the year 1929 in his native Germany by no less an authority than Philipp Gruenig and was imported to this country chiefly because of his good disposition which was desired to improve the breed in this country.

Muck's sire was Luz v Roedeltal and his dam Hella v d Winterburg. He is also known as the grandfather and the great-grandfather of the famous Ch. Dictator von Glenhugel, proving himself a top sire on both sides of the Atlantic.

In 1933 Baroness Brenda and Baroness Blenda v d Hoehen were whelped and Brenda produced well when bred to Troll v d Hoehen. Also it was the year twin-brothers, Alto and Ajax v Verstaame were born. All four of these Dobermans were bred well and made their contribution to the breed.

But perhaps the most significant event of the year 1933 was the whelping of yet another "Troll." This one, Troll v Engelsburg, became the outstanding stud dog in Germany from 1935 through 1937. He was sold to America, but not before being bred to everything of value in Germany. In fact, he was used to such an extent that at the 1938 Sieger show in Germany it was said that almost one half of all the dogs and bitches at the show were sired by him, including both the black Sieger and Siegerin, and the Second "V" dog, which was sired by him out of the fabulous Jessy v d Sonnenhoehe. Another daughter was Best of Breed winner! He is the only male in Germany up to that time that won Best of Breed at two consecutive shows; 1934 and 1935.

He was also the sire of the 1937 Reich Siegerin, Ossi v Stahlhelm, the fabulous Mona v d Rheinperle (later exported to Carl Muser in the United States) and Roland v Stahlhelm. When shown in the U.S. he racked up a show record second only to Jockel v Burgund.

Perhaps the most significant event of 1934 was the arrival of the Jan-Mar Kennels litter of three future champions, whelped in April. Nana, Napier and Nabob of Rhinegold were all destined to become show dogs important to the breed. Sired by Ch. Kurt v d Rheinperle-Rhinegold out of Miss Flash of Rhinegold, Napier and Nabob were to finish their championships the same year.

1934 was also the year Dietrich of Dawn was born and served well as a stud during his lifetime.

The following year, 1935, a litter of five future champions was whelped at the Lindenhof Kennels. Sired by Muck v Brunia out of Cora v Ruppersburg, this "F" litter produced Falko, Falk, Fritz, Fels and Flammchen v Lindenhof.

1935 was a banner year for the breed by virtue of Mona v d Rheinperle. Bred in Germany by Jakob Brunner, her sire was Troll v Engelsburg and her dam Kriemhilde v d Rheinperle. She came to America and was the treasure of Carl Muser at his Musbro Kennels.

German Sieger and American Champion Muck von Brunia, imported by Mr. and Mrs. Owen A. West of Chicago. Muck was considered the outstanding Doberman of the year 1929 by Philipp Gruenig. Whelped July 9, 1929; his sire was Luz v Roedeltal and his dam Hella v d Winterburg. Muck had a great influence on the breed both in his native Germany and the United States.

Ch. Steb's Top Skipper. This Westminster and Working Group winner is owned by Mr. and Mrs. J. Monroe Stebbins, Jr., of Long Island, New York.

She produced well for him and displayed her great beauty in the show ring where she obtained her championship in short order. Philipp Gruenig said of her, "Her back line and silhouette are A-1." and that, "she made a most pleasing appearance in the show ring."

During the year 1936 there was another "five-star litter" born in the United States. This one, sired by Kurt v d Schwartzwaldperle out of Madchen v Milde, was whelped in March of that year at the Gerdts Kennels and was indentified as the "H" litter. The names, all beginning with the same letter, which was a kind of custom in those days, contained Helgra, Helios, Hesta, Horst and Herra v Gerdts.

1936 saw the importation of Count Leo v d Donstadt and the outstanding American-bred bitch of the year, Orsova of Westphalia.

She excelled in the show ring and proved once again the great quality behind the Koningstad breeding which could be found behind her.

1937 was another great year. In Germany, Ferry v Rauhfelsen was whelped on January ninth. The sire was Troll v Engelsburg and the dam the famous Jessy v d Sonnenhoehe. His show record in Germany was impressive and upon his arrival in the United States he quickly attained his championship status. His greatest claim to fame perhaps was his Best in Show win at the 1939 Westminister Kennel Show in New York. Ferry was the first Doberman ever to win the top

One of the great heads of early days was that of Ch. Westphalia's Uranus. Owned and bred by F.F.H. Fleitmann.

award at the Garden, a feat not achieved again until his grandson, Ch. Rancho Dobe's Storm, won it for two consecutive years in 1952 and 1953.

1937 was a good year all around for the Doberman Pinscher. A total of 42 Dobermans won their championships in this country, including the very prominent Mona v d Rheinperle and Jessy v d Sonnenhoehe

It was Siegerin and Ch. Jessy v d Sonnenhoehe that made breed history in 1939 when bred to Pericles of Westphalia; the litter whelped in June of that year contained no less than six champions! They were Uranus, Jessy, Ursula, Undine, Umbra and Uganda. This was just a little more than one year after she whelped a record litter containing seven champions! The lucky seven litter was sired by Kurt v d Rhein-perle-Rheingold and arrived in February. The future champions were named Rani, Rehmha, Roxana, Rajah, Raswan, Rameses and Ramona. By the end of the year 1939, Jessy had whelped 13 champions within 24 months!

In March of 1939 the Glenhugel Kennels whelped a litter containing multiple champions. Sired by Blank v d Donstadt out of their Ch. Ossi v Stahlhelm, they finished three out of the "B" litter, namely Berta, Beth and Binchen, and all with the Glenhugel surname.

In 1939 champion titles were awarded to 43 Dobermans. This list included some of the most important dogs of the thirties. When considered with the 30 other dobermans which attained championship status during the first years of this decade, it is evident that the breed had made important strides. Many of the dogs whose names appeared on registration certificates were to appear as the important sires and dams during the "fabulous forties"!

In the late 1930's F.F.H. Fleitmann and Howard K. Mohr of the Westphalia Kennels in New York and the White Gate Kennels in Philadelphia put up considerable financial backing for the publication of an American translation of Philipp Gruenig's book, *The Dobermann Pinscher-History and Development of the Breed.* This was of great service to the breed since Mr. Gruenig's book was a comprehensive history of the breed and contained a year by year chronicle of all the top Dobermans from 1893 through 1937. Over four hundred entries were included and the text was liberally sprinkled with photographs of the old dogs.

Through these portals passed some of the most important Dobermans in the early history of the breed in this country. The "house of Westphalia" photographed in 1924 was the world-renowned kennel of Mr. F.F.H. Fleitmann which was managed for him by Ellie Buckley.

Mr. F.F. Hermy Fleitmann, one of the greatest world authorities on the breed that ever lived. Mr. Fleitmann, who died in 1976, fulfilled his last judging assignment at the 1970 North of England Dobermann Club show.

Ch. Ferry von Rauhfelson of Giralda in perfect show pose. Ferry, one of the earliest imports to this country from Germany, was not only a great dog in his own right, but did much to popularize the Doberman in this country. One of the great Dobermans of all time.

Ch. Westphalia's Raswan, a member of the famous "R" litter bred by the Westphalia Kennels; other champions were Radjah, Rembha and Ramona.

This book was updated through 1947 and updated again and re-issued in 1975. For those of you interested in the history of the breed this book is a must for the Doberman library since Mr. Gruenig not only wrote honestly about each dog, but researched his subject and knew most of the dogs personally.

THE FORTIES

The tremendous impact of imported stock, although narrowed down to a few exceptional imports, was still being felt at the beginning of the "fabulous forties." All one needed to do was to glance at the show catalogue for the May 1941, Morris and Essex Show, the year Anton Korbel judged the breed. Countless individual breeders are listed, all with their home-breds which account for a large portion of the 65 entries.

To encourage this trend of American-breds, Mrs. M. Hartley Dodge, who staged the M and E event on her fabulous estate in Madison, New Jersey, offered her M. Hartley Dodge, Jr., Memorial Trophy for First Prize in an American-bred class for Dogs and Bitches.

Also starring at this show were two exceptional imports, and the Specials Class of five entries included Ch. Ferry v Rauhfelson of Giralda, and Carl Muser's Ch. Mona v d Rheinperle.

But the classes displayed a wonderful representation of many of the top kennels of the early Forties among the entries. Pontchartrain, Rhinegold, Westphalia, Glenhugel and Marienland all listed in one or more of the classes.

Forest Hall had entered his Hallwyre Hamlet v Tyler, a Ferry son, and two Dobermans bred by Alfred Peter Knoop were entered by their owners. Blixen and Prancer of Barlynn were their names and the catalogue lists the date of birth as December 23, 1935, which is more likely the reason they were given names the same as Santa's reindeers!

The year 1941 was referred to by Peggy Adamson in one of her writings as "The Golden Year of the American Doberman." It was the year of the glorious bitch Dow's Illena of Marienland, and a year which boasted no less than seven top studs to enhance the future of the breed. Names like Westphalia's Rameses and Westphalia's Uranus, Favoriet v Franzhof (this Favoriet has an "e" in its name), Alcor v Millsdod, Emporer of Marienland, Domossi of Marienland, and of course Peggy Adamson's very own import, Ch. Dictator v Glenhugel.

These dogs, which were to reign all through the decade of the forties, represented the best Germany and all of Europe had to offer—and it was a proud and wonderful contribution.

Although Margaret K. Kilburn owned her first Doberman in 1939, it wasn't until the 1940's when she became known for her Kilburn Kennels. Her second Dobe was Ch. Dow's Illena of Marienland, dam of 12 champions. Within a five year period, three of her bitches produced 23 champions. Her Ch. Kilburn Audacity and Ch. Dow's Dodie v Kienlesberg accounted for 11 champions between them. Of the 23 champions whelped during this five year period, 12 were Group winners and eight won Best in Show awards.

Mrs. Paul Kilburn joined the Doberman Pinscher Club of America in 1940 after she first became interested in the breed and is a

The famous Dictator at the age of 10 months showing all the alert inquisitiveness characteristic of the breed. The owner, Peggy Adamson of the Damasyn Kennels in Roslyn Heights, New York.

Champion and Siegerin Ora v Sandberg-K Lindenhof, a red daughter of Ch. Moritz v Rodeltal. Ora was considered to be one of the most beautiful bitches ever imported to America and the last important import to America before World War II. She was winner of the DPCA Specialty Show in 1939 and was the third bitch to win a parent club Specialty (the first was Red Roof Hilda in 1924, the first DPCA Specialty, and the second bitch to win was Jessy v Sonnenhohe in 1937).

former delegate-at-large. She has served as a member of the last two Standard Revision Committees and has been a judge of the breed since 1943. One of her most recent assignments was at the 1973 DPCA Specialty Show in Washington, D.C., where she judged the Bitch Classes. Mrs. Kilburn is also a Board Member of the American Kennel Club.

Mr. Fleitmann's Westphalia Kennels scored in the 1940's with the aforementioned Westphalia's Rameses, C.D.X. Another Jessy son, sired by Ch. Kurt v d Rheinperle-Rhinegold, Rameses won the breed and fourth in the Working Group at the 1942 Westminster Kennel Club show. In addition to being one of the early obedience trained Dobermans that excelled equally in the show and obedience rings, Rameses was a potent sire and proved his value in this category as well.

An indication of just how popular the breed was becoming in this new decade can be seen not only from the number of entries in the two shows mentioned above but also by the fact that during the second half of 1940 another thirty Dobermans had been shown to their championships. Pontchartrain was well represented during this year with the title won by their Glenith of Pontchartrain, and Westphalia presented three title-holders, Rani, Rembha and Roxanna of Westphalia, all from one litter sired by Ch. Kurt v d Rheinperle-Rhinegold x Ch. Jessy v d Sonnenhoehe.

Opposite:
Ch. Ferry von Rauhfelson of Giralda, the first Doberman to win a Best in Show at Westminster—in 1939—photographed with his owner, Mrs. Geraldine Dodge, Giralda Farms, Madison, New Jersey. Ferry was one of the first great dogs in the history of the breed.

Cook of Gormley

Breite v Rupprechtheim, C.D. photographed in 1972. Bred and owned by Jim Roberts.

Erna von Graf Zeppelin, one of the early imports by the late Sydney Moss of the Verstaame Kennels in Los Angeles, California. Mr. Moss was one of the early presidents of the Doberman Pinscher Club of America.

"ERNA von GRAF ZEPPELIN"

Ch. Palanka's Hawkins v Eschen, a Ferry son owned by Ken and Fran Dyer. This dog was shown in the 1940's.

Another of the greats of the decade to finish in 1940 was Carl Muser's magnificent Black Ulan v d Rheinperle-Musbro. Ulan was sired by Ch. Kurt v d Rheinperle-Rhinegold x Ch. Mona v d Rheinperle.

In addition to those already mentioned there were several other exceptional Dobermans among the lists of champions produced. Some of these were Koenig v Heimdall, Tappo v Palank, Zita v Dombachtel, Cassie and Cora v Kienlesberg from the Dow Kennels, Maida v Coldod, Kurtson of Rhinegold, Assy v Allerblick, Riese v Lindenhof and both Berta and Binchen from the Glenhugel "five champions litter," and Beth and Bengal, from the same litter, which finished in 1942. Winner for outstanding show dog in 1941, however, was Ellie v Franzhof.

Twenty-seven champions were produced in 1942, with Westphalia once again in the lead with four winners. It is interesting to note that all of them were whelped by Ch. Jessy v d Sonnenhoehe again, two sired by Ch. Kurt v d Rheinperle-Rhinegold, and the other two by Pericles of Westphalia.

Other top contenders for excellence in the breed in 1942 were the Domstadt Kennels' Ferdinand v d Domstadt, Asta and Annabella of Spanaway, Dietrich v Koenigsheim, Fraulein v Dettershof, Heraldic of Het Loo, the Marienland Kennels' Ernestine, Dow's Dodie v Kienlesberg, Gessner's Rolf v Siegzel and the bitches Anne of Paulraine and Empress Rule of Rulego. Outstanding among the 1942 champions were Westphalia's Raswan, Undine and Rajah, who also got the "vote" as outstanding sire that year.

In 1943, of the 21 champions produced four carried the Marienland Kennels' name with Ajor of Pontchartrain representing Glenn Staines' important kennel. Westphalia was a double winner, with Westphalia's Jessy and Westphalia's Ursula finishing to championship.

By 1943 the war-time gas shortage began to take its toll on the show entries. With fewer champions being finished, the quality still remained high, and among the list of champions for 1943 many of the top kennels were represented. Emperor of Marienland, Cerita of Marienland and Dow's Illena of Marienland attained titles, as did Merak of Millsdod, Alcor of Millsdod and the A. Peter Knoop's Barlynn's Brenda.

The champions for 1944 numbered 33, with 22 in 1945, but with the amount of breeding now going on in the United States the number could have been a great deal higher. It became more and more obvious that the war was affecting the entries, and fewer dogs were being campaigned. The major kennels were still breeding, however. Westphalia, Marienland and Glenhugel were constantly being mentioned, and some of the new names included Falkenstein, Lakewood and Mannerheim.

Ch. Christie's Barrier (son of Ch. Christie von Klosterholz), owned by Brooke Bacon of Pemberton, New Jersey, and a show winner in the 1940's.

Winner in the 1940's, Ch. Wittland's Black King, the first champion for Leo Wittenberg of Hollis, Long Island, New York. Sired by the great Ch. Black Ulan v d Rhineperle-Musbro x Duchess Beauty of Zeider. Handled by A. Peter Knoop. King finished for his championship at 20 months of age with four Bests of Breed, a Group First and three Group Seconds.

Eight-month-old Redjack's Rain Flower, owned by Eileen Collins of the Redjack Kennels in Deaborn, Michigan, photographed in 1941. The sire was Ch. Damasyn Carly of Jerseystone x Redjack's Otillie.

One of America's earliest great Dobermans—Ch. Westphalia's Rameses, C.D.X., owned by Francis F.H. Fleitmann of Philadelphia.

1944 was the year the top stud, Favoriet v Franzhof, finished for his championship, along with Christie v Klosterholz, Doricka v d Elbe, Point Blank of Marienland, Abud v Samills and the great Dictator v Glenhugel.

In 1945 a bitch named Duvetyn of Stone Croft was an outstanding contender in the show ring while attaining her championship, as were Dow's Illisa of Westphalia, Marienland's Quintessence and a dog named Quo Shmerk v Marienland, later given the title of Dog of the Year by a group of judges in the Midwest before he had attained his title.

During the second half of the 1940's kennels such as Elblac became involved in the breed, as did Eleanor Houston Carpenter's Jerry Run Kennels, with her excellent Damon of Jerry Run finishing for his title in 1945. Damon's sire was Ch. Westphalia's Rameses and

Ch. Orsola of Westphalia, one of the early great bitches, owned by F.F.H. Fleitmann of the Westphalia Kennels.

Ch. Agitator of Doberland, bred and owned by Ivan Wolff of Forest Hills, New York and whelped in August of 1949. This red dog was by Dictator out of Pinsch of Doberland.

the dam was Ch. Assy v Illerblick. Westphalia's Apollo and Kama of Westphalia were popular studs during the late 1940's and helped contribute to the breed. We also see the Amerikeim Kennels listed in the 40's.

It was in 1948 that the name Ebonaire flashed on the scene. Not a kennel per se, Ebonaire was the prefix used by Judith Weiss; it identified a fine line of Dobermans over the next several decades.

The Ebonaire line was based on a Dictator granddaughter, Damasyn The Wild Wing. Two years later Judith Weiss purchased a red Dictator daughter, Damasyn The Flash. Bred to a great Solitaire son, she whelped a litter containing her Ebonaire's Flashing Star. Star became the dam of eight champions including her famous "Fencing"

Ch. Dow's Dodie v Kienlesberg, owned by Bert Dow of Davenport, Iowa, the dam of the famous "D" litter in the 1940's. Dodie was sired by Ch. Domossi of Marienland x Ch. Dow's Cassie v Kienlesberg. Bert Dow was president of the Doberman Pinscher Club of America in 1943.

and "Football" litters, including Ebonaire's Touchdown, Gridiron, Balestra, etc., all sired by another of the all-time greats, Ch. Steb's Top Skipper. Ebonaire's En Garde, a lovely bitch, and Ch. Ebonaire's Entertainer were also well known. En Garde, bred to her half-brother, Ch. Egothel's All-American, produced Entertainer, which Judith Weiss kept for herself, and he became the sire of eight champions during his 14 years.

Ebonaire Bravo, litter brother of Entertainer, was exported to Australia, and Judith Weiss is proud of his record in that country. Ebonaire prefixes precede the names of 22 champions to date and many obedience-title holders as well. In later years, Ed and Judy Weiss and daughter Robin are still active in Dobermans and are proud of the Ebonaire record.

CH. DICTATOR VON GLENHUGEL

The undisputed king of the 1940's was the great red Doberman Pinscher, Ch. Dictator von Glenhugel. Whelped in 1941, Dictator, as he was known the world over when people spoke of greatness in the breed, was a magnificent showdog, a top sire and was largely responsible for popularizing the red Doberman. Many of the earlier reds had been of poor coloration, but Dictator showed breed lovers what a good red could, and should, be.

Dictator, bred by John Cholley, sired champions in many countries of the world. His grand total was 52 champions, all sired out of less than one hundred litters. To prove his strong influence on his progeny, it need only be pointed out that over half of his get were also red.

Dictator was purchased in 1941 by Robert and Peggy Adamson of the Damasyn Kennels in Roslyn Heights, New York, and died in 1952. He was much loved and admired for the heritage he left to the breed.

The famous Ch. Dictator von Glenhugel with Granda von Palanka, C.D. photographed in 1943 training with their owner, Peggy Adamson, Damasyn Kennels, Roslyn Heights, New York.

Ch. Votan v Gruenewald II, bred by Earl Spicer and owned by Willie Deckert of Miami, Florida, in the 1940's. Sired by Ch. Dictator von Glenhugel out of Ch. Hanschen v Gruenewald.

Ch. Brown's Evangeline, C.D., bred by Eleanor Brown and owned by Peggy Adamson. A litter sister to Ch. Brown's Eric, this red bitch was from a Dictator daughter, Ch. Dow's Dame of Kilburn.

THE FIFTIES

CH. DAMASYN THE SOLITAIRE, C.D.X.

In 1951 another great Doberman was to come upon the scene from the Adamson's famous Damasyn Kennels in New York. Another of Dictator's red sons, Ch. Damasyn the Solitaire, C.D.X., was whelped by Ch. Damasyn The Sultry Sister, a Dictator granddaughter. Solitaire followed in his father's illustrious footsteps as a sire, with fifteen champion offspring, not only at Damasyn, but at other top kennels in the dog fancy. Solitaire was both a show dog and a top obedience contender, going all the way to the C.D.X. title.

Peggy Adamson, a judge, lecturer, writer, columnist and breeder of Dobermans since 1945 under her Damasyn kennel prefix, is also President of the Doberman Pinscher Club of America. She has served on the Governing Board for 19 years and has judged in many foreign countries as well as all over the United States. Her dedication to the breed is phenomenal and undisputed and her interests and talents have led to her serving the breed in many varied and important capacities.

Perhaps one of the most important functions in which Peggy Adamson has served the breed is as historian. There is no one who has collected as much breed information, photographs, memorabilia and general knowledge on the breed as she has. She is a prolific writer and has used this information and her talent to spread the word on the breed since she first became interested in Dobermans. Peggy Adamson was of tremendous help to the author in the compiling of this book and gave much time to supplying a great deal of her material and photographs for it. For this we should all be eternally grateful, as well as for the tremendous influence all of her Damasyn Dobermans have had on the breed. Hers is a contribution few can ever hope to equal or achieve.

AMERICAN, CANADIAN AND CUBAN CHAMPION
BORONG THE WARLOCK, C.D.

One of the most remarkable dogs in the history of the breed was for a long time the top-winning Doberman Pinscher of all time in this country. His name was Borong the Warlock, and he won his obedience degree in short order and his championship title in three countries.

Owned by Henry G. and Theodosia Frampton of Miami, Florida, that magnificent animal was a living legend in his own time. His fantastic show career included 230 Bests of Breed, 30 Specialty Show "bests," six all-breed Bests in Show and 66 Working Groups! He was the only Doberman ever to have won the Doberman Pinscher Club of America National Specialty Show three times, and in 1961 five Doberman specialists judged him Top in the breed in an annual Top Ten competition event. Needless to say, he was also one of the Top Ten in

Ch. Damasyn The Solitaire, C.D.X., 1951-1961, bred and owned by Peggy and Bob Adamson of the Damasyn Kennels in Roslyn Heights, New York. The magnificent headstudy portrays the classic beauty of the Damasyn Dobermans. By Dictator out of his granddaughter, Ch. Damasyn The Sultry Sister.

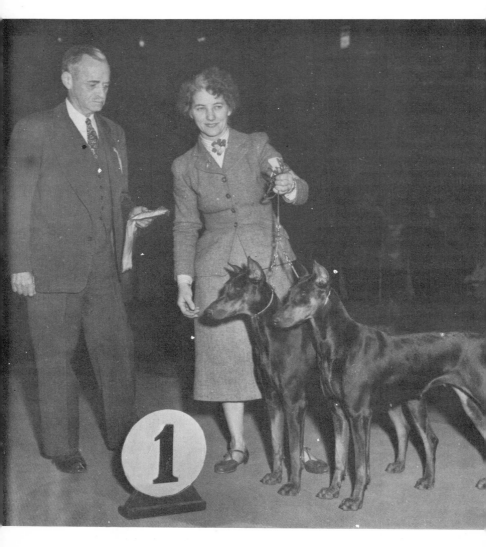

Best Working Dog Brace at the 1953 Westminster Kennel Club Show in Madison Square Garden was Tess Henseler's Ch. Frederica v Ahrtal and Ch. Friederun v Ahrtal. Miss Henseler was owner, breeder, handler and trainer of this magnificent pair of working dogs.

Ch. Bengel von Grosshugel, C.D., owned by George E. Harpham of Parma Heights, Ohio. Bengal actually was part of the "famous five" litter whelped at John Cholley's von Glenhugel kennels but a mistake over handwriting on a registration paper made the name come out as Grosshugel!

the Phillips System ratings over a four-year span. In 1962, when he was eight years of age, he won the Penn-Jersey Doberman Specialty for the third time and retired the Carl Muser Trophy which had been in competition since 1944.

He was one of a litter of five champions, and he finished for his American title at just 13 months of age with four major wins. His obedience title was won in three straight shows.

As a sire he also excelled, with 25 American champions to his credit, including three Best in Show winners. Obedience titlists were also among his offspring. His daughter, Ch. Jem's Amethyst v Warlock, was the top-winning Doberman bitch for the year 1963.

Warlock was known also for his temperament. He had always been a housedog and constant companion to the Framptons and traveled with them everywhere (including airplane, train and ship) as a good will ambassador for the breed. He was a credit to his sire, Ch. Astor v Grenzweg, C.D., and his dam, Ch. Florowill Allure, C.D.X.

INT. CH. DEFENDER OF JAN-HAR

International Champion Defender of Jan-Har was breeder-owner-handled to Best in Show wins six times during his show career. His first time shown, at ten months of age, he won Best of Breed at a Specialty Show over Best in Show competition. He also had 11 Best in Working Group wins and 10 Specialties to his credit. He was a Group winner from the classes and, with the exception of one Reserve Dog win, was undefeated in the breed classes during his career.

A panel of six renowned specialty judges voted unanimously that Defender was winner of the first Top Ten competition.

He was the sire of 21 champions including Jane Kay's top-producing bitch, Ch. Kay Hills Paint The Town Red, and grandsire of the Charles Etner's Ch. Kay Hill's Witch Soubretta. Defender was bred and owned by Jane and Harry MacDonald of Pontiac, Michigan, and was later sold to Dr. Wilfred Shute.

CH. RANCHO DOBE'S STORM

Storm was whelped on December 12, 1949. His breeders, Mr. and Mrs. Brint Edwards, owners of the Rancho Dobe Kennels in Van Nuys, California, bred their Ch. Maedel v Randahof to Ch. Rancho Dobe's Primo. There was trouble with the litter of 13 puppies and only a few survived. The single male left was Storm. The dam died a few days later, and Storm and his sisters had to be taken to a foster mother. In view of the trouble with the litter the Edwards decided to name the survivors after storms and winds. Just to break the "jinx" they registered the litter as having been born on the 12th instead of the 13th. Little did they imagine how much the number 13 would play in Storm's future! The litter consisted of 13 puppies, Storm became

BEST DOG IN SHOW

Alexander ©
DALLAS

Champion Kay Hill's Witch Soubretta, 1960-1972. Bred by Jane Kay and sired by Ch. Borong the Warlock x Kay Hill's Paint the Town Red, she was from a breeding that produced nine champions, three of which were Best In Show winners. She won the Doberman Pinscher Club of America Futurity Stakes in 1961 and was the DPCA Brook Bitch for 1968. She produced 18 AKC champions including five all-breed Best in Show winners, including the famous Ch. Dolph von Tannenwald. She was owned by Kay Etner, Tannenwald, Houston, Texas.

the Edward's 13th home-bred champion, he was the 13th Doberman handled to championship by Peter Knoop and his catalogue number was 13 at his first Westminster victory on his 13th time in the show ring, exactly 13 years since the day his grandfather, Ch. Ferry v Rauhfelsen of Giralda, became the first Doberman Pinscher ever to win Best in Show at the Garden!

Storm's Westminster win under judge Joseph Sims in 1952 was repeated in 1953 under judge James J. Farrell, Jr., over an entry of over 2,500 dogs, a Garden crowd of 12,000 spectators and a television viewing audience estimated at over one-half million people. His stud fee "soared" from one hundred to one hundred and fifty dollars!

During his ring career Storm was shown a total of 26 times and had 17 Bests in Show plus two Specialties. He was best in the Working Group 22 times!

Peter Knoop was handler for the great Storm. Peter had gotten his first exposure to Dobermans while working afternoons and weekends for Francis Fleitmann at his Westphalia Kennels while still in high school. Later he handled the breed on war patrols in the South Pacific. He owned his first Doberman in 1926 and had his own Barlynn Kennels in the early forties. Today Peter Knoop is an all-breed judge.

Storm was said to be a handler's "dream," and Storm and Peter made an incomparable pair in the show ring. He gaited flawlessly for Peter and baited perfectly to the rubber ball Peter held in his hand. He even responded to a wink of the eye. The fabulous Storm was never defeated in the breed during his entire career.

Storm's first show was in Yonkers in 1951, where he won the breed from the Puppy Class. Soon after he won his first Best in Show at the Wilmington Kennel Club show.

Storm was owned by Len Carey, an advertising executive and dog show judge since 1939, and owner of the Kurtiska Kennels which he established in 1936 in California. Storm lived with Len, his wife Shirley and son Jeff in Cos Cob, Connecticut, during most of his life and was always a house dog. Storm and his son, Geronimo, reigned supreme in the show ring—and at home!

The acclaim and publicity given to Storm had never been equalled in the breed. Both before and after his Garden victories he received the widest press coverage of any show dog in history at the time. He was the subject of two newsreels which were shown all over the world and was the featured star of an article in the February 9, 1953, issue of *Life* magazine with photographs by Philipe Halsman and Peter Stackpole; this was the only feature up until that time ever done on an animal.

Royal Doulton made him the subject of a magnificent ceramic model of the Doberman which featured his name on the right rear paw. It sold for $17.50 then, $31 today, and is available all over the world where Royal Doulton china is sold. Storm and Shirley Carey also appeared in advertising displays for Lucky Strike cigarettes.

Esquire magazine's Carl Perutz wrote articles on great dogs and said in his piece on Storm, ". . . whom we privately consider the greatest thing on four canine legs." Storm was written up and featured on the sports pages and the editorial pages of the New York

Ch. Rancho Dobe's Storm wins the 1952 Westminster Kennel Club show at Madison Square Garden in New York. This photograph was taken right after judge Sims gave the coveted rosette and trophies to Len Carey's magnificent Doberman Pinscher. Peter Knoop handled and show chairman John Cross looks on.

World-famous photographer Philippe Halsman is shown photograph-
ing Ch. Rancho Dobe's Storm for a *Life* magazine profile feature on the
dog in the February 9, 1950 issue. This article was the only text piece
ever done on an animal in that magazine until this time. The photograph was taken by John Baird, Mr. Halsman's assistant. Stormie was
owned by Len Carey of Greenwich, Connecticut.

The thrill of a lifetime! Winning at the Garden! Ch. Rancho Dobe's Storm wins Best in Show at the Westminster Kennel Club for the second consecutive time! This win under judge James Farrell. Peter Knoop handled Stormie to this second win for owner Len Carey of Connecticut and California, on February, 10, 1953.

newspapers, and the late MacDonald Daly wrote about Storm in great detail and in glowing terms in the English *Dog World*.

Storm's offspring were top show contenders in this country as well as being behind the top English kennels. Many of those were in Australia also. Percy Roberts, the famous judge, perhaps described it best when he said, "He is probably the best advertisement the Doberman ever had." Not only the best advertisement, but one of the best-remembered dogs in the history of the breed. Storm was afforded great acclaim, and he deserved every bit of it!

The great Ch. Rancho Dobe's Storm died of a heart attack on October 8, 1960, leaving a great void, but also leaving incomparable memories of his greatness in the hearts of his owners, his handler, and all of those who admired him so deeply. And that most assuredly includes the author of this book.

CH. RANCHO DOBE'S STORM COMPLETE SHOW RECORD

1951
Yonkers Kennel Club—Best of Breed
Wilmington Kennel Club—Best in Show under judge George Hartman
Penn-Treaty Kennel Club—Best of Breed
Westchester Kennel Club—Best in Group, judge Colonel William Meyer
Greenwich Kennel Club—Best in Show under judge Ray Patterson
Cape Cod Kennel Club—Best in Show under judge Madeleine Baiter
Mid-Hudson Kennel Club—Best of Breed
Naugatuck Valley Kennel Club—Best in Show under judge Alva Rosenberg
Ox Ridge Kennel Club—Best in Show under Mrs. Grace Bonney
Penn-Jersey DPBA Specialty—Best of Breed under Mrs. Geraldine Dodge
Union County Kennel Club—Best in Group under Alva Rosenberg

1952
Westminster Kennel Club—Best in Show
Hartford Kennel Club—Best in Show under judge Paul Palmer
Eastern Kennel Club—Best in Show under judge Harry Peters
Kennel Club of N. New Jersey—Best in Show under Mrs. Engle
Greenwich Kennel Club—Best in Show under judge Mrs. Frances Crane
Staten Island Kennel Club—Best in Show under Anna Katherine Nicholas
Morris and Essex—Best in Group under judge Joseph Quirk
Orange Empire Kennel Club—Best in Show under Wyman Tyler
Great Barrington Kennel Club—Best in Working Group under Selwyn Harris
Somerset Hills—Best in Show under judge Stanley Halle
Ox Ridge Kennel Club—Best in Show under Joseph Quirk
Valley Forge Kennel Club—Best in Show under Edgar Megargee
Philadelphia Kennel Club—Best in Group under judge Anton Korbel
Camden Kennel Club—Best in Show under Henry Stoecker

1953
Westminster Kennel Club—Best in Show under judge James Farrell
 . . . then retirement!

The great Best in Show winner Ch. Rancho Dobe's Storm poses for a Lucky Strike commercial with Mrs. Len Carey, wife of Stormie's owner

Ch. Rancho Dobe's Storm winning his first Best in Show at the 1951 Wilmington, Delaware Kennel Club show under judge George Hartman. At right is Christopher Ann Carey, daughter of Stormie's owner, Len Carey of Greenwich, Connecticut. Handler is Peter Knoop. Club officials complete the picture of this important win in the illustrious career of a great Doberman.

THE SIXTIES

CH. KAY HILL'S SOUBRETTA

Jane Kay bred Soubretta in 1960. The sire was the fabulous Tri-Champion Borong the Warlock and the dam her Kay Hill's Paint The Town Red. Soubretta, coming from such an illustrious background, was almost destined to make history herself. She won the Doberman Pinscher Club of America futurity stakes in 1961 and their Brood Bitch award for the year 1968. She was the dam of 18 American Kennel Club champions and a Bermuda champion as well. Among her get were five all-breed Best in Show winners, including Axel, Adlu, Bardolf, Bruno and the famous Dolph von Tannenwald.

Soubretta remains the top-producing bitch in the United States through the mid-1970's. Now owned by Kay and Charles Etner of the Tannenwald Kennels in Houston, Texas, Soubretta was purchased from Jane Kay when she was just seven weeks old; she was a house dog throughout her life. John Phelps Wagner, prominent working dog man, considered her the most perfect working dog he had ever seen.

Soubretta was a black and tan, but her red daughter Ch. Dulcie Von Tannenwald, granddaughter Ch. Gilde Von Tannenwald and a red son Erz Von Tannenwald live with Kay Etner today. They continue to use the Von Tannenwald suffix because of all the pine trees which encircle their home.

OTHER 1960's WINNERS

Another top bitch whelped in 1960 was Ch. Ebonaire's Honor Count. Winner of Best of Breed from the classes at the 1962 Westminster Kennel Club over 26 Specials, she finished her championship with four straight majors. Honor Count's dam was Ebonaire's Colonel's Lady, and her sire was Ch. Stebs Top Skipper. Top Skipper, along with Rancho Dobe's Storm, was largely responsible for siring England's greatest Dobermans when bitches they had bred were exported to England after World War II.

The Phillips System winners for 1963 pretty much reflected the dogs that had been winning during the early 1960's, with Ch. Singenwald's Prince Kuhio in command. He was number four Dobe in 1961 and at the 1963 Chicago International Show was Best of Breed, still winning "the big ones." He had many top show wins to his credit including Specialty Shows. He was owned by Bea and Dale Rickert.

Number three Doberman in 1961 was Charles O'Neill's Ch. Ebonaire's Touchdown. His winning continued through the first half of the 1960's as did Ch. Saratoga's Black Pirate. Pirate was owned by Fred and Vivien Reed who also owned Ch. Jussi vom Ahrtal. These two dogs enjoyed a wonderful winning streak on the Arizona circuit by winning Best of Breed or Best Opposite Sex in 12 out of 12 shows.

Ch. Ebonaire's Touchdown, multiple Best in Show winner and multiple Specialty Show winner. the famous Touchdown was one of the nation's Top Ten Dobermans for four consecutive years in the Phillips System; bred by Mr. and Mrs. Edward L. Weiss and owned by Charles A.T. O'Neill and Marie D. O'Neill of Philadelphia. The sire was Ch. Steb's Top Skipper x Ebonaire's Flashing Star.

Pirate also won the Groups at the Galveston and Dallas shows and Jussi the Groups at Austin and Longview.

By 1964 the "top contender title" went to Ch. Haydenhill's Hurrah. The Henry Framptons' Ch. Jem's Amethyst von Warlock was right up there with him, and everyone was delighted with her 1963 Best of Breed win at the Doberman Pinscher Club of Western Pennsylvania Specialty Show and her Best of Opposite Sex placement to Kuhio at the Chicago International, wins they repeated at this show in 1964. 1964 was a winning year for Ch. Mars of the Gladiators, Ch. Haydenhill's Harrigan and Ch. Ru-Mar's Tsushima!

CH. CASSIO VOM AHRTAL

On February 20, 1964, Cassio vom Ahrtal was born at Tess Henseler's Ahrtal Kennels in Ottsville, Pennsylvania. There were four puppies in Cassio's litter, and the other male died. From the very beginning, however, Tess Henseler had a "feeling" that this dog was going to be great, and she never considered selling him. At six months of age he won Best in Match to prove her right; he was off on his show career!

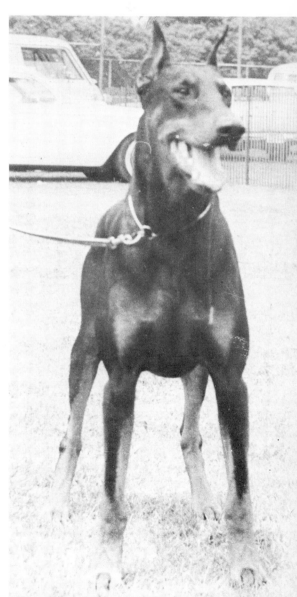

An informal photo of the great Ch. Cassio vom Ahrtal, owned, bred and shown during his ring career by Tess Henseler, Ahrtal Kennels, Ottsville, Pennsylvania.

Ch. Ru-Mar's Tsushima, C.D. pictured winning the Northern California Specialty Show in 1965 under judge Peggy Adamson. Bob Hastings handled for owner Margaret Carveth. The following month she went East for the first time and won the Westchester Kennel Club show. Johnnie McMillan photo.

At 13 months of age he won the breed at the Annapolis show over Specials and went on to win third in the Working Group. He had finished for his championship at 17 months with three majors. One of the majors was won at a Specialty Show. Even though Tess Henseler will be the first to tell you she has loved all her dogs over the years, there is no denying that Cassio was very special to her. He was a house dog, a constant companion to her and loved all the puppies—even kittens—at Ahrtal! His temperament was ideal and his affection also included children and the horses on the farm next to the kennels and runs.

Sire of 36 champions, Cassio has left his mark on the breed for many future generations. Several of the top kennels in the nation recognized the value of this stud and used him in their breeding programs.

When Cassio died on January 8, 1974, just a few weeks short of his tenth birthday, all those who had known this great dog felt a great sadness but looked further toward his 36 sons and daughters and 41 champion great-grandchildren to carry on the excellence and quality he had brought to the breed.

Tess Henseler was named Breeder of the Year eight times between 1954 and 1963 and has produced 63 champions and more than 50 obedience title holders during her more than three decades in the breed.

LADIES DAY IN DOBERMANS

In April of 1965 it became time for a bitch to top the competition in the show ring for Dobermans. The beautiful bitch to make the breakthrough was Ch. Ru-Mar's Tsushima, and the great day was when she topped an entry of 2,982 dogs to win Best in Show at the International Kennel Club of Chicago!

John Rendel, dog writer for the *New York Times*, in his report of the show said that Tsushima's win was the first time a Doberman had topped this show since it became a major dog show event. Tsushima, owned by Margaret Carveth of California, was bred by Marie and Rudy Wagner. Her sire was Ch. Rancho Dobe's Cello and her dam Ch. Jessamyn II v Ahrtal. Just under three years of age, she won the Working Group under judge Henry Stoecker and the coveted Best in Show rosette from judge Joseph Quirk. Both of them were quoted in the Rendel article as having superb showmanship, excellent movement and beautiful condition, high tribute to her owner and her breeders.

1964 seemed to be truly a year for the bitches to come into their own. The Top Ten Ratings in *Popular Dogs'* famous Phillips System showed that four of the Top Ten were bitches and, better still, two of the four had obedience degrees! In the all-breed ratings, Tsushima and Ch. Jem's Amethyst v Warlock ranked eighth and ninth. This was when the Doberman ranked 22nd in registrations with the American

Kennel Club with 4,185 recorded for that year. In spite of being #22, the breed accounted for more Best in Show wins than any of the other working breeds. During 1964 Dobermans won a total of 23 Bests in Show.

Tsushima's win had yet another effect on the breed. The trend toward fanciers wanting to buy bitches instead of dog's became a reality, with the demand for females far exceeding the supply!

Ch. Ru-Mar's Morgansonne, C.D., photographed in 1965, has sired 25 champions and was a Top Producing Stud in the Phillips System for 1967, 1968 and 1969. One of his most outstanding sons is Ch. Andelane's Indigo Rock, a Best in Show winner, whose litter sister was a Top Show Dog for 1965, all breeds, and a Best in Show winner also. Sonny's daughter, Ch. Rudy's Holli-Berri Florowill, was Top Producing Bitch for 1971 and for 1974 with 13 champion get to her credit. Many of Sonny's get are on their way up with Ch. Rudy's Holiday Spirit a Best in Show winner, Morgansonne Maid Marian a top winning bitch in Japan and Morgansonne's Kirby, a Japanese champion. Sonny is owned by Ruth Morgan of Carmichael, California.

MARKS-TEY KENNELS

1965 was a banner year for Joanna Walker's Marks-Tey Kennels also. In March of that year three litter brothers, all from her "H" litter, had racked up impressive wins. Marks-Tey Hanover won the breed at Saw Mill River Kennel Club in New York and Marks-Tey Hondo won the breed and the Working Group at the Nashville, Tennessee event.

Keith and Joanna Walker have been devoted to the breed for many years, and Joanna tied for first place with Barbara Flores as Leading Breeder for the 1974-1975 season, an honor awarded by the Doberman Pinscher Club of America. This same year the Walkers' Ch. Marks-Tey Vale won the title of Top Producing Dam.

CH. RU-MARS MORGANSONNE, C.D.

Ch. Ru-Mar's Morgansonne, C.D., was a winner in both the show and obedience rings and was a marvelous sire as well. Owned by Jack and Ruth Morgan, owners of the Morgansonne Kennels in Carmichael, California, Sonny earned the title of Top Producing Stud in the breed for three consecutive years—1967, 1968 and 1969—with at least five champion offspring finishing in each of those years. His total is 25 champion sons and daughters. One of the most famous of these is the outstanding Ch. Andelane's Indigo Rock, a Best in Show winner, owned by Robert Bishop of Dearborn, Michigan. His most outstanding daughter is Ch. Rudy's Holli-Berri Florowill, who was Top Producing Bitch for 1971 and 1974 with 13 champion get to her credit.

Many of Sonny's get have been exported to Japan, and Morgansonne's Kirby is a Japanese champion.

Ch. Ru-Mar's Morgansonne, C.D., is a litter brother to Ch. Ru-Mar's Tsushima, Top Show Dog for 1965 in all breeds, and a Best in Show winner.

THE VANDEVENTERS

One cannot speak of the 1960's without hearing the name of that outstanding husband-wife combination of professional handlers— Rex and Leota Vandeventer.

Between them the Vandeventers finished between fixty and sixty Dobermans during their handling careers, as well as many other breeds, which often appeared in the same Group or Best in Show rings in competition with each other. The famous Ch. Falstaff vom Ahrtal was among the first and with him they won 23 straight Bests of Breed, several Groups and a Best in Show. Other vom Ahrtal champions they handled were Faust and Bonaparte, the top producing bitch Ch. Kay Hill's Witch Soubretta, Rancho Dobe's Cello and Dow's Anchor v Riecke.

However, their very favorite was the great bitch Ch. Sultana von Marienburg. She was a house pet when not on the show circuit and before her retirement won 38 Bests in Show. In 1967 Rex showed Sultana to more Working Group Firsts than any other breed in that Group and she became winner of the Ken-L-Award trophy for that Group.

Rex also handled Soubretta's daughter Ch. Ru-Mar's Tsushima to three Best in Show wins and seven Groups. They also had the famous sixties winner Ch. Jem's Amethyst v Warlock for part of her show ring career.

All this helped Rex win the Handler of the Year award in 1967. Rex and Leota have retired from the handling profession and are looking toward their judging licenses in the 1970's, which seems a fitting and proper transition within the dog fancy they both enjoy so much. Their success is assured.

THE MARIENBURG KENNELS

The Marienburg Kennels in El Cajon, California, became active in the breed in 1963 with the arrival of their first litter. This kennel, not to be confused with the earlier Marienland Kennels in Baltimore, is owned by Mary M. Rodgers. There have been 22 home-bred champions finished under their banner between 1965 and 1975.

In the mid-sixties John F.K. Of Oklahoma was being shown, and in the following decade a marvelous succession of wonderful Dobermans have come along, including the incomparable American, Mexican and Canadian Ch. Sultana von Marienburg, Ch. Marienburg Maximilian, Ch. Marienburg Red Baron and Marienburg's One And Only, to name just a few. When Sultana died in 1974 her record stood at 37 All-breed Bests in Show, 92 Working Group Firsts, 36 Working Group Placements, 143 Bests of Breed and nine Specialty Show top awards. She was also the dam of four champions.

In 1973, within a three-month period, Marienburg finished three champions: Ch. Marienburg von Starker, Ch. Marienburg Only One and Ch. Marienburg Genghis Khan. One And Only and Khan are co-owned by Mary Rodgers and Moe Miyagawa, their handler. Mary Rodgers has also had her Marienburg dogs serve with the police dog squads in California. Marienburg's Ben Ghalli is with the Oceanside, California police department.

JUDGING DOBERMANS IN THE 1960'S

Anna Katherine Nicholas commented on judging Dobermans in her column in a Working Dog Issue of *Popular Dogs* magazine in which she singled out a few of her favorites which indicate the top Dobes of the day. Her article read in part:

"Judging Dobermans during this past decade has brought me the pleasure of going over some great ones. The mighty Touchdown was a tremendous favorite of mine for which I had much admiration. He

One of the all-time great bitches—American, Mexican and Canadian Champion Sultana von Marienburg, photographed at just under 10 years of age with Moe Miyagawa. Dam of four champion daughters, she was whelped in 1963. Sultana was the top-winning Best in Show Doberman of all time when she died in June, 1974. Bred by George E. Olenik, Sultana was Best of Breed winner at the 1967 Doberman Pinscher Club of America Specialty Show. Owned by the Marienburg Kennels; the sire was Ch. Steb's Gunga Din and the dam Farley's Princess.

Ch. Ebonaire's Balestra pictured winning Best of Breed under judge Ross Hamilton at the 1961 Southern Tier Kennel Club show. One of the famous "football and fencing" litter sired by Ch. Steb's Top Skipper x Ebonaire's Flashing Star, the Top Dam for 1960; the litter mates included Ch. Ebonaire's Touchdown, Gridiron, Flying Tackle and Touche. She is shown here handled by J. Monroe Stebbins, owner of her famous sire. Bred and owned by Judy and Ed Weiss, Ebonaire Kennels, Levittown, New York.

Opposite:
A classic headstudy of Ch. Ebonaire's Entertainer. Renowned in the breed, Entertainer was two years old when this photograph was taken. Owned and bred by Judy and Ed Weiss, Levittown, New York.

87

won a Specialty from me along with numerous other awards. Also, I especially was impressed by Ch. Tarra's Aventina, my Best of Breed several years ago at the Connecticut-New York Specialty. Such elegance, soundness, style and balance. Truly a picture bitch. Then there was Ch. Damasyn the Tartian, an EXCELLENT Doberman of power and substance. And, most recently, the glorious, beautiful Ch. Biggin Hill's Alarich, owned respectively by the O'Neills, the D'Amicos, Mr. Gustafson and Mr. and Mrs. Biggin. These Dobes are the ones I have especially enjoyed judging in the Sixties."

During the 1960's Charles E.T. O'Neill and his young daughter, Mari-Beth, were also active in the showing of top-winning Manchester Terriers. Their interest in both breeds carried over into the 1970's but had to be restricted when Charles became one of the Directors of the American Kennel Club. While this necessitated his absence from the show ring, he and his family are still much in evidence at many of the dog shows and especially at Doberman functions.

Charles O'Neill was a former Delegate to the American Kennel Club for the Doberman Pinscher Club of America and its President from 1965 to 1970. In 1975 he won a Gaines Medal for Good Sportsmanship awarded to him by the Quaker City Doberman Pinscher Club in Pennsylvania for outstanding contributions to the sport of dogs.

THE SEVENTIES

While Ch. Rancho Dobe's Maestro finished the 1960's as number 10 in the breed according to the Phillips System, by 1970 he was number one dog, all-breeds, and had been voted Top Winning Working Dog in the Kennel Review Hall of Fame, as he had been in 1967.

During this first year in the 1970's, Ch. Weichardt's A-Go-Go and Ch. Dolph von Tannenwald were moving up behind Maestro as numbers eight and nine. By the time the Phillips System finals were announced Go-Go and Dolph had reversed positions, with Dolph number two with three Bests in Show and Go-Go number three with one Best in Show.

Maestro, owned by Mr. and Mrs. Corky Vroom of El Monte, California, had won ten Bests in Show and 27 Group Firsts, amassing a total of 26,056 points in the Phillips System. This amazing score represented a point for each dog defeated in competition during the previous year, and made him the number two Dog in the Nation for 1970.

Dolph's position as number two Doberman also earned him the title of number six in the Top Ten Working Dog category, and Go-Go's record earned him number nine position in the Top Ten Working Dogs. Dolph had earned a total of 13,226 points and Go-Go, 11,930.

Interest in Dobermans was keen during this first year of a new decade and the breed moved up to number 14 in American Kennel Club registrations. From January 1, 1970 through December 31, 1970, 18,636 Dobermans had been registered with the AKC. This was a two-

Another Working Group win for E. Steven Barrett's Ch. Weichardt's A-Go-Go, C.D., at the 1970 Memphis Kennel Club show. Earl Graham photo.

position move up from the number 16 placing in 1969 when 14,232 Doberman Pinschers were registered according to their statistics. It was incredible to learn also that during this single year 1,056,225 dogs of all breeds had been registered, which gave everyone some indication about the popularity of dogs and dog shows and what the future decade would see.

CH. DOLPH VON TANNENWALD

It is amazing to contemplate the show record Dolph von Tannenwald could have amassed had he lived a long life, when one considers that upon his early demise he had probably defeated more Dobermans and more dogs in all-breed competition than any other Doberman. According to his record, when he died on June 3, 1972 he had won 28 Bests in Show, 209 Bests of Breed, six Specialty Show Bests of Breed and 78 Groups. This impressive tally of wins made him number one in the Phillips System ratings for 1971, number two Working Dog, and number three Dog in the Nation all-breeds. What particularly delighted his owners and Jeffrey Brucker, his handler, was that he was Top-Winning Sire for the same year.

There were many great moments and important wins during that illustrious career, including a Breed and Group Second win at Westminster. A dog of great stamina, Dolph was never perturbed by cross-country flights between shows and could always be counted on to both protect when necessary and to be sociable when the occasion demanded. His constant companion at home was a Chihuahua named Kat, and he was so well adjusted to the world that he needed only to be crated when benched at the shows.

Dolph was selected by Jeff Brucker and was an anniversary present from George West to his wife Sheila. When not with his handler, Dolph lived with the Wests at Muttontown, New York. The 27¼-inch, 73-pound dynamo that thrilled the show world unfortunately contracted cancer of the lungs. After a short hospitalization where the malady was discovered, Dolph went home to Jeff and Betty Brucker, where he died painlessly.

The Wests kept three daughters of Dolphs and a son, Lakewind's Count von West, to carry on, but none will ever take the place of their one and only Dolph, the dog they referred to as their "magnificent obsession!"

Opposite:
The top-winning Doberman Pinscher of all time! The late, great, Ch. Dolph von Tannenwald, pictured here winning at a 1970 show. Dolph, one of the Top Ten dogs in the Phillips System during most of his career, was handled by Jeffrey Brucker and was owned by George and Sheila West of Pound Ridge, New York.

PHILLIPS SYSTEM RATINGS FOR TOP-WINNING DOBERMANS

By the end of 1971 there was not too much of a change in the positioning of the nation's winners. 1971 was one of the years the author was editor of *Popular Dogs* magazine, which featured the famous Phillips System ratings of the top winning dogs in the United States. Part of my job was to tabulate show records of all the breeds and, while space only permitted the publication of the Top Ten in each breed, my records for the Doberman Pinschers at the beginning of 1970 included the top 25 Dobes. I list them here for the purpose of an extended look at the Doberman picture since most of the important kennel names of the era are represented along with the individual dogs which were making "history" for the breed. I am also including the number of Bests in Show and Working Group Firsts, as well as their point count. Bear in mind that each point represents a dog which has been defeated by them in the show ring while winning either a Best in Show, Specialty or Group Placement.

1. CH. DOLPH VON TANNENWALD: Total Points, 37,460; Bests in Show, 18; Group Firsts, 45.
2. CH. WEICHARDT'S A-GO-Go, C.D.: Total Points, 37,192; Bests in Show, 10; Group Firsts, 35.
3. CH. HOUSECARL HOPE OF DIVERSHA: Total Points, 19,073; Bests in Show, 15; Group Firsts, 31.
4. CH. ANDELANE'S INDIGO ROCK: Total Points, 13,098; Bests in Show, 6; Group Firsts, 16.
5. CH. AVENTINE'S TAMIKO: Total Points, 5,291; Bests in Show, 1; Group Firsts, 6.
6. CH. KAY HILL'S DEALER'S CHOICE: Total Points, 2,908; Group Firsts, 3.
7. CH. LU-ELL'S AMY LOU: Total Points, 2,533; Bests in Show, 2; Group Firsts, 3.
8. CH. MARIENBURG'S RED BARON: Total Points, 2,359; Group Firsts, 1.
9. CH. VOLTAIRE'S ADVENTURER: Total Points, 2,058; Bests in Show, 1; Group Firsts, 1.
10. CH. VON MAC'S MIKKI MAUS: Total Points, 1,961; Bests in Show, 1; Group Firsts, 2.
11. CH. TRANELL'S MAXWELL SMART: Total Points, 1,947; Group Firsts, 1.
12. CH. TEDELL PRIVATE LABEL: Total Points, 1,833; Bests in Show, 1; Group Firsts, 2.

Opposite:
Ch. Von Mac's Mikki Maus winning a Working Group at a Hutchinson, Kansas Kennel Club show. Handler, Betty Moore.

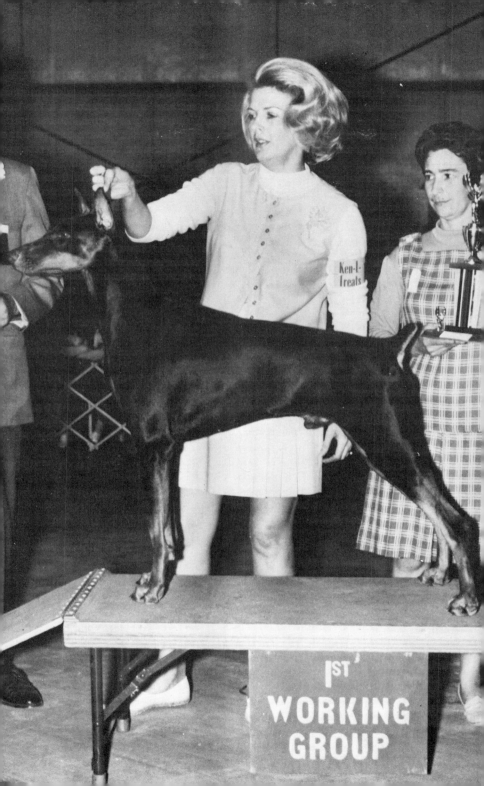

13. CH. MARKS-TEY VIXEN: Total Points, 1,676; Group Firsts, 1.
14. CH. FANFARE'S RINGMASTER: Total Points, 1,657; Bests in Show, 1; Group Firsts, 2.
15. CH. BELFORT'S ARTEMIS: Total Points, 1,499.
16. CH. THE MAESTRO'S REFLECTION: Total Points, 1,390; Group Firsts, 1.
17. CH. STAFFORD'S CAIRO: Total Points, 1,191.
18. CH. EIDO VON TANNENWALD, C.D.: Total Points, 1,161.
19. CH. BIGGIN HILL'S BECKETT: Total Points, 1,021; Group Firsts, 1.
20. CH. FLOROWILL T.N.T.: Total Points, 949; Group Firsts, 1.
21. CH. HOUSECARL HEATHER: Total Points, 921; Group Firsts, 2.
22. CH. BROWN'S A-AMANDA: Total Points, 882; Group Firsts, 1.
23. CH. HOTAI SWEET WILLIAM: Total Points, 881; Group Firsts, 2.
24. CH. DAREDOBE'S KASH: Total Points, 726; Group Firsts, 1.
25. CH. RIOBEAU'S VALLEY FORGE: Total Points, 702; Group Firsts, 1.

PHILLIPS SYSTEM RATINGS FOR TOP SIRES AND DAMS

By the end of 1971 the top sires and dams in the country were also evident on the scene, with their get winning all over the nation. On the top of the list was Ch. Dolph von Tannenwald, sire of eight champions during that calendar year and winner of the title of number one sire in the breed according to the Phillips System Ratings.

Ch. Highbriar Bandana and Ch. Gra-Lemor Demitrius v d Victor accounted for seven champions each in 1972, and the famous Ch. Cassio vom Ahrtal sired six champions. Champion studs, each responsible for siring three champions, were Ch. Alnwick's Black Fury Bismarck, C.D.; Ch. Damasyn Derringer, Ch. Haydenhill's Hurrah, Ch. Kay Hill's Takeswon To Nowon and Ch. Rancho Dobe's Maestro. These champions were to set the breed up in great style during the decade of the seventies.

Holding their own in great style, and keeping in mind that a bitch cannot whelp as often as a male can be used at stud, the Florowill Kennels' bitch Ch. Rudy's Holli-Berri Florowill produced four champions during 1971, making her Top Producing Doberman Pinscher bitch according to the Phillip System ratings. Carlatta v d Elbe, Dobereich's Duress, Hy-Vale Acres

Ch. Brown's A-Amanda winning Best of Breed at the 1971 Doberman Pinscher Club of America Specialty Show in Sacramento, California, under judge Rod Carveth. Charles A.T. O'Neill presents the trophy. Owners are Mr. and Mrs. John Brown, Mr. Brown handling.

Ilysa, C.D., Ch. Holly Wood's Miss Chocolate, Kimbertal's Liza von Bywyd, Marienburg's Inca, Ch. Marks-Tey Shay, Rio Beau's Kessie, Ch. Rudy's Christmas Angel, Ch. Stafford's Spitfire, Tamerlane Alert Abbie and Warlock's Black Orchid, C.D., each produced two champions.

OTHER WINNING DOBERMANS OF THE 1970's

Another Best in Show Doberman that helped to usher in the first half of the 1970's was Ch. Peri's Prince Temujin, owned by Marian Wallhofer of Pawling, New York. In 1973 "Bruiser" was number seven Doberman in Group and Best in Show competition. His show record includes 12 Bests of Breed, one Best in Show, two Group Firsts, two Group Seconds, three Group Thirds, and two Group Fourths, plus several Best of Opposite Sex wins.

Bruiser was the only dog shown from this first home-bred litter, and he has a C.D.X. daughter and a C.D. son so far in his stud record.

The 1970's also produced the winning Tri-International Champion Warlock's Diablo Rojo. "Red" as he was called by his owners, A.K. and Mary J. Bara of Houston, Texas, was featured on the cover of the March/April issue of *Top Dobe* in 1974 announcing that he was about to sit back and watch his youngsters come up in the show ring.

In 1971 American and Canadian Ch. Eido von Tannenwald, C.D.X., was winning laurels. He was the top-winning male Doberman in the Pacific Northwest for 1971 and 1972, the number four top-winning male Doberman in all of the United States for 1971 and number seven top-winning male Doberman in the U.S. for 1972. Eido was retired from the show ring in 1973 by his owners, Barbara and Gerald Gaines of Amor Natura Kennels, Tacoma, Washington. Eido was sired by Ch. Cassio vom Ahrtal out of Ch. Kay Hill's Witch Soubretta.

1972 produced a bumper crop of obedience dogs which also represented the top kennels in the nation. 405 Dobermans earned their Companion Dog titles that year, 89 went on to their C.D.X. degrees and 21 completed their Utility Dog requirements. It is gratifying to notice when scanning the list of title holders how many of them were also champions.

In 1973 two great beauties came into their own! Ch. Galaxy's Corry Missile Belle, who graced the cover of the Annual Spring Sta-

Eleanore Brown and her Ch. Brown's Gi Gi, the dam of Ch. Brown's A-Amanda (winner of the 1971 DPCA Specialty) and of Ch. Brown's B-Brian (winner of the DPCA Specialties in 1973 and 1975)—by two different sires! These triple Specialty wins meant that the Browns retired all the challenge trophies offered by the DPCA.

Ch. Peri's Prince Temujin, photographed winning his first points toward championship at one and one-half years of age under judge Robert Salomon at the 1971 Westbury Kennel Club Show. Co-owner with Marian Wallhofer of Pawling, New York is Marilyn Meshirer who handled Prince (otherwise known as Bruiser) to this first big win.

Ch. Welwyn Corette, one of the Top Ten Dobermans for 1974 and 1975. This beautiful bitch was sired by Ch. Tarrado's Corry out of Ch. Weichardt's A-Go-Go, C.D. Corette is owned by E. Steven Barrett, Palos Verdes Estates, California. Corette is pictured here winning the Breed at a 1975 show under judge Virginia Hampton.

tistics Issue of the *Doberman Quarterly*, and her equally beautiful sister, Ch. Galaxy's Corry Carina, literally swept over the show trail, beating stiff competition at all the major shows. They also shared the honor of being the only two bitches in the Top Ten polls that year.

Belle was number one Working Dog for 1973 and number one in points for all breeds. Carina was number seven. A male Doberman, Ch. Andelane's Indigo Rock, was number five. Three Dobermans out of the Top Ten is quite a showing!

Carina is co-owned by the Frank D'Amicos and Mrs. Cheever Porter of New York City. Jane Forsyth handled Carina for her owners. By September of 1974 Carina's record had reached 24 Bests in Show and 61 Working Group Firsts.

As this book goes to press in the mid-1970's, it is interesting to note the names of important kennels from the past few decades still

Ch. Civetta's Wolf Whistle of Kami, C.D. earned her Companion Dog title by seven months of age and her championship at twelve and one-half months. "Toot" went to Group First from the Puppy Class during her campaign for championship and has been in the Top Twenty Dobes list in *Top Dobe* magazine for two years. She is working for her C.D.X. degree as well.

ST OF
REED
OTO BY TATHAM

Ch. Damasyn The Jalli-Alli, C.D. and Damasyn The Christmas Carol, C.D., photographed in 1964 with their trainer and handler, Carol Selzle. The Dobes were bred by Peggy Adamson of the Damasyn Kennels in Roslyn Heights, New York.

The magnificent Ch. Tedell Eleventh Hour, bred by Theodora Linck, who co-owns him with Nancy Kibiloski. This striking black male made a breed record still unbroken as of the end of 1975. At eight months he was Best in Show at an all-breed show (under judges Leona Sharpley, Virgil Johnson and Charles Kellog). During his career he was shown by three prominent handlers: Bill Haines when he was a youngster and won his first Best in Show; Jane Kay during his early career, with several Specialty wins and Group Placings; and George Rood for the remainder of his ring career, during which he won the title of Number One Doberman in the country and Number Five Working Dog. He sired many champions, including Ch. Silent Sentry's Bikini, Best Puppy at the 1968 DPCA Specialty, and American and Canadian Ch. Misti Morn's Stormi Night, C.D., that won a Best in Show in Canada. The Tedell kennels are in Toledo, Ohio. Eleventh Hour was whelped in 1965 and died in 1974.

holding their own with top quality show dogs—"proof positive" that their breeding programs have produced dogs representing the criterions of the breed. We see names like Damasyn, Tedell, Marks-Tey, Gra-Lemor, Von Mac, Brandendorf, Hotai, Tarrado, Marien-burg, Tamarack, High Tor, Ahrtal, Ebonaire, Elfred, Biggin Hill, Galaxy and Zenodobe, to name a few.

It will be fascinating to watch in the years ahead the dogs that will end up victorious as top show dogs of the 1970's, the decade the glorious Dolph got off to such a fantastic start! How far Dobermans have come in less than a single century! What a wonderful tribute to breeders and owners who have persevered and, dedicated to the Standard, have brought the breed to what it is today.

But no matter how great the breed is in the future, we must never forget what the dogs from the past have given to that perfection. The Doberman has a royal heritage!

THE DOBERMAN PINSCHER TODAY

These chapters on the history of the Doberman through the years are by no means purported to be a *complete* list of all the excellent and influential Dobermans which have upheld the breed in this country—or any of the other countries—since it first came into prominence. The Doberman has gained such tremendous popularity so quickly that any list represented as being "complete" would be a gross misrepresentation.

All one needs to do is consult the lists of thousands upon thousands of registrations, champions and obedience dogs at the American Kennel Club to know that naming them all would be impossible. However, there have been certain dogs which made outstanding contributions by way of show records or stud services that must be considered as having had more than average influence on the breed during their lifetimes, and we have included as many of them as possible in an effort to present a true cross-section of the breed in all its majesty, either in photographs or in text.

The author pays tribute to the dogs and to their owners and handlers who so diligently guided their careers. But I would also like to pay tribute to any and all others which might have been unintentionally omitted from this book, or for reasons best known to their breeders and owners, never reached the spotlight. It is regrettable that many dogs, in every breed, never attain their claim to fame! But those of us who love this breed are, nevertheless, grateful to each and every one of them for their part in bringing the Doberman to its present state of magnificence!

3. THE DOBERMAN PINSCHER AROUND THE WORLD

THE DOBERMAN IN SWITZERLAND

While the exact date of the first importations to Switzerland is not recorded, by 1902 there was a sufficient number of interested Doberman owners to warrant formation of the Swiss Dobermannpinscher Club. The first breed registrations at that time were entries of four German imports, two males and two females, and one Swiss-bred bitch. As a matter of comparison, by 1912 there were 85 registrations and by 1932, 161. More than half of these were German imports during the first twenty years, and the restricted breeding of the few dogs and bitches available led to inevitable breeding problems.

The Dobermans were seldom true black in color, had spotted chests and frequently white paws. Godfried Liechti, an important breeder in Switzerland and owner of the Lentulus Kennels in Bern, referred in his writings to the Dobermans of that time as being "heavily overbuilt" and having "long, curly, and heavily underlaid coat, with a woolly undercoat."

Improvement came with the appearance of a bitch named Gertrud v Frauenlob, sired by the important German dog Leporello v d Nidda. Her influence on the breed held for many years throughout Switzerland. Also the introduction of Hellegraf v Thueringen and his son, Lord v Reid, added much improvement. These two important German dogs went back to Herr Otto Groeller's Freya.

Much needed "neck" was added to the breed when Godfried Liechti and three other breeders, Gutjahr, Gribi and a Miss Hermanhauser, used their dogs, Carlo, Leporello, Glocke II, Roland and Senta v Tale, in their breeding programs. Even though more neck was introduced at this time, heads still remained disproportionate, and the heavy bodies and bad, faded markings still persisted and were most obvious.

Around the turn of the century, in 1903 to be exact, a black dog named Graf Siggo v Hohenstien was whelped. Over his lifetime Siggo was known by many aliases so perhaps this worthy son of Prinz v. Ilm-Athen never got full credit for his contribution to the breed in Switzerland where his line was known for both a few coarse traits and a diabolical sharpness.

Gertrud II Frauenlob, a daughter of Leporello, carried on for her parents in benefiting the Swiss lines. Through her breeding to the dogs of Mr. Gutjahr's v Tale strain, she introduced quality and influenced the Lentulus lines. A German dog, Calo Frauenlob, whelped in 1908, was bred to her and saw great success in Switzerland, but died out in Germany. Her son, Roland v Tale, sired by the great Lord v Ried, brought the name Leporello to fame through his son, named Leporello v Tale.

In 1911, Glocke II v Tale, mentioned briefly before, was whelped and came to be a major influence in both the Lentulus and Baerenburg lines. She was a daughter of Gertrud II Frauenlob sired by Hans v Aprath.

In 1913, the black bitch Helda Lentulus, a Leporello v Tale and Glocke II v Tale daughter, came to fame by producing three important Swiss Dobermans named Miss Berneck, Budy Hambuehl and Bosco Hambuehl.

Max Heidenstien was whelped in 1914 and stood up well in the stud service department. He was the sire of Miss Berneck, one of the leading bitches in Switzerland to that date.

In 1918 Max Hambuelh was whelped and later distinguished himself as the sire of Bosco and Budy Hambuehl. In 1919 a decided influence was to appear with the whelping of Axel v Hindendorf. He and his son, Axel Kirchbuehl, benefited the breed immeasurably.

Of all the dogs, however, which were to leave their mark, perhaps Tasso v d WeissenElster and Helda Lentulus did the most to change the direction of the breed before 1920. After 1920 Helda's daughter, Miss Berneck, owned by Carl Wittwer and sired by the brown dog Max v Heidenstein, picked up where her mother left off and made a marked contribution to the breed, allowing them to be compared favorably at last with the quality stock of Germany.

In 1920 Miss Berneck was bred to Edelblut v Jaegerhof, the most popular sire in the country at the time and their union brought better pigmentation to the breed in Switzerland.

1920 was also the year that two good sires appeared in Switzerland, the black Dox v d Baerenburg and the brown Bosco Hambuehl. A black and a brown bitch also gained prominence: Dely v d Baerenburg, the dam of Gerda Lentulus and Emir Lentulus, and the brown Budy Hambuehl, which later gained fame as the dam of Axel Kirchbuehl. Emir was whelped in 1925 and excelled as both sire and show dog.

When Donar v Beundenfled was whelped on May 19, 1928, we find the result of one Swiss breeder's calculated breeding program. By

A personal post card sent to his Doberman friends the world over by Dr. Joseph Bodinebauer, "und Frau". Dr. Bodinebauer is a full professor specializing in animal behavior and is pictured on the card in his native Austria with his two Dobermans.

1928 the Swiss had realized the importance of once again introducing German bloodlines to their lines and went back to German studs. Donar's sire was Edel v d Barbarossahoehle, and his dam was Britta v Beundenfeld. This dog was beneficial to the breed by bringing back the Edelblut v Jaegerhof and Lux v d Blankenburg bloodlines.

In 1930 importations were made to Switzerland. Annerl v Zinsgut was the best bitch of her color this year and produced several litters in Switzerland during the following years. Angar von Angustenburg, a brown bitch whelped on July 25, 1930, was imported and, though her only claim to fame was as a producer, she did become a Swiss champion. She produced a famous trio of brown bitches named Alma, Asta and Annemirl v Sailerhaus when bred to Asso v Memminger-mau.

By 1931 the Swiss imported Egil zum Ziel from Germany, which brought additional improvement to the breed.

Then the war years. . . . While Switzerland was protected from all outside conflict by her wall of almost insurmountable mountains, breeders had to depend upon the stock on hand to continue their breeding programs.

Other kennels and their owners which must be mentioned when recalling the Swiss history of the Doberman are the Aris kennel owned by E. Gysin, Mr. Fluekiger's Hagburg line, the von Bruderholtz, Loosli, Brandis and Roth lines, C. Wittwer's Baerenburg Kennel, R. Thut's Berneck Kennel, F. Bigler's Beundenfeld Kennel and G. Schweizer's Kirchbuehl Kennel, all located in Bern, Mr. J. Buerki's Brandes Kennel in Rueegsauschachen, Mr. J.E. Albrecht's Hambuehe Kennel in Jegenstorg, and Mr. Guebi's Heidenstein Kennels in Lenbringen. All, through dedicated planning, added to the stature of the breed in their country.

THE DOBERMAN PINSCHER IN HOLLAND

Holland followed Switzerland by a very few years when it came to obtaining importations from Germany. And here again, it was the foresight of Herr Otto Groeller who sent some of his top stock to that

Alva vom Franckenhorst, SchH I, and 1973 Weltsieger at the World Dog Show. Bred by Sonja of the Netherlands.

country in 1904 that was responsible for getting the Dutch kennels off to a good start.

First to launch the breed in Holland was H. van der Hurk who adopted the kennel name of v Apolda, in deference to the town from which the dogs came. Along with Mr. A.A. Grasso and a few others who took a marked fancy to the breed, they imported Lotte v Thueringen, Casimir v Thueringen, Petronella v Thueringen, Glocke v Thueringen and Hermandad v Thueringen from Otto Groeller. They also imported Bobi v Fichtenhof, Elso v Hohenstein, Bodo v Hohenstein, Gerda v Friesland, Waldo v Hohenstein, and Sigrid v Saxonia.

There was enough interest in this important imported stock to cause the formation of a Doberman club by 1906. New member H. Kloeppel became a staunch supporter of the breed. About this same time, however, several imported dogs failed to produce the expected quality in the litters they were siring. It wasn't until the Sieger and Champion Troll v Albtal was imported that there was renewed interest in the breed in Holland.

The Dutch now had excellent stock from Troll and the v Jaegerhof and v Merseburg lines, and the quality of the Dutch-bred dogs could match the best from other countries. A brown bitch named Carmen v Kraichgau stood for top quality on the distaff side and her name could be found in the majority of pedigrees on the very best dogs Holland had to offer. Imported to Holland by Mr. H. Kloeppel of The Hague as a foundation bitch for his v Grammont Kennels, she is said to have deserved all the praise that was heaped upon her.

1906 was the year Wedigo II v Thueringen was born. A son of the famous Hellegraf and a grandson of Slenz, he marked the beginning of the Roemerschanz strain from which almost all of the important Dutch dogs are descended.

In 1908 Sepp v Kraichgau was bred. He belonged to Mr. Kloeppel also and had a great influence on the breed at that time. Mr. Kloeppel founded a great deal of his important stock on this stud. Sepp was sired by the famous Lord v Reid, imported to Germany, and himself a major influence on the breed in that country. Hella v d Roemerschanz was also whelped this year, sired by Wedigo v Thueringen x Dora II v Schwaben. She was said to be "stately," and this important brown bitch helped to build the breed in Holland.

In 1910 Rino v d Roemerschanz was whelped. A brown dog, he was known as the sire of Troll v Albtal who was considered to be of great influence on the breed in Holland.

By 1913 Fernando v Merseburg had arrived on the scene. Sired by Moritz v Burgwall and Adelgunde v Treuhort, this dog's success in Holland was based on his stud prowess and an excellent son, Rival's Adonis.

1915, with the devastating war approaching Holland, produced the brown dog Urian v Grammont. Sired by the excellent Edelblut v

Litta of Bamby's Pride, several times Best of Breed, who needs only one Championship Certificate to become a Dutch champion. This lovely import from Japan was shown in the Netherlands in 1973. Owner, Sonja of Dordrecht, the Netherlands.

Jaegerhof x Carmen v Kraichgan, he himself was short of leg. The condition was said to be pre-natal, and he was excellent in every other way. The condition was probably what we refer to today as chondrodysplasia, or dwarfism. It did not show up again, however, for four generations.

1915 also produced Undine v Grammont, a brown bitch whelped in the same litter which produced Ajax v Grammont, sire of Carlo v d Koningstad, the grandsire of Favorit v d Koningstad, perhaps one of the all time greats in the early days of the breed.

The famine was everywhere on the European continent by 1917, but it was the year of the birth of Ajax v Grammont. Sired by Rival's Adonis x Undine v Grammont, his substantial influence was expressed through the very excellent Carlo v d Koningstad and through progeny exported to Belgium and later to America.

Angola v d Grammont was a brown litter-sister to Ajax and was subsequently exported to America, where she went to the White Gate Kennels in Philadelphia, but not before she had whelped Elfreida, Favorit and Ilisa v d Koningstad.

As the war came closer to the borders of Holland, the great dogs they had imported from Germany suddenly seemed in jeopardy. By 1919 most of the best dogs from both Germany and Holland were sent to America to assure their survival.

The best black dog in 1920 was Benno v d Roemerhof, bred in Holland and later exported to America when he was five years of age. Benno and Ilissa of Westphalia were the only foreign-bred Dobermans ever to have a Sieger title conferred upon them by a German breed organization.

It was also during 1920 that Elfreida v d Koningstad was whelped on October 14th. She was an outstanding show bitch and produced admirably through an excellent son, Big Boy of White Gate, which was sired by Claus v d Spree. She was exported to the United States and added greatly to the breed there.

1921 produced the important brown dog Favorit v d Koningstad, whelped June 19th. The dog was so great he was also exhibited in Germany with great success before being sent to America, where he was regarded as the best stud to come from overseas. Many of his get were sent back to Germany where they were later shown with equal success in that country. It was said that Favorit did for America what Horst v Stresow did for Russia. That is to say that these two dogs were of strong potency in the future generations of the breed and strong in passing on their individual desirable traits important to the breed at the time.

During the breed's reign in Holland, therefore, the important kennels were Rivals Kennel owned by Mr. van der Schoot in Francker and the v d Roemerhof Kennels owned by Mr. La Noble, as well as those already mentioned.

The Dutch club, the Nederlandsche Dobermannpinscher Club, maintains the stud book for Holland which, with its hundreds of entries dating back to the early imports, is accurate proof of the popularity of the breed in that country.

THE DOBERMAN IN CZECHOSLOVAKIA

The Doberman reached Czechoslovakia by 1914, and a dog named Fels v d Krenzhorst was famous in that country as a stud. Sired by Wotan v Thueringen, he went back to the best of the German lines with this Thueringen blood.

By 1916, with the appearance of Sidi Meierhoefer (whelped on July 21 of that year) the breed took yet another step ahead in the breed. Sired by Rudi v Bayern x Hexe v Muehlbergwarte, this bitch became a prime producer for the Czecholslovakie Falkenstein kennels.

In 1918 a blue bitch, whelped on April 12 and named Meta v Ostersee, came along to head up a long line of quality Czech Dobermans. Shortly thereafter Angola v d Dreiflussestadt came along to also play an important part in the breed.

In 1920 an important "coup" was made by the Czechoslovakian breeders. A fine dog named Alex v d Finohoehe was born. On paper his pedigree could not be surpassed. He was sired by a dog named Achim v Langerode out of Leddy v d Blankenburg. For some odd reason he went virtually unnoticed and completely unappreciated in his native Germany. A Czech purchased him at a very nominal cost and he went on to great fame in Czechoslovakia. Bred to the best bitches, he did much to improve the breed and root out the vicious blood brought in by the Roland dog a few years back. He is said to have stabilized the breed through his progeny, including his son, Stolz v Roeneckenstein, Ari and Alto v Sigalsburg, Modern v Simmenau, Lux II and Lotte II v Simmenau, Dora Veckardtsburg and so on through succeeding generations. His blood was said to be important to the breed in every way and in each of his attempts at reproduction. Philipp Gruenig said after seeing the dog in 1927 that with the exportation of Alex Germany had lost one of its best sires of all time. High praise indeed!

The first fawn, or Isabella, Doberman and the second brown dog were also influential in the breed in this country. Gilka v d Sternalee was whelped December 4, 1920. Sired by Zeus v Parthengrund out of Meta v Ostersee, Gilka and her son, Fels v d Kreuzhorst, were important to the breed. The brown litter sister, Goldelse v d Sternallee, became the dam of one of the top Dobermans of this time, Artus v Friedeck.

1920 was a good year for the breed in Czechoslovakia. Not only did the important dogs already mentioned do their part, but 1920 was also the year that another brown bitch came into being. Whelped on January 15, Lola v d Goldenen Hoehe went on to serve the interests of the breed in every way possible. She was perhaps best known as the dam of a daughter named Nixe Meirling, who picked up where her mother left off as a brood matron making a contribution to the betterment of the breed.

Joan McDonald Brearley with Ch. Damasyn The Forecast (pictured on the cover) and a red. Photo by Miceli Studios, Ltd.

In 1921 Angola v d Dreifluessestadt was whelped and became important to the breed. Her sire was Harras v Ostersee x Freya v Rottal.

1922 was the year of the whelping of Fels v d Kreuzhorst. Though out of a fawn mother, he proved his dominance in the breed by producing all black progeny. 1922 was also the year for another brown stud to come into prominence in Czechoslovakia. Artus v Friedeck, whelped January 2nd, was sired by Salto v Rottal and Goldelse v d Sternallee. Since his paternal lines were all brown in color, his progeny were also brown, and he became known through the excellence of a particularly good brown daughter, Bora v d Goldflagge. Bora was said to be the best Doberman in Czechoslovakia, and was owned by Mr. Hosch in Bruenn.

By 1925 another top bitch had come along. Whelped in May of that year, Blanka v Korsika, a daughter of Artus v Friedeck, was to become famous as the dam of Beno z Nameste, after a mating to Dar z Isonzo. Dalila z Isonzo was another top bitch, always at her best in the show ring.

This succession of excellent sires and dams meant that by 1925 the Czechs had made excellent progress in breeding by properly cross breeding their imports and thereby establishing a line of native-bred dogs which would carry them through to World War II. Following the war the breed progressed on a small scale with records and listings available in that country.

THE DOBERMAN PINSCHER IN RUSSIA

One of the first Dobermans to be exported to Russia was the bitch Elfriede v Elsass, whelped on August 15, 1914. Her sire was the great Modern v Ilm-Athen x Nora v Elsass, which assured the Russians of getting off to a rather good start with the bloodlines she carried into their country. Through Elfriede's brown daughter, Lotte II v Stresow, she became the grandmother of a dog which was to establish a very active and important Russian strain that was to become known and respected far and wide in Russia. This dog, named Horst v Stresow, was whelped on December 9, 1922. His sire was Troll v d Blankenburg.

The eminent Doberman authority at the time, Philipp Gruenig, highly revered today through his important writings on the breed, described Horst as ". . . the modern Dobermann's pioneer in the Soviet Republics. Compact and correct, tight of back with straight and strong legs, chest both wide and deep. . . his progeny, especially the dogs of the Arbet strain, were a true and constant reflection of himself in both their external traits and appearance. . . with the few bitches available he worked marvels of both quantity and quality."

Another important stud that worked wonders for the breed in Russia was to soon appear on the scene. An excellent dog named

Artus v Eichenhein. Artus was whelped on February 2, 1923 and was sired by the great Lux v d Rochsburg out of Asta v d Rochsburg. When he was two years of age he was imported to Russia and caused a good deal of comment in his new domain in Leningrad with owner L. Henningson at the Arbet Kennels. He was a rather large dog and, according to Mr. Gruenig, lacked compactness because of his size, but he did well for the Russian strains.

Asta v d Spree, a black bitch whelped on April 20, 1920, proved to be one of the strongest foundation bitches in this country. Her sire was Burschel v Simmenau out of Fanny v d Blankenburg.

Bona v Seehagen, a Lux daughter of half brother-sister breeding, proved to be of high value to the Russian breeding program. Her sire was Lux and the half-sister dam was Adda v d Blankenburg.

DOG SHOWS IN RUSSIA

Russia acknowledges both local and national champions, and these regional titles can be won many times, though there is usually only one regional show per year. Every few years there is a show called an All National, and the national champion from this show is the top winning dog. Dogs are rated excellent, very good, fair, poor or unacceptable, depending on both performance and conformation.

Russia held its first dog show in 1923, and shows have survived all regimes and political changes, though they are on a smaller scale than in other countries. As elsewhere in the world, the dedicated core of devoted breeders managed to preserve the important bloodlines during the various wars.

In Russia if you wish to buy a dog you must do so through a local dog club, and the cost will depend on the quality and success of its sire and dam. You must register the dog with the club after receiving the dog's papers and, if you wish to breed it, you must consult with the Breeding Section of the same local club. Dogs which are permitted to be bred must have a show mark of X, or V.G. for males and G. for bitches as well as obedience and utility degrees. Dogs are registered with three independent branch organizations under Toy, Hunting or Service Dog categories and then individually by breed. These Service Dog clubs can be found in all major cities of Russia and are the central body overseeing all the activity under the name of the Federation of Service Dog Breeding.

There is no advertising of "puppies for sale" since there is always a demand for puppies and, therefore, the need to advertise is unnecessary. Russian show dogs are a healthy lot—since veterinary care is free.

THE DOBERMAN IN JAPAN

In 1931 a dog named Desir v Glueckswinkel was whelped in Germany. Desir and his litter-sister, Daisy, became Sieger and Siegerin for that year and were both sold abroad. Daisy was exported to America and Desir was sold to a Japanese sportsman who used him extensively at stud with bitches that had also been imported from Europe to establish the breed in Japan.

Over the years Japan imported quite a few top quality dogs and bitches from Europe and the United States, but during the late 1960's reports began to filter back to the United States about over-breeding and indiscriminate breeding to the point that Americans became skeptical about sending dogs there. Several prominent breeders in different breeds actually went over to Japan to investigate the situation, and not all of the reports were good. Also, the dog welfare organizations looked into the matter to try and determine the truth. The Japanese became suspect both for the huge amounts of money they were willing to pay and for the great number of dogs in all breeds they wanted to buy.

However, what they do have going for them is that they are able to purchase many excellent Dobermans from some of our top kennels. Ruth and Jack Morgan sent over Morgansonne's Kirby, who quickly attained his Japanese championship. A son of Ch. Ru-Mar's Morgansonne, C.D., was sent to Japan after winning a Best in Show in this country, and Morgansonne's Maid Marian soon became one of the top-winning bitches there. A Morgansonne granddaughter, Ch. Belinda's Mis Behavin has also been exported to Japan.

In the mid-1970's there are quite a few Dobermans in Japan. One young man, Keizo Sasade of Osaka, is a member of the Doberman Pinscher Club of Sacramento and the Doberman Pinscher Club of Western Japan. He is owner of Champion Brookwood's San Marin and imports a number of quality Dobermans from the United States.

THE DOBERMAN IN SOUTH AFRICA

One of the first Dobermans on record in South Africa was a black dog named Balmung v Zinsgut, whelped on March 13, 1924. His sire was Rival v Kranichsteing and his dam was Brangaerie v Weingarten. Balmung was shipped to South Africa at an early age and quickly became a champion in that country.

The Dobermann Club of South Africa was founded in 1932 in Johannesburg, and today is the largest breed-club in South Africa. Its membership is approximately 450, ranging throughout the southern parts of the continent. This large club membership is testimony to the surge of popularity in this breed in recent years along with the increasing necessity for guard dogs.

The club has an Obedience Committee which keeps busy overseeing training schools in Cape Town, Durban, Benoni and Johannesburg. The main group operates out of Johannesburg, where every Sunday morning as many as 135 Dobermans are trained in "action

Damasyn The Bat pictured with her son, Japanese Grand Champion (1951-1952) and American Champion Mikado v d Elbe. They are pictured here with their handler Tashichiro Matsumoto. The Bat was bred by Mrs. Earl Downing of Kansas City, Kansas and was the dam of seven champions.

dog events" to perfect their performances as true working dogs. The other schools handle an average of thirty dogs every week.

The aims and particular function of the South African club actually evolved in 1971 when the Council of the club realized that the sudden growth in popularity of the breed necessitated the dog being presented at all times in the best possible light—therefore a controlled,

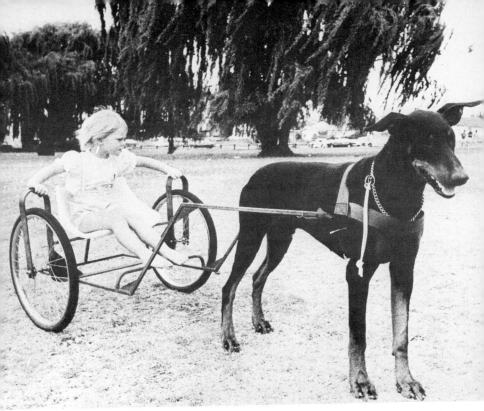

Ready for the race. . . in South Africa! Brutus of Quintre and his charge are ready for the sulky races, a regular feature of some of the South African sporting events. This photograph was taken in 1972 and submitted by J.P. Schlesinger, former President of the Doberman Club in that part of the world.

obedient guard dog was what they wished the breed to be. The club was constantly being asked to aid in the selection of puppies and to advise on the care and keeping of the dogs, and they were provided with the best possible method of "controlling" the advancement of the breed in the world of dogs once they had become club members.

Through this concentrated effort to put both the breed and the club in "the public eye," the Doberman has continued to enjoy an important place in the lives of the South Africans as both a working and companion dog. This was accomplished largely through action dog displays of obedience training held in conjunction with other working dog clubs and sponsored or supported by the dog food companies. These displays present the most impressive programs for interested audiences, over and above the regular obedience and working dog trials. With this thinking came the introduction of sulky racing for the Doberman.

South Africa's first sulky or "chariot" race for Dobermans featured eight specially constructed sulkies and specially fitted harnesses on eight of the more sturdy Dobermans. The sulky riders were children of the owners, and they delivered the "stand-stay" command at the starting line. The owners, once they were 50 yards down the 100 yard track, called their dogs while running for the finish line and the dogs were off and running.

Doberman sulky racing has proven to be so popular in South Africa that a race was held in conjunction with the Duban Horse Race over a July weekend before a crowd of 17,000 people. J.P. Schlesinger, now living in England but a resident of South Africa in the early 1970's, reported in an article he wrote recently that the crowd literally went wild and gave a standing ovation to the victors of the day during the two heats. The event was considered a huge success as the crowd cheered its approval.

Numerous other events were staged to establish the worth of these fabulous working dogs. Often children were used as trainers in the demonstrations to attest to the tractability of the dog when in a close relationship with the very young. Attack routines simulating their effectiveness when tracking down convicts or lost persons were given. Other police work involving a dog being parachuted into certain trouble areas by helicopter was presented as well as the film entitled "The Doberman Gang." A team of 12 Dobermans often gave demonstrations in obedience and guard dog work. In fact, The Dobermann Club of South Africa was invited to present a display at the Goldfields Championship Show in August of 1974 before the Minister of Sport, the first Cabinet Minister on record to ever make an official visit to a dog show.

One of the interesting items listed as an objective of the club in South Africa reads as follows: "To protect and advance the interests of the breed in both beauty and obedience by the holding of dog shows, match-meetings and working trials. . . " They record their entries as Obedience and Beauty as compared to our Obedience and Conformation.

In 1973 at the August 25th and 26th show held in conjunction with the Goldfields Kennel Club Championship Show, Mr. Herman L. Fellton, from Marietta, Georgia, U.S.A. (and DPCA 2nd Vice President), judged the breed. At a banquet after the show both Mr. and Mrs. Fellton spoke before the club, giving their impressions of the comparisons of Dobermans in South Africa, Europe and the U.S.A. The club's match-meetings are held in March. The club publishes a magazine called *Dobe Globe* and a club newsletter. Due to the great advances and popularity in the breed, by the end of 1974 the formation of another Doberman club to be called the Doberman Club of the Cape was accepted by the club as a means to better serving those fanciers in that area, which had heretofore been restricted by K.U.S.A.

Members of the Dobermann Club of South Africa put their dogs through their precision work at a sporting event. These demonstrations by this very active club are popular features.

It is unquestionably this concentrated effort on the part of the devoted members of the breed in South Africa which has, and will continue, to present the breed in the best possible light on that continent, and will preserve the breed's natural instincts as a true working breed.

ROCCO—AFRICA'S SKY-DIVING DOBERMAN

Rocco is the name of South Africa's Para Dog. This fantastic black and tan Doberman that parachutes out of a plane to participate in a mock attack on a field below is a main attraction promoted by

The Dobermann Club in South Africa to help popularize the breed. Owned and trained by Mr. D.A. Kloeck, Rocco leaves the aircraft in the skydiver's arms and attached to his equipment by quick-releasing clips. Once the parachute opens and the skydiver is stable Rocco is slowly lowered by an 18 foot static line so that both can land separately. The impact of landing is far less severe for a dog with four legs than it is for a human with two.

Mr. Kloeck quite naturally had to find a dog of stable temperament to perform this feat. First Rocco was given a trial flight in a plane to see how he took to the air. To help him associate the flights with pleasant experiences, the first venture was made in a doorless plane used by skydivers. Rocco was given a specially designed harness which allowed complete freedom, provided firm support for the chest and stomach areas and made sure that Rocco would be tilted slightly forward so he would be sure to land on his forefeet first. The first jump was a huge success. . . Rocco no sooner landed on the ground than he was back in the plane waiting to go up again!

This initial event took place at an air field on the outskirts of Johannesburg with the plane flying at an altitude of 2500 feet. On the first flight, as Rocco was lowered on the static line he realized as he got to the diver's feet that it was his last link with "life" and instinctively sank his teeth into the diver's boot at the ankle and clutched his paws around his leg! It required much shaking loose on the part of the diver to break free of his grip and continue to lower Rocco to the full 18 foot distance! This happened only twice, as after that Rocco was content to drift down to earth as master of all he surveyed.

Early in 1971 The Dobermann Club arranged a day of dog activities and demonstrations at a sporting event, and Rocco's jump and his mock attack were to be the highlight. By this time Rocco had come to love the jumps because his reward was the attack on the fake criminal in the field below. By the day of the show he was in full command and delighted the spectators as the terrorist attack took place. On completing his tenth jump Rocco was awarded his "A" license and his "wings" and is recognized as a fully-fledged parachutist. He was presented with his own logbook in which all statistics and personal data regarding each jump are recorded and signed by the pilot, the skydiver and Rocco himself!

On one other occasion all did not go well and wind conditions were responsible for both Rocco and the diver landing in a treetop. Much to the amazement of all, Rocco was very calm and complacent while they waited for the local fire department to rescue them. His trainer, Mr. Kloeck, made an interesting observation which clearly illustrates the natural instincts of Rocco for the performance of each jump. At about 40 feet above the ground Rocco begins to move his legs as a means of preparing himself for a balanced landing. So precise was Rocco in this reaction that the skydiver came to know from

Rocco's actions just how many seconds were left before landing without consulting his altimeter.

Mr. Kloeck observed that "again one wonders whether we credit our dogs with the intelligence they really possess."

Rocco's real name is Lescaut's Mecki vom Forellenbachle, and he was bred in Germany. He was cropped there and selected to be sent to Mr. Kloeck by Herr Valentine Stefan, the Hauptzuchtwart for the German Verein. Whelped on December 3, 1969, he was flown to South Africa at eight weeks of age. His training was begun by Mr. Kloeck when he was just 10 months old, and he was ready for his first jump just eight months later. Mr. Kloeck started the training by getting Rocco used to the harness. He wore it on all occasions and under different conditions; while at play, eating, exercising, etc. Then Rocco was lowered from a balcony to help him get used to being held in suspension with the harness as his only support and to simulate the lowering on the 18 foot static rope during the actual parachute jump. Then came his friendship with his skydiver, who was advised to carry on a conversation with the dog during the jumps to give reassurance in the wide open spaces.

This remarkable dog has provided much excitement for the crowds that have witnessed his jumps over the years. But perhaps never more than on that first parachute jump at the day of the dog show when the first parachute out of the plane failed to open and the

A demonstration of an attack on a fugitive at the 1972 Rand Show in South Africa, put on by the Dobermann Club of South Africa.

The Dobermann Club of South Africa in formation for one of their exciting demonstrations at a South African sporting event. This demonstration was at the 1972 Rand show.

crowds gasped in horror! It was quickly explained however that the first chute was actually a streamer which indicated weather and wind conditions. All heaved a sigh of relief when skydiver and Rocco bailed out next and floated safely to earth as intended!

DOBERMANS IN EAST AFRICA

The Doberman was first seen in any numbers in East Africa in and around Kenya in the early 1950's. However, before the emergency over the native uprisings was declared in 1953, the breed was little known there. There were a few breeders, but the breed in no way could be considered as popular or established and the dogs were put to no special use as working dogs.

Once the emergency was declared the need for forceful service dogs became apparent and the Doberman suddenly came into its own. The police obtained four trained police dogs from South Africa; three were Dobermans and the fourth a Doberman/Bloodhound cross. By the time they arrived by airplane, they were needed for immediate service.

They more than proved their worth as tracking dogs during the first few weeks of police work and, needless to say, were much feared by the natives. As tension grew in and around Nairobi it was found that only the homes that were guarded by these dogs were free of the danger of native attack. Mrs. J. Harding, a member of the Doberman Club of Great Britain, was a resident in Kenya during the early 1950's and when it came time to return to Britain, she turned over her 100 pound Doberman to the police staff.

They had found the Doberman so successful in their work that they were now breeding them, and Mrs. Harding's dog was used at stud and then sent on to do guard duty at the Williamson's diamond mine in Tanganyika. Many Dobermans are used throughout Africa to guard the diamond mines.

By 1956 the police had bred and specially trained several Dobermans, with a total of 10 tracker dogs and three wind scenters, with others coming up in the ranks. Dobermans have always been found to be of great use as trackers in the jungles, and most all of the police forces in this area have continued their use over the years.

Mrs. Ernest Lau of Hawaii shows her two Dobermans, which were among the first shown on the Hawaiian Islands. They are Champions Apollo of Silvergate and Asta of Mauno Loa. Apollo (on the right) won Best in Show under judge Arthur Zne at the 1933 Hawaiian Kennel Club show held at the Civic Auditorium.

Malaysian Champion Chocolate Soldier of Bamboo River, whelped in August, 1963. He is pictured with his owner, Mr. Yin EE Guan. Bred by Mr. A.H. Ritchie, the sire was Barrimilne Ghenghis Khan x Ha Liam of Bamboo River.

THE DOBERMAN IN MALAYSIA AND SINGAPORE

The first two Dobermans registered with the Kennel Association in Malaysia were imported from South Africa. The year was 1947 and the kennel records listed the dogs as Dobermanns, with the double "n" and omitting the word Pinscher. These two original arrivals

Von Klebons Dark Jaspar, owned by Mr. Benny Yeoh of Kuala Lumpur, Malaysia. The sire was Int. Ch. Delderland Black Regal x Australian Ch. Delderland Black Hera. The breeder was Mrs. Jackie Perry of Kuala Lumpur, Malaysia.

were of Dutch origin and were owned by an English rubber planter who initiated the breed in that country under the kennel name of Von Revillo.

It wasn't until 1952 that the next importations reached Malaysia, and they came from Germany. These German dogs were quickly followed by several puppies which had been purchased in England. These original dogs started the basic interest in the breed and more and more imports were brought in from both England and Germany. The quality, however, remained the same until the progeny of the imported dogs from the English Tavey and Barrimilne bloodlines began to come through. Oddly enough, it was to be a German import that was to attain the first championship title in Malaysia for the breed. Ch. Errol vom Furstenfeld was their first recorded champion, and it was two years before another champion appeared on the show scene. His name was Ch. Chocolate Soldier of Bamboo River, and he was sired by Barrimilne Ghenghis Khan.

Mr. A. Ritchie was the owner of the Bamboo River Kennels and established a firm base for the breed in Malaysia between 1963 and 1968. The Bamboo River name can be found behind many of the Dobermans found in Malaysia today, a famous one being another son of Ghenghis Khan named Ch. Flashing Gem. Gem's son, Ch. Traysan's Flashing Gem II, won two Bests in Show in succession. Credit is also due to his dam, Dauphiness of Canistar, who won Best in Show at 14 months of age at her very first dog show! Unfortunately for the breed, the Dauphiness died while whelping the litter with Gem II, and her tragic demise was considered a great loss to future breeding programs.

It was in 1967 that Mrs. Jackie Perry imported her first Doberman from England to Singapore. This was Ch. Carrickgreen Champignon. This lovely bitch was to be the foundation of her Von Klebong Kennels. This bitch was not her first Doberman, nor was it her first experience at breeding. There had been other Doberman litters, but not of the quality desired by Mrs. Perry; Champignon changed all that. More bloodlines were then imported from England and a serious breeding program was underway to establish the Von Klebong line. Mrs. Perry purchased two bitches from the Tavey line and two from the Carrickgreen line. To round out the breeding program she also imported a dog from Australia that, to use Mrs. Perry's words, "put Dobes on the map in this part of the world!"

His name was Australian Champion Delderland Black Regal, and he proceeded to gather Best in Show awards in amazing succession. "Humphrey," as he was called, was so close to what Mrs. Perry desired for her breeding that she obtained a top bitch from Regal's breeder, Mrs. Rita Komduur in Queensland. This top bitch was Australian Champion Delderland Black Hera. Bred to Ch. Vondobe The Maharajah, Hera had produced just this one litter in her native Australia. Mrs. Perry chose as her stud the United States import Sojole's Bukkles of Marks-Tey.

Australian, Singapore and Malaysian Champion Delderland Black Regal, an Australian import, pictured winning Best in Show under judge Stanley Dangerfield. Bred by Mrs. O. Komduur, Regal is owned by Mrs. Jackie Perry, Kuala Lumpur, Malaysia.

Ebonstorm's The Honey Buck photographed at 11 months of age. Owned by the Warren Andersons of Sydney, Australia.

Opposite, above:
Malaysian Champion Von Klebons Dark Heritage, owned and bred by Mrs. Jackie Perry of Kuala Lumpur. The sire was Sojole's Bukkles of Marks-Tey and the dam was Australian Champion Delderland Black Hera.

Opposite, below:
Malaysian Champion Von Klebongs Dark Havov, bred and owned by Mrs. Jackie Perry of Kuala Lumpur, Malaysia. The sire was Sojole's Bukkles of Marks-Tey (imported from the U.S.A.) and the dam was Australian Champion Delderland Black Hera.

Black Hera's Australian litter produced two Australian champions and two international champions. Mrs. Perry's first litter of nine also produced good results. The first to enter the show ring was a bitch shown in Singapore who won Best in Show at nine months of age. This was followed a few weeks later by a litter brother that won Best in Show at a show in Malacca, a town just south of the capital. At 11 months Mrs. Perry's bitch, which was her choice to keep from this outstanding litter, took Best in Show her first time out. Her second show she placed Reserve to the Best in Show Alsatian, and at her third show she won Best in Show once again. Having attained her title in three shows, "Paula" was retired to the whelping box. But Mrs. Perry was far from finished with this litter. At the very next dog show she entered the male she had chosen to keep from this litter and he won his title and Best in Show!

Paula had her fifth litter in November, 1975, at the age of eight. . . still in the best of health and top condition. She is a wonderful brood bitch and her offspring are winning in the show rings.

During 1975 Mrs. Perry added a brown dog from Australia to her kennel. He is a grandson of the U.S. import Sojole's Bukkles of Marks-Tey. Also present are Damasyn Bo-Tandy of Ardon and Marks-Tey Yancey. These dogs are to be bred to a bitch Mrs. Perry purchased on a recent trip to England. The bitch carries both the Triogen and Tavey lines and was bred to the U.S. import to England, Phileens Duty Free of Tavey.

As is her custom, Mrs. Perry will retain a dog and a bitch from this breeding. When bred to her Marks-Tey and Damasyn lines they should, she believes, give her exactly what she has hoped for and will be appreciated by the international judges which officiate at the Malaysian and Singapore dog shows.

Mrs. Perry has exported Dobermans to various countries in the area, as well as some which have found their way to England and the United States (and one to Kenya) with their new owners. They are doing well in foreign competition.

In December, 1975, Mrs. Perry judged the breed at a Doberman Specialty Show in Manila, and in 1976 she will go to Australia to judge the breed in that country. It is Mrs. Perry who has coined one of the author's favorite phrases. . . she calls the people devoted and dedicated to the breed her "dobermaniac friends!"

Mrs. Perry is owed a debt of gratitude by the Doberman fancy for she is surely the guiding force behind the breed in that part of the world. Her effort at obtaining the very best bloodlines without regard to time, trouble or expense is to be commended. She is surely the pillar of the breed. While she reports that keeping Dobermans in top condition in that tropical country is not easy with both coat and skin problems, they are nonetheless completely enamored of the breed and consider themselves a cult unto themselves!

THE DOBERMAN IN THE WEST INDIES

The first Doberman in Trinidad was named Duchess of Scott. Brought to the island in the early 1950's by an American couple that wanted first of all a good watch dog, this brown/rust bitch excelled at her position as family guard and helped popularize the breed in that country at about the same time the breed was gaining popularity in England.

Singapore Ch. Von Klebongs Allusion at three months. Whelped in March, 1970, the sire was Template of Tavey x Seeker of Tavey. Bred by Mrs. Jackie Perry of Kuala Lumpur, Malaysia.

Mrs. Winifred Scott succeeded in buying Duchess from the American couple with the intention of breeding her. Mrs. Scott obtained a stud dog from England, which unfortunately died before any mating occurred. It was 1954 before the Scotts succeeded in getting another Doberman from England for Duchess. This dog was named Lion of Branda, and he was a black and tan. Neither of these dogs was shown, but they did well as guard dogs protecting their home.

The fourth Doberman to arrive in the West Indies was a black and tan bitch named Bowsmoor Charmer, also imported from Great Britain. Charmer also had a C.D. title and was the property of Mrs. Jane Jones, wife of a veterinarian on the island. Mrs. Jones bred to Lion of Branda to establish her breeding kennel, which bore the "of the Main" suffix. While Mrs. Jones' main objective was to breed the much-needed and highly sought-after guard dogs for the island, Charmer was shown sparingly and did win a few times over the limited competition at island shows.

While Mrs. Jones admitted that Charmer was by no means a "perfect specimen," she did possess and pass on to her progeny the desired characteristics of the guard dog, and Mrs. Jones made a trip

Bucky, one of the greatest dogs ever to be imported in Trinidad and Tobago, sitting with the Dobermann Club's Challenge Trophy which he won in 1969, 1970, 1971 and 1972. The trophy was a Best in Show award won outright. He is owned by Frank Thompson of Trinidad.

Opposite:
Damasyn Androcles, one of the first Dobermans to reach Puerto Rico, was sired by Ch. Checkmate's Count von Glam x Damasyn The Strawberry Tart, C.D. Pictured here with handler Ben Burwell in 1966.

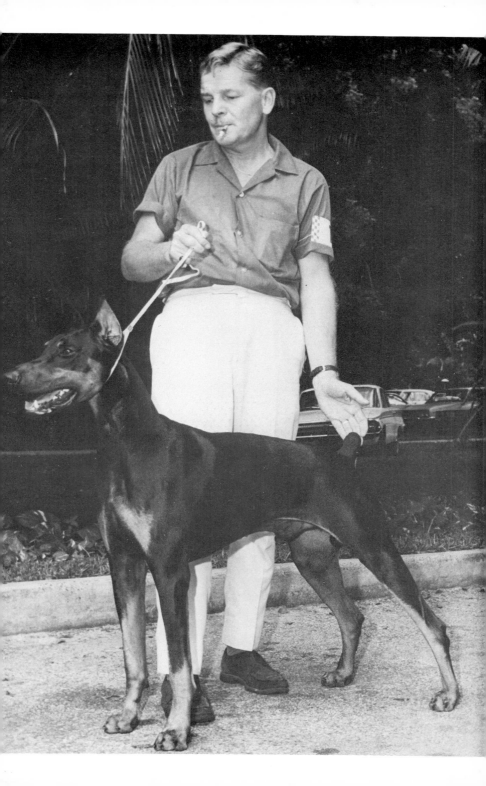

to England to secure another stud for her. She purchased Mahadeo Chessman. This brown/rust dog did some winning in England and, together with Duchess, produced the first impressive line of Dobermans to bring credit to the Trinidad and Tobago scene, which are prominent on up into the seventies.

Coral of the Main, whelped in February, 1956, established a great line of Dobermans on the island for Mr. James Gooding, of the "of Brook" kennel suffix. Coral was by Lion of Branda x Bowsmoor Charmer. Mr. Gooding also bred Ch. Gloss of Brook, C.D., one of three great sisters produced by Coral of the Main from three different sires.

Another quality representative of the line started by Coral was Ch. Angelique Des Iles. Her daughter Countessa won a Championship Certificate at the 1972 Doberman Specialty Show under American judge Norman Biggin. Angelique's death in 1972 brought an end to a show career which included many Best in Show awards as well as the end to an impressive record as a top-producing dam.

Angelique, for instance, was the granddam of Nada The Lilly of Rosfa, a black and tan bitch which won a C.C. in 1972, and represents the quality Dobermans which represent the breed in the West Indies during the present decade.

Champion Damasyn The Honeybuck was sent to Trinidad by Peggy Adamson and has many wins to his credit in that country, including a Best in Show.

DOBERMANS IN AUSTRALIA

The Australians, of course, spell the name of the dog in the British manner, which is with the double "n," and have also dropped the "pinscher" as have all other countries other than the United States. They also do not crop the ears as is the European tradition.

Best Puppy at the 1974 First National Doberman Show was six-month-old Prima Coya, owned by Hedi Wetherall of Melbourne, Australia, under judge Peggy Adamson. Prima Coya is now a champion.

Khamaviro Dari, photographed in 1972 by his co-owners Mrs. R. McCarthy and Mrs. J.M. Gray of N.S.W., Australia.

The Doberman is not terribly popular in some circles "down under." As recently as 1970 the Country Shire Council's Association wanted all Dobermans sterilized. They all agreed that Dobermans should be classified as "killers" and placed under the same rigid controls as are the Shepherds. They firmly believe the Doberman to be a definite threat to Australian livestock in the outlying areas. We can only hope the attitude is changing with each passing day.

One of the leading kennels in the country is the Dobeherr Kennels of Mrs. Laurel Wicks, N.S.W. Dobeherr began several years ago with the purchase of a bitch puppy, Glenunga Gay Baroness. She was the result of a breeding between two imports from England, Bronvorny's Black Prince and Carissima of Tavey. Both parents were strongly linebred to Tavey's Stormy Achievement, a son of Ch. Rancho Dobe's Storm. Black Prince was a son of Achievement.

The Baroness was successful in the show ring and quickly earned her Australian championship. She was a dual Best Exhibit in Show winner and Challenge Bitch and R.U. Non-Sporting Group in the 1967 Brisbane Royal National Show.

When the time came to breed her Mrs. Wicks went to Tavey's Stormy Perfection, an import from Britain, and a son of Tavey's Stormy Achievement. This breeding led to a partnership between Mrs. Wicks and Mrs. Brenda Sender, the woman who had imported Stormy. The breeding was successful and produced two outstanding specimens, Australian Ch. Dobeherr Royal Presto and Australian Ch.

Dobeherr Royal Perfecta. Presto went Best Exhibit in Show at the Non-Sporting Championship Show in 1972. Perfecta was Best of Breed at the 1970 P.A.L. International and Challenge Bitch winner at the 1971 P.A.L. International. Their litter brother, Dobeherr Royal Pharoah, won the C.C. at the 1972 P.A.L. International.

A repeat breeding of Stormy and Baroness produced another pair of top winners, Australian Champions Dobeherr Fireball and Dobeherr Cyclone Lola. Fireball won the C.C. at the 1973 P.A.L. International, and Lola was Reserve. Fireball went Best Exhibit in Show at the 1973 Canberra Non-Sporting and Working Dog Club, and Lola was Best Exhibit in Show at the Sunbury, Victoria event. Australian Ch. Dobeherr Thunderball was another outstanding dog from this second litter.

Shanzu Tafethali, whelped in August, 1973. Bred and owned by Mrs. Janne Gray, Shanzu Kennels, New South Wales, Australia.

Therefore, it was not unlikely that a third breeding of these two dogs should take place when it was found they "nikked" so well. This breeding resulted in Australian Ch. Dobeherr Stormy Lustre, who won Best Exhibit in Show at the 1973 Non-Sporting Dog Club of N.S.W. and in 1974 at the Dobermann Club Show of N.S.W. championship event. She was also winner of the Challenge Certificate for bitches at the 1975 North of the Harbour Winter Classic.

All told, the Dobeherr Kennels have produced over 15 champions to date and there are many plans ahead for breedings from original outcrosses with the hope of returning the Stormy Achievement line.

Janne Gray is owner of the Shanzu Kennels in New South Wales. She has done considerable breeding and shows a great deal as well. Some of her top home-breds are Shanzu Jamo, Zaidi, Verdene, Tafethali, Wanawake and Vitu to name just a few. Shanzu Tumbuka is one

Tavey's Stormy Perfection, an import from the United Kingdom, and stud behind many of Australia's best Dobermans. His sire was Ch. Tavey's Stormy Achievement and his dam the U.S.A. import to England, Westwinds Quintessence of Tavey. Stormy is owned by R. and L. Wicks.

of her brood bitches which has been producing well. Janne Gray co-owns Khamaviro Dari with Mrs. R. McCarthy and Haida Induna with Denise Irons. Her son, Bruce, helps with the training of the dogs also.

The Grays are responsible for bringing many Australians into the breed through the sale of their puppies.

The Gray's Shanzu Verdene, from a January, 1975 breeding, is being shown in both conformation and obedience classes. Verdene is owned by Greg Royall. Many of these dogs are seen regularly in junior handling classes with the children of their owners.

Other exhibitors of Dobermans in Australia are C. Curtis, Lynarcl Annej, K. Newman, David Goldie, Larry Mojses (owner of an 8-year-old C.D.X. Doberman), Bob Donnelly and Mr. and Mrs. G. Derrick. Kennel names that figure prominently in the Australian home-bred strains are Vondobe, Kurtavey, Chaquen, Mandobe, Tabou, Doberleibe, Nibelungen, Zareba's Vangeire, Biyugal, Bonhaven, Waldenstein, Chacomb, Denecourt, Ehrengarde, Sharonacy and Yarrabrae, to mention a few.

Peggy Adamson's Damasyn line is represented in Australia also. Her excellent Damasyn Bo-Tandy was exported to Australia several years ago.

THE DOBERMAN PINSCHER IN ISRAEL

The Doberman Pinscher ranks number four in popularity in Israel's Top Ten favorite dog list! Mr. Avi Marshak of Tel-Aviv (a member of the Israel Doberman Club) tells me there are many, many Dobermans in Israel, and that over the years they have imported quite a few dogs from both the United States and Germany to help establish the breed in their country.

It was in the second half of the 1940's that Mr. Mannfred Josephs joined the Israeli police force and served for six years as a dog

Two Israeli Dobermans wait for the command to attack during a training lesson. Trained Dobermans have been used for many years by the Israeli police force with great success.

Doberman training in Israel—a bevy of Dobes circle in on an aggressor with raised fist.

Mr. Mannfred Josephs, in charge of dog training in the Israeli police force for six years, puts a Doberman through its paces.

trainer for them—with Dobermans, of course. Mr. Josephs was a top breeder of Dobermans in Israel and was highly respected by his fellow breeders and police officers for his work with the Doberman. Mr. Josephs immigrated to Philadelphia, Pennsylvania, in 1953, where he lived until his death a few years ago.

The Israel Doberman Club is a member of the all-breed Israel Kenel (their spelling) Club, which in turn is a member of the F.C.I. It was founded in 1973 by Mr. Marshak and several other Doberman fanciers. There are four Doberman dog shows each year, and the stud book registers around 300 dogs each year. It is difficult to say when the very first Dobermans were seen in Israel, but it is believed to be around 1940.

THE DOBERMAN IN PUERTO RICO

The first Doberman Pinschers seen in Puerto Rico arrived around 1958 or 1959. Shortly thereafter they began appearing at the Kennel Club of Puerto Rico dog shows and now, about twenty years later, account for one of the largest entries of any breed at the shows. When the Doberman judging begins, the crowds gather to watch this impressive dog compete.

Four people are largely responsible for the gain in popularity of this breed. The late Jose Alfaro was a man who admired the Doberman greatly and brought much knowledge and information on the breed to the island where Alexis Rodriguez, a director of the all-breed club, had the good sense to import top dogs from Jane Kay's Kay Hill Kennels in the states to be trained by the greatest owner-handler of all time on the island, Luis Puig, a Cuban living in Puerto Rico. Senor Puig got into the breed in 1966, finished two champions in Puerto Rico and has been devoted to the breed over the years.

In 1974 Caesar Sierra, also a Cuban living in Puerto Rico and a great admirer of the Doberman, organized the Doberman Pinscher

Texas von Haus Viking, pictured at four months of age and winner of the Futurity at the Clube Bandeiranto Dobermann show (Sao Paulo, Brazil) under judge Suzanne Blum. The sire was Alisaton's Infrared out of Naja von Haus Viking. Owned by Professor Strenger.

Vega de la Morliere, a top Doberman in France, and winner at the 1973 Dortmund World Show. A champion in France and vice-championne du Monde. Owned by M.M.A. Demangeat of Orvault-Nantes, France.

Mexican Ch. Robin Prince Brown, a red dog, pictured winning Best in Show at the 1975 Cria-Mex Show under judge Mrs. D. Brown of Australia. Dr. Lorenza Rocca handled for owner Joaquine Albarazo. Trophy's presented by Club President Ing. Robin F. Hernandez.

club. He owns and shows two Cassio grandsons, Kaisar von Schuman and Marienburg Schroeder von Schuman. The breed club founded by Senor Sierra has created much new interest in the breed, with many of the Puerto Rican owners and exhibitors coming to the States to show here as well as on their island.

OTHER COUNTRIES

There are, of course, evidences of Dobermans being imported by people in such countries as Belgium, Austria and Italy around the same time as they were appearing in other European countries as word of this handsome, near perfect working dog spread. However, they were so few in number that no substantial written records could

Gilberto Comallonga pictured in Cuba in 1948 with his beloved Cuban Ch. Damasyn Venture—three times Best in Show in that country and never defeated. Senor Comallonga, Batista's Minister of Agriculture, and his dogs disappeared after the Castro take-over, and Mrs. Adamson has never heard from him again.

be found to accurately document their progress over the years to be included in this book.

We are sure, with each passing year, their popularity grows and the breed increases in number along with their universal appeal.

4. THE DOBERMAN IN GREAT BRITAIN

One of the first Doberman Pinschers ever seen in the British Isles was at the 1933 Kennel Club show at the Crystal Palace in London. The famous writer Elizabeth Craig, Mrs. A.E. Mann in private life, exhibited the only dog of German origin at the show. It was, of course, a Doberman Pinscher, and it caused a sensation!

However, it wasn't until several years later that they appeared in Great Britain in any substantial number. In fact, it was only after World War II that the breed really caught the fancy of British dog-lovers and especially the fancy of Fred and Julia Curnow, who were to become its most dedicated and successful breeders over the following several decades.

BRITISH DOBERMAN CLUBS

The Dobermann Club in England was founded in 1948, right after World War II, by Fred and Julia Curnow and a small group of enthusiasts eager to further develop the breed in Britain with imports they had secured from both Germany and Holland. In that first year of the "senior" club's existence there were about twenty to twenty-five members who adhered to the German name of Dobermann, spelled with the double n and dropping the word Pinscher as well.

By the mid-1970's membership in the Dobermann Club had risen to around 600, with members from Europe and a few in Australia, South Africa, Rhodesia and Malaya. Registrations at the Kennel Club run about 2,000 per annum, though this is only a slight indication of the actual number of Dobermans in the British Isles. The club has a very active Working Dog membership, and they run their own working tests as well as support three dog shows a year, one of which is a championship event.

In addition to the keen competition in the working and obedience fields, the club also boasts among its members the top winners in the show ring, with many of the dogs winning both in and out of their breed. Dobermans in England win top honors among all the breeds. Perhaps the best example of this in recent times is Ch. Flexor Flugelman, owned by David Crick. This magnificent dog was 1973 Best of Breed at Crufts and is a Working Group winner as well.

Mr. R.G. Hodges, president of the Dobermann Club, is a gentleman who has shown and worked Dobermans since the mid-fifties and maintains an active and interested part in the club and in the good and welfare of the breed in Great Britain.

Other Doberman clubs in Great Britain are the North of England Dobermann Club and the Midlands Dobermann Club. There is also a Welsh Dobermann Club and the Scottish Dobermann Club. While many members belong to one or more of these clubs, each club is permitted to send a delegate to attend an annual meeting to serve on a Breed Council.

FOREIGN JUDGES

In spite of the relatively few championship shows held each year, the British are not adverse to inviting foreign judges recognized as experts in their field to adjudicate at their Specialty Shows.

Championship show winning Borain's Born Forth, daughter of Ch. Royaltain's Babette of Tavey and dam of Borain's Hot Chocolate and Borain's Raging Calm. Bred and owned by Mrs. Pat Gledhill of Oxfordshire, England.

Three international judges pose for a picture with Dudley Wontner-Smith (far left), prominent British fancier and Doberman club official. Left to right: Peggy Adamson, DPCA President, U.S.A., who judged the North of England Dobermann Club show in 1972; standing is Willi Rothfess, a top German Doberman fancier and judge; and Margaret Bastable of England, the only woman licensed to judge Dobermans in Germany.

This came about in 1967 when the North of England Dobermann Club was the first to invite a foreign judge to officiate. Ernst Wilking, President of the German Verein, presided in the ring. In 1970 the Swiss judge Francis Fleitmann was invited, in 1971 it was Professor Bodingbauer of Austria and in 1972 America's Peter Knoop officiated and drew their largest entry up to that time. In 1973 Mrs. Robert (Peggy) Adamson judged their summer show, and in the spring of 1974 Willi Rothfuss, a past-president of the Dobermann Verein of Germany was invited. Foreign judges are popular in Great Britain and undoubtedly would be even more popular were it not for the great expense of importing judges from overseas for these clubs with rather small budgets.

There are over fifty shows where Dobes can win Championship Certificates during the course of a show season, in addition to the Specialties held by the individual breed clubs. In order to earn a championship each Doberman must win three C.C.'s under three different judges.

Damasyn Bo-Tandy, litter sister of Ch. Damasyn Bo-Tairic and Bo-Tassi, was exported to the Andersons in Australia to improve the breed in that country. Bred by Peggy Adamson of the Damasyn Kennels in Roslyn Heights, New York.

Opposite:
A lovely headstudy of Shanzu Vitu, owned by David Goldie of New South Wales, Australia.

Shanzu Wanawake, photographed in 1975 at six months of age. Bred and owned by Janne Gray, New South Wales, Australia.

EAR CROPPING

It is important to note that in England, as throughout Europe and Africa, ear-cropping is not permitted. While Bermuda is a British possession, dogs are shown there with cropped ears, especially if they have been imported from the United States. However, there have been periodic attempts to outlaw earcropping on all breeds of dogs in Bermuda.

MODERN BRITISH KENNELS

While the six-month quarantine laws in Great Britain remain rigid and definitely affect the number of imports to that country, the Doberman Pinscher in the 1970's is definitely showing remarkable improvement over the post-World War II dogs which were imported

Roanoke Starlight, a typical quality Doberman puppy from the Richardson's Roanoke Kennels in Essex, England.

Mrs. Dorothy P. Parker of Norfolk, England, with three of her beloved Dobermans, Ch. Tavey's Stormy Medallion, Ch. Hensel Midnight Max, and Marsh Meadows Shoemaker.

when the breed first found its way to England in numbers. It wasn't until 1975 that a Doberman won the Working Group. Ch. Flexor Flugelman won the Group at the Crufts show, the world's largest dog show.

Flugelman is owned by David Crick of Avon and has an impressive show record. As of the end of 1975 he had three Bests in Show and 14 Challenge Certificates in addition to his Working Group win at Crufts. He is a grandson of the great English dog Ch. Acclamation of Tavey, who in turn was sired by American Champion Stebs Top Skipper x Orebaugh's Raven of Tavey, a bitch also imported from the U.S.A.

There is no denying that the American stock imported by the British has added size, stature and substance to the breed and that

The top-winning Doberman in England. . . Ch. Flexor Flugelman, winner—as of November, 1975—of 14 Challenge Certificates and three Bests in Show. He won the Working Group at the 1975 Crufts show as well, the first time that a Doberman has achieved this honor. Flugelman is a grandson of the great English producer, Ch. Acclamation of Tavey, who is by American Champion Steb's Top Skipper x Orebaugh's Raven of Tavey, a bitch Mr. Fred Curnow imported to England from the U.S.A. Flugelman's owner is David L. Crick, Flexor Farm, Avon, United Kingdom.

the British Dobermans now have a great deal more "freedom of movement." The original British stock was inclined to be smallish and rather "thick." Lighter markings than desired are still a problem at times, as well as hip dysplasia. Planned breeding and dedication to breeding out these problems has helped the situation enormously.

Mrs. Daisy Richardson, one of the first people interested in the Doberman breed back in 1947, and her son Jimmy run the Roanoke

Kennels in Essex, and have seen the benefits of good breeding over the years. The Richardsons purchased their first Doberman in 1953, and it was the beginning of what was to become a long succession of top show dogs. Their Roanoke Kennels by 1975 had become about the largest Doberman Kennels in all of Britain, housing approximately twenty Dobermans. Their aim has always been to breed the best to the best to ensure conformation according to the Standard, as well as the correct temperament, since so many of their dogs are sold as companions as well as show dogs.

The Richardsons export a few dogs each year to the United States and Canada, and with James as their handler in England the Roanoke Dobermans are winning. The actual list of their wins over the past three decades is too long to include here, but it is impressive and stands well for the success of their breeding program.

The Richardsons consider their Roanoke Bobadilla as being as close to perfection as they have come so far but, needless to say, they are still striving for an even more "perfect" Doberman.

In addition to training and showing all the Roanoke Dobes, James is a championship show judge and is active in two local groups, the Suffolk Kennel Association and the Colchester C.S., and actively participates in the ring craft classes.

Fred and Julia Curnow, along with the Richardsons, the late Mrs. Porterhouse, Harry Darbyshire of the Bowesmoors line and Eileen and Phil Edwards with their Phileens prefix can all take a major share of credit for the popularity and progress in breeding in those early days.

Other active kennels of more recent establishment have made their contribution as well. Mrs. D.P. Parker and Miss C. Parker have been in the breed since the early 1960's and are known for their excellent specimens. They include Ch. Tavey's Stormy Medallion and his son, Ch. Hensel Midnight Max, to name just two. It was Stormy Medallion which started Mrs. Parker in Dobes when she purchased him from Mr. and Mrs. Curnow at 10 weeks of age.

Mrs. Parker is a great advocate of the Doberman starring as a working dog and has many stories to tell regarding their proficiency as shepherds and herders as well as companions in the home and with children. She works closely in the breed with her friend Mrs. Neave, and together they are producing quality show dogs as well.

Charles and Blanche Wileman, owners of the Russtun Dobermanns, are breeders and exhibitors of show quality stock. Apart from their activity in the show rings, they are the Southern Area Rescue Agents for the Dobermans in their area. Part of the public feels that Dobermans cannot be rehabilitated and many end up in their hands after having been abandoned. They work diligently to place these deserted dogs in permanent homes. They are alarmed by the increasing numbers fitting into this "unwanted" category as the breed con-

English Champion Royaltain's Babbett of Tavey, whelped in August, 1968. She was the foundation bitch for the Borain strain of Dobermans owned and bred by Mrs. Pat Gledhill of Oxfordshire, England. She is the granddam of Ch. Royaltain's Highwayman of Borain, Borain's Hot Chocolate and Borain's Raging Calm.

Opposite, above:
Roanoke Remus, whelped in June, 1969, and sired by Ch. Heidiland Trouble Spot x Ch. Cadereyta of Roanoke. Owned and bred by Mr. James and Mrs. D.C. Richardson of the Roanoke Kennels in Essex, England.

Opposite, below:
Borain's Hot Chocolate, winner of two Championship Certificates whelped in February, 1973. This lovely red and tan was bred and owned by Mrs. Pat Gledhill, Oxfordshire, England.

153

tinues to grow in popularity. Their lines are based mainly on the Tavey bloodlines, and their puppies are sold largely to show-potential homes.

Mr. and Mrs. Bernard Spaughton own the Frankskirby Dobermanns in Kent, England. Mr. Spaughton saw his first Doberman when he worked in the livestock department at the A.W. Gamage London General Stores. It was a large red/brown dog just out of quarantine and about to be sent to an American in the Embassy. If he recalls correctly, the dog's name was Vulture von Gruenewald, with some Sieger Gerd v Sporthof in his pedigree. He was called "Der Guerher" while they had him in their charge, and the foreman took him home over the weekend where he tried him for pointing and retrieving in the fields with great success. Mr. Spaughton says he had a

Top Sire in the breed in England, Ch. Acclamation of Tavey, whelped in 1958 and owned by Mrs. J. Curnow of Sussex, England. Acclamation deserves acclamation as the sire of 32 champions, a feat that will, in the opinion of Fred Curnow, never be excelled in Britain.

English Champion Roanoke Bobadilla, which in the opinion of breeder-owner James Richardson came closest to being their ideal of the perfect Doberman. Whelped in May of 1968, the sire was Roanoke Nayrilla Apollo x Ch. Cadereyta of Roanoke. Bobadilla was the winner of eight Challenge Certificates, and seven Reserve C.C.'s. Co-owned by Mr. James and Mrs. D.C. Richardson, Roanoke Kennels, Essex, England.

curl wave on the back of his neck going in the correct direction and down the sides of his neck curling back toward his head. From the day Mr. Spaughton first laid eyes on this dog he could think of nothing but owning one of his very own some day.

World War II accounted for an even longer wait before this desire was to become a reality. Mr. Spaughton moved to Horton Kirby after the war and there chanced to meet Triogen Test Run on the street one day. She didn't really want Mr. Spaughton to pass by and eventually came over a wall at him and stood on his back with her teeth near the back of his neck to get this across to him! Mr. Spaughton gave in to her demand and they became friends for life after this first encounter.

When Test Run had puppies Bernard and Joyce Spaughton went to see them at Mrs. B. Panton's and the Spaughtons were hooked! A red bitch puppy named Nina stood on Mr. Spaughton's feet and they considered this prophetic. Nina went home with them and their Frankskirby Kennels was established.

Nina was shown only in the "beauty ring." After Nina gave birth to a litter of puppies sired by Ch. Iceburg of Tavey at the age of four, their breeding program was underway. Nina and all her offspring have been natural guard, gun and companion dogs. The Spaughton's Tessa and Juno were new additions to their kennel in 1975 as Nina reached her twelfth birthday that year.

Joyce Spaughton is a judge, and her first assignment was at a Dobermann Club Rally in 1975. She was judge again at the Alexandra

English Ch. Demo's Skipper, whelped in January, 1972 was Top Winning Doberman in 1973 and Top Winning Champion Doberman in 1974. This home-bred black and tan is the only Doberman to hold a "Daily Express Trophy" for Best Puppy in Show which he won at the 1972 Richmond show (London) over a record entry of 382 puppies of all breeds. When retired at stud at just over two years he had a show record of 10 Challenge Certificates, three Reserves and a Junior Warrant, and he is already the sire of C.C. and first prize winners in England and Ireland. Owned by Mr. Michael J.R. Turner, Herefordshire, England.

Palace show in April, 1976. Bernard Spaughton judged the breed for the first time in December, 1974, when 60 Dobermans showed up for his initial assignment.

Mr. Spaughton, with the help of what he refers to as "people who know Dobes well," has since 1965 put together the most remarkable pedigree of Dobermans ever compiled. The paper which traces the breed back to its earliest days in 1898 is over six feet long. While it is a remarkable piece of work, we are at a loss as to how it could be published within a book. At any rate, it is a heritage for the breed and a monumental piece of work which was of great value to the author in the writing of this book and surely to all who have worked on it or have had the privilege of viewing it.

It begins with the arrival of their Nina van Frankskirby and traces back over four hundred generations, including great, great grandchildren. All those people involved in putting this chronology of our breed together deserve much credit for this remarkable work.

A young show ring hopeful for the mid-1970 dog show season, Mrs. Dorothy P. Parker's Royaltain Artful Gypsy, a son of Ch. Hensel Midnight Max and grandson of Ch. Tavey's Stormy Medallion. Mrs. Parker's kennel is in Norfolk, England.

THE TAVEY KENNELS

The most dominant and undisputable influence of the Doberman breed in Britain has persisted through the excellent breedings of the Tavey Kennels. While all the Tavey dogs are registered in the name of Mrs. Julia Curnow, there is no denying the guiding force behind the operation provided by her husband, Fred Curnow.

In 1947 the Curnows imported three bitches, all in whelp, from Germany and Holland. Unfortunately, one litter was lost while the bitch was sitting out the six months quarantine. In spite of this disappointment, the Curnows purchased another couple of bitches to help establish their Tavey bloodlines and form the basis of a quality Doberman kennel.

Around this same time, while they were planning their long-range breeding program, the Curnows formed the Dobermann Club

Ch. Triogen Tuppeny Treat photographed at 11 months of age, winner of six Challenge Certificates. The sire was Ch. Acclamation of Tavey x Triogen Teenage Wonder. Owner, Mrs. Jean M. Scheja, Dorset, England.

Opposite, above:
English Champion Royaltain's Highwayman of Borain, whelped in June of 1971. Foundation dog at Mrs. Pat Gledhill's kennels in Oxfordshire, England.

Opposite, below:
English Champion Caderyta of Roanoke, whelped in May, 1964 and winner of three Challenge Certificates and three Reserve C.C.'s. Bred by John Hodson and owned by Mr. James and Mrs. D.C. Richardson, Roanoke Kennels, Essex, England. The sire was Ch. Tumlow Impeccable x Heidi of Tickwillow.

with a total of 24 breed admirers in 1948. Julia Curnow became the secretary of the club and continued to hold that position for the next 23 years. Fred Curnow was chairman for 21 years and served as its president for another three years.

It was while the Curnows were traveling in Europe that they first saw the Doberman and fell in love with the breed. It was at this same time, 1947, that they decided to introduce the breed into Great Britain. As the breed caught on thanks to their presentation, more and more imports were obtained from Germany. However, during regular business trips to the United States, and especially after judging at several dog shows in the U.S., Fred Curnow came to the decision that the American bloodlines were definitely superior to the European lines. He returned to England and in 1956 sold all the dogs they had and began all over again—with American imports.

The more elegant type, both larger and with more substance, revolutionized the breed in Great Britain, and within a few years the Curnows were winning Best in Show awards at the championship shows with amazing regularity—and against entries well over the 5,000 mark!

Ch. Iceberg of Tavey, whelped in September, 1963 and winner of 33 Challenge Certificates. Iceberg was Dog of the Year all-breeds for 1965 in Great Britain. Owned by Mrs. Julia Curnow of Sussex, England. Her Tavey Kennels are world-famous.

The Curnows adhered to a system uniquely their own, but one which worked. They would not buy females sight unseen, but would attend shows in the United States, decide on a bitch they would like to buy, conclude the transaction, have her mated to a dog of their own selection and, when proved to be in whelp, have her flown over to the quarantine kennels near their home.

Although the dams had to spend the six months at the quarantine station, it is permitted to remove the puppies born to them at six weeks of age. The Curnows did this, and with excellent results. This permitted them to raise the litters in their own kennel under their close supervision and at little risk to the welfare of the puppies.

One of the first litters from the United States was out of American Champion Rustic Adagio, sired by the great dog American Ch. Rancho Dobes Storm. All five puppies from this outstanding litter became champions, forming a successful pattern which did so much to establish the breed in England.

The Tavey Kennels also hold two other breed records in Great Britain that they are very proud of. One is the show record of their remarkable Ch. Iceberg of Tavey. Iceberg won 33 Challenge Certificates and innumerable Best in Show awards. The greatest thrill provided for them was when he won the Dog of the Year Competition for all breeds in 1965. This award is granted on a points basis covering wins over the space of a 12 month show season.

The second distinction brought home to their Tavey Kennels was the record achieved by Ch. Acclamation of Tavey. Acclamation sired 32 champions during his lifetime, a feat Mr. Curnow believes will go unchallenged in Britain for a long time to come, if ever.

But as always the Curnows are looking ahead. Looming high on the horizon are two other personally important males. Champion and Obedience Champion Jupiter of Tavey is the only Doberman in Britain and, as far as is known, in Europe which has become both a breed and obedience title holder in keen competition. The other star at their kennels is the only male they purchased in America, Vanessa's Little Dictator of Tavey, that they brought home with them in 1963. He is still alive and well and ruling the roost at Tavey as a house guard dog and companion. The Curnows speak of his glorious temperament and his love for his family.

Mrs. Curnow is also a judge of the breed and officiates at the important shows where her placings are highly regarded. With their many years of devotion to the breed and the great contribution to the breed through their excellent breeding, it is only natural that they should be respected for their integrity which will go down in British dog history.

Jean Faulks, who handled Lorelei of Tavey for the Curnows, did much to popularize the working abilities of the Doberman in England. Lionel Hamilton Renwick was also breeding good stock in the

Roanoke Tamarix in beautiful show stance; Nina, a brown and tan bitch, was born August 22nd, 1974 and was bred by her owners, Mr. James and Mrs. D.C. Richardson of the Roanoke Kennels in Essex, England. The sire was Cameron's Snoopy of Tinkazan x Samtrenno Snowflake of Roanoke.

A handsome trio of Dobermans which made their mark in the dog world of South Africa: South African Champion Brutus of Quintre of the Magaliesberg, C.D.X., South American Champion Carinn of Bohemia of the Magaliesberg, C.D.X. and Magaliesberg Tania of Apolda. All owned and trained for show and obedience by J.P. Schlesinger, now of London, England.

Tinkazan Tabora, whelped in August, 1973 by breeder Mrs. Jean Scheja. Campaigned in 1975 by owner-handler Mr. James Richardson who handles all of the Roanoke Dobermanns from the kennel co-owned by himself and his mother, Mrs. D.C. Richardson in Essex, England. The sire was Cameron's Snoopy of Tinkazan x Ch. Tinkazan Serengetti. Tabora was a Junior Warrant winner and has four Challenge Certificates.

Vånessa's Little Dictator of Tavey, imported to England by Mrs. Julia Curnow of the Tavey Kennels in Sussex. Dictator was whelped in 1963.

early days along with the Curnows. It was Mr. Renwick who imported Britta v d Heerhoff in whelp to start his Birling Kennels. Excellent Dobes like Birling Rebel, Rogue and Rachel followed in his line.

Alpha of Tavey, whelped in 1948, became the basis of Eva Would's kennel in England. She finished Champions Claus, Day, Daybreak Caprice and Helena, all of Cartergate.

A returning soldier brought Ulf v Margarethenhof to England with him. After the customary quarantine, he was offered, free of charge, to several Doberman fanciers because of his aggressive nature. The Curnows recommended Sgt. Harry Darbyshire, a renowned police dog handler. After having bitten the sergeant several times, Ulf was given to a constable in Surrey, where within one year "Peter," as he was now called, became the first Doberman to become a working trials champion. He was used extensively at stud and sired many excellent working-type Dobermans that also served well in constabularies.

Top working dogs during this time were Hawk of Trevellis, Gurnard Gloomy Sunday, Dollar Premium, Tavey's Stormy Jael, Yuba

Adonis, Dandy of Dovecote and Jupiter of Tavey, among others. Jupiter of Tavey held the record of being the only dual champion Doberman in the world for many years, with titles in both breed and obedience. Ch. Tavey's Stormy Master was also a well-known obedience winner, as were Maverick The Brave, Heiner Rustic, Annastock Moonraker and a couple of bitches owned by Dudley Wontner.

Ch. Elegant of Tavey was the first champion bitch C.C. winner and was never defeated after winning that first C.C. at Crufts in 1953. Names of other breeders supporting the breed in those days included Betty Harris, Jane and Greg Parks, Alf Hogg, Phillippa Thorne Dunn, Dorothy Horton and Jean Ryan.

Other important early imports to Britain were Derb and Beka v Brunoberg, Bruno v Ehrgarten, Prinsess Anja v t Scheepjeskerk, Iris v Wellborn, Angela v Kastanienhof, Wilm v Forell, Bill v Blauenblut, Pia v Dobberhof, Roeanka v d Rhederveld, Waldox v Aamsveen, Vilja Germania, Ditta v Scholzback, Timo v d Brunoberg, Treu v d

Ch. Tavey's Badge, photographed in 1972. Breeder was Mrs. Julia Curnow, Tavey Kennels, Sussex, England. Mrs. S. Somerfield of Sussex is the owner. Diane Pearce photograph.

Roanoke Halcyon, whelped in May, 1971 and pictured winning Best Opposite Sex in Show at the 1974 Romford event. Sired by Roanoke Nayrilla Apollo x Roanoke Ramona. Bred and owned by Mr. James and Mrs. D.C. Richardson, Roanoke Kennels, Essex, England.

Opposite, above:
Cameron's Snoopy of Tinkazan, owned by Mrs. Jean M. Scheja, Tinkazan Kennels, Dorset, England.

Opposite, below:
Roanoke Double Diamond, born in April, 1968 at the kennels of Mr. James and Mrs. D.C. Richardson, Essex, England. The sire was Ch. Iceberg of Tavey x Tavey's Stormy Nadia.

Tavey's Stormy Nadia, bred by the Curnows and owned by Mr. James and Mrs. D.C. Richardson, Roanoke Kennels, Essex, England. Whelped in August, 1964, she was sired by Ch. Tavey's Stormy Achievement x Ch. Tavey's Stormy Wrath.

Steinfurthohe, Centa v Empsperle, Ritter v d Heerhof, Donathe v Begertal, Gin v Forell, Britta v d Heerhof, Astor v d Morgansonne and Alex v Rodenaer.

Perhaps the most important of these was Tasso v d Brunoberg, a brother of the famous Troll, imported by the Curnows. Tasso produced many champions including Lyric, Lustre and Precept Pilot, all bearing the Tavey suffix, and the working trial bitch mentioned earlier, Lorelei of Tavey owned by Jean Faulks.

OTHER ACTIVE BRITISH KENNELS TODAY

The Derek Kings own, breed and show their Dobermans with the Studbriar prefix. Four of their Dobes qualified for the 1976 Crufts show. Their bloodlines are based on the Curnows' stock, using the Curnow's Phileens Duty Free of Tavey as a stud. Duty Free is out of American stock, the sire being Tarrado's Corry and the dam Kay Hill's Outrigger. They are also known for Ch. Studbriar Chieftain, who has four C.C.'s and five Reserve wins to his credit.

Both Margaret and Derek King are breed judges, and Mr. King is Doberman columnist for the English *Dog World.* In the mid-70's they

Ch. Hensel Midnight Max in show stance at eight years of age. Max and his sire, Ch. Tavey's Stormy Medallion, trace their bloodlines back to famous U.S. Ch. Rancho Dobe's Storm, the Westminster Kennel Club winner. Owned by Mrs. Dorothy P. Parker of Norfolk, England. Photograph by well-known British dog photographer, Diane Pearce.

were busy exhibiting three of their top Dobes, Studbriar The Red, Studbriar The Dilemma and Ariki Arataki.

Another advocate of the potential of Duty Free as a sire was Sara Mitchell, who bred her bitch Sophie to him in 1974. Sara Mitchell has the Copper Bronze Kennels and is proud that Copper Bronze Sophie has won consistently in A.O.C. class under both national and international judges when they officiate in England.

Margaret and Harry Woodward own the Achenburg lines, with their stud Champion Triogen Tornade siring Jack Anory, Juliette and Gordini, all bearing the Achenburg prefix. Their Achenburg Kennel is also the home of Kenstaff Tornado of Achenburg, who took the show ring by storm as a puppy, winning six times Best Puppy in Show and Puppy Stakes, plus numerous Best of Breed and Best in Show wins. These were topped by 85 Junior Warrant points as of 1974.

Brian and Vi Blachford are owners of the Drumpellier Kennels and have several promising Dobes following a successful show season in 1974 with Drumpellier Anhel and Drumpellier Alcorjet. They also own Tinkazan Serenata.

The Tinkazan Kennels are owned by Jean M. Scheja. A brown and tan Canadian import, Cameron's Snoopy of Tinkazan, made his show debut in 1975 and is at stud at her kennel.

Pat Gledhill's Borain Dobermanns use Ch. Royaltain's Highwayman of Borain as their stud force. His brown and tan daughter, Borain's Hot Chocolate (whelped in 1973), is an exciting showgirl at the kennel. In 1974 she was Best Bitch at the North of England Dobermann Club championship show and the Dobermann Club open show, as well as accumulating two C.C.'s and other wins.

Margaret Bastable and her Barrimilne Kennels have enjoyed success in the show ring for many years. In the 1970's some of the Barrimilne studs were Timo von der Brunoburg, Baron von Bavaria and German Champion Greif von Hagenster, Schutzhund I. Greif was

Crufts Show, 1975, Derek King handled his black and tan bitch, Ariki Arataki, to First in the Novice Bitch Class at nine months of age. She is the youngest Dobe to qualify at Crufts to date. Her sire was Ch. Studbriar Chieftain x Ch. Treasurequest Christal. Margaret and Derek King's kennel is in Bucks, England.

English Champion Triogen Tuppeny Feast, bred by Alf Hogg and owned by Mr. James and Mrs. D.C. Richardson, Roanoke Kennels, Essex, England. The sire was Ch. Acclamation of Tavey x Triogen Teenage Wonder.

sired by German Champion Bonni von Forell x German Champion Dona vom Eichenhain. Mrs. Bastable is a recognized authority on the breed, especially on the breed in England, and is the only woman licensed to judge the breed in Germany.

Other showing kennels in the mid-1970's are Haward Curtis and his Kirnvar Kennels, the Illustria Kennels of Mr. and Mrs. M.J. Garrod, Hilary Partridge and his Pompie Dobermanns, T.J.H. Anderson with the Leafayer prefix, Paul and Eileen Eales and their Ironman Dobermanns, Jean and Jack Linger and the Greenling line, Lynda and Jim Clar and their Dekaos Dobes, Mr. and Mrs. K.V. Frankland who own Linhoff, Roger Skinner and his Ikos dogs, Pat and Ed Jenner and their Nivelle Dobermanns, J. McManus and the Metexa lines, Maureen and Ken Bennett, Mrs. Flora Auld and the Auldrigg Dobermanns, Jim and Marty Burrell with the Jimartys and Valenia and Alan Harle.

Show catalogues reveal the names of the Highroyd dogs owned by Mr. T.J. Lam, Mike Turner's Demo Dobermanns, Mrs. E. Edward's Phileen Dobermanns and Ken and Sheila Cole with their Kaybar Dobermanns.

Mrs. Neave of Suffolk, England, with her young dog Chevington Royal Septre.

BRITISH REGISTRATIONS

To document the growth of the Doberman in Britain, one need only refer to the registrations in the breed over a twenty year period. In 1951, after only a few years while the breed was "catching on," the registrations were 94. Two decades later, in 1971, the total registrations were 1,566. We hesitate to venture a guess as to what they will be in another twenty years.

DOBERMANS IN SCOTLAND

Soon after its initial appearance in England the Doberman reached Scotland. Some of the early Doberman champions were Ch. Carrickgreen Confederate, Crontham King, Clanguard Commanche, Audrigg Corsair and Clanguard Cadet.

The Richardson's English Ch. Triogen Tuppeny Feast. Sired by Ch. Acclamation of Tavey x Triogen Teenage Wonder. The Richardson's Roanoke Kennel is in Essex, England.

English Champion Studbriar Chieftain photographed after winning his third Challenge Certificate and Best in Show at the Scottish Dobermann Club Championship Show. This photograph was autographed by George Chakaris when he was using some of the dogs belonging to Derek and Margaret King of Bucks, England, in a film he was making there. Chieftain's sire was Ch. Iceberg of Tavey x Eikon Jests Amazon.

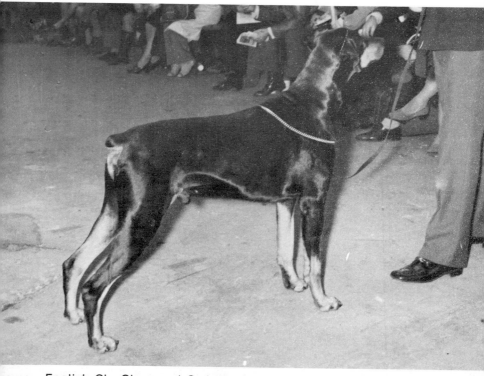

English Ch. Clanguard Cadette, famous show dog (one of the best ever). Owned by a Scotsman, Mr. D. Montgomery of Glasgow, Scotland.

We must remember that the growth was not as rapid as it could have been because of transportation problems, but the names of the top British kennels spread to the Scottish dog world to establish their earliest kennels.

While the count of Dobermans in Scotland might not be considered as great in number, there is certainly enthusiasm for the breed, at least to the point where we find the organization and existence of a Scottish Dobermann Club. This group is headed by Mr. R.C. Lang, in Lanarkshire, Scotland, who is active in the club and the breed.

The Hopemanne Dobermann Kennels are located in Moray, Scotland and are owned by Laurie Ann Marker, wife of a Royal Air Force man. The Markers and their young daughter have attended several dog shows in Scotland, though they have not as yet exhibited extensively.

Mrs. Marker says she likes to keep her dogs for obedience work and the bitches for the show ring. Their bloodlines are chiefly Triogen. Their Triogen Tory Majority is five-and-a-half years of age. Bluey, as she is called, rules the roost at Hoppemanne, along with her daughter, Hopemanne Happy Hazel. Hazel's litter sister, Hopemanne Happy Helga, was exported to the United States to Mrs. Anne David of Redwood City, California. Their youngest bitch is Hopemanne Olympic Silver, who for some strange reason is called Kleiner. Kleiner is a full sister to Hazel, but out of another litter. The sire of both of Bluey's daughters was Linhoff the Saracen. Another male at Hopemanne was Triogen Timely Arrival. Until he met with an unfortunate accident in December, 1974, "Kurt" could usually be seen patrolling on the roof of the Markers' house on the Scottish shore, built just 30 feet above sea level. The Hopemanne Dobermanns love to run on the sandy beach below the house, which keeps them in top condition.

Eventually the Markers hope to open their own breeding and boarding kennels and intend to import some American bloodlines to form a nucleus of stud force for Dobermans in their part of the world.

Best Brace at a 1946 Canadian show was Dirk and Dash, owned by C.W. Kelly of Vancouver, Canada. These two American and Canadian Champions were Dictator sons out of Ch. Olivia of Marienburg.

5. THE DOBERMAN PINSCHER AS A WAR DOG

It is difficult at times to envision our beautiful Dobermans as war dogs now that it is over a quarter of a century since the end of World War II when the Doberman was adopted as the official dog of the U.S. Marine Corp. But, lest we forget the outstanding heroic services these dedicated dogs performed under war-time conditions, we must make some of their remarkable feats under fire a matter of record.

TYPES OF SERVICES IN ANCIENT TIMES

We can go back many centuries before World War II to acknowledge the effective uses of dogs during wartime, when they were employed as both defense and attack dogs. Plutarch and Pliny both wrote about war dogs that carried messages in their collars hundreds of years ago. Attila the Hun used enormous guard dogs to watch over his camp whenever he went on a rampage. The Romans used them in war and peace as sentry dogs, stationing them in the towers in the walls around that great ancient city. Marco Polo marched through Asia accompanied by enormous Molossian mastiffs.

At times the war dogs were dressed in various forms of armor which bore spikes, knives, etc., and they cut quite a swarth through the land soldiers when called upon to do so. William the Conqueror was accompanied by Bloodhounds during his campaign in England; these were to be used for sentry duty. The Turks also used dogs for attack during their assault on the Austrian patrols

Opposite:

"Peppy," listed as missing in action for three days during front line action on Guam during World War II, heroically made his way back to camp after being lost in the jungles. Here he is greeted by his handler after being treated for a bullet wound in his left ear. Official U.S. Marine Corps photo.

Soldiers and their "devil dogs" take a short rest before moving on during hostilities on Guam Island during World War II. Official U.S. Marine Corps photo.

In Italy in 1800 there was a dog named Moustache used during the Italian Consulate Campaign that not only tracked down spys but was later decorated during the battle of Austerlitz for having grabbed the flag when he saw the standard bearer fall and an enemy soldier about to reach for it!

Satan was the name of a World War I dog which is said to have helped the allies at the battle of Verdun. The dog was sent out to a headquarters far behind the lines with a message for help after all other methods of communication had been cut off as a result of constant bombardment from enemy guns. Satan came back and was hit as he crept his way toward the trench where his master was hiding. Satan's owner was killed as he called encouragement to the dog, but Satan succeeded in returning to the trench. In his collar was the message that help was on the way, and two baskets strapped to his body contained two carrier pigeons. The exact position of the enemy artillery was written on a slip of paper and placed in the containers on the pigeons' legs and the birds released. Shortly thereafter the German guns were blasted out of commission.

THE "EARTHBOUND" GRAF ZEPPELIN

The story of the "earthbound" Graf Zeppelin comes to us by way of Arthur Roland, dog writer for the newspaper *The Sun*, who wrote for the fifth edition of *The Story of Pedigreed Dogs*, published in 1940.

The item concerns the heroism and keen intelligence of a Doberman Pinscher named Graf Zeppelin that served with the Nationalist Army in China. The dog had a reputation for intelligence and, as Arthur Roland put it, "true grit."

Graf was born in Weimar, Germany in 1933. He was exported to San Francisco in 1935, and in 1937 was shipped off to China. By 1939 Graf had learned to take orders in the dialects of Peking and Canton, as well as English and his native German. In two years of constant service to his American volunteer master he saved him twice from injury and possible death and on one occasion rescued his entire company.

This occurred when the outfit was trapped in a river bed in Honan Province by a superior enemy force. Graf was sent with a dispatch for help to a town 18 miles away! His outfit was rescued within sixty hours after his departure for the town, in which they all hadn't set foot for over a week.

EUROPEAN WAR DOGS

Russia, France, Holland, Belgium, Italy and Germany all have used dogs in times of war. Germany had an especially well organized war dog corps and during World War II sent many war dogs to Japan to be used against the Americans during our confrontations in the Pacific Theatre of war.

Russia trained what they referred to as anti-tank dogs which they used extensively during World War II. Anti-tank dogs went into the face of oncoming tanks with explosives tied to their backs. They were trained to crawl beneath the tanks; the moment they did so the explosives were set off, blowing the dog, the tank and its occupants to bits. Germany also used anti-tank dogs.

Mr. Bernard Spaughton, of the Frankskirby Kennels in England, personally corroborates the fact that during World War II the Germans also trained Dobermans to be used against the enemy forces in Holland. The dogs had one hundred pounds of T.N.T. tied to their backs and a trigger set to go off if anyone touched their collars. The more fortunate of these dogs were herded into empty tank compounds and fed from the ends of long poles over the sandbags until such time as they were friendly enough to be fed by hand. Then the Royal Engineers who had rescued them would carefully approach them and remove the explosives without having to grab them by the collars. Many dogs were saved in this manner.

Five such dogs were handed over to the U.S. Army and another five were kept by the British Army of the Rhine. Two eventually went back to England on a tank landing craft with someone who is still in Dobermans today but wishes to remain anonymous. We cannot help but wonder why he wishes to remain anonymous for what can only be regarded as a tremendous act of compassion in trying to save and rehabilitate Dobermans which in their innocence had done their duty and served so well.

WAR DOGS IN GREAT BRITAIN

While the English Channel eliminated the need for widespread use of sentry or guard dogs during the war, the British still made good use of trained dogs by utilizing their services as ambulance dogs. The dogs carried first aid equipment to the wounded to be used until the medics could reach them, located wounded under bombed buildings and sought out unconscious wounded in open fields or where they might be hidden from normal view.

WORLD WAR II AND THE ROLE OF THE MILITARY DOG

When war was declared by the United States after the bombing of Pearl Harbor on December 7, 1941, it occurred to more than one dog fancier that there was a place for the dog when it came to defending our country. Their loyalty, their desire to please, their ability to scent and track, their extraordinary strength and endurance, their insatiable curiosity and acute hearing all could be harnessed into a dependable "living machine" which could be trained to do the work of anywhere from two to a dozen men.

THE FORMATION OF DOGS FOR DEFENSE

Strange as it may seem, it was a stage actress that first came up with the idea for an organization which would serve the purpose of supplying dogs to serve in the armed forces. Helen Mencken, of the American Theatre Wing, thought that such a voluntary organization could be mustered from the ranks of the nation's kennel owners, who would know of a constant supply of dogs required for such work. She was absolutely correct in this assumption.

The organization was called Dogs for Defense, Incorporated. Listed among its founding members were some of the biggest and most important members of the dog show world, as well as many others who wished to contribute their efforts to this cause. While the

Sentry dogs were trained to come back to their handlers with the aid of a silent whistle. In this photograph the trainer recalls. his Doberman Pinscher by this method. Official U.S. Marine Corps photograph.

initial response from the Army was disappointing when Miss Mencken first approached Quartermaster General Gregor, the group went on to train 200 dogs for sentry duty and proudly presented them to the Quartermaster Corps.

AN OFFICIAL "ABOUT FACE"

Once the dogs had a chance to prove what they could do, the Army placed an order for two thousand. Before long the canine ranks had swelled to 125,000! By the end of the war the Army, Navy and Marines had requested—and received—over 250,000 military dogs to serve side by side with the men.

Naturally, as the number of dogs requested far exceeded the number of qualified trainers within the ranks of the Dogs for Defense organization, the job of training the dogs had to be turned over to the armed forces. The role of the organization became more of a question of finding sufficiently qualified dogs and trainers to work with the soldiers, and of offering advice on the general care and capabilities of the dogs themselves. Dogs for Defense became the sole procurement agency for the armed forces. Names like K-9 Corps and Devil Dogs became popular jargon whenever talk of the war was brought up in the course of conversation.

Many of the larger breeds were accepted into the corps, especially the German Shepherd and Doberman Pinscher, and a list of specifications was written up for the dogs to meet in order to qualify for active duty. The dogs had to be between one and five years of age, 50 pounds or over and 20 inches or more at the withers. They must have had distemper or have been innoculated against it and had to be free of worms and skin trouble. Of course they could not be gun shy or afraid of noise and thunder, and were not to be too friendly either.

One of the casualties of war. . . a wounded Marine Corps war dog named Corporal Kurt is hospital bound. Trained to follow either of his two Marine partners—and to take orders only from them—Kurt suffered a fractured back and was taken back to his kennel on this jeep ambulance during hostilities on Guam. Official U.S. Marine Corps photo.

Marine Raiders and their devil dog partners walk along a jungle path on Bougainville toward the front lines during World War II. These marine war dogs and their trainers were the first to arrive and fought fearlessly side by side during this island confrontation. Official U.S. Marine Corps photo.

THE NEED FOR A WAR DOG FUND

As the organization grew so did expenses. It became more and more apparent that a subsidy was necessary if they were to carry on their tremendous work. While none of the officers or regional directors for Dogs for Defense were salaried and all dogs were donated to the service, expenses were incurred and something had to be done about it.

A War Dog Fund was set up within the organization to help defray expenses. Here again the list of founding members reads like the K-9 Blue Book—Mr. and Mrs. William A. Rockefeller, Mrs. David Wagstaff, Mrs. William J. Warburton, Mrs. Cheever Porter, Mrs. Sherman Hoyt, Miss Laura Delano, Mrs. Marian Foster Florsheim, Mr. and Mrs. W. French Githens and the Frelinghuysens were among the elite who were anxious to support the War Dog Fund.

The offices were at 22 East 60th Street in New York City, where Harry I. Caesar served as its president. A.M. Lewis was treasurer, Mrs. Milton Erlanger was in charge of finance, William E. Buckley was counsel, George F. Foley was director at large and Leonard Brumby was field secretary. Mrs. William H. Long, Jr., served as secretary.

Roland Kilbon was in charge of publicity, and through his efforts the organization became well known. Kennel clubs donated part of the revenue from their shows to them, "In Memorium" donations were received, the Westminster Kennel Club show featured a Parade of War Dogs and a booth for the organization was set up at "The Garden" to tell the general public all about the War Dog Fund and its parent organization. Trophies were also donated and many publications both in the dog world and in the public press donated free advertising space for this worthy cause.

The money garnered from these efforts was not only used for necessary expenses, but helped pay the expenses incurred in securing the dogs and in shipping them. The War Dog Fund of Dogs for Defense also gave the dogs at home that did not qualify for active service a chance to make a "contribution." Owners donating specified sums of money received a certificate stating that their dog helped to procure a dog for active service. Their "rank" in the War Dog Fund was listed as follows:

DONATION	ARMY	NAVY
$1	Private	Seaman
$2	Private First Class	3rd Class Petty Officer
$3	Corporal	2nd Class Petty Officer
$5	Sergeant	Chief Petty Officer
$10	Lieutenant	Ensign
$15	Captain	Lieutenant
$20	Major	Commander
$25	Colonel	Captain
$50	Brigadier General	Rear Admiral
$75	Major General	Vice Admiral
$100	General	Admiral

(*These ranks are not exactly equivalent.*)

So the dogs contributed on both the war front and the home front. Dogs for Defense helped in active service, and the War Dog Fund organized the home front.

THE CLASSIFICATIONS OF SERVICE

There were many names given to the war dogs—military dogs, service dogs and an individual name for each that was trained to a single special field. Perhaps the most versatile of all were the dogs referred to as the commandos.

The *commandos* were of extremely high intelligence and capable of responding successfully to a wide range of commands. They would attack on commands given verbally, by whistle and by touch and were trained to advance through fire and water, climb ladders, jump, guard and to hold at bay and retrieve. They could also track, scout and do sentry duty. Truly they were the most "all-around" dogs in the service.

The *command dog* should not be confused with the commandos. The command dog is a dog which has been trained to attack on command from a trainer and also to stop the attack on command.

Just as the command and the commando dogs should not be confused, we must not confuse the *attack dog* with the *assault dog*. The assault dogs were used in the fields and jungle to flush out the enemy

One of the first photographs released of the Marine Corps "devil dogs" in training at Camp Lejeune, North Carolina, during World War II. Training included landing operations, sentry duty, scout and messenger duties, first aid treatment and locating wounded Marines. This photo shows the dogs and their trainers being put through a close order drill to get them used to discipline. Official U.S. Marine Corps photo.

Ruff, with his trainers PFC Glen Dodge of Oklahoma City and PFC Curtis Eldredge of Philadelphia, serving in Bougainville. Donated to the Marine Corps by Clyde Folmar of Torrington, Connecticut for service in World War II.

from foxholes, trenches, etc., while the attack dogs were trained to attack upon encountering the enemy in the field whether their trainers were with them or not.

Stake dogs were those "staked-out" in an area where no more was expected of them than to sound an alarm by barking at the approach of an intruder. These stake dogs were used to guard the supply units, ammunition depots, military barracks, etc. In other words, they merely alerted personnel on the premises to the arrival of visitors or the enemy. These dogs were also referred to as yard dogs, guard dogs, etc.

Patrol dogs were the canines that accompanied soldiers while patrolling an area. The area could be within our own boundaries or along the front line of battle or a country boundary. They are not to be confused with the sentry dog.

A *sentry dog* is trained to work with his trainer and handler in the guarding of a specified area. Sentry dogs are also usually trained as scout dogs since their duties are so similar, with neither of them being trained to attack or allowed to bark.

In spite of all the sophisticated weapons of war, incorporating fantastic aerial photography, mighty tanks and long-range firearms, there was still an important place for the *scout dog* during World War II. Since boundaries and "county lines" were non-existent in enormous square miles of jungle, there was one way, and only one way, of

At the 1944 Cleveland Classic show banquet, Dick Webster congratulates Clyde Henderson on his triumphant return to the U.S. after taking the 1st Platoon of Marine Corps Dobermans over to the Pacific war theatre. The newspaper account of the story in the *Cleveland Plain Dealer* featured a full page picture of the great Dictator with the headline, "The Marines have Landed!"

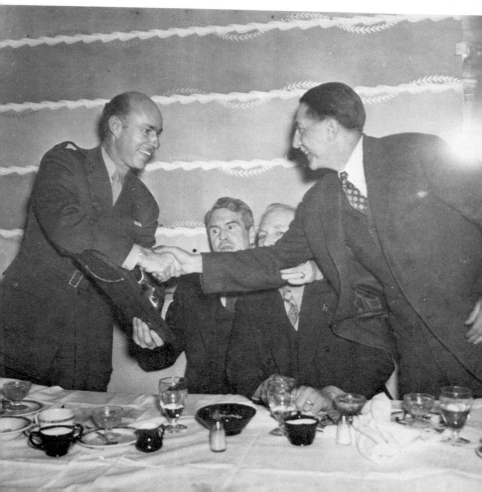

ferreting out the enemy, and that was by man himself—and his friend the dog!

These highly trained scout dogs were taught to seek out and find the enemy, and could do this for distances of anywhere from 500 yards to half a mile. They were trained to react to both live and dead scents. By live scent we mean the dog was trained to locate the presence of a person or object; a dead scent was when the dog was expected to locate the position where a person or object *had* been. These scents included soldiers as well as booby traps, weapons caches, food, mines, military equipment or tripwires, as well as the wounded.

The way in which the scout dog alerted his trainer could vary. Some of the dogs were taught to hang on to the sleeve of their trainer, or to go "on point" the way a hunting dog might, or perhaps give no more of a signal than raising the hackles and bristling the coat. But one way was forbidden—the dog must never bark!

The method of training was usually taught by working the dog in what was referred to as a "scent cone," a cone-shaped area with its apex at the point of location of the object and spanning downwind from that point. The dog, of course, became more anxious as it came closer to the actual scent.

In addition to perfect health, the scout dog had to be at least 60 pounds and 23 or more inches at the withers. Either sex was acceptable if they were between one and three years of age, and the females, of course, had to be spayed at least 90 days before their induction. The dogs also had to indicate a rather aggressive attitude with a mental capacity of learning more than one hundred commands after a twelve week training course.

So successful were these scout dogs during war-time conditions that additional research was conducted to further utilize their talents. Tests were conducted to see if it would be possible to have the dogs work alone or use a man-to-animal communications system which would maintain contact between the two by means of a small transistor which would automatically enable the dog to work far

Opposite:
"Andy," a Marine Corps devil dog, saved a Marine Corps tank platoon from annihilation on Bougainville during World War II. Andy and his trainer share a moment of relaxation in this official Marine Corps photo. Many of these dogs were returned to their owners after the victory.

Opposite:
Guarding a prisoner! The scene was the Westminster Kennel Club show during World War II, when famous dog trainer Lieut. Willy Necker gave a demonstration of the U.S. Coast Guard war dogs guarding prisoners. The dogs were trained at the Curtis Bay Training Station in Maryland.

below:
Hunting for snipers on Guam Island during World War II, this Doberman war dog rests for a moment along with his human and canine companions. These dogs played a major role in tracing down the Japanese snipers during the struggle. Official U.S. Marine Corps photo.

ahead of his trainer and/or the patrol. These and other studies were being discussed in terms of future potential for the scout dogs which distinguished themselves so well on the battlefield after their rigorous training at Fort Benning, Georgia, Training Headquarters.

Mine detector dogs were used to locate land mines and booby traps as well as tripwires which might be laid across a field. During the war some of our scout dogs were also trained and used for this purpose.

The Americans used *ambulance dogs* in some instances. They were trained to travel right up along the front lines to tend to the wounded and can be credited with saving many lives.

One of the lesser known services performed by our wonderful war dogs was that of *blood doner*. The dogs were seldom the same ones sent out into the field to serve under fire (unless there was some dire emergency in the field of operations), but rather were a select group which was kept at the school or field headquarters and cared for and fed with great care and attention. Their state of health was constantly being checked.

The blood reserves at the canine blood bank were used either in direct transfusions to the injured dogs or in direct transfusions during surgery.

We know of a veterinary school in Maisons-Alfort, France, where a staff of 25 dogs were on hand to supply the necessary blood required for life-saving duties at the school. It was reported that these husky canines supplied nearly two hundred pints of blood for the school's blood bank over a six-month period.

There is hardly a veterinarian in practice today who does not know where he can acquire this precious blood when required to save a canine life, even though few of them maintain dogs expressly for this purpose on their premises. It is interesting to note that these dogs are serving each other so admirably, as well as serving mankind in so many other ways.

Serving in a less significant manner, but not less faithfully, were the countless brave *mascot dogs* which followed the troops from town to town and camp to camp. Many a dog was adopted by the G.I.s and traveled across foreign lands with them, sometimes under secret conditions and sometimes as very vocal comrades chasing alongside the road during the long marches.

Many a dog also found itself aboard ship and on its way to strange countries as mascot of a ship, and many of these beloved mascots found their way home to America with the G.I.s. There is no doubt about it: in their own special way, they also served.

"Who, me?" says one-year-old Alcyon, photographed by her owner, Mrs. Janet M. Skidmore of Norwalk, Connecticut.

Ch. Damasyn Jalli's Jayna, owned by Manuel Miyeres of New Orleans, Louisiana. This lovely bitch is pictured winning at a show in the 1960's. Her sire was Ch. Damasyn Carly of Jerseystone x Ch. Jalli Alli, C.D., and she is litter sister to Damasyn Jalli's Jaimie and Damasyn Jalli's Jing Jing, C.D., SchH I.

6. THE DOBERMAN PINSCHER AS A WORKING DOG

There is no denying that those of us who adore the Doberman Pinscher get a thrill whenever we see a show dog moving around the ring and "strutting his stuff." They are impressive to look at and always command the admiration of those at ringside no matter what the competition.

But for those of us who take our admiration of this breed to the fullest extent, we must confess that the Doberman is truly at his magnificent best when he is doing what he was bred to do—WORK! A working dog "doing what comes naturally" is a joy to behold, and over the years we have trained our Dobermans to do a multitude of working jobs that make us truly proud of their ability, intelligence and desire to please their owners as well as carry out commands.

We have domesticated the Doberman Pinscher to the point where he can be considered a companion and house dog, where almost inherently he protects the family and the house. American Kennel Club obedience training comes almost as "second nature" to the average Doberman. As the tremendous interest in the breed continues to grow with each passing year, we are observing the comparative ease with which almost all Dobermans can be trained to carry out the most difficult and most exacting requirements for whatever task they are asked to perform or in whatever position they are asked to serve.

During the years of the Doberman's development they have been required to perform not only complicated and difficult jobs, but to perform in the most unusual situations and to serve in most important capacities. With each passing year their purposes increase and they keep adding to their talents. Those of which we can be most proud are discussed in this chapter to help us fully appreciate this remarkable working dog.

THE DOBERMAN AS A PACK DOG

Perhaps the most vivid account of Doberman pack dogs is recorded with the Dobermann Club of South Africa and relates the

The Russtun Dobe "gang" with the real boss of the outfit, the Dachshund Bruno, in Hants, England.

Opposite:
Ebonaire's Bagheera
pictured winning
Junior Showmanship
competition with her
owner-handler, 12-
year-old Robin Weiss
of Levittown, New
York. Sired by Ch.
Ebonaire's
Entertainer; the dam
was Debbie Duchess
v Palen.

marvelous hikes of three of their club members. Jonathon Schlesinger, Chris Lee and John Flach, their Dobermans Brutus, Jason and Faust, all made newspaper headlines in their country when they set out with their dogs on a hike covering 150 kilometers (about 90 miles). The trek began at Port Edward and took them over rugged terrain, ending at Mpandi five days later.

Men and dogs carried food and water enough for the trip, along with tents, sleeping bags, snakebite kits and, quite naturally, a few cameras.

Two months of training preceded the hike, with 20-kilometer walks through the Magaliesberg territory over weekends. But the warm-up walking was only partially useful since it in no way could simulate the rocky crags and steep inclines they would encounter on the actual hike. It was also the first time the hike had been made with dogs. Needless to say, the dogs did very well.

Where the mountains were virtually impassable at certain points, the dogs, securely harnessed to their owners, were raised and lowered over the crags with the help of the three men. The dogs also wore special leather boots made for them to protect their feet on certain parts of the trail.

Dogs and owners both loved the adventure so much that no sooner had they returned from the original trip (along what is referred to as the Wild Coast of South Africa) than they began planning a second pack walk a few months later from Lochiel, near the Swaziland border. Jonathon Schlesinger currently resides in London and is no longer able to accompany his contemporaries in their positive attempts to prove the ability of the Doberman as a pack dog. But history records the initial attempts which proved to all that the Doberman is tough and able to keep up with the best of them!

THE DOBERMAN AS A HUNTER

While the Doberman Pinscher is used extensively as a working and guard dog, there have been Dobermans successfully trained as hunting dogs. There are those who have actually seen Dobermans go "on point" and have had excellent results using them for retrieving.

There is no doubt of their value in this pursuit in Africa, where Dobermans have been used on all kinds of small game. Their speed and power permit them to be successful with larger animals as well. Their phenomenal talent when tracking in either the city or the jungle is well known, and there is no reason to believe they are any less able to do the same in the fields.

DOBE TRACK RECORD

While Bloodhounds are reported to have the keenest noses for tracking down human victims in distress or fugitives from justice, it is actually a Doberman Pinscher which holds the record for sticking to a scent and tracking down a thief.

Detective-Sergeant Herbert Kruger trained his Doberman, Sauer, to follow a scent. In 1925, by scent alone he tracked for over 100 miles across the Great Karroo in South Africa and brought his owner to the criminal.

DOBERMANS AS HERDING DOGS

Mrs. D.P. Parker of Norfolk, England, tells us the story of a Doberman that caught sight of a lamb caught up in a barbed wire fence and actually stood on the bottom row of wire until the lamb managed to wriggle free of it. This seems to be a case of pure, intelligent reasoning on the part of the Doberman, although it is too often said that dogs cannot reason.

Mrs. Parker also relates the story of a keeper at the Thefford Chase forest in England. This forest of several miles in area is inhabited by semi-wild deer. Unfortunately, each year many of these deer are injured by cars or by poachers taking pot shots at them, with the result that many are cruelly and painfully injured and wander off in pain. This particular keeper, who had been impressed with the intelligence of the Doberman, bought a puppy from Mrs. Parker several years ago and finds that the Doberman has taken it upon himself to round up and stand guard over injured deer in the forest until the keeper either puts them out of their misery or nurses them back to health.

Another customer of Mrs. Parker uses his Dobermans to shepherd over 400 of his sheep. He reports that he would not go back to Collies since having Dobermans that "use their heads and never tire."

MOVIE STAR DOGS

In 1927 Carl Spitz started the Hollywood Dog Training School, still one of the largest and oldest institutions of its kind. Since 1962 it has been run by his son, Carl Spitz, Jr. Mr. Spitz received his early training instruction in his native Germany starting in 1919 and has ever since then been associated with the training of dogs.

In 1926 he immigrated to the United States and for one year trained dogs in Chicago. The move to California and the formation of his Hollywood training school followed the next year. Some of the dogs Mr. Spitz has trained include the two Great Danes for *Big Boy* with Al Jolson; the Saint Bernard in the first *Moby Dick* with Lionel Barrymore; Toto the Cairn Terrier belonging to Judy Garland in *The Wizard of Oz*; Buck, the dog lead in the Clark Gable movie *The Call of the Wild*; and the Great Dane in *The Most Dangerous Game*, to name a few.

In 1941 the War Department Quartermaster Corps requested that Mr. Spitz organize the first continental platoon of war dogs in Stock-

Maverick, Marauder and Mystique (a black and tan, a red and a fawn) pictured at six weeks of age. Bred by Patricia D. Edwards, D.V.M., owner of the Barchet Kennels in Snellville, Georgia. Dr. Edwards has been breeding and showing Dobermans since the mid-1960's.

Opposite:
Irish Jig of Aramis photographed taking Winner's Dog honors at the October, 1975 Catonsville Kennel Club show. Terry Lazzaro handled for owner Robert Ranciato of North Haven, Connecticut. William Gilbert photograph.

ton, California. He later organized another in Pomona. In 1942 it was off to Washington to help with the training of the first men and dogs for the K-9 Corps and to help draft the first instructions for war dog training. In 1943 Carl Spitz assisted the U.S. Marine Corps in training their first combat war dog platoon, which served so well in Bougainville.

Two blind persons make their first attempt at crossing a busy street with their Pathfinder guidedogs, the project established by the late Glenn Staines. This photograph was taken in 1950.

Mr. Spitz first began judging the obedience classes around 1935 and wrote a book on obedience training in 1938. This book was updated recently. One of his most recent judging assignments was at the 47th Annual Specialty Show and Obedience Trial of the Doberman Pinscher Club of America in Maumee, Ohio, on October 5th, 1972.

When speaking of Dobermans as working dogs and recalling Carl Spitz and his Hollywood Training School, we must realize that the trained movie dogs have not always worked to the advantage of their breed.

It seems that whenever a "vicious" dog is required for the plot of a movie its always a "snarling" Doberman pictured lungeing at the end of a leash with teeth bared. An October, 1975, telecast of a film entitled *They Only Kill Their Masters* was aired on CBS-TV and "starred" Doberman Pinschers. The film contained such detrimental phrases in reference to the dog as "ate the lady," and "vicious attack." This certainly is no help in our efforts to educate the public to the fact that only trained Dobermans attack on command and the temperament of the average Doberman will blend remarkably well with a family routine and way of life.

202

"Arnold," one of Glenn Staines most famous guide dogs for the blind in his famous Pathfinder project. Arnold is pictured here in the late 1930's with his harness on. Photo courtesy of the Thornes.

DOBERMAN PINSCHERS AS GUIDE DOGS FOR THE BLIND

There is no doubt about the mental capacity of the Doberman when it comes to serving as a guide dog for the blind. They have the intelligence to assume any and all the responsibilities required and certainly possess the dedication and loyalty to their master. In fact, they have too much loyalty! Agencies supplying guide dogs for the blind in this country are quick to tell you this, and then add that they possess too much dedication! They profess that the Doberman Pinscher becomes overly-protective of the master and cannot be completely depended upon in this regard.

There is no doubt that over the years the Doberman HAS been used and in some cases has proved successful. But we must assume that these agencies, which have come to the point where they breed their own dogs for the blind, know what they are talking about. Their breeding programs consist largely of German Shepherds, Labradors and Golden Retrievers. Therefore we must assume, generally speaking, that guide dog work is not one of the Doberman's chief working functions and not every Doberman suits this profession.

DOBERMAN GUIDE DOGS IN RUSSIA

In 1960 the All-Russian Society of the Blind, located in Veshnyaki, a community near Moscow, founded the Central School to Train Dogs to Guide the Blind. The director, Nikolai Orekhov, has devoted several decades to working for the blind. His school covers many acres

Studbriar The Red, winner of one Challenge Certificate at the 1975 Bournemouth Championship Show at 13 months of age. His sire was Phileen's Duty Free of Tavey x Tavey's Renaissance; bred by Mrs. M.L. King and Mrs. J. Curnow. This lovely red and tan dog is pictured here at 10 months of age, and is owned by Margaret and Derek King, Burghfield, Bucks, England.

Opposite:
Ch. Carosel In The Spotlight pictured winning at a 1975 dog show on the way to her championship. Carosel finished with a five-point major as Best of Winners at the November Motor City Kennel Club show. She is handled by her co-breeder, Carol Selzle, and is owned by Mrs. Susan P. King of Saratoga Springs, New York.

Working Dobermans of the Oceanside, California Police Department. Left to right: officer Larry Hanson with Marienburg's Ben Ghalii, their trainer Fon Johnson of San Diego, and officer John Wheelock with Sultan. Beh Ghalli was bred by Mary Rodgers. The sire was Ch. Damasyn Bo-Tairic of Ardon x Marienburg's Rachel.

and is surrounded by a board fence; it features open-air cages for the dogs, an administration building, a veterinary center and a small building for the students that come there to be taught along with their dogs.

The blind pay nothing for their guide dogs, and the State even pays for their transportation to and from the school as well as room and board while they are in training.

Before the blind arrive to be instructed along with their new lead dog, much training has gone into the making of a good guide for the blind. It costs the school 320 rubles (about $120) to keep and train each dog. The school has a "mock village" in which the dogs become acquainted with fences, ditches, sidewalks, curbs, stones, posts, pits, a railway platform, staircases and an old bus. Once trained on their "home territory," the dogs are taken into a nearby town and exposed to the same circumstances with the public at large.

At the conclusion of their three-month training period, the dogs meet their new masters. The blind owners are introduced to their new companions and are trained along with them during an intensive 12-day indoctrination. The blind are given a theoretical course in the proper handling of the dog, walking with it and feeding and caring for it properly. They are also taught the training methods for the dog so that the dog may continue to function correctly. Each of the 12 days, under the close guidance of the instructor, the blind person not only works with the dog but determines whether or not they are socially agreeable to each other. If so, the student is given a collar, leash, muzzle and other equipment needed to care for the dog. The new owner can also expect that the dog has been taught to take good care of him—Russian guide dogs are taught to nudge bus passengers with their noses if after a reasonable time no one has offered their master a seat!

The school trains an average of 80-100 dogs a year on a budget of approximately 75,000 rubles a year, which includes staff salaries for approximately 16 to 20 instructors. The school requires that the dogs be between one and three years of age. The best workers are the East European Shepherd dogs, Dobermans, Collies, Airedales and the indigenous Black Terrier. When he leaves the school with his master the dog wears a badge on the breastplate of his harness; it is a white oval with a red cross in the center and bears the words "Guide for the Blind."

THE WORKING DOG IN RUSSIA

Russians have always made good and extensive use of dogs as working animals. There is a Soviet club which consists entirely of owners of working dogs; it has a membership in excess of 15,000. Over 6,000 of these members are in Moscow or its immediate vicinity. The dogs which are specified as working dogs include those that are bred, trained and owned by those people interested in having the dogs qualified to do either guard duty or rescue work.

The Russians have always preferred the large breeds of dogs to the hunting or fancy toy breeds and take great pride in the degree to which their guard dogs respond to their duties. They consider savagery as a sign of character rather than a fault and encourage it in breeding programs. For many decades the Russians have been mixing bloodlines in order to introduce this highly aggressive quality into all the large breeds.

Ch. Barchet Maverick winning five points at the 1974 Chagrin Falls, Ohio Kennel Club show. Bred and owned by Patricia D. Edwards, D.V.M. of Snellville, Georgia.

Opposite:
Class winner at the 1973 Doberman Pinscher Club of the Tappen Zee show was Gemae Beelzebub, owned by Dr. Howard Cohen and handled by his daughter.

By introducing the blood of the Caucasus and Central Asian Sheephounds to the normally accepted breeds they have produced a hybrid known as the Black Terrier. The Russian Black Terrier is so ferocious that it is also referred to, even by the Russians themselves, as "the black devil!" According to the Russians about five different breeds went into the Black Terrier, but they are not admitting which five. Suffice it to say that it is menacing and that it is a guard dog to be reckoned with. It is a dog they claim to be a guard dog supreme.

THE NOSE KNOWS! — SNIFFING OUT NARCOTICS

Not only are dogs good at following the scent on a trail left by a human, they are also excellent at sniffing out drugs and narcotics for police and customs officials. Wherever there is a problem or suspicion of the trafficking of narcotics, the "narc squad" comes into play. Their record of success is phenomenal and is responsible for the confiscation of great caches of narcotics each and every year, both on the local level all over the United States and at points of entry on all of our borders.

The United States Air Force had a Security Police compound operated at Fort Benning, Georgia. A 15-week training program there produced dogs which could sniff out narcotics and were used to demonstrate this work at Air Force bases with a narcotics problem all over the country. Films for distribution to other Air Force installations were also made at Fort Benning with this in mind.

The narcotics squad can be trained to uncover several different varieties of narcotics during the course of service, depending on the area in which they are required to work.

PRISON DOGS

Several of our prisons keep dogs to accompany guards on their patrols. These prison dogs are trained to bark and to hang on to escaped prisoners.

POLICE DOGS

Dogs have been used for police work for hundreds of years in both Europe and the United States. There are many ways that a dog can assist a policeman in his work, all the way from the most basic requirements right on up to highly trained and executed work requiring superb keeness and physical stamina.

Policemen frequently use dogs while making their normal rounds, such as checking stores for forced entry or checking out apartment houses, warehouses or shopping centers and industrial complexes. They are also used by the police for crowd control. Contrary to popular opinion, not just Bloodhounds are used for tracking

Damasyn The Redstone Rocky with his police partner Arthur O'Keefe. Rocky was one of the first San Francisco police dogs. Regrettably Rocky was killed by a bullet in the line of duty, but not before causing quite a stir as a police dog and by bringing a great deal of credit to the force. Bred by Peggy Adamson.

Ch. Ebonaire's His Excellency winning the Breed at the New Brunswick Kennel Club show several years ago. The sire was Ch. Ebonaire's Entertainer x Debbie Duchess v Palen. Handled by Ed Weiss, who co-owns him with Judy Weiss and Irma Walen.

Opposite:
Mystique, a six-week-old fawn bitch, hasn't quite decided how she likes posing for her photograph in a basket. Bred by the Barchet Kennels; owned by veterinarian Patricia Edwards of Snellville, Georgia.

down escaped criminals, missing children or campers! Most dogs have great scenting ability, and the Doberman Pinscher is no exception!

Patrol dogs are also referred to as compound dogs, warehouse dogs, etc., but these names usually apply to dogs which work outside and by themselves. True security or patrol dogs are those which work indoors with a trainer or company guard. Therefore the name guard dog also applies.

R.H. MACY & CO.'S GUARD DOGS

R.H. Macy and Company, the world's largest department store, has a motto—"It's Smart to be Thrifty," and thrifty is what they decided to be back in October of 1952 when they purchased their first four Doberman Pinschers to patrol the store after hours. As a result, they have saved hundreds of thousands of dollars in stolen merchandise from the "sleep-ins" alone! Sleep-ins are the burglars who enter the store just before closing time and stay overnight, packing up the merchandise they are after and then leaving the store shortly after it opens in the morning. In addition, the dogs have saved the store much money by preventing damage by discovering machines that had been left on after closing and locating smoldering fires and water flows. They also have quite a record on recovering runaway children who try to hide in the store overnight to frighten their parents.

The four original Dobermans were purchased fully trained for their service in the store. All subsequent Dobermans—and there have been over twenty of them—have been trained by Macy detectives assigned to the Canine Corps. The training classes are held on the roof of the Macy building, where the kennels are located among the Manhattan skyscrapers. Their training is extensive and includes basic obedience, exercises, searching, finding, flushing and attack on a prowler on command.

The Dobermans are also trained as stake outs for entrances and exits which are easily accessible to thieves and are sometimes stationed at the top of escalators where they listen for sounds from the floor below. The dogs are also trained to obey any and all of the detectives with the Corps. . . there are no one man - one dog teams.

Each detective is specially trained for the proper care and handling of the dogs. Particular attention is paid to their paws and claws, keeping nails cut short so that they can move silently across the bare floors of the store without being heard. Their lithe movement and sleek coat ensure maximum efficiency and their ability to withstand heat also is an asset. When the store is closed each evening and the air conditioning is turned off during the summer months, heat builds up in the store. They are bothered much less by heat than, for instance, a German Shepherd, and this is one of the reasons why Macys selected this particular breed.

Two Macy detectives and their canine guards complete a patrol outside the building to make sure everything is in order. These dogs are trained to obey any of the detectives. . . there are no one man-one dog teams.

The dogs are also of importance to the store when it is time for the store detectives to take large sums of money to the bank or to supervise the transporting of valuable merchandise. The dogs accompany the men on these missions as well.

The naming of the dogs is synonymous with the various Macy brand names, such as Red Star, Thrifty, Lily White, Cash, etc. The dogs are all valuable living examples of these Macy trademarks familiar to wise shoppers all over the world!

Phileen's Duty Free of Tavey, photographed at 18 months of age. This important stud dog from American stock was sired by Ch. Tarrade's Corry x Kay Hill's Outrigger and is owned by Blanche and Charles Wileman, Russtun Dobermanns, Hants, England.

Opposite:
Ch. Alisaton's
Intrepid Lad pictured
winning at the
August, 1975 Sand
and Sea Kennel Club
show with owner-
handler Gwyn Lynn
Satalino of Old
Westbury, New York.

THE DOBERMAN AS A FAMILY GUARD DOG

As a guard dog the Doberman Pinscher reigns supreme!

We have already discussed its guard dog duties with the police and in industry, so now let us discuss the Doberman Pinscher as a guard dog in the home. We have often heard that the Doberman "cannot be trusted;" that sooner or later they "turn on their owners;" or that they cannot be both a guard dog and a canine companion for the children. Such is not the case. If a Doberman is properly trained, treated well and bred well there is no reason at all why it cannot become both a member of the family and its protector. Care must be taken to see that the dog is properly initiated into the family, that it does not become too devoted to any one member of the family and that it very definitely knows when it is to defend the family and what it is to defend it against! While perfectly capable of making these distinctions, it will take time and patience on the part of the entire family to establish this pattern of behavior so that no mistakes are made.

While the Doberman Pinscher can be the perfect answer to your quest for both a guard dog and a companion dog for the whole family, we must also bear in mind that to be a good watch dog the Doberman need not show any signs of outward aggression or viciousness. I have seen too many cases of people becoming victimized by their own dogs, actually afraid of disciplining the dog for fear the dog would turn on them! All you need is a dog that is keen and alert to potential danger, not one that is ready to fly at anyone who makes a sudden or questionable move.

For one thing, the Doberman Pinscher looks the part of a guard dog! He is impressive and, with his sleek coat and proud carriage, every muscle and every move he makes indicate power. The Doberman instantly suggests that he is in command, and this formidable appearance is itself a great deterrent to crime! In fact, so many people buy Doberman Pinschers as guard dogs for the home that the demand almost exceeds the supply. Unfortunately, this demand leads to many instances where improperly trained animals are sold to uneducated buyers that do not put the dogs to proper use.

By the mid-1970's legislation was being sought in many states to require the licensing of guard dogs and dog training schools. This is so we can all be absolutely certain that dogs sold to the public and represented as "trained guard dogs" are actually trained properly and according to methods which allow the dog to perform as a guard dog when required to do so. Yet the dog should also be able to live within a family unit without risk to the family itself. The unreliable, unstable guard dog has become such a threat to society that *Homelife* magazine asked me to write an article about guard dogs in 1974. The article reads as follows:

THE GUARD DOG
A Safety Measure or Potential Danger to Your Family?

There hasn't been a thief in the history of crime who wouldn't choose to burglarize a dark, empty house or apartment rather than one with a snarling, barking, lunging guard dog ready to tear into him the moment he stepped inside!

More and more families are buying—or in some instances renting—guard dogs to protect themselves and their homes as crime reports reveal that burglaries are zooming to an alarming all-time high. While guard dogs are a definite deterrent to crime, both at home and in the streets, caution must be advised before you introduce a guard dog into your family life.

Special considerations and responsibilities are involved when turning over potentially dangerous protective duties to a guard dog. For instance, if you have not purchased a properly trained guard dog, your "safety measure" could turn into a troublemaker. Quite suddenly you could discover you are harboring an attack dog which would intimidate your friends and neighbors and present a possible menace to your entire family.

Just as you are responsible for injuries inflicted by any of your pets, the guard dog that breaks loose and attacks someone on the street, or bites an invited guest, the behavior of your guard dog would also be, undeniably, yours. After all, innocent bystanders should not have to be victimized by ferocious guard dogs no matter how dedicated they are to serving their masters. The extent of your liability in case of injury would depend on the individual circumstances and the damages. Therefore, it would be wise before bringing a guard dog into your home to have your lawyer reread your insurance policy to make sure that you have maximum coverage in this category.

It is also essential for you to check out the reputation of the school and the credentials of the trainers where your guard is to be purchased. If you already own a guard dog it is still not too late to do it *now!* Many excellent schools can be located in the yellow pages of the telephone book listed under "Pet and Dog Training." A visit to the school can help you make your decision and any reliable organization will be happy to answer your questions and inform you as to what you can expect in the way of behavior and protection from the guard dog they might sell you.

If you have any doubts about being able to cope with a guard dog, risk robbery or resort to other protective measures rather than face the possibility of a tragic accident due to a lack of knowledge on your part or your inability to keep a dog under control. Such a tragedy could haunt you and your family for the

The best of everything. . . one of each color in the Doberman spectrum! This litter, containing all four colors, was sired by American and Canadian Ch. Misti Morn's Stormi Knight, American and Canadian C.D. Stormi was Ch. Tedell Eleventh Hour's first champion. Stormi is owned by Beverly Capstick, Lutzyn Kennels, Delano, Minnesota.

Opposite:
Two-month-old Judd, known later in the show ring as Scudamore Wheel of Fortune. Owned by Mrs. James G. Skidmore II of Norwalk, Connecticut. Photograph by Ruth Damico.

rest of your lives! But remember also that the properly trained guard dog *can* live within the family unit without danger to anyone, *can* learn to differentiate between welcome friends and someone breaking in with criminal intent, and *can* and *does* represent one of the most inexpensive and effective crime-fighters available, a guard ready to lay down its life to protect its family and their home!

BUYER BEWARE!

As the need and desire for guard dogs continue to grow in the world today, we have become aware of a frightening and most unfortunate situation. Aside from all of those wanting to buy a guard dog and who do so through the regular known sources, we are now aware that, especially in some of the larger cities, unscrupulous people are going to the local pounds and humane societies and are acquiring all available Doberman Pinschers.

Dobermans are not readily taken into private homes, especially when a majority of the public believes them to be vicious or hard to handle. When someone comes along who is willing to take a full grown Doberman, the societies are usually very happy to place them. However, what they do not know is that in many cases these Dobermans are taken to be re-sold as trained guard dogs, when actually all the training they have had is by the person who has salvaged them from the pound, trained them as little as possible by their own questionable methods and then sold them at considerable profit. Often trainers use them as "demonstration dogs," but more often they are not completely trainable and are sold as quickly as possible since their unfortunate backgrounds and poor training make them unreliable guards. Tragic results have occurred from this unfortunate practice, and it goes a long way to giving the breed a bad name that it does not deserve.

7. THE DOBERMAN IN OBEDIENCE

Carl Muser of West Englewood, New Jersey was the founder and guiding force behind America's first training club devoted to the working dog. The First Working Dog Club of America was organized by him on April 7th, 1935, and its fame was soon known over the entire Eastern seaboard.

The purpose of the club was to encourage and promote the owning, exhibiting and training of working dogs. The club held dog trials periodically and put a strong accent on the good behavior of the dog in both the show ring and all phases of its private and public life. The relationship between owner and dog was of prime importance to Mr. Muser, and his idea was for a dog to be a pleasure to those around it rather than merely a powerful source of energy uncontrolled and rather a nuisance at times.

The First Working Dog Club of America held training classes every Saturday and Sunday afternoon from three to five o'clock at the training field owned by Carl Muser's Musbro Kennels, and Mr. Muser and his staff of trainers supervised the systematic training of the dogs. Initial membership dues were five dollars plus twenty-five cents for each lesson. Private lessons were available during the week for those who could not come on the weekends or for dogs with special problems requiring special training.

While the main objective of the training was to produce a companion dog, the foundation of all the training was obedience. About 60% of the time was spent with obedience. The training was based on the latest scientific methods without stiff penalties and certainly no physical abuse or whippings. Short and sharp commands were the basis of their successful results.

The goal was to achieve success on 15 different points, including heeling on and off leash, sitting, lying down both on command and for three minutes, coming when signaled and stopping when signaled, retrieving an object over obstacles and carrying it through a group of people, refusing food from strangers and not touching food when found on the ground. There was also training for jumping over obstacles on command, retrieving an article over an obstacle and back

First in the Working Group from the Puppy Class—and at just 11 months of age! Pictured here is Ch. Civetta's Wolf Whistle of Kami, C.D. with judge Robert Salomon awarding this wonderful win at the 1973 Riverhead Kennel Club show. Handled by Kay Martin, her breeder and co-owner with Richard Orlander.

A training lesson in protecting a child being conducted by Carl Muser, director of the first dog training club in the United States. This photograph taken in 1932 demonstrates how two Dobermans are taught to prevent a kidnapper from wheeling off a baby in a kidnap attempt.

again and surrendering it to the trainer. They were also taught not to be gun shy, not to flinch at unexpected loud noises, trailing both on and off lead and identifying a single object from among several belonging to the owner. These points were all preliminary to the Companion Dog degree and to any future police work.

The training courses were divided into two sections, general obedience and protection, and were of about two months duration, covering five individual courses. Dogs successfully completing the first four courses could qualify for the Schutzhund degree.

Carl Muser advocated that no dog was too sharp or too vicious. He believed that if a dog was said to be that way, then the real fault was with an improper trainer or an aggressive person that forced their attention on the dog. He declared that the working dog's instincts were genuine and good and that every dog was man's best friend when correctly treated and trained and could be a real companion and friend.

With such high ideals as the goal for every dog that trained at the Musbro Kennels, there is little wonder that The First Working Dog Club of America set such a fine example and helped to ensure the future aims of other working dog clubs all over the nation.

TRAINING YOUR DOBERMAN

There are few things in the world a dog would rather do than please his master. Therefore, obedience training, or even the initial basic training, will be a pleasure for your dog, if taught correctly, and will make him a much nicer animal to live with for the rest of his life.

WHEN TO START TRAINING

The most frequently asked question by those who consider training their dog is, naturally, "What is the best age to begin training?" The answer is "not before six months." A dog simply cannot be sufficiently or permanently trained before this age and be expected to retain all he has been taught. If too much is expected of him, he can become frustrated and it may ruin him completely for any serious training later on, or even jeopardize his disposition. Most things a puppy learns and repeats before he is six months of age should be considered habit rather than training.

THE REWARD METHOD

The only proper and acceptable kind of training is the kindness and reward method which will build a strong bond between dog and owner. A dog must have confidence in and respect for his teacher. The most important thing to remember in training any dog is that the quickest way to teach, especially the young dog, is through repetition. Praise him when he does well, and scold him when he does wrong. This will suffice. There is no need or excuse for swinging at a dog with rolled up newspapers, or flailing hands which will only tend to make the dog hand shy the rest of his life. Also, make every word count. Do not give a command unless you intend to see it through. Pronounce distinctly with the fewest possible words, and use the same words for the same command every time.

Include the dog's name every time to make sure you have his undivided attention at the beginning of each command. Do not go on to another command until he has successfully completed the previous one and is praised for it. Of course, you should not mix play with the serious training time. Make sure the dog knows the difference between the two.

In the beginning, it is best to train without any distractions whatsoever. After he has learned to concentrate and is older and more proficient, he should perform the exercises with interference, so that the dog learns absolute obedience in the face of all distractions. Needless to say, whatever the distractions, you never lose control. You must be in command at all times to earn the respect and attention of your dog.

HOW LONG SHOULD THE LESSONS BE?

The lessons should be brief with a young dog, starting at five minutes, and as the dog ages and becomes adept in the first lessons, increase the time all the way up to one-half hour. Public training classes are usually set for one hour, and this is acceptable since the full hour of concentration is not placed on your dog alone. Working under these conditions with other dogs, you will find that he will not be as intent as he would be with a private lesson where the commands are directed to him alone for the entire thirty minutes.

If you should notice that your dog is not doing well, or not keeping up with the class, consider putting off training for awhile. Animals, like children, are not always ready for schooling at exactly the same age. It would be a shame to ruin a good obedience dog because you insist on starting his training at six months rather than at, say, nine months, when he would be more apt to be receptive both physically and mentally. If he has particular difficulty in learning one exercise, you might do well to skip to a different one and come back to it again at another session. There are no set rules in this basic training, except, "don't push!"

WHAT YOU NEED TO START TRAINING

From three to six months of age, use the soft nylon show leads, which are the best and safest. When you get ready for the basic training at six months of age, you will require one of the special metal-link choke chains sold for exactly this purpose. Do not let the word "choke" scare you. It is a soft, smooth chain and should be held slack whenever you are not actually using it to correct the dog. This chain should be put over the dog's head so that the lead can be attached over the dog's neck rather than underneath against his throat. It is wise when you buy your choke collar to ask the sales person to show you how it is put on. Those of you who will be taking your dog to a training class will have an instructor who can show you.

To avoid undue stress on the dog, use both hands on the lead. The dog will be taught to obey commands at your left side, and therefore, your left hand will guide the dog close to his collar on a six-foot training lead. The balance of the lead will be held in your right hand. Learn at the very beginning to handle your choke collar and lead correctly. It is as important in training a dog as is the proper equipment for riding a horse.

WHAT TO TEACH FIRST

The first training actually should be to teach the dog to know his name. This, of course, he can learn at an earlier age than six months, just as he can learn to walk nicely on a leash or lead. Many puppies will at first probably want to walk around with the leash in their mouths. There is no objection to this if the dog will walk while doing it. Rather than cultivating this as a habit, you will find that if you don't make an issue of it, the dog will soon realize that carrying the lead in his mouth is not rewarding and he'll let it fall to his side where it belongs.

Ch. Damasyn The Boatswain, bred and owned by Peggy Adamson at her Damasyn Kennels in Roslyn Heights, New York. Bo was by Ch. Damasyn Derringer x Damasyn The Li'l Red Lampchop. He sired Ch. Damasyn Bo-Tairic, Bo-Tai, Bo-Tassi and Bo-Tandy, in one litter, and Ch. Damasyn The Ardon Arondi and Arori in another litter. Both litters were out of Ch. Brown's Wendy, C.D.

BJ's the Godfather pictured going Best of Winners on the way to championship at the 1975 Susque-Nango Kennel Club show. The sire was Ch. Damasyn The Troycen and the dam BJ's Gift of Joy. Owners are Mr. and Mrs. John Monsolino of New York City.

We also let the puppy walk around by himself for a while with the lead around his neck. If he wishes to chew on it a little, that's all right too. In other words, let it be something he recognizes and associates with at first. Do not let the lead start out being a harness.

If the dog is at all bright, chances are he has learned to come on command when you call him by name. This is relatively simple with sweet talk and a reward. On lead, without a reward, and on command without a lead is something else again. If there has been, or is now, a problem, the best way to correct it is to put on the choke collar and the six-foot lead. Then walk away from the dog, and call him, "Pirate, come!" and gently start reeling him in until the dog is in front of you. Give him a pat on the head and/or reward.

Walking, or heeling, next to you is also one of the first and most important things for him to learn. With the soft lead training starting very early, he should soon take up your pace at your left side. At the command to "heel" he should start off with you and continue alongside until you stop. Give the command, "Pirate, sit!" This is taught by leaning over and pushing down on his hindquarters until he sits next to you, while pulling up gently on the collar. When you have this down pat on the straightaway, then start practicing it in circles, with turns and figure eights. When he is an advanced student, you can look forward to the heels and sits being done neatly, spontaneously, and off lead as well.

THE "DOWN" COMMAND

One of the most valuable lessons or commands you can teach your dog is to lie down on command. Some day it may save his life, and is invaluable when traveling with a dog or visiting, if behavior and manners are required even beyond obedience. While repeating the words, "Pirate, down!" lower the dog from a sitting position in front of you by gently pulling his front legs out in front of him. Place your full hand on him while repeating the command, "Pirate, down!" and hold him down to let him know you want him to *stay* down. After he gets the general idea, this can be done from a short distance away on a lead along with the command, by pulling the lead down to the floor. Or perhaps you can slip the lead under your shoe (between the heel and sole) and pull it directly to the floor. As the dog progresses in training, a hand signal with or without verbal command, or with or without lead, can be given from a considerable distance by raising your arm and extending the hand palm down.

THE "STAY" COMMAND

The stay command eventually can be taught from both a sit and a down position. Start with the sit. With the dog on your left side in the sitting position give the command, "Pirate, stay!" Reach down with the left hand open and palm side to the dog and sweep it in close to his nose. Then walk a short distance away and face him. He will at first, having learned to heel immediately as you start off, more than likely start off with you. The trick in teaching this is to make sure he hears "stay" before you start off. It will take practice. If he breaks, sit him down again, stand next to him, and give the command all over again. As he masters the command, let the distance between you and your dog increase while the dog remains seated. Once the command is learned, advance to the stay command from the down position.

THE STAND FOR EXAMINATION

If you have any intention of going on to advanced training in obedience with your dog, or if you have a show dog which you feel you will enjoy showing yourself, a most important command which should be mastered at six months of age is the stand command. This is essential for a show dog since it is the position used when the show judge goes over your dog. This is taught in the same manner as the stay command, but this time with the dog remaining up on all four feet. He should learn to stand still, without moving his feet and without flinching or breaking when approached by either you or strangers. The hand with palm open wide and facing him should be firmly placed in front of his nose with the command, "Pirate, stand!" After he learns the basic rules and knows the difference between stand and stay, ask friends, relatives, and strangers to assist you with this exercise by walking up to the dog and going over him. He should not react physically to their touch. A dog posing in this stance should show all the beauty and pride of being a sterling example of his breed.

FORMAL SCHOOL TRAINING

We mentioned previously about the various training schools and classes given for dogs. Your local kennel club, newspaper, or the yellow pages of the telephone book will put you in touch with organizations in your area where this service is performed. You and your dog will learn a great deal from these classes. Not only do they offer formal training, but the experience for you and your dog in public, with other dogs of approximately the same age and with the same purpose in mind, is excellent. If you intend to show your dog, this training is valuable ring experience for later on. If you are having difficulty with the training, remember, it is either too soon to start—or YOU are doing something wrong!

Ch. Marienburg's Red Baron pictured winning the Working Group at the 1971 Yuma Kennel Club show with handler Mike Shea. Whelped in 1969, Baron's sire was Ch. Gra-Lemor Demetrius v d Victor x Marienburg's Inca. Breeders were John King and the Marienburg Kennels. This magnificent multi-Specialty and Group winner is owned by Joseph Ciaccio and the Marienburg Kennels, El Cajon, California.

Mexican Champion Robin Prince Brown wins another Best in Show at the 1975 San Migueldle Allende Show under the prominent Mexican judge Senora Thelma von Thaden. Dr. Lorenzo Roca handled for owner Senor Joaquin Alverez.

ADVANCED TRAINING AND OBEDIENCE TRIALS

The A.K.C. obedience trials are divided into three classes: Novice, Open and Utility.

In the Novice Class, the dog will be judged on the following basis:

TEST	MAXIMUM SCORE
Heel on lead	35
Stand for examination	30
Heel free—on lead	45
Recall (come on command)	30
One-minute sit (handler in ring)	30
Three-minute down (handler in ring)	30
Maximum total score	200

If the dog "qualifies" in three shows by earning at least 50% of the points for each test, with a total of at least 170 for the trial, he has earned the Companion Dog degree and the letters C.D. (Companion Dog) are entered after his name in the A.K.C. records.

After the dog has qualified as a C.D., he is eligible to enter the Open Class competition, where he will be judged on this basis:

TEST	MAXIMUM SCORE
Heel free	40
Drop on Recall	30
Retrieve (wooden dumbbell) on flat	25
Retrieve over obstacle (hurdle)	35
Broad jump	20
Three-minute sit (handler out of ring)	25
Five-minute down (handler out of ring)	25
maximum total score	200

Again he must qualify in three shows for the C.D.X. (Companion Dog Excellent) title and then is eligible for the Utility Class, where he can earn the Utility Dog (U.D.) degree in these rugged tests:

TEST	MAXIMUM SCORE
Scent discrimination (Article #1)	30
Scent discrimination (Article #2)	30
Directed retrieve	30
Signal exercise (heeling, etc., on hand signal)	35
Directed jumping (over hurdle and bar jump)	40
Group examination	35
Maximum total score	200

For more complete information about these obedience trials, write for the American Kennel Club's *Regulations and Standards for Obedience Trials*. Dogs that are disqualifed from breed shows because of alteration or physical defects are eligible to compete in these trials.

THE COMPANION DOG EXCELLENT DEGREE

There are seven exercises which must be executed to achieve the C.D.X. degree, and the percentages for achieving these are the same as for the U.D. degree. Candidates must qualify in three different obedience trials and under three different judges and must have received scores of more than 50% of the available points in each exercise, with a total of 170 points or more out of the possible 200. At that time they may add the letters C.D.X. after their name.

THE UTILITY DOG DEGREE

The Utility Dog degree is awarded to dogs which have qualified by successfully completing six exercises under three different judges

Damasyn The Sheik photographed at 10 months of age on the porch of his owner's home in Arlington, New Jersey. This lovely, dog, owned by Frank Dayton, was sired by Dictator out of Damasyn The Song.

at three different obedience trials, with a score of more than 50% of available points in each exercise, and with a score of 170 or more out of a possible 200 points.

These six exercises consist of Scent Discrimination, with two different articles for which they receive thirty points each if successfully completed; Direct Retrieving, for 30 points; Signal Exercise for 35 points; Directed Jumping for 40 points and a Group Examination for 35 points.

THE TRACKING DOG DEGREE

The Tracking Dog trials are not held, as the others are, with the dog shows, and need be passed only once.

The dog must work continuously on a strange track at least 440 yards long and with two right angle turns. There is no time limit, and the dog must retrieve an article laid at the other end of the trail. There is no score given; the dog either earns the degree or fails. The dog is worked by his trainer on a long leash, usually in harness.

8. THE DOBERMAN AS A SCHUTZHUND

Schutzhund training for Doberman Pinschers is the answer for those who wish to have the most completely trained dog possible, a dog that excels beyond the show ring and obedience training and goes on to accomplish the ultimate in all-around working dog purpose and function.

WHERE IT ALL BEGAN

The origin of the Schutzhund training was in Europe. At the turn of the century the German Working Dog Association, referred to as the DVG, established the standard for working dogs, which included police work as well. Special attention was given to the dog's use with his fellow man and to the general behavior of the dog. Particular attention was paid to temperament, courage, protection drive, fighting drive, toughness, sharpness, responsiveness, absence of fear, flight reflex and eagerness to please. It was in this way possible for them to determine the character of the dog and to what extent it could be utilized as a true working dog.

It was on these fundamentals that the DVG and the national breed organizations in Europe instituted a controlled breeding program to achieve this end, with one of the prerequisites being that no litter or dog could be registered in their association unless both parents were registered also, and only after having passed a working dog trial. The European trial tests include Schutzhund Trials, Police Work Trials, Herding Dog Trials and other service dog tests which are designed to measure the extent to which each dog qualifies in all the above mentioned categories pertaining to their character development and behavior patterns.

THE EUROPEAN FCI

The Federation Cynologique Internationale, or FCI, with its headquarters in Belgium, set up the rules for the organization in that country, the rest of the European countries and a total of 37 nations around the world. The FCI accepts all internationally recognized working breeds of dogs that are at least 18 inches at the withers as well as those listed in the Working Group. The FCI was instrumental in helping the comparable American organization in getting its start and is still an influence today.

THE NORTH AMERICAN WORKING DOG ASSOCIATION

The North American Working Dog Association, Inc., or NASA, was founded on January 1, 1971 with the helpful assistance of the European organization and has fashioned itself in their successful image. NASA is an independent non-profit organization which sets the standards for all training and sanctioning of the Schutzhund trials on the North American continent and is the parent organization for all the local or regional Schutzhund training clubs all over the United States, Mexico and Canada in accordance with rules and regulations acceptable to the FCI. In the beginning the licensed judges of Europe officiated at the early NASA trials to ensure correct procedures and even today frequently adjudicate at Schutzhund trials.

In the few short years since 1971, when NASA came into being, it has grown to amazing proportions with interest keen and widespread. While Mexico is considered a single district, Canada has been divided into Eastern, Central and Western regions and the United States has been divided into nine regions to better serve the membership.

NASA AND THE DOBERMAN PINSCHER CLUB OF AMERICA

The Doberman Pinscher Club of America immediately recognized the value of NASA training for our breed and was one of the founding members of this organization dedicated to an even more advanced working dog. The DPCA was, as a matter of record, the very first parent breed club to join forces with this association.

NASA PRINCIPLES AND OBJECTIVES

Adhering strictly to the idea of "a sound mind in a sound body" for dogs as well as humans, NASA has a strict and dedicated approach to training and training methods. NASA deplores the present day "commercial" attack or guard dog training and labels it incomplete and unjust. They consider their training program a form of sport and offer their training only through membership in NASA clubs and not to the general public.

From the beginning their objective has been to consider the *dog* and the *sport* as important, without any commercialization of the training practices. Their paramount interest is the overall betterment of the working dog physically and mentally, with an eye to the dog's added usefulness to society and to the country.

Damasyn Jalli's Jing Jing, C.D. and SchH I, owned by Larry Mc-Kinney. This lovely blue female was the first Doberman bitch ever to earn the SchH I title. The sire was Ch. Damasyn Carly of Jerseystone x Damasyn Jalli-Alli, C.D.

THE SCHUTZHUND DEGREE

Now recognized all around the world, the Schutzhund degree is highly esteemed. There are three parts to it: Tracking, Obedience and Protection. The dog's keenest senses can be tested and measured in the field under the requirements of the Schutzhund tests. A dog that works well will breed well and fulfill its purpose in life. We can think of no better way to assure the future of the working dog than to see it measure up to these requirements and to pass this versatility on to their progeny. The Schutzhund, or SchH, degree is something to be proud of!

NASA AND OTHER OBEDIENCE DEGREES

NASA encourages owners to earn all possible obedience degrees. They respect the achievement, and there is no doubt that it is of value in going on to Schutzhund titles. They state that while training for the SchH degree it is also possible to earn the C.D.X. and T.D. degrees, since the requirements for these AKC titles account for about two-thirds of the requirements for one of the Schutzhund degrees. NASA considers Schutzhund training as a further extension of the American Kennel Club obedience titles. Of late more and more of the dog owning public have come to realize the value of field trials in promoting the better all-around hunting dog.

WHAT EXACTLY IS A SCHUTZHUND?

A Schutzhund is NOT an attack or guard dog! A Schutzhund is a dog which has earned a valid, recognized Schutzhund degree in an official Schutzhund Trial sanctioned by NASA. He is a highly trained animal conditioned to perform equally well in an AKC obedience ring, on tracking grounds, in search or rescue circumstances and in protecting his owner, family and home. This includes use of force or detaining an intruder when necessary, and the knowledge to cease when the assailant stops struggling. He attacks only on command unless he or his master is directly threatened. Even with all this highly specific training, he is still considered to be an accepted member of the family.

THE SCHUTZHUND TRAINER

Perhaps the most specific requirement of a Schutzhund trainer is patience, patience to work with and train a working dog over and beyond the requirements of AKC obedience training. A great deal of additional satisfaction can be gained by this demanding advanced training, which adds to the challenge. Schutzhund training is not for everyone.

WHEN TO START SCHUTZHUND TRAINING

While puppies are brought on to the field at anywhere from three months of age on to give them exposure to future training conditions, serious training should only be started between nine months and one year of age. At this time the dog is mentally alert and agreeable to precise training and it is obvious whether or not he is physically capable of pursuing the training course.

SCHUTZHUND TITLES AND NASA REQUIREMENTS

The Schutzhund Trials are a test of the training accomplishments. When a trial is sanctioned by NASA, after a Practice Schutzhund Trial, a licensed judge officiates and is permitted to award Schutzhund degrees to qualifying dogs. At such a trial a dog may earn SchH degrees, AD Endurance Test, FH or Advanced Tracking Dog or the INT, the International Degree. There are also PD I PD II awards for Police Dog tests.

SCHUTZHUND A

This is a beginner's exercise almost identical to Schutzhund I but leaving out the tracking exercise. There are two sections, *Obedience* (B) and *Protection* (C), each counting 100 points for a score of 200.

Obedience includes heeling on and off leash at normal, fast and slow paces, including walking through a group of people. A gun will be fired when the dog is off leash; if the dog should shy, he would fail the test. There are two exercises in which the dog sits and downs while heeling, the handler continuing on. On the sit the handler will return to the dog and on the down the dog will be called to the handler.

There is a retrieve over a 39'' jump for an article and a retrieve on the flat. The dog must also upon command leave the handler, going at least 25 paces away and dropping on command. The handler must pick the dog up. The last exercise is the long down stay with the handler some distance away with his back to the dog. The dog remains while another dog goes through his paces.

In *Protection Work* the dog must first locate the Decoy who is hiding in the field. The dog must just bark, not bite. In the next exercise the dog heeling off-lead must attack the Decoy, who will come out of hiding to attack the handler. The dog will be hit with a switch; he must not show fear. The dog must stop his aggression on command. The Decoy will then run away, acting in a belligerent manner, and the handler will send the dog after the man to attack and hold.

SCHUTZHUND I

This is the first degree for a protection trained dog. He must be at least 14 months old to participate in the trial and must pass a temperament test. There are three sections: *Tracking* (A), *Obedience* (B) and *Protection* (C), each counting 100 points for a score of 300. A dog must receive a passing score of 70 points for sections A and B and 80 points for section C.

In *Tracking* the dog must follow an unmarked track of at least 400 paces while on a 20' lead. There are two turns, and the track must be at least 20 minutes old. The track is laid by his own handler and two articles are dropped which must be located by the dog.

Obedience includes heeling on and off leash at normal, fast and slow paces, including walking through a group of people. A gun will

International Champion Curt v d Schwarzwaldperle, SchH and P.H., imported and owned by the Rupprechtheim Kennels. Curt was photographed here in 1942.

be fired when the dog is off leash; if the dog should shy, he would fail the trial. There are two exercises in which the dog sits and downs while heeling, the handler continuing on. On the sit the handler will return to the dog and on the down the dog will be called to the handler. There is a retrieve over a 39" jump for an article and a retrieve on the flat. The dog must also upon command leave the handler, going at least 25 paces away and dropping on command. The handler must pick the dog up. The last exercise is the long down stay with the handler some distance away with his back to the dog. The dog remains while another dog goes through his paces.

In *Protection Work* the dog must first locate the Decoy who is hiding in the field. The dog must just bark, not bite. In the next exercise, the dog heeling off-lead must attack the Decoy, who will come out of hiding to attack the handler. The dog will be hit with a switch; he must not show fear. The dog must stop his aggression on command. The Decoy will then run away, acting in a belligerent manner, and the handler will send the dog after the man to attack and hold.

SCHUTZHUND II

This is the second degree for a protection trained dog. The dog must have already passed the test for Schutzhund I to work for this title. As in Schutzhund I, there are three sections: *Tracking* (A), *Obedience* (B) and *Protection* (C), each counting 100 points for a score of 300. A dog must receive a passing score of 70 points for sections A and B and 80 points for section C.

In *Tracking* the dog must find two lost articles over a strange trail approximately 600 paces long and at least thirty minutes old, while on an 11-yard lead. The strange trail includes two right angles to the right or to the left.

Obedience includes heeling on and off leash at normal, fast and slow paces, including walking through a group of people. A gun will be fired when the dog is off leash (but not in the crowd exercise); if the dog should run away from his handler when the gun is shot, he would fail the test and be excused. There are two exercises in which the dog sits and downs while heeling, the handler continuing on. On the sit the handler will return to the dog, and on the down the dog will be called to the handler. There are three exercises requiring the dog to retrieve an article. On the first the dog will retrieve a 2.2-pound wooden dumbbell over a flat ground. On the second the dog will be required to retrieve a 1 pound, 7 ounces wooden dumbbell with a free jump over a hurdle 40" high. On the third the dog is required to climb over a 64" jump and retrieve an object belonging to the dog handler. The dog must also do a go-away, leaving his handler on command and advancing at least 30 paces in the indicated direction in a fast gait and on command lying down. The last exercise is the long down stay, with the handler some distance away with his back to the dog. The

One of the early Schutzhund dogs, Ch. Kaspar v Lobensteirn, SchH, owned by Mr. C.W. Harris of Winston-Salem, North Carolina.

dog remains while another dog goes through his paces.

In *Protection Work* the dog must first locate the Decoy who is hiding in the field. The dog must just bark, not bite. In the next exercise the handler will leave the dog guarding the suspect while he, the handler, investigates the suspect's hiding-place. The suspect then attempts to escape and the dog has to stop him by seizing him. As soon as the suspect stops escaping, the dog has to stop his aggression without command. The suspect will then attempt to attack the dog with a stick or whip, and the dog immediately has to attack the suspect to prevent him from further aggressive action. At this time the dog is hit several times. The next exercise is the transport of the suspect with the dog and handler approximately 40 paces behind the suspect. Following the transport, the handler will be attacked by the suspect—which the dog is to prevent. On the Courage Test, the dog is sent after the suspect, who is about 50 paces away. The dog has to seize the suspect firmly until called off by his handler.

SCHUTZHUND III

This is the most advanced degree possible in Schutzhund work. A dog must have completed the requirements for the Schutzhund II to earn this title. There are three sections: *Tracking* (A), *Obedience* (B) and *Protection* (C), each counting 100 points for a score of 300.

In *Tracking* the dog must search for three lost articles on a track approximately 1,200 paces long and at least 50 minutes old. The dog may be worked off leash or on an 11-yard lead.

Obedience includes heeling on and off leash at normal, fast and slow paces, including a walk through the crowd. A gun will be fired and the dog is to show no reaction to the shot. There are two exercises in which the dog sits and downs while heeling. On the sit out of motion the handler picks the dog up; on the down out of motion the handler will call the dog to him. There are two additional exercises in which the dog is given the command to stand while heeling, one while heeling at a walk and another at a run. The handler will return to the dog on the stand exercises. There are three exercises including a retrieve. The dog must retrieve a 4.4-pound dumbbell over the flat ground, a 1.7-pound dumbbell with a free jump over a 40'' jump and his handler's article after climbing over a wall 71'' high. The go-away is similar to Schutzhund II exercise except the dog must go away from his handler 40 paces. The last exercise is the long down stay with the handler 50 feet away out of sight of his dog. The dog remains while another dog goes through his paces.

In *Protection Work* the dog must first locate the Decoy who is hiding in the field. The dog must just bark, not bite. In the next exercise the handler has to search the Decoy's hiding-place, and while this is being done the Decoy is to break away and run; the dog has to stop the Decoy. Then the Decoy has to stop his escape and the dog has to stop his aggression. At this time the Decoy is to attack the dog with his stick and the dog has to apprehend the Decoy again. Following this is the transport of the Decoy with dog and handler following about 50 feet behind. After the transport follows the attack on the handler by the Decoy. Included in this exercise is the sending of the dog after another suspect who also strikes at the dog. The dog has to hold this suspect. The dog is also scored on his over-all combativeness during the protection portion of this work.

ENDURANCE EXAMINATION (AD)

The Endurance Examination shall prove that the dog is capable of performing a physical effort to a certain degree without afterwards showing extreme exhaustion or fatigue. This Examination shall be held on roads and paths of as many different surfaces as possible. The distance to be covered shall be 12.4 miles (20 kilometers) with three rest stops, at which time the dogs will be examined by the judge whether they show any signs of fatigue or other problems which would eliminate them from the test.

Following the completion of the running portion of the examination, the dogs shall go through some basic obedience work, including off-leash heeling and a retrieval of a dumbbell or object over a 39" jump. This shall be done after the dogs have completed all of the 12.4-mile distance and have had a short period of rest.

To participate in this examination the dog must be at least 12 months old and be in good health and physical condition. The dogs are to be on leash and gait at a speed of about 6.2 miles per hour on the *right* side of the handler, either with the handler running or on a bicycle. The dogs, on a loose leash, shall be allowed some forging (forward pulling), though the dogs shall not be allowed to lag all (or most of) the time. Once one half of the distance has been covered, there is a break of ten minutes, with a break of 15 minutes given at the end of the running exercise. The judge, ideally, will follow the dogs all the distance, and he must be present at the rest periods. A car shall be available to pick up the dogs who are unable to complete the full distance.

The examination is considered "not passed" if the dog lacks all temper and toughness, shows signs of exceptional fatigue, and/or could not keep the speed of 6 miles per hour, but needed much more time. Duration of the entire Endurance Examination shall be two hours.

FIRST NASA WOMAN JUDGE

In the January-February, 1976 issue of the *NASA NEWS*, the name of Salle Richards of Pine City, New York, was listed as an Apprentice Judge. With this announcement Salle Richards becomes the first woman Schutzhund judge in this country.

SOME AMERICAN TITLE HOLDERS

Frederick's Son Ausslander, owned by Rosalie G. Simpson of Los Altos Hills, California, is the only Doberman Pinscher to have both a U.D.T. and the SchH III titles. He is also a member of the drill team trained by his owner and discussed later. Mrs. Simpson also co-owns with Linda Simpson Lazzarini a Doberman named Little Mist v Frederick; it is a U.D.T. dog, a ScH II title holder and also a member of their famous drill team.

Little Mist von Frederick, UDT, SchH II pictured at four months of age performing at a California veteran's hospital with her owner and trainer, Mrs. Rosalie G. Simpson of Los Altos Hills, California. Mist grew up to be a member of Mrs. Simpson's 25-member drill team.

Outgoing President Charles A.T. O'Neill congratulates and introduces incoming President Peggy Adamson at ceremonies following the 1972 DPCA Convention. A Rich Bergman photograph.

The judging panel at the 1959 Top Ten Doberman Competition. Seated at the judges' table, from left to right, are Helen Kamerer, Elanor Carpenter, the late John Cholley, E. Lundberg, Peggy Adamson, and the late Frank Haselman.

Ch. Damasyn Carly of Jerseystone winning the Stud Dog Class at the 1970 DPCA Specialty Show. He is pictured with get from three different bitches; Ch. Damasyn The Jalli-Alli, C.D.; Francis Willmeth's Ch. Centre Candy of Brandy; and Larry Glardy's Damasyn The Tartnsweet. Charles A.T. O'Neill presenting the trophy; Intersex Judge Charles Etner holding a ribbon; and Patrick Doniere is handling Carly.

Claudio Arno owns Frederick's Stregga, C.D.X. and SchH I; Lorraine Lydon's dog, Frederick's Question Mark, has both these titles also. Merilyn Blake has another American-bred bitch with a SchH I title; her name is Flashburn's Delilah.

Peggy Adamson bred and owns Damasyn Jalli's Jing-Jing, C.D. and SchH I, that was handled for her by Larry McKinney. She received her title under the Swiss judge Zaver Blasi on June 11, 1972, at the Southern California Schutzhund Club trial and is the first blue Doberman to receive a Schutzhund degree in the United States. She is also the first to have breed champions as parents—her sire was Ch. Damasyn Carly of Jerseystone and her dam Ch. Damasyn the Jalli-Alli, C.D.

Griffin's Dillon, SchH II, A.D., C.D., was the first Doberman to earn a SchH II degree, won in November, 1975 under judge Nero Lindblad. Owner Lorene Griffin is also proud of the fact that Dillon was the first Doberman to earn a rating of "Excellent," with a score of 290. It is additionally important to make a matter of record the fact that the first *two* Dobermans to earn SchH II titles were owned and trained by a husband and wife team, the above mentioned Lorene Griffin and her husband Larry. Dog number two was named Casey.

NASA HEADQUARTERS

For anyone wishing to start a Schutzhund club when there is none in your area, NASA encourages correspondence with their headquarters at 1677 North Alisar Avenue, Monterey Park, California 91754. They also invite memberships at a small fee, entitling members to copies of the bi-monthly publication *NASA NEWS*, edited by Alfons Ertelt.

Mr. Ertelt is the German-born Schutzhund enthusiast who has played a major role in the formation of the club in California and also the SV or Verein fur Deutsche Schaferhunde in Germany. He imported V Fee vom Stauderpark, SchH III, A.D. in 1966, a daughter of the dog which was the foundation of his kennel in Nibelung, Germany.

For those who wish to own the "total" working dog by taking obedience training beyond the AKC requirements, membership and participation in the trials offered by this organization is the answer. Their motto reflects the strong and true purpose of their existence—"Nothing else is so POWERFUL as an idea whose time has come." Schutzhund training is undeniably the ULTIMATE for today's working dog.

9. DOBERMAN DRILL TEAMS

There is virtually no one who is not thrilled by the sight of precision-trained Dobermans going through their exercises in a well-planned and executed performance. Anyone who was present at the Westminster Kennel Club shows years ago and saw the 16-dog drill team trained by Tess Henseler will never forget the experience. The crowds at the show in Madison Square Garden in New York City were delighted with their exhibition, and the applause rang from the rafters.

As Doberman fanciers increase in numbers, so do the ranks of obedience dogs and those who wish to see their dogs perform in unison with others of the breed, and we are beginning to see new interest in drill teams.

At the 1975 Doberman Pinscher Club of America National Specialty Show in San Diego, California, on October 25th and 26th, there was a most impressive demonstration by the Doberman drill team from the San Francisco Bay Area. The participants began their performance with precision marching followed by agility exercises which included scaling walls and jumping through barrels and paper hoops.

One of the participants, Frederick's Timbrel, U.D., owned and trained by Linda Lazzarini, completed its repertoire by finishing with an egg in its mouth. Linda Lazzarini, as was pointed out by Linda Lewis in a story about this team in the December, 1975 issue of *Front and Finish*, is the only person known to have trained a Doberman to carry a raw egg in its mouth without a crunch!

The Doberman drill team was created and brought together by the late Frederick Simpson and his wife, Rosalie, in July, 1968 along with Walt Nagle. After the demise of her husband, Rosalie Simpson continued with the group as trainer, and it is she more than anyone else who is responsible for the success of the team.

The original team consisted of 16 men, women and Doberman Pinschers drilling under a team captain, Susan Feusse. Their first public appearance was in October of 1968 at the Santa Clara, California dog show in the Parade of Champions. They took first place in the Open Marching Division. This performance was followed by one at

So fast it's almost a blur! Frederick's Tabhitha, U.D., four-year-old Doberman jumping through a covered hoop six-feet high. This amazing feat was performed as part of the drill team exhibition held in conjunction with the Doberman Pinscher Club of America National Specialty Show held in San Diego, California in October 1975. Tabhitha was also First Place winner in Utility A in the obedience classes held at this show. Tabhitha is owned by Rosalie Simpson, founder and trainer of the drill team, Los Altos Hills, California.

the Golden Gate show at the Cow Palace in San Francisco and by many others. These resulted in a number of awards for their excellence in performance.

In 1970 Paul Romera became the drill captain for the team, and a succession of appearances followed along with an invitation to appear at the 1971 Doberman Pinscher Club of America Specialty Show in Sacramento, California. At the October, 1975 DPCA Convention in San Diego, Robert Lazzarini served as the drill captain. The team at present consists of 20 members on the team, four flag bearers and the drill captain.

Their efforts do not go unappreciated in California. They have now won a total of 16 first prizes as a precision marching unit and one second place in 17 parade appearances in their area. They perform also by invitation at schools, hospitals and, of course, at dog shows. They have performed on four different occasions at the annual Golden Gate Kennel Club show, at the Cabrillo Doberman Pinscher Club show and at the Sacramento Doberman Pinscher Club show.

All members of the present team either have, or are, working on their obedience degrees. There is already one U.D. performing with the group and one Doberman with a C.D.X., T.D., SchH I and FH to his credit. Their ages range from 11 months to 7½ years.

Past Doberman greats which have brought such high praise to the unit are Ru-Mar's Pandora, C.D.X., Frederick's Son Ausslander and Little Mist von Frederick, U.D.T., SchH II, who had eight high

Another of the great Dobermans on the California Doberman drill team is Frederick Son Auslander, U.D.T. SchH III, the only Doberman to earn those titles. "Hassan" is pictured here going over a seven-foot jump during training. He is owned and trained by Mrs. Rosalie Simpson, Los Altos Hills, California. Mrs. Simpson has finished some forty dogs with Tracking Degrees, one of which became the only Doberman to be awarded the German Tracking Degree, F.H.

California drill team Captain Robert Lazzarini and his wife, Linda Simpson Lazzarini, with their drill team dog Moira, photographed in Los Altos Hills, California. This famous drill team performed at the 1975 Doberman Pinscher Club of America Specialty Show.

Fredericks Timbrel, U.D. jumping over barrels for a 14½-foot span. This four year old Doberman is owned by Linda Simpson Lazzarini, a member of Rosalie Simpson's famous drill team, which performs all over California at various dog shows and sporting events.

A dramatic moment at Westminster Kennel Club in 1959—Tess Henseler's famous Doberman drill team! These 16 Dobermans put on an amazing performance for the crowds and all but two of the dogs were owned and trained by Tess Henseler. At times it was difficult for Miss Henseler to get people to work with the team because of the reputation the Doberman breed had at that time. But what better way to prove their working ability, stable temperament and great beauty than by this amazing exhibition at dogdom's "show of shows"!

The twenty-dog drill team of California passing in review at the October, 1975 Doberman Pinscher Club of America National Specialty Show. Team Captain is Robert Lazzarini, and the founder and trainer of the team is Mrs. Rosalie Simpson of Los Altos Hills, California.

trial scores and attained the SchH II title at 11 years of age. She was on the drill team from the age of four months until retirement at the ripe old age of 12!

Other team members performing at the 1975 National Specialty were Sasha, owned by Roy Epperson; Benji, owned by Johnn Dodd; Frederick's Timbrel, U.D., owned by Linda Simpson Lazzarini; and Frederick's Tabhitha, C.D.X., owned by Rosalie Simpson.

Drill teams are a revelation to those just becoming interested in our breed, and the impression they make is a lasting one. There are great rewards for the owners and trainers as well when they see these dogs at the peak of their abilities as working dogs. We hope to see many more Doberman drill teams in the future!

10. THE STANDARD FOR THE BREED

The very first Standard toward perfection for the Doberman was composed in Germany, its native land, in the year 1899. This Standard was used in all countries including the United States until 1935, when the first American Standard was submitted to the American Kennel Club for approval. With 36 years behind it as a criterion for the breed, it was almost a foregone conclusion that certain adjustments had to be made for future generations. However, it is fascinating to read what was considered to be the ideal working Doberman.

THE GERMAN STANDARD

GENERAL APPEARANCE — The Dobermann Pinscher should be built muscular and powerful, but not clumsy and massy; neither should he be greyhound-like. His appearance must indicate swiftness, power and endurance. Temperament should be lively and ardent. *Height* at the shoulder: Males 21.6 to 25.6 inches; females, 18.9 to 21.6 inches. *Length* from occiput to first joint of tail about 27.5 inches.

TAIL — Cropped, not longer than 5.9 inches.

HEAD — Top of head must be flat or may be slightly arched, but the forehead must be broad; stretched long, the head must go over into a not too pointy muzzle. *Cheeks* must be flat but very muscular. A dog of about 19.7 inches in height at the shoulder should measure about 16 inches around the forehead. The length of the head, from occiput to the tip of the nose should be 9.9 to 10 inches.

BITE — Must be very powerful, well developed and closing right. Lips lying close to the jaw, not drooping.

EYES — Must be dark brown, medium sized, with an intelligent, gentle but energetic expression.

EARS — Cropped, not too short, not too pointy.

THE AMERICAN STANDARD

The American Standard for the breed compiled during 1935 also included a list of Doberman "faults," though no actual disqualifications were listed. The Standard in this country was revised in 1948

Taphria of Marks-Tey, owned by Joanna and Keith Walker of Centralia, Illinois. The sire was Ch. Stacy's Taurus of Marks-Tey x Ch. Marks-Tey Valika, C.D.X.

Opposite:
Magnificent headstudy of a typical Damasyn Doberman. This one of Damasyn The Waltzing Raven, bred by Peggy Adamson and owned by Joseph Rapisarda of Hillsdale, New Jersey. Photograph by William Brown.

with adjustments in size and head and more attention to the dog being "fearless and aggressive" though not "shy or vicious." Obviously we were coming around to the greater use of the dog as a guard even though the dog was beginning to appear with more and more regularity in the show ring.

The Standard was revised once again, in 1969, to place emphasis on teeth. It actually requires a tooth count with a disqualification for four or more missing teeth. This specific emphasis on teeth has caused a great controversy among breeders and especially dog show judges. It was in this 1969 revision that shyness and viciousness as disqualifications were omitted and left to the discretion of the judge should he wish to dismiss a dog from the ring on either of these conditions.

DOBERMAN PINSCHER STANDARD
(Adopted October 1969)

GENERAL CONFORMATION AND APPEARANCE — The appearance is that of a dog of medium size, with a body that is square; the height, measured vertically from the ground to the highest point of the withers, equalling the length measured horizontally from the forechest to the rear projection of the upper thigh. *Height* at the withers—*dogs* 26 to 28 inches, ideal about 27½ inches; *bitches* 24 to 26 inches, ideal about 25½ inches. Length of head, neck and legs in proportion to length and depth of body. Compactly built, muscular and powerful, for great endurance and speed. Elegant in appearance, of proud carriage, reflecting great nobility and temperament. Energetic, watchful, determined, alert, fearless, loyal and obedient.

The judge shall dismiss from the ring any shy or vicious Doberman.

SHYNESS — A dog shall be judged fundamentally shy if, refusing to stand for examination, it shrinks away from the judge; if it fears an approach from the rear; if it shies at sudden and unusual noises to a marked degree.

VICIOUSNESS — A dog that attacks or attempts to attack either the judge or its handler, is definitely vicious. An aggressive or belligerent attitude towards other dogs shall not be deemed viciousness.

HEAD — Long and dry, resembling a blunt wedge in both frontal and profile views. When seen from the front, the head widens gradually toward the base of the ears in a practically unbroken line. Top of skull flat, turning with slight stop to bridge of muzzle, with muzzle line extending parallel to top line of skull. Cheeks flat and muscular. Lips lying close to jaws. Jaws full and powerful, well filled under the eyes.

EYES — Almond shaped, moderately deep set, with vigorous, energetic expression. Iris, of uniform color, ranging from medium to

D.V. Sieger for 1973, International Champion, Schweizer Sier, and SchH III— Afra v Bavaria, photographed in her native Germany. Bred by Hans Wiblishauser who is owner of the von Bavaria Kennels in West Germany.

darkest brown in black dogs; in reds, blues, and fawns the color of the iris blends with that of the markings, the darkest shade being preferable in every case.

TEETH — Strongly developed and white. Lower incisors upright and touching inside of upper incisors—a true scissors bite, 42 correctly placed teeth, 22 in the lower, 20 in the upper jaw. Distemper teeth shall not be penalized.

DISQUALIFYING FAULTS — Overshot more than 3/16 of an inch. Undershot more than 1/8 of an inch. Four or more missing teeth.

NECK — Proudly carried, well muscled and dry. Well arched, with nape of neck widening gradually toward body. Length of neck proportioned to body and head.

EARS — Normally cropped and carried erect. The upper attachment of the ear, when held erect, is on a level with the top of the skull.

BODY — Back short, firm, of sufficient width, and muscular at the loins, extending in a straight line from withers to the slightly rounded croup.

WITHERS — Pronounced and forming the highest point of the body. *Brisket* reaching deep to the elbow. *Chest* broad with forechest well defined.

RIBS — Well sprung from the spine, but flattened in lower end to permit elbow clearance. *Belly* well tucked up, extending in a curved line from the brisket. *Loins* wide and muscled. *Hips* broad and in proportion to body, breadth of hips being approximately equal to breadth of body at rib cage and shoulders. *Tail* docked at approximately second joint, appears to be a continuation of the spine, and is carried only slightly above the horizontal when the dog is alert.

FOREQUARTERS — Shoulder blade sloping forward and downward at a 45 degree angle to the ground meets the upper arm at an

The 1964 German Bundessiegerin, Citta Germania.

angle of 90 degrees. Length of shoulder blade and upper arm are equal. Height from elbow to withers approximately equals height from ground to elbow. *Legs*, seen from front and side, perfectly straight and parallel to each other from elbow to pastern; muscled and sinewy, with heavy bone. In normal pose and when gaiting, the elbows lie close to the brisket. *Pasterns* firm and almost perpendicular to the ground. *Feet* well arched, compact and catlike, turning neither in nor out. Dewclaws may be removed.

HINDQUARTERS — The angulation of the hindquarters balances that of the forequarters. *Hip Bone* falls away from spinal column at an angle of about 30 degrees, producing slightly rounded, well-filled-out croup. *Upper Shanks*, at right angles to the hip bones, are long, wide, and well muscled on both sides of thigh, with clearly defined stifles. Upper and lower shanks are of equal length. While the dog is at rest, hock to heel is perpendicular to the ground. Viewed from the rear, the legs are straight, parallel to each other, and wide enough apart to fit in with a properly built body. *Cat Feet*, as on front legs, turning neither in nor out. Dewclaws, if any, are generally removed.

GAIT — Free, balanced, and vigorous, with good reach in the forequarters and good driving power in the hindquarters. When trotting, there is strong rear-action drive. Each rear leg moves in line with the foreleg on the same side. Rear and front legs are thrown neither in nor out. Back remains strong and firm. When moving at a fast trot, a properly built dog will singletrack.

COAT, COLOR, MARKINGS — *Coat,* smooth-haired, short, hard, thick and close lying. Invisible gray undercoat on neck permissible. *Allowed Colors* — Black, red, blue and fawn (Isabella). *Markings* — Rust, sharply defined, appearing above each eye and on muzzle, throat and forechest, on all legs and feet, and below tail. *Nose* solid black on black dogs, dark brown on red ones, dark gray on blue ones, dark tan on fawns. White patch on chest, not exceeding ½ square inch, permissible.

FAULTS — *The foregoing description is that of the ideal Doberman Pinscher. Any deviation from the above described dog must be penalized to the extent of the deviation.*

DISQUALIFICATIONS — *Overshot more than 3/16 of an inch; undershot more than 1/8 of an inch. Four or more missing teeth.*

THE BRITISH STANDARD FOR THE DOBERMANN

CHARACTERISTICS — The Dobermann is a dog of good medium size with a well-set body, muscular and elegant. He has a proud carriage and a bold, alert temperament. His form is compact and tough and owning to his build capable of great speed. His gait is light and elastic. His eyes show intelligence and firmness of character, and he is loyal and obedient. Shyness or viciousness must be heavily penalized.

HEAD AND SKULL: Has to be proportionate to the body. It must be long, well filled under the eyes and clean cut. Its form seen from above and from the side must resemble a blunt wedge. The upper part of the head should be as flat as possible and free from wrinkle. The top of the skull should be flat with a slight stop, and the muzzle line extend parallel to the top line of the skull. The cheeks must be flat and the lips tight. The nose should be solid black in black dogs, solid brown in brown dogs, and solid grey in blue dogs. Head out of balance in proportion to body, dish-faced, snipey or cheeky should be penalized.

EYES — Should be almond-shaped, not round, moderately deep set, not prominent, with vigorous, energetic expression. Iris of uniform colour, ranging from medium to darkest brown in black dogs, the darker shade being the more desirable. In browns or blues the

D.V. Sieger and Bundessieger Chico v Forel, an International Champion as well; bred by the late Ernst Wilking, famous German breeder and judge.

colour of the iris should blend with that of the markings, but not be of lighter hue than that of the markings. Light eyes in black dogs to be discouraged.

EARS — Should be small, neat and set high on the head. Erect or dropped, but erect preferred.

BODY — Should be square, height measured vertically from the ground to the highest point of the withers equalling the length measured horizontally from the forechest to rear projection of the upper thigh. The back should be short and firm with the topline sloping slightly from the withers to the croup; the female, needing room to carry litters, may be slightly longer in loin. The belly should be fairly well tucked up. Ribs should be deep and well-sprung, reaching to elbow. Long, weak or roach backs to be discouraged.

MOUTH — Should be very well developed, solid and strong, with a scissor bite. The incisors of the lower jaw must touch the inner face of the incisors of the upper jaw. Overshot or undershot mouths, badly arranged or decayed teeth to be penalized.

NECK — Should be fairly long and lean, carried erect and with considerable nobility, slightly convex and proportionate to the whole shape of the dog. The region of the nape has to be muscular. Dewlap and loose skin are undesirable.

FOREQUARTERS — The shoulder-blade and upper arm should meet at an angle of 90 degrees. Relative length of shoulder and upper arm should be as one, excess length of upper arm being much less desirable than excess length of shoulder blade. The legs, seen from the front and side, are perfectly straight and parallel to each other from elbow to pastern, muscled and sinewy, with round bone proportionate to body structure. In a normal position and when gaiting, the elbow should lie close to the brisket.

HINDQUARTERS — Should be parallel to each other and wide enough apart to fit in with a properly built body. The hip bone should fall away from the spinal column at an angle of about 30 degrees. Croup well filled out. The hindquarters should be well developed and muscular, with long bent stifle and their hocks turning neither in nor out. While the dog is at rest, hock to heel should be perpendicular to the ground.

FEET — Fore-feet should be well arched, compact and cat-like, turning neither in nor out.

GAIT — Should be free, balanced and vigorous with good reach in the forequarters, and driving power in the hindquarters. When trotting, there should be a strong rear action drive with rotary motion of the hindquarters. Rear and front legs should be thrown neither in nor out. Back should remain strong and firm.

TAIL — The tail should be docked at the first or second joint and should appear to be a continuation of the spine, without a material drop.

COAT — Should be smooth-haired, short, hard, thick and close lying. Invisible grey undercoat on neck permissible.

COLOUR — Colours allowed are definite black, brown or blue with rust-red markings. Markings must be sharply defined and appearing above each eye and on the muzzle, throat and fore-chest, and on all legs and feet, and below the tail. White markings of any kind are highly undesirable.

WEIGHT AND SIZE — Ideal height at withers: males 27 inches; females 25½ inches. Considerable deviation from this ideal to be discouraged.

FAULTS — Shyness or viciousness must be heavily penalized. Head out of balance in proportion to body, dish-faced, snipy or cheeky should be penalized. Light eyes in black dogs to be discouraged. Over-

Borain's Raging Calm, winner of two Championship Certificates and a Junior Warrant holder. Whelped in March, 1974. The Borain Dobermans are bred and owned by Mrs. Pat Gledhill of Oxfordshire, England.

shot or undershot mouths, badly arranged or decayed teeth to be penalized. Dewlap and loose skin are undesirable. Long, weak or roach backs to be discouraged. White markings of any kind are highly undesirable.

It is interesting to compare the British and American Standards. The British have no disqualifying faults, only undesirables or "to be heavily penalized" requirements. Most outstanding is, of course, the difference in ears. Dogs which have had their ears cropped can not be shown in England. The weight and size categories vary, and there is no mention of the fawn color as yet in the British Standard.

11. DOBERMAN TEMPERAMENT AND BREED CHARACTERISTICS

Perhaps no other breed of dog has been so maligned and misunderstood as the Doberman Pinscher. The stories of their supposed viciousness are widespread and varied and have persisted through all the years of its existence, and the breed has obviously suffered from it. As more and more Dobermans are pressed into guard dog duty because of soaring crime rates, their image as fierce protectors —the ultimate in attack dogs—grows. Many people think of them as ready to sink their teeth into any trespasser or even the next-door neighbor who drops by to borrow a cup of sugar.

The tag "guard dog" sometimes puts an unfortunate stigma on a breed and seems to indicate the tendency to attack with or without cause. Actually there is a big difference between a guard dog and an attack dog, and the uneducated public is unable to make this distinction. There are, of course, Dobermans that have been mistreated, mistrained or misunderstood by their owners, who should not have chosen this breed in the first place. Philipp Gruenig, the wise old German judge, breeder, author and profound student of the breed, said, "Not everybody is suited to the ownership of a tempermental dog and that is exactly as it ought to be."

We who know and understand the breed today are also aware that the Doberman is not a breed for everyone. To get the best out of a Doberman it must be properly handled, correctly trained and well disciplined. The owner that is not willing or able to devote sufficient time to a Dobe's education should settle for a less rambunctious breed. Almost a century of planned breeding has gone into making it the dog it is today: protective, fearless, intelligent, companionable, aggressive yet not quarrelsome and a thing of beauty with boundless energy and instant responses to the world around it. It should not have to live down a reputation for viciousness because so many have fallen into the wrong hands.

Ch. Doricka v d Elbe, owned and bred by Hans Smidt of Downington, Pennsylvania.

Reproduction of a painting of American and Canadian Ch. Damasyn The Elf, C.D., by M. Huff. This lovely Dictator daughter out of Damasyn The April Rain was owned by Helen Kamerer of Carmel, California. The Elf is a sister to Ch. Damasyn The Ember.

Opposite:
A classic photo of taken several years ago of two great obedience Dobermans—Aleric v Ahrtal, C.D.X., T.D., and Champion Elektra v Ahrtal, C.D. Owned and trained by Miss Tess Henseler, Ahrtal Kennels, Ottsville, Pennsylvania. Aleric's sire was Ch. Delegate v d Gibe x Kriemhild v Ahrtal, C.D. and Elektra's sire was Ch. Dorian v Ahrtal x Meadowmist Belladonna.

Much discussion should preceed the purchase of a Doberman Pinscher. Beyond the initial attraction to the breed itself it should be determined, if it is to live with a family, whether each member of that family is capable of handling a Dobe and is willing to care for it as well as enjoy its company. If it is to be a guard dog it must be decided that the training will be given at an accredited school experienced in teaching properly the techniques the Doberman will need to function in society. If it is to be a show dog, it must also be schooled in the proper manner to meet the demands that will be made on it to assure success when the time comes to meet the temperament requirements called for in the American Kennel Club approved Standard.

Part of the misunderstanding on the part of the public in regard to the temperament of the Doberman is a result of its meteoric rise in popularity. It was virtually impossible to educate the public as the breed came up in the ranks. The responsibility at this point in the breed's development lies almost exclusively with the breeders, clubs and individual owners. With an eye toward assisting in this endeavor, the Doberman Pinscher Club of America has devised a plan whereby its members can test the temperament of the dogs they breed.

THE DPCA TEMPERAMENT TESTING PROGRAM

In 1973 at the National Convention, the Doberman Pinscher Club of America's Board of Directors voted to establish the Register of Merit Study Committee (to be known also as ROM) as a regular standing committee of the parent club. Along with a major objective of creating an award to be bestowed upon Doberman Pinschers possessing ideal temperament, sound conformation and trainability,

Peggy Adamson "at home" at Damasyn with a trio of her top adult dogs, Easter Bonnet, Solitaire and Brown's Evangeline, and a puppy.

their aim during their first official year was toward the devising of temperament tests for Dobermans.

These tests are designed to estimate the dog's response, when in a working environment, to various situations which might arise for the first time. These temperament tests measure the reaction to playfulness, non-threatening strangers, a change in handlers, sound, sudden visual stimuli, changes in footing and to a threatening stranger.

The committee supplies the test requirements to the chapter clubs where the temperament tests are actually conducted. The ultimate goal is to come closer to producing the ideal combination of both working and show dog. Anyone wishing to test their dogs need only contact the club for full particulars.

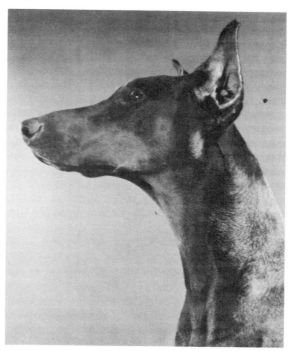

Impressive headstudy of Ch. Triadel Honey B's Blak Rites, owned by Donna Smith of Edmonton, Alberta, Canada.

DOBERMAN SIZE

During the 1960's and early 1970's, as the Doberman's popularity grew by leaps and bounds, there was a great deal of concerned discussion regarding the apparent increase in the size of the dog.

The surge in popularity for Dobermans as guard dogs on the part of the public has leaned toward the bigger Doberman and unfortunately some of the breeding has seemed to go along with this trend. Too many Dobermans are seen that far exceed the heights called for

Damasyn Panzer, a fawn dog photographed at seven months of age with his handler. The dam was Cameo's Tanya and the sire was Damasyn Intrepid. Owned by Melinda and John Aron.

in the approved Standard. Along with the increase in size comes a natural increase in weight. The result is obviously an excess of Dobermans being marketed that are too large and too heavy for anything *but* guard work or pet stock. Naturally this deviation from the Standard is a cause for concern among dedicated breeders.

Although the Doberman started out as a small-to-medium dog when Herr Dobermann embarked on his breeding program, the ultimate aim was for the Doberman to be larger. The DPCA Standard revisions accommodate the natural increase in size. Since the 1935 and 1948 revisions there has been no further need for any increase in size. Dobermans meeting the present approved height and weight requirements are perfectly capable of guard dog responsibilities as well as any other working dog services which might be required of them.

Size and weight in the Doberman must be strictly adhered to in any breeding program if the Doberman is to maintain the classic symmetry that has come to exemplify the breed. After almost a century of hard work in developing this magnificent dog, it would be a crime to see it get out of hand as a result of irresponsible breeding to produce a "big" guard dog—when "bigger" certainly does not mean "better!"

DOBERMAN COATS

Color seems to play a definite part in the care and condition of the Doberman coat. Reds are said to carry the heaviest coats, with blacks next and the blues and fawns with the lightest and thinnest. Perhaps all of us with an interest in Dobermans have heard the bad joke—and always from bald men, naturally—that they are not bald, they are fawn Dobermans.

Careful attention to diet and grooming are necessary to preserve the blue and fawn coats. Fawns and blues must be fed additional supplements of oil and suet, and they require a weekly bath using a medicated shampoo. The shampoo provides best results when left on for a time, followed by a thorough washing and then blown dry. Warm olive oil should then be rubbed thoroughly into the coat until it is completely absorbed. The olive oil rub may be indicated between baths as well in particular areas which indicate dryness or friction.

Under normal circumstances the above should be sufficient care to preserve a normal coat on the fawns and blues. Any additional trouble would indicate a trip to the veterinarian for special care.

DOBERMAN COLORS

According to the Standard for the breed approved by the American Kennel Club, there are four approved colors: black, red, blue and fawn. However, one need not be around Doberman people for very long before realizing that there are those who call the reds "browns" and the fawns "Isabellas." Why this should be the case is a wonder, for we are all AKC oriented. But nonetheless, the reds ARE referred to by some as browns, and Isabella is heard almost more often than fawn, except by those strict adherents to breed propriety!

Perhaps part of the confusion between the red and the brown coloration can be attributed to the fact that from the beginning of the breed in Germany the reds were called browns, even by authorities such as Philipp Gruenig who used the term brown throughout his book on the breed. As for the fawn color, Mr. Gruenig in all instances where he makes mention of a fawn puts the word "Isabella" immediately following it in brackets. Such is the case with the A.K.C. Standard. The word fawn is immediately followed by (Isabella).

In ancient history it is not quite clear which came first, the term fawn or Isabella, but it is believed to be Isabella as a result of the story circulated regarding the Spanish Queen Isabella.

As the story goes, when the capital of Spain was surrounded by the enemy during the war with the Moors, Queen Isabella announced that she would not change her linen until the siege was over—no matter how long that would be. Historians will tell you it was a period of three years before the hostile forces were completely dispersed! So it is not hard to imagine that the color of the Queen's linen most assuredly had turned to the color of parchment, or fawn color, much the same shade as our Doberman dogs!

Another side to the same story, if we might digress for a moment to another member of the animal kingdom, is that Queen Isabella ordered all of Spain's royal horses to be of her favorite color—a shade of yellow, or cream, greatly resembling what we have come to call Palamino in our American horses. As a result of the great influence Spain had over all of Europe during the reign of Queen Isabella, the yellow horses became known as Isabels, or Ishbels, in deference to her wishes. When the Spanish Conquistadors arrived on the American shores in the years following Columbus' discovery of America, they brought with them their Isabel horses. On occasion they escaped or bred with other escaped Spanish horses and the natural succession to our Palaminos followed.

Since our Dobermans (those that are fawn in color, that is) resemble the color of parchment and the Isabel horses, they have been referred to as Isabellas.

In 1912 the first Isabella was born in Germany, but the fawns never were appreciated or acceptable in European countries, especially in the early years. However, as long as the color appeals to even a single breeder, and especially now that the American Standard recognized it, there will be fawn Dobermans. Even though the fawn color is not accepted in Germany even today, Philipp Gruenig saw their existence as inevitable. He wrote: "It is indeed a matter of regret that the various breed organizations will not tolerate this beautiful fawn color. . . Our Dobermann could only profit by permit-

Barbara Schmidt "at home" in Kentucky with her two Ch. Dictator von Glenhugel offspring—Damasyn The Tazh and Ch. Damasyn The Ballad.

ting this color to assume its rightful place in the spectrum of the breed."

Once the Doberman Pinscher Club of America accepted the fawn Doberman and it was approved by the American Kennel Club as an addition to the revised Standard in 1969, admirers of this color were "off and running" to help establish it in the breed. The Long Island Doberman Pinscher Breeders and Fanciers Association placed an advertisement in the 1970 Working Dog Issue of *Popular Dogs* magazine offering a Sunray Trophy with a value of one hundred dollars to the owner of the first fawn Doberman Pinscher to gain its championship.

MELANISM

Every once in a while the word melanism is heard when breeding Dobermans is mentioned or contemplated. Melanism in the Doberman Pinscher is seen in the presence of an all black dog, or one with decidedly indistinct markings or with tan coloration absent entirely.

Melanin is a dark pigmentation which colors the hair and/or the skin black. Melanin is produced by a special cell, called a melanocyte, which is derived from the neural crest and migrates to the basal cell layer of the epidermis, or skin.

The melanocyte is a melanin-producing and melanin-containing cell that in its earliest form is called a melanoblast. The small organelles are called melanosomes and possess tyrosinase activity, and this enzyme catalyzes the tyrosine to melanin. When the melanin formation is complete the melanosomes are dense black. Melanin formation is affected by and is under the control of melanin-stimulating hormones which are produced in the intermediary lobe of the pituitary gland and can be influenced by the diseases of the pituitary glands and by other endocrine glands.

By way of comparison, the opposite of melanism would be albinism, which means no pigmentation at all, resulting in an all white dog. The albinistic dog has pale "pink" eyes and a virtually colorless skin. The lucistic dog has white hair but blue eyes.

Therefore, the Doberman with an over-abundance of pigmentation can be said to be a melanistic dog, as a result of a condition known as melanism. Fortunately, through better breeding and more knowledgable breeders in today's enlightened era, melanism is a rarity, but its existence should be realized and recognized by all those who intend to become active in the breeding of dogs.

A dog named Rappo v d Blankenburg, whelped on March 8, 1918, and a half brother to the famous Lux v d Blankenburg that died in Detroit in 1931, was one of the first known melanistic dogs in the United States. He was used as a stud in his native country and then shipped to America at an early age. Although completely black in color, he was used at stud because of his other fine traits and did at-

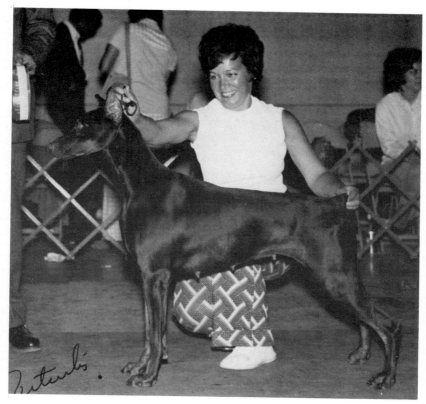

Ch. Richwyn's Desiree, a red bitch bred and owned by Pat Gwyn of Canyon, Texas. Desiree is handled here by L. Ruth Morris for this win at the 1973 Hutchinson Kennel Club show under judge Ed Bracy. Desiree was a Group winner from the classes on the way to her championship.

tain his championship in this country much to the dismay of other breeders both here and in his native Germany. Again we quote the breed expert, Philipp Gruenig, who wrote of this: ". . . the reader can supply his own comment on the American conception of Dobermann perfection when we learn that he became an American champion."

FLAVISM

In direct opposition to melanism, or a progressive turning to a solid black color, we have a condition known as flavism. Flavism is a tendency to yellow color, a general progressive weakening of the color factor. Flavism tends to be the term applied to the fading or

Ch. Marks-Tey Valika, C.D.X. Valika is a sister to Keith and Joanna Walker's great bitch, Vale. The Marks-Tey Kennels are in Centralia, Illinois.

paling of color, while a condition known as Lenchaemia constitutes a total absence of color. The only corrective measure in either case is proper selective breeding.

TEETH

One of the great controversies in the breed during the early 1970's concerned the Doberman's dentition, following the 1969 revision of the Standard declaring four or more missing teeth a disqualification. It goes without saying that a guard dog which may be called upon to hang on to a "prisoner" certainly must have teeth with which to do it.

However, the objections seem to come from those who have observed some judges which have put all the emphasis on teeth instead of judging the entire dog. Some judges notice spaces between teeth and rule out the dog entirely. They would rather not "take a chance" of putting up a dog with missing teeth when there are others in the ring to choose from without risk.

We have all known dogs which have lost teeth through decay or as fence-fighters or "chewers" that lose or break teeth trying to bite through chain-link fencing, but judges are sometimes reluctant to detemine what the cause might be. They automatically write it off as a hereditary fault. It is a simple matter for a judge to subtract missing teeth from the total number required, without always having to do a tooth-by-tooth count.

Since bad dentition and bad bites are so hard, and take so long to breed out of a line, we can't put too much emphasis on the importance of a dog having the required number of teeth—forty-two and correctly placed!

In Germany no dog with even a single missing tooth is permitted to be bred. In fact, at the 1973 meeting of the Dobermann Verein a suggestion was made to permit the breeding of Dobermans with less than full dentition, and it was voted down almost unanimously. Perhaps more serious consideration should be given to the revision in the American Standard which permits as many as three to be missing before a disqualification is made.

Problems with bites and dentition were almost inevitable as the Doberman grew in size over the years and the head became more refined. Philipp Gruenig was one of the first to point out that with this refinement there would be the natural tendency for less than a complete set of teeth. . . that heredity would eventually omit teeth as the jaw bone lengthened. Genetically the Doberman was regarded as having a short or medium-sized head, but it is now a long-headed breed, and those that believe too much emphasis is being put on teeth think that allowances must be made for it.

The fact remains that if the Standard is designed to produce the "perfect" Doberman, the dogs which are bred toward this goal should have all the necessary teeth required for a "perfect" dog. Shouldn't teeth be as important as toes? What judge would put up a dog with a missing toe, or a polydactyl—a dog with seven toes? If two testicles are required, why not forty-two teeth? Teeth are a most important defense for every breed of dog and never more so than with a breed expected to defend or attack.

DOBERMAN POPULARITY

As this book goes to press the Doberman fancy is astonished to find that the breed is approaching the position of being in the Top Five of American Kennel Club registrations. During 1974 the breed

The handsome Elfred's Telstar photographed at seven years of age. The foundation dog of Jane N. Benfield's Telstar Kennels, he had to be retired from the show ring due to an injury when he had 10 points toward his championship. He is the sire of champion and pointed get.

showed the largest registration increase of any breed, moving up to sixth place from number eight where it was during 1973. A more than ten-thousand-dog increase was shown in the final A.K.C. figures, bringing the total registration for 1974 to 45,110.

While the Doberman has been seen making a steady climb up the registration ladder, the responsibility of being one of the Top Five or even one of the Top Ten dogs in the nation is not to be taken lightly. It can mean disaster if breeding gets out of control and leads to Dobermans suddenly turning up in pounds, turned loose, sold under their true value in pet shops or being used in experimental laboratories.

Part of the increase in popularity is due, of course, to the demand for guard dogs, as well as dog lovers discovering that the Doberman is such an ideal family dog. However, the situation suddenly makes it the responsibility of every Doberman owner and breeder to keep the dangers of over-popularity in mind and to do their part in educating the general public on the need for restraint in breeding and the proper care and handling of the dogs they sell or own.

12. THE DOBERMAN PINSCHER CLUB OF AMERICA

In 1921, at a meeting during the Westminster Kennel Club show, George H. Earle III (later Governor Earle) and a group of Doberman fanciers got together and formed the Doberman Pinscher Club of America. In 1922 they adopted the Standard for the breed set up by the Germans and managed to administer to the breed under their requirements until 1935 when the first official American Standard was drawn up by the DPCA and approved by the American Kennel Club. Both the 1935 and 1938 Standard revisions called for height adjustments as well as other minor changes, and the revision of 1969 recognized the fawn or Isabella and made four or more missing teeth a disqualification.

Right from the start the DPCA had a firm hold on its members and offered a fine program for the control and monitoring of the breed without having to limit the purpose of this marvelous working dog either outside or within the dog fancy. Membership in the parent club reached over 1300 by 1975. In 1944, it became necessary to sanction many chapter clubs and provisional local clubs to keep a close eye on breed activities all over the nation, and it is these smaller clubs and the diligent workers in them that are responsible for both its popularity and the strict adherence to breeding to the Standard.

As an aid toward this goal, the parent club offers far more than lip service or breed status. In addition to an Annual Convention, Specialty Show, Futurity Stakes and Obedience Trial held by a "host club" in a different part of the country every October, the DPCA also plans two to three Regional Symposiums each year, conducts a Doberman Temperament Testing Program via its Register of Merit Study Committee, supplies educational materials and publications for nominal fees, sponsors Annual Awards for members, publishes a periodical, *DPCA Pipeline* and distributes a *DPCA Yearbook* containing an explanation of the parent club functions and a *Breeders Directory* to aid interested parties in the purchase of a Doberman Pinscher.

THE DPCA YEARBOOK

Each October, after the Annual Convention, the DPCA publishes their annual *Yearbook* as a service to its members as well as to the general public. The *Yearbook* publishes a complete list of elected officers and Board of Directors for the coming 12-month period, as well as the name and address of the delegate to the American Kennel Club.

It also publishes the names and addresses of the Project Secretaries, which include the Membership Secretary, Recording Secretary, Corresponding Secretary, Chapter Club Secretary, Regional Symposium Chairman and the Director of Public Relations for the club. Along with a descriptive paragraph explaining the function and services of each of the major projects and special programs are listed the Directors or Secretaries of the Annual Futurity Stakes, the Educational Materials Publications, *Yearbook* and *Breeders Directory* editor, *Pipeline* editor, Obedience Chairman, National Convention and Specialty Show Coordinator, Bench Show Chairman, Annual Award Chairman for Obedience, Conformation and Junior Showmanship and the contact for the programs available to the DPCA chapters.

The *Breeders Directory* was originally conceived to assist those who wished to buy a Doberman from reputable breeders in good standing with the parent club. It is listed alphabetically by state and then by country around the world. The *Breeders Directory* has also proved to be a great aid in locating stud service. Breeders listed in this *Directory* are known to have signed a statement to the effect that they do not sell Dobermans for re-sale nor permit their studs to be used by anyone who does, and that they do not sell to or service bitches owned by dog dealers or suppliers to pet shops.

DPCA ARCHIVES

For many years now the parent club has been encouraging the collecting and preserving of valuable items such as photographs, magazines, catalogues, etc., of historial interest. Past-president Dr. Wilfrid Shute in 1967 appointed Mrs. Nancy Hogans as head of an Archives Committee to pursue this endeavor. There had been attempts in 1955 and in 1966 to do this, but it has only been during the 1970's that any significant progress has been made.

Each October at the Annual Convention of the parent club these archives are put on display for all members to peruse with the hope of encouraging others to loan or donate any valuable items they might possess to further the collection. The project, supported by the DPCA, is able to purchase other items as well to further preserve the history and heritage of the breed. These parent club appropriations can at times involve hundreds of dollars to secure and a great deal of time for proper recording and cataloguing. All this is done with the ultimate goal of one day having a permanent location for the archives, where they can be viewed and enjoyed on a full-time basis.

The committee's solicitation of old Doberman statues, prints, paintings, trophies, marked catalogues for both point and match shows, books, magazines, pedigrees, pictures of show and obedience winners from yesteryear, stories about famous kennels, films or slides brings a great response from Doberman people. The future looks bright for this important and active committee.

Australian Dog writer Dora Mitroi hosting a party after the 1974 Australian National show with judge Peggy Adamson and the breeders of the Best of Breed winner, Mr. and Mrs. Eric Archibald.

JOINING THE DPCA

Membership in the Doberman Pinscher Club of America is relatively simple for the dedicated owner. The Membership Secretary receives and processes membership applications, forwarding them to the Board for approval. Once approved, the applicant receives a

Ch. Mark's Tey High Hat finishing for his championship under judge Peggy Adamson at the 1963 Metropolitan Washington Associated Specialty Clubs show. Handled for owners Mr. and Mrs. A. Schilling by J. Monroe Stebbins, Jr.

Opposite:
Ch. Von Mac's Rusty pictured winning at the 1970 Doberman Pinscher Club of Houston Specialty Show. Rusty is owned by Evelyn Collier of San Antonio, Texas.

membership kit acquainting him or her with the intents and purposes of the DPCA. Annual dues are ten dollars a year; the sponsorship of two DPCA members is required.

The main objective of the club is to encourage and promote the breeding of purebred Dobermans and "to do all possible to bring their natural qualities to perfection." Members also have an opportunity to participate in the process of revising the breed Standard and/or to vote on recommended changes should they become necessary. This same vote includes any proposed changes to the Constitution, a vote in the election of judges for the Annual Specialty Show, Obedience Trial and Futurity and a vote in the annual election of officers and board members. Members also have the opportunity to buy a listing in the *Yearbook Breeders Directory* when requirements are met and to compete for the club's Annual Awards. Membership includes free copies of the *Pipeline* and a copy of each new edition of the *Yearbook* and *Breeders Directory*.

For those wishing to become even more active in club activities special reduced rates are offered on educational materials and free copies of all information concerning the DPCA, including the breed Standard, Constitution, decals and color charts.

The DPCA is a non-profit organization incorporated under the laws of the State of Michigan. This national club boasts members in almost all of the 50 states and many foreign countries. The chapter clubs number about forty. It is organized and operated on a participative basis but governed in its management and administration by the elected Board of Directors.

AFFILIATIONS

The Doberman Pinscher Club of America is a member of the American Kennel Club and is the only national Doberman breed club which is recognized and sanctioned by them.

The DPCA is also a founding member of the North American Working Dog Association, referred to also as NASA, and is the first parent breed club to join this association which encourages the overall betterment of the working dog mentally as well as physically.

The DPCA is also a member of the American Dog Owners Association, whose objectives are to protect the breeding and exhibiting of dogs as a non-commercial venture and to engage in educational and legislative activities geared to the promotion of the welfare of dogs.

CLUB CONTACTS

For those wishing to contact the parent club it is advised that you write directly to the American Kennel Club, 51 Madison Avenue, New York, New York, 10010 for the name and address of the current Corresponding Secretary of the Doberman Pinscher Club of America or that you request from the AKC the current issue of their *Yearbook* so that you may contact the secretary of the local chapter in your area regarding any information you might want.

CHAPTER CLUB ROSTER

ATLANTA DPC. . . AZTEC DPC OF SAN DIEGO. . . CABRILLO DPC, INC. (Monterey Peninsula). . . CALIFORNIA—SIERRA DPC (San Bernardino County). . . CAVALIER DPC (Tidewater, VA). . . CUYHOGA VALLEY DPC (Akron, OH). . . DESERT VALLEY DPC, INC. (Phoenix, AZ). . . DP BREEDERS ASSOC. OF PENN-JERSEY INC.. . . DPC OF CHARLOTTE, INC.. . . DPC OF CONN.-NEW YORK, INC. (NY City & Long Island). . . DPC OF DALLAS. . . DPC OF FLORIDA, INC. (Miami area). . . DPC OF GREATER KANSAS CITY, INC.. . . DPC OF GREAT WICHITA. . . DPC OF HOUSTON. . . DPC OF THE INDIAN NATION, INC. (Okla. City area). . . DPC OF INDIANA, INC. (Indianapolis). . . DPC OF LOUISIANA, INC. (New Orleans). . . DPC OF MICHIGAN (Detroit). . . DPC OF MISSOURI (St. Louis). . . DPC OF THE NATIONAL CAPITAL AREA, INC. (Washington, D.C.). . . DPC OF NORTHERN CALIFORNIA, INC.

Damasyn's Jalli's Jaimie, bred and owned by Peggy Adamson of Roslyn Heights, New York. Sire was Ch. Damasyn Carly of Jerseystone x Ch. Damasyn Jalli-Alli, C.D.

Civetta's Outfax, C.D., First Graduate Novice at the 1973 Doberman Pinscher Club American National Specialty Show. She is pictured here with Kay Martin, her handler and trainer, and co-owner Arnold Orlander.

Selfaire's Black Onyx, C.D.X., High in Trial at the 1972 Cedar Rapids Kennel Club show under judge Clarence Alexander. Robert T. Self is the owner, trainer and handler.

(San Francisco Bay)... DPC OF THE PACIFIC NORTHWEST, INC. (Portland)... DPC OF THE ROCKY MOUNTAIN AREA, INC. (Denver)... DPC OF SACRAMENTO, INC.... DPC OF ST. JOSEPH VALLEY (South Bend, IN)... DOBERMAN SPORTSMEN'S CLUB OF DETROIT, INC.... FINGER LAKES DPC, INC. (Central & Western NY)... FLORIDA WEST COAST DPC, INC.... GREATER TWIN CITIES DPC (Minn.-St. Paul)... ILLINI DPC, INC. (Greater Chicago)... KEYSTONE DPC (Berks County)... LAKE SHORE DPC (Cleveland)... LOS ANGELES DPC, INC.... MAUMEE VALLEY DPC (Toledo)... METROPOLITAN BALTIMORE DPC, INC. ... MIAMI VALLEY (Cincinnati)... OIL CAPITOL DPC, INC. (Tulsa)... PILGRIM DPC (Boston, MA area)... POTOMAC VALLEY DPC, INC. (Northern VA)... PUGET SOUND DPC (Seattle-Tacoma)... QUAKER CITY DPC, INC. (Philadelphia area).

The great dog Ch. Dictator von Glenhugel, a sire of 52 champions and a sensation in the forties! Purchased at five months of age by Peggy and Bob Adamson for their famous Damasyn Kennels in Roslyn Heights, New York. Dictator was one of the most important dogs in the history of the breed. His sire was Ch. Blank v d Domstadt x Ch. Ossi v Stahlhelm.

DPCA PROVISIONALLY RECOGNIZED LOCAL CLUBS

DPC OF GREATER DAYTON INC.. . . DPC OF LAS VEGAS. . . DPC OF MEMPHIS. . . DPC OF SANTA CLARA VALLEY. . . DPC OF THE TAPPAN ZEE (Carmel, NY area). . . NASHVILLE DPC. . . SAN FERNANDO VALLEY DPC. . . SANTA ANA VALLEY DPC (Orange County). . . TUSCON DPC.

DPCA ANNUAL FUTURITY STAKES

The Futurity Stakes, held each year at the DPCA Convention, were instituted to encourage the breeding of the best possible Dobermans through rewarding DPCA members with a substantial cash award for their efforts. For this reason, the Stakes are weighted heavily in favor of the breeder, who is the one that chooses the sire, nominates the litter, raises the puppies, and often pays the nomination fee of each individual puppy. However, recognition should be given to the sire for his genetic contribution and to the owner of the individual Doberman in developing it to its greatest inherited potential. The quality of the individual animal is the result of the combined efforts of these three.

A summary of the more pertinent rules for the stakes follows. For complete rules, nomination forms and answers to related questions, contact the Futurity Director of the DPCA.

THE STAKES ARE ENTERED BY NOMINATION OF A LITTER BY THE BREEDER, WHO MUST BE A MEMBER OF THE DPCA. THE SUBSEQUENT NOMINATION OF AN INDIVIDUAL PUPPY IS MADE BY THE OWNER, WHO NEED NOT BE A MEMBER OF THE DPCA.

Litter nominations must be made *prior* to whelping. The envelope postmark is considered the nomination date. Any puppy from a valid litter nomination is eligible for nomination to the Stakes regardless of ownership.

Individual puppy nominations must be made before they reach FOUR MONTHS OF AGE. Again, the postmark determines the nomination date. If ownership changes after nomination, full particulars must be received by the Futurity Director at least one month before the Stakes.

A nominated puppy is eligible to compete in the first Futurity Stakes held on or after it reaches six months of age, and in only this Stakes.

NOTE—When buying a puppy, determine if the litter has been nominated *and* if the individual puppy has been nominated.

Nomination fees are $5.00 for the litter and $5.00 for an individual puppy. Fees must accompany nominations. The puppy nomination fee covers its entry in the Futurity competition (indicate as Addition-

Champion Hagen v Ahrtal, bred and owned by Tess Henseler of the Ahrtal Kennels in Ottsville, Pennsylvania. This Delegate x Isis dog was one of the true "greats" in the breed.

al Class) but the puppy must also be entered in a regular class in the Specialty Show or Obedience Trial and this entry fee paid. Three-quarters of the nomination fees are returned as prize monies with one-quarter being retained for operating expenses including judging costs.

The Stakes have four age divisions which are (in months) 6-9, 9-12, 12-15, and 15-18. Each age division has four classes: Black Dogs, AOC Dogs, Black Bitches and AOC Bitches. A Winner and a Reserve Winner are selected for each age division and Stake prizes awarded.

Winners from the 6-9 and 9-12 divisions compete for the BEST FUTURITY PUPPY title and award. Winners from the 12-15 and 15-18 divisions compete for the BEST FUTURITY JUNIOR title and award. From the Best Futurity Puppy and the Best Futurity Junior the GRAND PRIZE FUTURITY WINNER is selected.

Eight Dobermans receive a total of 11 Stakes awards with each award being proportioned on a 3-2-1 basis to the breeder, owner and owner of the sire.

GRAND PRIZE FUTURITY WINNERS

The First Futurity was incorporated in 1959 by Molly Farrell and that year was won by the bitch Jessie Vom Ahrtal, owned by Mr. and Mrs. Stanley Cohen. Tess Henseler was the breeder. A list of Futurity winners in the years that followed is given here:

1960 *Roark's Achilles von Pia,* owned by W.R. Roark, the breeder.

1961 *Highbriar Halla,* a bitch, owned by Mrs. H. Linck and Betsy Thomas, also the breeders.

1962 *Wendolyn Vom Ahrtal,* a bitch bred by Tess Henseler and owned by Ethel Bergman.

1963 *Elfred's Mr. Victory,* owned by Mr. and Mrs. C.A. Bodar and bred by the Elfred Kennels.

1964 *Kay Hill's Study in Wine,* a bitch bred by Jane Kay and owned by Warren and Bettye Sears.

1965 *Ch. Kay Hill's Takeswon to Nowon,* also bred by Jane Kay and owned by Mrs. Michael Pym.

1966 *Toledobe's Quarter Back,* bred by Patrick and Judy Doniere and co-owned by Judy Doniere and Charles A.T. O'Neill.

1967 *Tevrac's Tahita,* bred by Margaret Carveth and owned by Mr. and Mrs. Fred Simpson.

1968 *Von Mac's Mikki Maus,* bred by Florence McDonald and owned by Florence Groce.

1969 *Ch. Elfred's Nikki,* bred and owned by Ellen Hoffman's Elfred Kennels.

1970 *Encore's Mystic Melody,* a bitch bred by Antonia McMorris and owned by Nell Hampton.

1971 *Sassy's Silhouette v Greenlace,* a bitch bred by Shirley Cota and Glorida Hernandez and owned by George and Phyllis Riley.

1972 *Castelane Querida Miranda,* a bitch bred by Shirley Clardy and owned by Doris Booher and Judy Doniere.

1973 *Centre Shirlee of Castlelane,* bred by Joann and Gwyn L. Satalino and owned by J. McQueen and F. Willmeth.

1974 *Alisaton's Intimate Miss,* owned by Joann and Gwyn L. Satalino.

Best Brace in Show at the 1964 Sussex Hills Kennel Club Show under judge Mrs. Flora Bonney were Peggy Adamson's two superbly matched reds, Damasyn the Jalli-Alli, C.D., and Damasyn The Christmas Carol, C.D. This was their first time shown as a brace. The following year they won Best Working Brace at Westminster. Handled for the owner by Carol Selze.

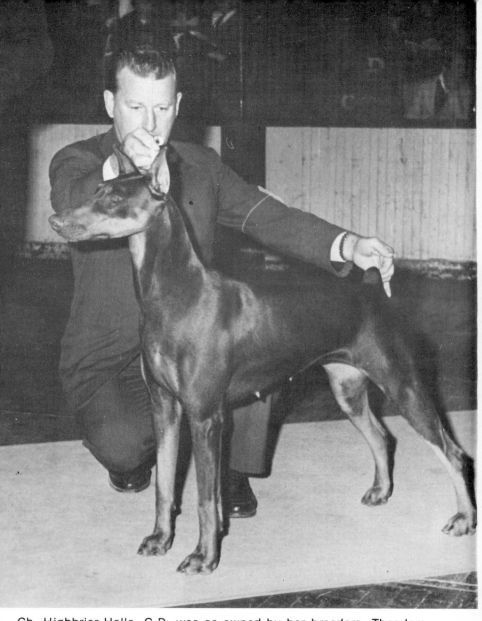

Ch. Highbriar Halla, C.D. was co-owned by her breeders, Theodora Linck and Betty Thomas. A red sired by the Best in Show Ch. Florian v Ahrtal, C.D., Halla was whelped in 1960. In 1961 she was the Doberman Pinscher Club of America Grand Futurity Winner and Best Puppy. During a short show ring career she won several Bests of Breed and Group Placings. Bred to Ch. Highbriar Minois, she produced one champion, Highbriar Major Dare, and by Ch. Felix v Ahrtal she produced Ch. Highbriar Valencia.

BEST OF BREED WINNERS FROM 1924 TO 1975 DOBERMAN PINSCHER CLUB OF AMERICA SPECIALTY SHOWS

DATE	NAME OF DOG	NAME OF OWNER
1924	Red Roof Hilda	George H. Earle, III
1925	Apollo v Schuetzeneck	Dr. R.C. Bauman
1926	Hella of Pontchartrain	Glenn S. Staines
1927	Claus v Sigalsburg	E.J. Robinson
1928	Ch. Claus v Sigalsburg	E.J. Robinson
1929	Alphabet of Dawn	Kettie Kove Kennels
1930	Modern v Simmenau Rhinegold	J.C. Zimmerman
1931	Ch. Hamlet v Herthasse	M.V. Reynolds
1932	Ch. Hamlet Herthasse	M.V. Reynolds
1933	Dash of Bardo	Jos. A. Stoffel
1934	Ch. Muck v Brunia	Owen A. West
1935	Jockel v Burgund	Owen A. West
1936	Ch. Jockel v Burgund	Owen A. West
1937	Ch. Jessy v d Sonnenhohe	F.F.H. Fleitmann
1938	Ch. Rigo v Lindenhof	Ray Soldwell
1939	Ora v Sandberg-Lindenhof	A.D. Nast, Jr.
1940	Ellie v Granzhof	Miss Charlotte V. Bergen
1941	Cerita of Marienland	Marienland Kennels, R.C. Webster
1942	— — —	— — —
1943	Ch. Dow's Dodie v Kienlesberg	Bert T. Dow
1944	Ch. Dictator v Glenhugel	Capt. & Mrs. Bob Adamson
1945	— — —	— — —
1946	Ch. Alcor v Millsdod	Mrs. A. Ernest Mills
1947	Ch. Quo Shmerk v Marineland	Rupprechtheim Kennels
1948	Ch. Alcor v Millsdod	Mrs. A. Ernest Mills
1949	Ch. Jet v d Ravensburg	Mr. & Mrs. Walter A. Dencker
1950	Ch. Jet v d Ravensburg	Mr. & Mrs. Walter A. Dencker
1951	Ch. Kitchawan's Cara Mia	Kitchawan Kennels
1952	Ch. Meadowmist Elegy	Mrs. Wilhelm F. Knauer
1953	Ch. Rontyelee Lady Alleyne	Bishop C.C. Alleyne
1954	Ch. Dortmund Delly's Colonel Jet	Boxdob Kennels
1955	Ch. Dortmund Delly's Colonel Jet	Boxdob Kennels
1956	Ch. Borong the Warlock, C.D.	Henry G. & Theodosia Frampton
1957	Ch. Borong the Warlock, C.D.	Henry G. & Theodosia Frampton
1958	Ch. El Campeon's Diosa	Mr. & Mrs. George S. Forbes
1959	Ch. Haydenhill's Diana	Mr. & Mrs. Robert Sikes
1960	Ch. Borong the Warlock, C.D.	Henry G. & Theodosia Frampton
1961	Ch. Brown's Bridget	Col. R.B. Hoover & Hazel C. Samara
1962	Ch. Singendwald's Prince Kuhio	Singenwald Kennels
1963	Ch. Singendwald's Prince Kuhio	Singenwald Kennels
1964	Ch. Jem's Amythest v Warlock	Henry G. & Theodosia Frampton
1965	Ch. Ru Mar's Tsushima, C.D.	Margaret Carveth
1966	Ch. Toledobe's Linebacker	Loren D. Nickols
1967	Ch. Sultana von Marienburg	Mary M. Rodgers
1968	Ch. Sultana von Marienburg	Mary M. Rodgers
1969	Ch. Rosevale's Little Nip of Loron	Ronald & Loretta Batacao
1970	Ch. Checkmate's Nite Cap	Jim Roe
1971	Ch. Brown's A-Amanda	Eleanor Brown
1972	Ch. LuJoe's Stinger	Jack and Louise Strutt
1973	Ch. Brown's B-Brian	Eleanor Brown
1974	Ch. Loran's Aviator	Helen F. Kamerer & Náncy Hogans
1975	Ch. Brown's B-Brian	Eleanor Brown

Ch. Galaxy's Corry Missile Belle, owned by Elaine Herndon and handled by her breeder, Claire McCabe. Belle is pictured going Best of Winners on the way to her championship under judge Ron Carveth at the 1971 Doberman Pinscher Club of America Specialty Show. She was Winners Bitch over 162 entries for her first points from judge Peggy Adamson at this show at 14 months of age.

14-month-old Marks-Tey Brut, sired by Ch. Marks-Tey Shawn, C.D. x Ch. Marks-Tey Vale. Owned and bred by Keith and Joanna Walker, Centralia, Illinois.

Opposite:
Ch. Highbriar Valencia, a vivacious black and tan bitch who finished for her championship in five weekends, going Best of Breed her first time in the ring. After attaining her title she was leased twice by Theodora Linck (her co-breeder with Betsy Thomas) and bred to Ch. Cassio v Ahrtal. The resulting litters were the first to be registered under the Tedell banner. She produced three champion sons: Ch. Tedell Red Carpet (owned and handled by Barbara Shourt), Ch. Tedell Private Label (owned by Stuart Rogell), and Ch. Tedell Eleventh Hour, a dog that made history in the breed.

Ch. Damasyn Bo-Tairic of Ardon pictured winning on the way to his championship with handler Carol Selzle. The owner is Peggy Adamson; the sire Ch. Damasyn The Boatswain x Ch. Brown's Wendy, C.D.

Ch. Ebonaires' Touchdown pictured winning Best in Show at a 1961
event. Owned by Marie and Charles A.T. O'Neill of Philadelphia.

Selfaire's Poppy, U.D., highest scoring dog in trial at the 1970 Cedar Rapids Kennel Club show under judge Laddie Scheffel. Owner Robert Self handling.

Bigge v d Muhlenbirke, C.D.X., highest scoring dog in trial at the 1975 Paper Cities Kennel Club Show under judge Herbert Semper. Robert T. Self handling. Mr. Self is co-editor and publisher of *Front and Finish*, the dog trainer's newspaper published in Galesburg, Illinois.

Peggy Adamson, the "first lady of Dobermans" receives a plaque at the Santa Barbara Kennel Club show where the largest entry (116) of Dobermans at an all-breed show were entered for her assignment. The plaque read: "Presented to Peggy Adamson for her untiring efforts and interest over the past 25 years as a judge, breeder and exhibitor of Doberman Pinschers. Santa Barbara, California, July 31, 1966." Included in this photograph of prominent Doberman fanciers over the years are Club Chairman Sidney Heckert (in center) with Maxine Cunningham, President of the Orange County Doberman Club on the right, holding the trophy with Peggy Adamson.

A historic meeting of important Doberman people in Cologne, Germany on November 4, 1972. Seated on each side of Dudley Wontner-Smith, Chairman of the North of England Dobermann Club, is Peggy Adamson from the U.S.A. (who judged the British Specialty that year) and on the left is Werner Niermann, President of the Dobermann Vereine. The occasion was the first night of the Bundesseiger Show that year. Herr Niermann judged in Baltimore, Maryland that year also.

Jerry Smith's 4½-month-old Damasyn Intrepid, photographed in Sunnyvale, California.

Opposite:
Ch. Marienburg's Only One, whelped in 1971, pictured finishing for her championship under judge John Cassevoy and. Handled by Moe Miyagawa, who co-owns her with her breeder Mary Rodgers, owner of the Marienburg Kennels in El Cajon, California. The sire was Ch. Marienburg's Red Baron and the dam, American, Mexican and Canadian Ch. Sultana v Marienburg.

HIGHEST SCORING DOG IN TRIAL— DOBERMAN PINSCHER CLUB OF AMERICA SHOWS

YEAR	DOG'S NAME	OWNER'S NAME
1937	Ducat v d Rheinperle	Frank L. Grant
1938	Duke of Schroth Valley	Henry G. Schmitt
1939	Princess B Wilhelmina	H.E. Crebs
1940	King IV, CDX	Harry Carson
1941	Tiger of Pontchartrain	Willy Necker
1942	No Event	
1943	Ch. Danny v Neckerheim	Lester Erhardt
1944	Princess B Wilhelmina	Hugh E. Crebs
1945	No Event	
1946	Ines Gozo de Feliz	Dorothy H. Pagel
1947	Firtz v Darburg	Gilbert F. Berger
1948	Ch. Assault v Aleck, CDX	Clarence C. Alexander
1949	Von Ritter	Anthony Wilkas
1950	Abbenoir	Mr. & Mrs. Frank H. Grover
1951	No Trial	
1952	Teresa v Mac, CDX	Mr. & Mrs. Joseph McKann
1953	Beechurst's Ajax the Great	Beechurst Kennels
1954	Creb's Betty Girl	Hugh E. Crebs
1955	Readington's Dynamite, UD	Barrierdobes Kennels
1956	No Trial	Mr. & Mrs. F.H. Grover
1957	Guiding Eye's Magdolin	Lewis & Bessie Fowler
1958	No Trial	
1959	Titan of Ashworth	Mr. & Mrs. Luke Reilly
1960	Rad's Friendly Jest of Summer	Velma Janek
1963	Ch. Commando's Silver Sandal	Melvin & Virginia Spafford
1964	Val Jan's Amber	Robert T. Self
1965	Ch. Commando's Silver Sandal, UDT	Melvin & Virginia Spafford
1966	Ch. Commando's Silver Sandal, UDT	Melvin & Virginia Spafford
1967	Little Mist v Frederick, UDT	Rosalie & Fred Simpson
1968	Azteca's Bellona, CD	Teresa Nail
1969	Countess Misty of Manistee, CDX	Robert & Patricia Schultz
1970	Ava Danica Hartmann, UD	Genevieve C. McMillen
1971	Ronsu's Clipper Blue Jacket	Wayne Boyd
1972	Schauffelein's Dilemma	Leon K. Matthews
1973	April Acres Black Magic	Rickie L. Brooks
1974	April Acres Black Magic, CDX	Rickie L. Brooks

13. BUYING YOUR DOBERMAN PINSCHER

There are several paths that will lead you to a litter of puppies where you can find the puppy of your choice. Write to the parent club and ask for the names and addresses of members who have puppies for sale. The addresses of breed clubs can be obtained by writing the American Kennel Club, 51 Madison Avenue, New York, N.Y. 10010. They keep an accurate, up-to-date list of reputable breeders from whom you can seek information on obtaining a good healthy puppy. You might also check listings in the classified ads of major newspapers. The various dog magazines also carry listings and usually a column each month which features information and news on the breed.

It is to your advantage to attend a few dog shows in the area where purebred dogs of just about every breed are being exhibited in the show ring. Even if you do not wish to buy a show dog, you should be familiar with what the better specimens look like so that you may at least get a decent looking representative of the breed for your money. You will learn a lot by observing the dogs in action in the show ring, or in a public place where their personalities come to the fore. The dog show catalogue will list the dogs and their owners with local kennel names and breeders whom you can visit to see the types and colors they are breeding and winning with at the shows. Exhibitors at these shows are usually delighted to talk to people about their dogs and the specific characteristics of their particular breed.

Once you have chosen your breed above all others because you admire its exceptional beauty, intelligence and personality, and because you feel the breed will fit in with your family's way of life, it is wise to do a little research on it. The American Kennel Club library, your local library, bookshops, and the breed clubs can usually supply you with a list of reading matter or written material on the breed, past and present. Then, once you have drenched yourself in the breed's illustrious history and have definitely decided that this is the breed for you, it is time to start writing letters and making phone calls to set up appointments to see litters of puppies.

A word of caution here: don't let your choice of a kennel be determined by its nearness to your home, and then buy the first cute puppy

An all blue litter of puppies belonging to Robert and Leslie F. Lloyd of Milford, Connecticut.

that races up to you or licks the end of your nose. All puppies are cute, and naturally you will have a preference among those you see. But don't let preferences sway you into buying the wrong puppy.

If you are buying your dog as a family pet, a preference might not be a serious offense. But if you have had, say, an age preference since you first considered this breed, you would be wise to stick to it. If you are buying a show dog, all physical features must meet with the Standard for the breed. In considering your purchase you must think clearly, choose carefully, and make the very best possible choice. You will, of course, learn to love whichever puppy you finally decide upon, but a case of "love at first sight" can be disappointing and expensive later on if a show career was your primary objective.

To get the broadest possible concept of what is for sale and the current market prices, it is recommended that you visit as many kennels and private breeders as you can. With today's reasonably safe, inexpensive and rapid non-stop flights on the major airlines, it is possible to secure dogs from far-off places at nominal additional charges, allowing you to buy the valuable bloodlines of your choice if you have a thought toward a breeding program in the future.

While it is always safest to actually *see* the dog you are buying, there are enough reputable breeders and kennels to be found for you to buy a dog with a minimum of risk once you have made up your mind what you want, and when you have decided whether you will buy in your own country or import to satisfy your concept of the breed Standard. If you are going to breed dogs, breeding Standard type can be a moral obligation, and your concern should be with buying the best bloodlines and individual animals obtainable, in spite of cost or distance.

It is customary for the purchaser to pay the shipping charges, and the airlines are most willing to supply flight information and prices upon request. Rental on the shipping crate, if the owner does not provide one for the dog, is nominal. While unfortunate incidents have occurred on the airlines in the transporting of animals by air, the major airlines are making improvements in safety measures and have reached the point of reasonable safety and cost. Barring unforeseen circumstances, the safe arrival of a dog you might buy can pretty much be assured if both seller and purchaser adhere to and follow up on even the most minute details from both ends.

Two two-day-old Doberman puppies whelped at the Marks-Tey Kennels of Keith and Joanna Walker in Centralia, Illinois. These typical Marks-Tey puppies were sired by Ch. Stacy's Taurus of Marks-Tey.

Damasyn The Wishing Ring photographed at two months of age. Bred and owned by Peggy Adamson, Roslyn Heights, New York.

THE PUPPY YOU BUY

Let us assume you want to enjoy all the cute antics of a young puppy and decide to buy a six-to-eight-week-old puppy. This is about the age when a puppy is weaned, wormed and ready to go out into the world with a responsible new owner. It is better not to buy a puppy under six weeks of age; it simply is not yet ready to leave the mother or the security of the other puppies. At eight to twelve weeks of age you will be able to notice much about the appearance and the behavior. Puppies, as they are recalled in our fondest childhood memories, are gay and active and bouncy, as well they should be! The normal puppy should be interested, alert, and curious, especially about a stranger. If a puppy acts a little reserved or distant, however, such

A three-week-old puppy bred and owned by Robert and Leslie Lloyd of Milford, Connecticut. The sire was Ch. Zenodobe's Arius x Sethanie Happy Hour, C.D.

Ch. Damasyn The Sonnet, C.D. and Ch. Damasyn The Sage, C.D., litter mates and great grandchildren of the famous import, Sieger and International Champion Muck v Brunia.

act need not be misconstrued as shyness or fear. It merely indicates he hasn't made up his mind whether he likes you as yet! By the same token, he should not be fearful or terrified by a stranger—and especially should not show any fear of his owner!

In direct contrast, the puppy should not be ridiculously over-active either. The puppy that frantically bounds around the room and is never still is not especially desirable. And beware of the "spinners"! Spinners are the puppies or dogs that have become neurotic from being kept in cramped quarters or in crates and behave in an emotionally unstable manner when let loose in adequate space. When let out they run in circles and seemingly "go wild." Puppies with this kind of traumatic background seldom ever regain full composure or adjust to the big outside world. The puppy which has had the proper exercise and appropriate living quarters will have a normal, though spirited, outlook on life and will do his utmost to win you over without having to go into a tailspin.

Nine-month-old Drumpellier Anhel and three-month-old Bon-Bon, bred by the B. Blachfords at their Drumpellier Kennels. Owned by Mr. and Mrs. R.E. Bates of Hants, England.

If the general behavior and appearance of the dog thus far appeal to you, it is time for you to observe him more closely for additional physical requirements. First of all, you cannot expect to find in the puppy all the coat he will bear upon maturity. That will come with time and good food, and will be additionally enhanced by the many wonderful grooming aids which can be found on the market today. Needless to say, the healthy puppy's coat should have a nice shine to it, and the more dense at this age, the better the coat will be when the dog reaches adulthood.

Look for clear, dark, sparkling eyes, free of discharge. Dark eye rims and lids are indications of good pigmentation, which is important in a breeding program, and even for generally pleasing good looks.

When the time comes to select your puppy, take an experienced breeder along with you if this is possible. If it is not possible, take the Standard for the breed with you. Try to interpret the Standard as best you can by making comparisons between the puppies you see.

Check the bite completely and carefully. While the first set of teeth can be misleading, even the placement of teeth at this young age can be a fairly accurate indication of what the bite will be in the grown dog. The gums should be a good healthy pink in color, and the teeth should be clear, clean and white. Any brown cast to them could mean a past case of distemper and would assuredly count against the dog in the show ring and against the dog's general appearance at maturity.

Puppies take anything and everything into their mouths to chew on while they are teething, and a lot of infectious diseases are transmitted this way. The aforementioned distemper is one, and the brown teeth as a result of this disease never clear. The puppy's breath should not be sour or even unpleasant or strong. Any acrid odor could indicate a poor mixture of food, or low quality of meat, especially if it

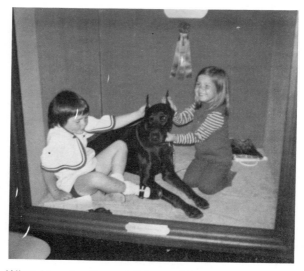

What is cuter than children with their dogs? Here little Marilyn Wallhofer of Pawling, New York, introduces her dog, Ch. Peri's Prince Temujin, to her young friend, Susan Forsyth, at a dog show for the public at the Manhattan Savings Bank in 1973.

is being fed raw. Many breeders have compared the breath of a healthy puppy to that of fresh toast, or as being vaguely like garlic. At any rate, a puppy should never be fed just table scraps, but should have a well-balanced diet containing a good dry puppy chow and a good grade of fresh meat. Poor meat and too much cereal or fillers tend to make the puppy too fat. We like puppies to be in good flesh, but not fat from the wrong kind of food.

It goes without saying that we want to find clean puppies. The breeder or owners who shows you a dirty puppy is one from whom to steer away! Look closely at the skin. Rub the fur the wrong way or against the grain; make sure it is not spotted with insect bites or red, blotchy sores or dry scales. The vent area around the tail should not show evidences of diarrhea or inflammation. By the same token, the puppy's fur should not be matted with dry excrement or smell of urine.

True enough, you can wipe dirty eyes, clean dirty ears and give the puppy a bath when you get it home, but these things are all indications of how the puppy has been cared for during the important formative first months of its life, and can vitally influence its future health and development. There are many reputable breeders raising healthy puppies that have been reared in proper places and under the proper conditions in clean housing, so why take a chance on a series of veterinary bills and a questionable constitution?

MALE OR FEMALE?

The choice of sex in your puppy is also something that must be given serious thought before you buy. For the pet owner, the sex that would best suit the family life you enjoy would be the paramount

"Who Goes There?" This inquisitive puppy was bred by owner Grace Joffe, Liquorish Dobes, Miami, Florida.

Ch. Marienburg's Maximilian, a red and rust Dobe whelped in June of 1965. This marvelous specimen was the sire of eight champions. The sire was Baron Leverett von Mott x Marrero's Dark Princess. Maximilian was bred and owned by the Marienburg Kennels of Mary Rodgers in El Cajon, California.

choice to consider. For the breeder or exhibitor, there are other vital considerations. If you are looking for a stud to establish a kennel, it is essential that you select a dog with both testicles evident, even at a tender age, and verified by a veterinarian before the sale is finalized if there is any doubt.

The visibility of only one testicle, known as monorchidism, automatically disqualifies the dog from the show ring or from a breeding program, though monorchids are capable of siring. Additionally, it must be noted that monorchids frequently sire dogs with the same deficiency, and to introduce this into a bloodline knowingly is an unwritten sin in the fancy. Also, a monorchid can sire dogs that are completely sterile. Such dogs are referred to as cryptorchids and have no testicles.

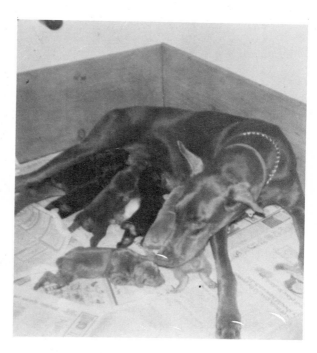

Storm Suns Ginger Brand with her first litter, which contained all four colors. Bred and owned by Mrs. Charles LaPlant of Shortsville, New York.

If you want the dog to be a member of the family, the best selection would probably be a female. You can always go out for stud service if you should decide to breed. You can choose the bloodlines doing the most winning because they should be bred true to type, and you will not have to foot the bill for the financing of a show career. You can always keep a male from your first litter that will bear your own "kennel name" if you have decided to proceed in the kennel "business."

This beautiful bitch is Marks-Tey Simona at the age of three and one-half months. Her sire was Ch. Laur-ik Procyon of Marks-Tey x Ch. Marks-Tey Yarmine. Bred and owned by Keith and Joanna Walker, Marks-Tey Dobermans, Centralia, Illinois.

An additional consideration in the male versus female decision for the private owners is that with males there might be the problem of leg-lifting and with females there is the inconvenience while they are in season. However, this need not be the problem it used to be—pet shops sell "pants" for both sexes, which help to control the situation.

THE PLANNED PARENTHOOD BEHIND YOUR PUPPY

Never be afraid to ask pertinent questions about the puppy, as well as questions about the sire and dam. Feel free to ask the breeder if you might see the dam, the purpose of your visit to determine her general health and her appearance as a representative of the breed. Ask also to see the sire if the breeder is the owner. Ask what the puppy has been fed and should be fed after weaning. Ask to see the pedigree, and inquire if the litter or the individual puppies have been registered with the American Kennel Club, how many of the temporary and/or permanent inoculations the puppy has had, when and if the puppy has been wormed and whether it has had any illness, disease or infection.

You need not ask if the puppy is housebroken. . . it won't mean much. He may have gotten the idea as to where "the place" is where he lives now, but he will need new training to learn where "the place" is in his new home! And you can't really expect too much from puppies at this age anyway. Housebreaking is entirely up to the new owner. We know puppies always eliminate when they first awaken and sometimes dribble when they get excited. If friends and relatives are coming over to see the new puppy, make sure he is walked just before he greets them at the front door. This will help.

The normal time period for puppies around three months of age to eliminate is about every two or three hours. As the time draws near, either take the puppy out or indicate the newspapers for the same purpose. Housebreaking is never easy, but anticipation is about 90 per cent of solving the problem. The schools that offer to housebreak your dog are virtually useless. Here again the puppy will learn the "place" at the schoolhouse, but coming home he will need special training for the new location.

A reputable breeder will welcome any and all questions you might ask and will voluntarily offer additional information, if only to

Four-year-old Marilyn Wallhofer wins first prize in the 1972 Junior Handling competition at the Riverview Doberman Pinscher Club show. Her bitch is named Berghof's Star Sapphire, owned by Terri Wallhofer.

And this is what Santa found at the Ferrari's house! Ten Doberman puppies sired by Damasyn The Russian out of Damasyn Remarkable. These three-month-old puppies are truly remarkable!

brag about the tedious and loving care he has given the litter. He will also sell a puppy on a 24-hour veterinary approval. This means you have a full day to get the puppy to a veterinarian of your choice to get his opinion on the general health of the puppy before you make a final decision. There should also be veterinary certificates and full particulars on the dates and types of inoculations the puppy has been given up to that time.

PUPPIES AND WORMS

Let us give further attention to the unhappy and very unpleasant subject of worms. Generally speaking, most all puppies—even those raised in clean quarters—come into contact with worms early in life. The worms can be passed down from the mother before birth or picked up during the puppies' first encounters with the earth or their kennel facilities. To say that you must not buy a puppy because of an infestation of worms is nonsensical. You might be passing up a fine animal that can be freed of worms in one short treatment, although a heavy infestation of worms of any kind in a young dog is dangerous and debilitating.

The extent of the infection can be readily determined by a veterinarian, and you might take his word as to whether the future health and conformation of the dog has been damaged. He can prescribe the dosage and supply the medication at the time and you will already have one of your problems solved. The kinds and varieties of worms and how to detect them is described in detail elsewhere in this book and we advise you to check the matter out further if there is any doubt in your mind as to the problems of worms in dogs.

1 ½-year-old Jamey LaPlant obviously enjoys visiting rights in the whelping box with Stormy and her 10 puppies at the LaPlant's Storm Sun Kennels in Shortsville, New York.

VETERINARY INSPECTION

While your veterinarian is going over the puppy you have selected to purchase, you might just as well ask him for his opinion of it as a breed as well as the facts about its general health. While few veterinarins can claim to be breed conformation experts, they usually have a good eye for a worthy specimen and can advise you where to go for further information. Perhaps your veterinarian could also recommend other breeders if you should want another opinion. The veterinarian can point out structural faults or organic problems that affect all breeds and can usually judge whether an animal has been abused or mishandled and whether it is oversized or undersized.

I would like to emphasize here that it is only through this type of close cooperation between owners and veterinarians that we can expect to reap the harvest of modern research in the veterinary field.

Ebonaire's Bravo was exported by breeders Ed and Judy Weiss to Australia at three and one-half months of age. He is pictured here nine months later after settling into his new home with owners Mr. and Mrs. M. McNichol of Melbourne. Bravo has become the sire of many Australian champions.

Most reliable veterinarians are more than eager to learn about various breeds of purebred dogs, and we in turn must acknowledge and apply what they have proved through experience and research in their field. We can buy and breed the best dog in the world, but when disease strikes we are only as safe as our veterinarian is capable—so let's keep them informed breed by breed, and dog by dog. The veterinarian represents the difference between life and death!

THE CONDITIONS OF SALE

While it is customary to pay for the puppy before you take it away with you, you should be able to give the breeder a deposit if there is any doubt about the puppy's health. You might also (depending on local laws) postdate a check to cover the 24-hour veterinary approval. If you decide to take the puppy, the breeder is required to supply you with a pedigree, along with the puppy's registration paper. He is also obliged to supply you with complete information about the inoculations and American Kennel Club instructions on how to transfer ownership of the puppy into your name.

A typical inquisitive three-month-old Dobe puppy bred by the Dama-syn Kennels, Roslyn Heights, New York.

Russtuns
Aurora and
Tavey's Iona,
owned by
Blanche and
Charles
Wileman,
Russtun
Dobermanns,
Hants, England.

Some breeders will offer buyers time payment plans for convenience if the price on a show dog is very high or if deferred payments are the only way you can purchase the dog. However, any such terms must be worked out between buyer and breeder and should be put in writing to avoid later complications.

You will find most breeders cooperative if they believe you are sincere in your love for the puppy and that you will give it the proper home and the show ring career it deserves (if it is sold as a show quality specimen of the breed). Remember, when buying a show dog, it is impossible to guarantee nature. A breeder can only tell you what he *believes* will develop into a show dog. . . so be sure your breeder is an honest one.

Also, if you purchase a show prospect and promise to show the dog, you definitely should show it! It is a waste to have a beautiful dog that deserves recognition in the show ring sitting at home as a family pet, and it is unfair to the breeder. This is especially true if the breeder offered you a reduced price because of the advertising his kennel and bloodlines would receive by your showing the dog in the ring. If you want a pet, buy a pet. Be honest about it, and let the breeder decide on this basis which is the best dog for you. Your conscience will be clear and you'll both be doing a real service to the breed.

BUYING A SHOW PUPPY

If you are positive about breeding and showing your dog, make it clear that you intend to do so so that the breeder will sell you the best possible puppy. If you are dealing with an established kennel, you will have to rely partially if not entirely on their choice, since they know their bloodlines and what they can expect from the breeding. They know how their stock develops, and it would be foolish of them to sell you a puppy that could not stand up as a show specimen representing their stock in the ring.

However, you must also realize that the breeder may be keeping the best puppy in the litter to show and breed himself. If this is the case, you might be wise to select the best puppy of the opposite sex so that the dogs will not be competing against one another in the show rings for their championship title.

Anxious mother checks on eating habits of her litter which was sired by American import Phileen's Duty Free of Tavey. Bred and owned by Charles and Blanche Wileman, Russtun Dobermanns, Hants, England.

THE PURCHASE PRICE

Prices vary on all puppies, of course, but a good show prospect at six weeks to six months of age will sell for several hundred dollars. If the puppy is really outstanding, and the pedigree and parentage is also outstanding, the price will be even higher. Honest breeders, however, will be around the same figure, so price should not be a deciding factor in your choice. If there is any question as to the current price range, a few telephone calls to different kennels will give you a good average. Breeders will usually stand behind their puppies; should something drastically wrong develop, such as hip dysplasia, etc., their obligation to make an adjustment is usually honored. Therefore, your cost is covered.

Photographed in 1966, Ch. Damasyn The Boatswain's beautiful daughters out of Ch. Brown's Wendy, C.D. From left to right, Rory, Rondi, Rissi, and Raini when they were one year old.

THE COST OF BUYING ADULT STOCK

Prices for adult dogs fluctuate greatly. Some grown dogs are offered free of charge to good homes; others are put out with owners on breeders' terms. But don't count on getting a "bargain" if it doesn't cost you anything! Good dogs are always in demand, and worthy studs or brood bitches are expensive. Prices for them can easily go up into the four-figure range. Take an expert with you if you intend to make this sort of investment. Just make sure the "expert" is free of professional jealousy and will offer an unprejudiced opinion. If you are reasonably familiar with the Standard, and get the expert's opinion, between the two you can usually come up with a proper decision.

Buying grown stock does remove some of the risk if you are planning a kennel. You will know exactly what you are getting for your foundation stock and will also save time on getting your kennel started.

14. GROOMING THE DOBERMAN PINSCHER

Contrary to the belief of many people new to the Doberman Pinscher breed, the Doberman *does* require grooming, whether it is to be a show dog or just a family companion. Shorthaired breeds shed coat just as do the longhaired breeds. A rather frequent brushing is therefore necessary to remove the dead hair, encourage the new hair growth and keep the skin supple and clean. The rubber curry comb is best for a daily rubbing down to keep the coat sleek and clean. Bathing is seldom necessary unless the dog has gotten into some sort of situation where an odor has been left behind on the coat and/or skin. Normally a general going-over with the curry comb will take care of the daily grooming, especially for the pet Doberman.

GROOMING THE SHOW DOG

Grooming for the show ring is something else again. Preparation cannot start a day or two before the show if you expect your dog to look its best. The daily going over with the rubber curry comb is a must for the show prospect. Additional care is also essential and should start when the dog is still a puppy.

Since the show dog will be spending a great deal of time on the grooming table, it is important that you teach it at an early age how to not only jump up onto it when required (and jumping down on command when grooming is completed), but that it get used to standing still on the table for as much time as is necessary to accomplish the required grooming.

Start by trimming off the eyebrow hairs and the whiskers with curved blunt-end scissors. There is no "sound" involved in this procedure and it will get the dog accustomed to your working around its eyes and ears.

Next get after the areas which need to be trimmed. With thinning shears trim the areas where the cowlicks appear. Cowlicks are the areas where hairs turn up or away from "the lay of hair" to grow in another direction. On the chest is the most obvious example, where the cowlicks or little swirls of hair all come together. Trim this out with the shears and also the ridge that runs from the base of the ear

Ch. Checkmates Beau Geste pictured winning under judge Peggy Adamson. This Dion son was bred and is owned by Bill Haines of Ohio.

down the neck. Very carefully thin it out until it seems to blend in with the rest of the coat. The neck also requires this thinning at times.

There "normal" cowlicks are not to be confused with the occasional cowlicks found on other areas of the body and which are not disqualifications in the show ring or mentioned in the Standard for the breed. They are still undesirable, and serious consideration should be given to their occurrence in show dogs.

There are also areas on the Doberman which must be clipped before an appearance in the show ring. While electric clippers are used by the experienced groomer, beginners are strongly urged to use hand clippers. I have seen such havoc wrought on dogs by inexperienced or careless people with electric clippers in their hands that I cannot advise using them. The proper use and handling should be learned first-hand from an experienced person and practiced weeks before show time so that your "beginner's mistakes" can be remedied before show time! Clipper burns and cuts are nasty and painful injuries, and I repeat my request that you learn at the elbow of an experienced Doberman owner, since you will be working on many tender and important areas of the dog's body, such as the area around the ears. As with shorthaired cats, the edges of the ears should be trimmed as close as possible to the actual edge. The inner ear must also be trimmed and so must the hairs at the base of the inside or opening of the ear.

Hopefully you will start your clippers ahead of time so that the dog will become accustomed to the sound before you approach him. If you notice any apprehension at all, you can plug the ears with wads of cotton to help cut down the noise. If the dog is still uneasy, use the clippers in another area before approaching the head.

There may be hairs to be clipped off on the stomach and the back of the pasterns. Hair in this area should be removed as well as any hair between the toes.

The Doberman tail needs trimming with scissors. Stray hairs may extend straight out from the very end or hairs may grow too long around the sides. Eveness on all sides and the leveling off of the end is what is required for the smooth look. Scissors should also be used to trim down the raised hairs along the shanks. These hairs may extend from around the vent area down toward the hocks and should be scissored off so that the hair blends in smoothly with the rest of the coat.

Once again, the best possible method of learning how to trim the Doberman is to observe an experienced groomer willing to share his knowledge and expertise with you. Many breeders offer this service to those people who buy puppies from them and realize the advantage of Dobermans bearing their kennel names looking their very best in the show ring. This service should be discussed at the time you purchase your puppy and again several weeks before you intend to start showing your dog.

OTHER GROOMING POINTS

I have always saved the grooming of the feet until the very last of the grooming session. We must assume that whether your dog is a pet or for show a weekly cleaning of the ears and cutting the nails will have become a routine matter. Dogs are extremely cautious about their feet since they are such an important part to their survival, so it is wise to get them used to having their nails cut at a very early age. A weekly cutting of the nails will keep them as short as they should normally be, yet without causing excess bleeding since the cuticle will not grow too long when the nails are kept cut back.

The same routine applies to the cleaning of the teeth. Teeth should be checked on a regular basis so that large deposits of tartar do not accumulate and require major scaling sessions, either before shows or on a frequent schedule. Diet and chemical content of the drinking water in your area can influence tartar or coloration, and it might be wise to consult your veterinarian on any possible adjustment which could modify the situation if it is having an adverse effect on your dog's teeth.

THE DAY OF THE SHOW

With all of the above taken care of prior to the day of the show, it should only be necessary to give the dogs a few last minute touches once you arrive at the show grounds and prepare to go into the ring. A last minute going over with a show coat pad (sold at all pet shops and most show ground concessions) will usually put that lovely last minute shine on the coat and show up any stray hairs you might have missed during your trimming and scissoring session. Trim these stray hairs off and as a final touch, when necessary, rub a little dab of petroleum jelly over the dog's nose to make it shine and remove any traces of "salt" which might have accumulated from his panting during the car trip to the show.

15. GENETICS

No one can guarantee the workings of nature. But, with facts and theories as guides, you can plan, at least on paper, a litter of puppies that should fulfill your fondest expectations. Since the ultimate purpose of breeding is to try to improve the breed, or maintain it at the highest possible standard, such planning should be earnestly done, no matter how uncertain particular elements may be.

There are a few terms with which you should become familiar to help you understand the breeding procedure and the workings of genetics. The first thing that comes to mind is a set of formulae known as Mendelian Laws. Gregor Mendel was an Austrian cleric and botanist born July 22, 1822 in what is now named Hyncice and is in Czechoslovakia. He developed his theories on heredity by working for several years with garden peas. A paper on his work was published in a scientific journal in 1866, but for many years it went unnoticed. Today the laws derived from these experiments are basic to all studies of genetics and are employed by horticulturists and animal breeders.

To use these laws as applicable to the breeding of dogs, it is necessary to understand the physical aspects of reproduction. First, dogs possess reproductive glands called gonads. The male gonads are the testicles and there are produced the sperms (spermatozoa) that impregnate the female. Eggs (ova) are produced in the female gonads (ovaries). When whelped, the bitch possesses in rudimentary form all the eggs that will develop throughout her life, whereas spermatozoa are in continual production within the male gonads. When a bitch is mature enough to reproduce, she periodically comes in heat (estrus). Then a number of eggs descend from the ovaries via the fallopian tubes and enter the two horns of the uterus. There they are fertilized by male sperm deposited in semen while mating, or they pass out if not fertilized.

In the mating of dogs, there is what is referred to as a tie, a period during which anatomical features bind the male and female together and about 600 million spermatozoa are ejected into the female to fertilize the ripened eggs. When sperm and ripe eggs meet, zygotes are created and these one-celled future puppies descend from the fallopian tubes, attach themselves to the walls of the uterus, and begin the developmental process of cell production known as mitosis. With all inherited characteristics determined as the zygote was formed, the dam then assumes her role as an incubator for the developing organisms. She has been bred and is in whelp; in these circumstances she also serves in the exchange of gases and in furnishing nourishment for the puppies forming within.

Let us take a closer look at what is happening during the breeding process. We know that the male deposits millions of sperms within the female and that the number of ripe eggs released by the female will determine the number of puppies in the litter. Therefore, those breeders who advertise a stud as a "producer of large litters" do not know the facts or are not sticking to them. The bitch determines the size of the litter; the male sperm determines the sex of the puppies. Half of the millions of sperm involved in a mating carry the characteristic that determines development of a male and the other half carry the factor which triggers development of a female, and distribution of sex is thus decided according to random pairings of sperms and eggs.

Each dog and bitch possesses 39 pairs of chromosomes in each body cell; these pairs are split up in the formation of germ cells so that each one carries half of the hereditary complement. The chromosomes carry the genes, approximately 150,000 like peas in a pod in each chromosome, and these are the actual factors that determine inherited characteristics. As the chromosomes are split apart and rearranged as to genic pairings in the production of ova and spermatozoa, every zygote formed by the joining of an egg and a sperm receives 39 chromosomes from each to form the pattern of 78 chromosomes inherited from dam and sire which will be reproduced in every cell of the developing individual and determine what sort of animal it will be.

To understand the procedure more clearly, we must know that there are two kinds of genes—dominant and recessive. A dominant gene is one of a pair whose influence is expressed to the exclusion of the effects of the other. A recessive gene is one of a pair whose influence is subdued by the effects of the other, and characteristics determined by recessive genes become manifest only when both genes of a pairing are recessive. Most of the important qualities we wish to perpetuate in our breeding programs are carried by the dominant genes. It is the successful breeder who becomes expert at eliminating undesirable genes and building up the desirable gene patterns.

We have merely touched upon genetics here to point out the importance of planned mating. Any librarian can help you find further information, or books may be purchased offering the very latest findings on canine genetics. It is a fascinating and rewarding program toward creating better dogs.

16. THE POWER IN PEDIGREES

Someone in the dog fancy once remarked that the definition of a show prospect puppy is one third the pedigree, one third what you see and one third what you *hope* it will be! Well, no matter how you break down your qualifying fractions, we all quite agree that good breeding is essential if you have any plans at all for a show career for your dog! Many breeders will buy on pedigree alone, counting largely on what they themselves can do with the puppy by way of feeding, conditioning and training. Needless to say, that very important piece of paper commonly referred to as the pedigree is mighty reassuring to a breeder or buyer new at the game or to one who has a breeding program in mind and is trying to establish his own bloodline.

One of the most fascinating aspects of tracing pedigrees is the way the names of the really great dogs of the past keep appearing in the pedigrees of the great dogs of today—positive proof of the strong influence of heredity and witness to a great deal of truth in the statement that great dogs frequently reproduce themselves, though not necessarily in appearance only. A pedigree represents something of value when one is dedicated to breeding better dogs.

To the novice buyer or one who is perhaps merely switching to another breed and sees only a frolicking, leggy, squirming bundle of energy in a fur coat, a pedigree can mean everything! To those of us who believe in heredity, a pedigree is more like an insurance policy—so always read them carefully and take heed!

The size of this book prevents reproducing pedigrees of all the important Dobermans which have left their mark in the breed over the years, but we do include a few of the early prominent dogs and a few pedigrees which indicate the cross-breedings of some of the important kennels during the years when the Doberman breed was taking hold in this country and establishing itself as a prominent member of the Working Group.

For the even more serious breeder of today who wishes to make a further study of bloodlines in relation to his breeding program, the American Kennel Club library stud books can and should be consulted. However, we hope that the selection of those included in this book will be of interest.

CH. RANCHO DOBE'S STORM

Ch. Rancho Dobe's Primo

Ch. Alcor v Millsdod

Ch. Westphalia's Uranus

Ch. Maida v Coldod

Ch. Rancho Dobe's Kashmir

Int. Ch. Roxanna's Emperor v Reemon

Rhumba of Rancho Dobe

Ch. Maedel v Randahof

Mr. Butch v Rittenhouse

Sgr. Ch. Ferry v Raufelsen of Giralda

Kara v Randahof

Ch. Indra v Lindenhof

Sgr. Ch. Muck v Brunia

Mitzi of Lawnwood

Ch. Maedel von Randahof, dam of the famous Ch. Rancho Dobe's Storm, owned by the Edwards of California.

Ch. Rancho Dobe's Roulette, a half-sister to the famous Ch. Rancho Dobe's Storm, whom she rivalled for show-win records! Owned by the late Vivian Edwards of Los Angeles, California.

Ch. Rancho Dobe's
Presto, brother of
Ch. Rancho Dobe's
Primo (also owned
by the Edwards of
Rancho Dobe Kennel
fame).

Magnificent headstudy of
Ch. Favoriet von Franzhof,
a red son of Ch.
Westphalia's Uranus,
owned by the Westphalia
Kennels.

Stormie and his handler Peter Knoop go for a run in Greenwich, Connecticut. This was a part of the conditioning of the great Ch. Rancho Dobe's Storm, twice a Westminster Best in Show winner.

Owner Len Carey and Stormie at home in Greenwich, Connecticut. This photograph was taken by a *Life* magazine photographer for a feature article on Stormie which appeared in a 1950 issue.

Opposite:
An informal photographed captured after the second winning of "the Garden"! Shirley Carey and Stormie pose for the news photographers after his 1953 victory.

Ch. Derek of Mark's Tey, sired by Ch. Brown's Eric x Ch. Damasyn the Waltzing Brook, C.D. Derek sired Tamerlane Alert Abbie out of Ch. Ladaska's Ebony Charm. He is owned by Keith and Joanna Walker, Mark's Tey Dobermans, Centralia, Illinois.

AMERICAN & CANADIAN CH. BUSHIDO YODAN

SIRE

Ch. Highbriar Bandana
- **Ch.** Felix Vom Ahrtal
  - **Ch.** Lakecrest's Thunderstorm
    - **Ch.** Rancho Dobes Storm
    - **Ch.** Apache Lady Of Lakecrest
  - **Ch.** Willa Vom Ahrtal
    - **Ch.** Dorian Vom Ahrtal
    - **Ch.** Electra Vom Ahrtal
- **Ch.** Highbriar Constant Comment
  - **Ch.** Florian Vom Ahrtal, CD
    - **Ch.** Lakecrest's Thunderstorm
    - **Ch.** Willa Vom Ahrtal
  - **Ch.** Highbriar Tea For Two CDX
    - **Ch.** Steb's Top Skipper
    - Highbriar Stormette

Am. & Can. Ch. Hotai Sweet William

Hotai Sibyl Selene
- **Int. Ch.** Kohlen
  - **Ch.** Lakecrest's Thunderstorm
    - **Ch.** Rancho Dobes Storm
    - **Ch.** Apache Lady Of Lakecrest
  - Dobe Acres Chi-Chi
    - **Ch.** Dobe Acres Delmira
    - Dobe Acres Pretty Girl
- Tamerlane Alert Abbie
  - **Ch.** Derek of Mark's Tey
    - **Ch.** Brown's Eric
    - **Ch.** Damasyn The Waltzing Brool
  - **Ch.** Ladaska's Ebony Charm
    - Rauschbaum Prinz v. Dresden
    - Borong The Saucy Susan, CD

DAM

Highbriar Mustang
- **Ch.** Felix Vom Ahrtal
  - **Ch.** Lakecrest's Thunderstorm
    - **Ch.** Rancho Dobe's Storm
    - **Ch.** Apache Lady Of Lakecrest
  - **Ch.** Willa Vom Ahrtal
    - **Ch.** Dorian Vom Ahrtal, CD
    - **Ch.** Elektra Vom Ahrtal, CD
- **Ch.** Highbriar Constant Comment
  - **Ch.** Florian Vom Ahrtal, CD
    - **Ch.** Lakecrest's Thunderstorm
    - **Ch.** Willa Vom Ahrtal
  - **Ch.** Highbriar Tea For Two, UD
    - **Ch.** Steb's Top Skipper
    - Highbriar Stormette, CDX

Queen of Spades II

Fritz's Dobie Debonaire
- Eric Von Maximilian, CD
  - Baron Maximilian
    - Dobe Acres Mozecho
    - Red of Windy Acres
  - Lady Chela v. Pontchartrain
    - Alexis Von Aned
    - Dobe Dawn of Delaware
- Princess Doty Madchen Plaas
  - Quinacres Carioca
    - Highbriar Night Hawk
    - Ching Von Spitz
  - Ty-Ty Schon Madchen
    - Kieth Van Plaas
    - Bro-Ken H's Schon Madchen

Ch. Felix vom Ahrtal, sire of 29 champion sons and daughters and over 100 champion grandchildren! Bred and owned by Tess Henseler of the Ahrtal Kennels in Ottsville, Pennsylvania.

Opposite:
Beautiful headstudy of Ch. Dagobert vom Ahrtal, who was famous in the breed several years ago. Owned by Tess Henseler, Ahrtal Kennels, Ottsville, Pennsylvania. The sire was Ch. Delegate v d Elbe x Meadowmist Isis of Ahrtal.

CHAMPION DEREK OF MARKS TEY

Brown and Rust

28½ inches

Ch. Derek of Marks Tey
- Ch. Brown's Eric
  - Ch. Dictator v Glenhugel
    - Ch. Blank v Domstadt
    - Ch. Ossi v Stahlhelm
  - Ch. Dows Dame of Kilburn
    - Ch. Dictator v Glenhugel
    - Ch. Dows Dodie v Kienlesburg
- Ch. Damasyn the Waltzing Brook C.D.
  - Ch. Damasyn the Solitaire
    - Ch. Dictator v Glenhugel
    - Ch. Damasyn the Sultry Sister
  - Damasyn the Winter Waltz
    - Ch. Dictator V Glenhugel
    - Damasyn the Wild Wing

Breeder - Owner
Joanna Walker, Marks-Tey Dobermans
Rt. 4 Salem, Illinois - Phone 2591

Ch. Damasyn The Solitaire, C.D.X., and Ch. Brown's Evangeline, C.D., both owned and handled by Peggy Adamson. "Evvie" was Dictator's 49th champion, and she was out of his granddaughter, Ch. Damasyn The Sultry Sister. Damasyn The Solitaire was sire of Ch. Damasyn The Waltzing Brook, C.D. The Waltzing Brook is the dam of Ch.

A classic profile photograph of the great Ch. Dictator von Glenhugel, sire of 52 champions. Imported by Peggy and Bob Adamson of Roslyn Heights, New York.

Ch. Mark's Tey Melanie, dam of eight champions and one of the top brood bitches at the Mark's Tey Kennels of Keith and Joanna Walker in Centralia, Illinois.

Ch. Carla von Glenhugel, full sister to the famous Ch. Dictator von Glenhugel; owned by the Radford Kennels in Nashville, Tennessee back in the 1950's.

Ch. Edah v Trail, dam of three champions, all sired by Ch. Dictator von Glenhugel, and known as the "B" litter. They were champions Brenda, Bonnie and Burt v Trail; owned by T. and E. Holliday of Los Angeles, California.

Opposite:
Ch. Marks-Tey Vale, winner of the 1974-1975 Top Producing Dam award from the Doberman Pinscher Club of America. Her breeder, Joanna Walker, tied for First Place as Leading Breeder of the Year for the club as well. Vale's sire was Gra-Lemaire Demetrius v d Victor x Ch. Marks-Tey Melanie.

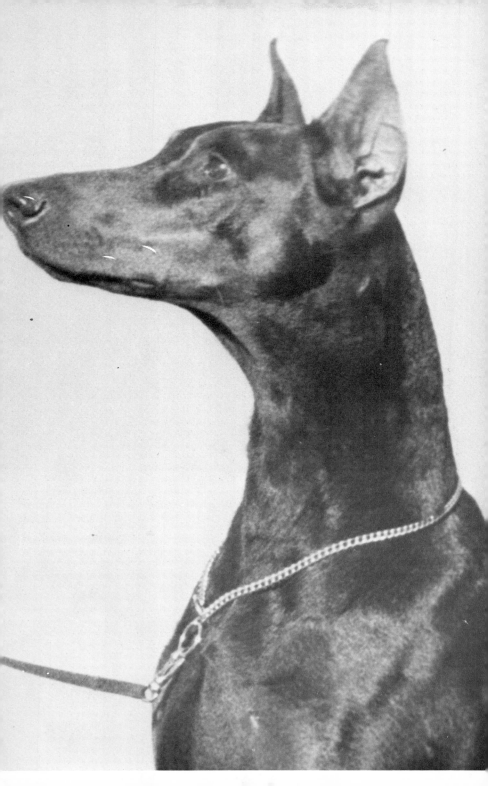

CH. AXEL VON TANNENWALD

SIRE: CH. D-Dow's Bonaparte of Falstaff

- **CH. Falstaff v Ahrtal**
  - CH. Delegate vd Elbe
    - CH. Kama of Westphalia
      - CH. Westphalias Uranus
      - Alma v Molnar
    - CH. Belydia v Elbe
      - CH. Domossi of Marienland
      - CH. Dorica vd Elbe
  - Meadowmist Isis of Ahrtal
    - CH. Emperor of Marienland
      - CH. Domossi of Marienland
      - CH. Westphalias Rhemba
    - Dow's Ditty of Marienland
      - CH. Dictator v Glenhugel
      - Dow's Dodie of Kienlesburg
- **CH. Brown's Feegee**
  - CH. Kilburn Cameron
    - CH. Alcor v Millsdod
      - CH. Westphalias Uranus
      - CH. Madia v Coldod
    - CH. Kilburn Audacity
      - CH. Emperor of Marienland
      - CH. Dow's Illena of Marienland
  - CH. Brown's Belinda
    - CH. Emperor of Marienland
      - CH. Domossi of Marienland
      - CH. Westphalias Rhemba
    - CH. Dow's Dame of Kilburn
      - CH. Dictator v Glenhugel
      - CH. Dow's Dodie of Kienlesburg

DAM: CH. Kay Hill's Witch Soubretta

- **TRI-INT.CH. Borong the Warlock**
  - CH. Astor v Grenzweg
    - SGR.&CH. Bordo vd Angelburg
      - SGR. Casso v Kleimwaldheim
      - Hertha vd Brunoburg
    - Illa vd Leinenstadt SCH II
      - Dreby vd Brunoburg
      - Gradin v Paulindorf
  - CH. Florowill Allure
    - CH. Damasyn the Sage
      - CH. Dictator v Glenhugel
      - Damasyn the Song
    - TRI-INT.CH. Damasyn the Pert Patrice
      - CH. Meadowmist Elegy
      - CH. Damasyn the Sonnet
- **CH. Kay Hill's Paint the Town Red**
  - INT.CH. Defender of Jan Har
    - CH. Saracen of Reklaw
      - CH. Dictator v Glenhugel
      - Kay of Reklaw
    - CH. Cissi of Jan Har
      - INT.CH. Brigum of Jan Har
      - Kilburn Jiffy
  - CH. Westerholz Elita
    - INT.CH. Beltane of Tamarack
      - CH. Ximines of Elblac
      - Zita of Elblac
    - CH. Erica of Damhof
      - CH. Kama of Westphalia
      - Topaz of Westphalia

Ch. Axel v Tannenwald, owned by Betty Moore of Houston, Texas. Axel's illustrious show career included 18 Bests in Show (five all-breed and 13 Specialties), 29 Group Firsts, 26 Group Seconds, 15 Group Thirds and eight Group Fourths. Axel was listed among the Top Ten Dobermans in the Phillips System for five consecutive years, 1965-1969. He died in May, 1973, at ten years of age.

Ch. Duvetyn of Stonecroft, owned by Francis F.H. Fleitmann, and the second of only three Dobermans ever to win the Westchester Kennel Club show. Dictator was the first, Duvetyn second and Tsushima was third.

Ch. Meadowmist Elegy, owned by Ginnie Knauer, and a son of her famous Ch. Emperor of Marienland. Photographed at the Bucks County Kennel Club show in May, 1951.

Ch. Echo of Marienland, owned by Colonel Lambert Caine. Echo was a litter sister to the famed Ch. Emperor of Marienland and was bred by Richard Webster.

Best of Breed at the 1944 Doberman Pinscher Club of America Specialty Show held in Chicago Illinois was Ch. Dictator von Glenhugel, owned by Peggy Adamson of the Damasyn Kennels in Roslyn Heights, New York, and pictured with him here. His breeder, John Cholley, handled him to this wonderful win under the late judge Anton Rost.

The great Ch. Emperor of Marienland, bred by Dick Webster at his famous Marienland Kennels in Baltimore during the early days of Dobermans. Emperor was sired by Ch. Domossi of Marienland out of Ch. Westphalia's Rembha; Emperor was owned by Ginnie Knauer.

Eleanor Carpenter's Assy v Illerblick pictured in a sylvan setting many years ago.

Dominican Champion Blackjax Ace O'Spades wins Best of Breed at a 1975 show in the Dominican Republic. Bred by Nancy Flax of Maryland, Ace is owned by Cesar Sierra of Puerto Rico and handled by his daughter Yvonne, who is active as a junior handler.

Best in Show at the 1976 Japanese Kennel Club Specialty Show was two-year-old Break of South Dobes, Japanese-bred red male owned by H. Itani. Pictured on the left is breeder M. Minami; the handler is K. Kasumi. Peggy Adamson was the first woman ever to be allowed to judge in Japan.

Ch. Maida von Coldod, owned by Mrs. A.E. Mills and photographed in 1941.

Opposite:
Peggy Adamson's favorite headstudy of her beloved Ch. Dictator von Glenhugel. This sire of 52 champions was bred by John Cholley and purchased by the Adamsons in 1941 when he was just two months old. Dictator was at the peak of his success in the 1940's and ranks with the all-time greats in the history of the breed.

The winners at the 1943 Kennel Club of Philadelphia show were Ch. Domossi of Marienland (pictured with Dick Webster) and on the right, Ch. Westphalia's Ursala with Howard Mohr. Col. Dodson was the judge.

Ch. Damasyn The Sonnet, C.D., a red daughter of Ch. Dictator von Glenhugel out of Damasyn The Song. Co-owned by Peggy Adamson and Agnes Johnson Eathorne, Sonnet was handled by her breeder, Mrs. Adamson, to her championship by 19 months of age. Bred only once, she produced two champions; one, the famous American, Canadian and Cuban Ch. Damasyn The Pert Patrice, C.D.X., the granddam of the equally famous Warlock.

CH. GRA-LEMOR DEMETRIUS V D VICTOR

Ch. Damasyn Derringer

Duke of Lombardi

Ch. Damasyn The Solitaire

Stark's Black Beauty

Damasyn The Tcheska

Ch. Steb's Captain Treble

Damasyn The Royal Flush

Jerry Run's Boto Sprite

Ch. Steb's Top Skipper

Ch. Dortmund Delly's Colonel Jet

Damasyn The Easter Bonnet

Venture's Blue Waltz

Ch. Rebel of Jerry Run

Ch. Venture of Jerry Run

Ch. Damasyn The Solitaire, C.D.X., sire of 15 champions; this magnificent animal was bred and owned by Peggy Adamson of the Damasyn Kennels in Roslyn Heights, New York. The sire was Ch. Dictator von Glenhugel x Ch. Damasyn The Sultry Sister. Solitaire was whelped in 1951 and died in 1961. This photograph was taken in 1955 by William Brown.

Damasyn The Easter Bonnet, a bitch from the first litter sired by the great Ch. Rancho Dobe's Storm out of Damasyn Sikhandi, and the only sister of the famous Ch. Damasyn The Solitaire, C.D.X. The Easter Bonnet was famous as the dam of another great dog, Ch. Steb's Top Skipper.

Ch. Gra-Lemor Plain 'n' Fancy Lil Eva. She is sister to the famous Ch. Gra-Lemor Demetrius, top show-winner in the 1970's.

Headstudy of Peggy Adamson's famous Ch. Damasyn Derringer, sire of 17 champions.

Damasyn Carly of Jerseystone pictured winning on the way to his championship under the late judge Alva Rosenberg at the 1970 Kitaning Show. Bred and owned by Peggy Adamson. He is handled here by Pat Doniere for the Dennis Clardys of St. Joseph, Missouri. Carly is a son of the famous Ch. Damasyn Derringer and is sire of 17 champions.

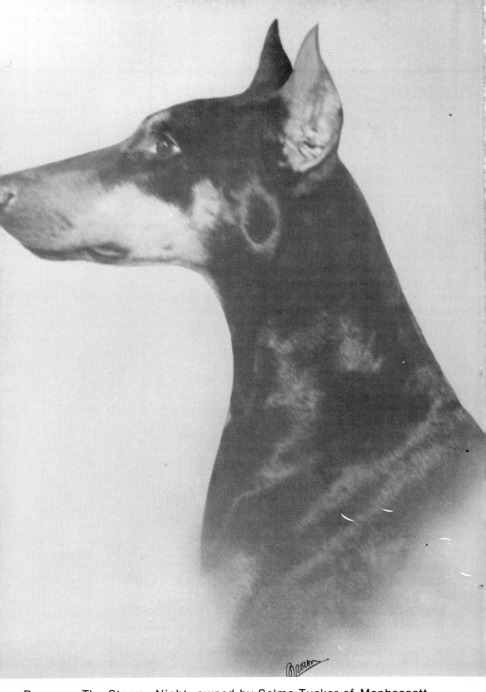

Damasyn The Stormy Night, owned by Selma Tucker of Manhassett, Long Island, New York. The sire was Ch. Rancho Dobe's Storm x Damasyn Sikhandi. It was the first litter to be sired by Storm. Stormy Night is a litter brother to Damasyn Easter Bonnet. Bred by Peggy Adamson of Roslyn Heights, New York.

Ch. Alisaton Kinderwicke is pictured going Best of Winners at the Doberman Pinscher Club of America 1973 Specialty Show from the Bred by Exhibitor Class. She finished for her championship with three majors, always owner-breeder-handled. The sire was Ch. Damasyn The Troycen x Ch. Arabar's Impertinence. The young owner is Gwyn Lynn Satalino of Old Westbury, New York.

17. BREEDING YOUR DOBERMAN

Let us assume the time has come for your dog to be bred, and you have decided you are in a position to enjoy producing a litter of puppies that you hope will make a contribution to the breed. The bitch you purchased is sound, her temperament is excellent and she is a most worthy representative of the breed.

You have taken a calendar and counted off the ten days since the first day of red staining and have determined the tenth to fourteenth day, which will more than likely be the best days for the actual mating. You have additionally counted off 65 to 63 days before the puppies are likely to be born to make sure everything necessary for their arrival will be in good order by that time.

From the moment the idea of having a litter occurred to you, your thoughts should have been given to the correct selection of a proper stud. Here again the novice would do well to seek advice on analyzing pedigrees and tracing bloodlines for your best breedings. As soon as the bitch is in season and you see color (or staining) and a swelling of the vulva, it is time to notify the owner of the stud you selected and make appointments for the breedings. There are several pertinent questions you will want to ask the stud owners after having decided upon the pedigree. The owners, naturally, will also have a few questions they wish to ask you. These questions will concern your bitch's bloodlines, health, age, how many previous litters if any, etc.

THE HEALTH OF THE BREEDING STOCK

Some of your first questions should concern whether or not the stud has already proved himself by siring a normal healthy litter. Also inquire as to whether or not the owners have had a sperm count made to determine just exactly how fertile or potent the stud is. Also ask whether he has been X-rayed for hip dysplasia and found to be clear. Determine for yourself whether the dog has two normal testicles.

When considering your bitch for this mating, you must take into consideration a few important points that lead to a successful breeding. You and the owner of the stud will want to recall whether she has had normal heat cycles, whether there were too many runts in the litter, and whether Caesarean section was ever necessary. Has she ever had a vaginal infection? Could she take care of her puppies by herself, or was there a milk shortage? How many surviving puppies were there from the litter, and what did they grow up to be in comparison to the requirements of the breed Standard?

Don't buy a bitch that has problem heats and has never had a litter. But don't be afraid to buy a healthy maiden bitch, since chances are, if she is healthy and from good stock, she will be a healthy producer. Don't buy a monorchid male, and certainly not a cryptorchid. If there is any doubt in your mind about his potency, get a sperm count from the veterinarian. Older dogs that have been good producers and are for sale are usually not too hard to find at good established kennels. If they are not too old and have sired quality show puppies, they can give you some excellent show stock from which to establish your own breeding lines.

Damasyn Intermezzo, sired by Ch. Damasyn The Troycen and Damasyn The Kindl. Owned by Barry and Jim Pollack of Aspen, Colorado.

THE DAY OF THE MATING

Now that you have decided upon the proper male and female combination to produce what you hope will be—according to the pedigrees—a fine litter of puppies, it is time to set the date. You have selected the two days (with a one day lapse in between) that you feel are best for the breeding, and you call the owner of the stud. The bitch always goes to the stud, unless, of course, there are extenuating circumstances. You set the date and the time and arrive with the bitch *and* the money.

Standard procedure is payment of a stud fee at the time of the first breeding, if there is a tie. For the stud fee, you are entitled to two breedings with ties. Contracts may be written up with specific conditions on breeding terms, of course, but this is general procedure. Often a breeder will take the pick of a litter to protect and maintain his bloodlines. This can be especially desirable if he needs an outcross for his breeding program or if he wishes to continue his own bloodlines if he sold you the bitch to start with, and this mating will continue his line-breeding program. This should all be worked out ahead of time and written and signed before the two dogs are bred. Remember that the payment of the stud fee is for the services of the stud—not for a guarantee of a litter of puppies. This is why it is so important to

"Please don't eat the daisies!" Roanoke Nayrilla Wild Melody, the patient observer, and Roanoke Starlight at 10 weeks of age, do not seem to know that flowers are not to be disturbed. Both puppies whelped in 1966 and both sired by Vanessa's Little Dictator of Tavey. Melody's dam was Ch. Opinion of Tavey and Starlight's was Ch. Cadereyta of Roanoke. Owned by the Richardsons, Roanoke Kennels, Essex, England.

Champion Ebonaire's Laurel, owned by Alton Anderson of New City, New York. The sire was Ch. Damasyn Bo-Tairic x Ebonaire's Betsy Ross, C.D. Photograph by Mr. Anderson, well-known dog photographer.

Bluebell, the donkey, visits the Drumpellier Doberman puppies in their run in Hampshire, England. These puppies were bred by their owners, Brian and Vi Blachford.

make sure you are using a proven stud. Bear in mind also that the American Kennel Club will not register a litter of puppies sired by a male that is under eight months of age. In the case of an older dog, they will not register a litter sired by a dog over 12 years of age, unless there is a witness to the breeding in the form of a veterinarian or other responsible person.

Many studs over 12 years of age are still fertile and capable of producing puppies, but if you do not witness the breeding there is always the danger of a "substitute" stud being used to produce a litter. This brings up the subject of sending your bitch away to be bred if you cannot accompany her.

The disadvantages of sending a bitch away to be bred are numerous. First of all, she will not be herself in a strange place, so she'll be difficult to handle. Transportation if she goes by air, while reasonably safe, is still a traumatic experience, and there is the danger of her being put off at the wrong airport, not being fed or watered properly, etc. Some bitches get so upset that they go out of season and the trip, which may prove expensive, especially on top of a substantial stud fee, will have been for nothing.

If at all possible, accompany your bitch so that the experience is as comfortable for her as it can be. In other words, make sure before setting this kind of schedule for a breeding that there is no stud in the area that might be as good for her as the one that is far away. Don't sacrifice the proper breeding for convenience, since bloodlines are so important, but put the safety of the bitch above all else. There is always a risk in traveling, since dogs are considered cargo on a plane.

HOW MUCH DOES THE STUD FEE COST?

The stud fee will vary considerably—the better the bloodlines, the more winning the dog does at shows, the higher the fee. Stud service from a top winning dog could run up to $500.00. Here again, there may be exceptions. Some breeders will take part cash and then, say, third pick of the litter. The fee can be arranged by a private contract rather than the traditional procedure we have described.

Here again, it is wise to get the details of the payment of the stud fee in writing to avoid trouble.

The famous sire, Ch. Kilburn Cameron, owned by Edward F. Ackerman of Louisville, Kentucky.

THE ACTUAL MATING

It is always advisable to muzzle the bitch. A terrified bitch may fear-bite the stud, or even one of the people involved, and the wild bitch may snap or attack the stud, to the point where he may become discouraged and lose interest in the breeding. Muzzling can be done with a lady's stocking tied around the muzzle with a half knot, crossed under the chin and knotted at the back of the neck. There is enough "give" in the stocking for her to breathe or salivate freely and yet not open her jaws far enough to bite. Place her in front of her owner, who holds onto her collar and talks to her and calms her as much as possible.

If the male will not mount on his own initiative, it may be necessary for the owner to assist in lifting him onto the bitch, perhaps even in guiding him to the proper place. But usually, the tie is accomplished once the male gets the idea. The owner should remain close at hand, however, to make sure the tie is not broken before an adequate breeding has been completed. After a while the stud may get bored, and try to break away. This could prove injurious. It may be necessary to hold him in place until the tie is broken.

Damasyn The Strawberry Tart, C.D., photographed in 1964 at the age of 5½ years. She is famous as the dam of Am. and Can. Ch. Damasyn The Tartian. Her sire was Ch. Damasyn The Solitaire, C.D.X., and her dam Damasyn The Tcheska. Bred and owned by Peggy Adamson, Damasyn Kennels, Roslyn Heights, New York.

We must stress at this point that while some bitches carry on physically, and vocally, during the tie, there is no way the bitch can be hurt. However, a stud can be seriously or even permanently damaged by a bad breeding. Therefore the owner of the bitch must be reminded that she must not be alarmed by any commotion. All concentration should be devoted to the stud and a successful and properly executed service.

Many people believe that breeding dogs is simply a matter of placing two dogs, a male and a female, in close proximity, and letting nature take its course. While often this is true, you cannot count on it. Sometimes it is hard work, and in the case of valuable stock it is essential to supervise to be sure of the safety factor, especially if one or both of the dogs are inexperienced. If the owners are also inexperienced it may not take place at all!

Marine Captain Robert Adamson, Peggy Adamson's husband (rarely seen in connection with canine activities of any type) pictured with Dictator and Lieut. L. Wilson Davis (on the left), who was honored for his command of all the war dogs in the Southwest Pacific. "Tator," photographed here in May, 1944, helped recruit dogs for the Marines during World War II.

Opposite:
The "First Lady" of Dobermans—Peggy Adamson of Damasyn Kennel fame photographed at the Kamerer home in California in 1967 with Ch. Damasyn The Ardon Arondi, a full sister to Ch. Damasyn Bo-Tairic of Ardon.

ARTIFICIAL INSEMINATION

Breeding by means of artificial insemination is usually unsuccessful, unless under a veterinarian's supervision, and can lead to an infection for the bitch and discomfort for the dog. The American Kennel Club requires a veterinarian's certificate to register puppies from such a breeding. Although the practice has been used for over two decades, it now offers new promise, since research has been conducted to make it a more feasible procedure for the future.

Great dogs may eventually look forward to reproducing themselves years after they have left this earth. There now exists a frozen semen concept that has been tested and found successful. The study, headed by Dr. Stephen W.J. Seager, M.V.B., an instructor at the University of Oregon Medical School, has the financial support of the American Kennel Club, indicating that organization's interest in the work. The study is being monitored by the Morris Animal Foundation of Denver, Colorado.

Dr. Seager announced in 1970 that he had been able to preserve dog semen and to produce litters with the stored semen. The possibilities of selective world-wide breedings by this method are exciting. Imagine simply mailing a vial of semen to the bitch! The perfection of line-breeding by storing semen without the threat of death interrupting the breeding program is exciting, also.

As it stands today, the technique for artificial insemination requires the depositing of semen (taken directly from the dog) into the bitch's vagina, past the cervix and into the uterus by syringe. The correct temperature of the semen is vital, and there is no guarantee of success. The storage method, if successfully adopted, will present a new era in the field of purebred dogs.

THE GESTATION PERIOD

Once the breeding has taken place successfully, the seemingly endless waiting period of about 63 days begins. For the first ten days after the breeding, you do absolutely nothing for the bitch—just spin dreams about the delights you will share with the family when the puppies arrive.

Around the tenth day it is time to begin supplementing the diet of the bitch with vitamins and calcium. We strongly recommend that you take her to your veterinarian for a list of the proper or perhaps necessary supplements and the correct amounts of each for your particular bitch. Guesses, which may lead to excesses or insufficiencies, can ruin a litter. For the price of a visit to your veterinarian, you will be confident that you are feeding properly.

The bitch should be free of worms, of course, and if there is any doubt in your mind, she should be wormed now, before the third week of pregnancy. Your veterinarian will advise you on the necessity of this and proper dosage as well.

Lynarcl Annej, nine weeks old with breeder C. Curtis in New South Wales, Australia.

PROBING FOR PUPPIES

Far too many breeders are overanxious about whether the breeding "took" and are inclined to feel for puppies or persuade a veterinarian to radiograph or X-ray their bitches to confirm it. Unless there is reason to doubt the normalcy of a pregnancy, this is risky. Certainly 63 days are not too long to wait, and why risk endangering the litter by probing with your inexperienced hands? Few bitches give no evidence of being in whelp, and there is no need to prove it for yourself by trying to count puppies.

ALERTING YOUR VETERINARIAN

At least a week before the puppies are due, you should telephone your veterinarian and notify him that you expect the litter and give him the date. This way he can make sure that there will be someone available to help, should there be any problems during the whelping. Most veterinarians today have answering services and alternate vets on call when they are not available themselves. Some veterinarians suggest that you call them when the bitch starts labor so that they may further plan their time, should they be needed. Discuss this matter with your veterinarian when you first take the bitch to him for her diet instructions, etc., and establish the method which will best fit in with his schedule.

DO YOU NEED A VETERINARIAN IN ATTENDANCE?

Even if this is your first litter, I would advise that you go through the experience of whelping without panicking and calling desperately for the veterinarian. Most animal births are accomplished without complications, and you should call for assistance only if you run into trouble.

When having her puppies, your bitch will appreciate as little interference and as few strangers around as possible. A quiet place, with her nest, a single familiar face and her own instincts are all that is necessary for nature to take its course. An audience of curious children squealing and questioning, other family pets nosing around, or strange adults should be avoided. Many a bitch which has been distracted in this way has been known to devour her young. This can be

Damasyn Infuriator, owned by Bob and Evelyn Stolting of Bayville, New York. The sire was Ch. Damasyn The Solitaire, C.D.X., x Steb's Remarkable Sparkle.

Ch. Steb's Captain Treble, litter brother to the famous Steb's Top Skipper. In Treble's one litter he produced Damasyn The Cheska, dam of the famous Ch. Damasyn Derringer. Unfortunately, Treble died shortly after making his championship.

the horrible result of intrusion into the bitch's privacy. There are other ways of teaching children the miracle of birth, and there will be plenty of time later for the whole family to enjoy the puppies. Let them be born under proper and considerate circumstances.

LABOR

Some litters—many first litters—do not run the full term of 63 days. So, at least a week before the puppies are actually due, and at the time you alert your veterinarian as to their arrival, start observing the bitch for signs of the commencement of labor. This will manifest itself in the form of ripples running down the sides of her body, which will come as a revelation to her as well. It is most noticeable when she is lying on her side—and she will be sleeping a great deal as the arrival date comes closer. If she is sitting or walking about, she will perhaps sit down quickly or squat peculiarly. As the ripples become more frequent, birth time is drawing near; you will be wise not to leave her. Usually within 24 hours before whelping, she will stop eating, and as much as a week before she will begin digging a nest. The bitch should be given something resembling a whelping box with layers of newspaper (black and white only) to make her nest. She will dig more and more as birth approaches, and this is the time to begin making your promise to stop interfering unless your help is specifically required. Some bitches whimper and others are silent, but whimpering does not necessarily indicate trouble.

THE ARRIVAL OF THE PUPPIES

The sudden gush of green fluid from the bitch indicates that the water or fluid surrounding the puppies has "broken" and they are about to start down the canal and come into the world. When the

Theresa Ferrari of Manhassett, Long Island and two puppies from their latest litter—just three months old. The sire was Ch. Damasyn The Russian out of Damasyn Remarkable.

water breaks, birth of the first puppy is imminent. The first puppies are usually born within minutes to a half hour of each other, but a couple of hours between the later ones is not uncommon. If you notice the bitch straining constantly without producing a puppy, or if a puppy remains partially in and partially out for too long, it is cause for concern. Breech births (puppies born feet first instead of head first) can often cause delay or hold things up, and this is often a problem which requires veterinarian assistance.

FEEDING THE BITCH BETWEEN BIRTHS

Usually the bitch will not be interested in food for about 24 hours before the arrival of the puppies, and perhaps as long as two or three days after their arrival. The placenta which she cleans up after each puppy is high in food value and will be more than ample to sustain her. This is nature's way of allowing the mother to feed herself and her babies without having to leave the nest and hunt for food during the first crucial days. The mother always cleans up all traces of birth in the wilds so as not to attract other animals to her newborn babies.

However, there are those of us who believe in making food available should the mother feel the need to restore her strength during or after delivery—especially if she whelps a large litter. Raw chopmeat, beef boullion, and milk are all acceptable and may be placed near the whelping box during the first two or three days. After that, the mother will begin to put the babies on a sort of schedule. She will leave the whelping box at frequent intervals, take longer exercise periods, and begin to take interest in other things. This is where the fun begins for you. Now the babies are no longer soggy little pinkish blobs. They begin to crawl around and squeal and hum and grow before your very eyes!

It is at this time, if all has gone normally, that the family can be introduced gradually and great praise and affection given to the mother.

BREECH BIRTHS

Puppies normally are delivered head first. However, some are presented feet first, or in other abnormal positions, and this is referred to as a "breech birth." Assistance is often necessary to get the puppy out of the canal, and great care must be taken not to injure the puppy or the dam.

Aid can be given by grasping the puppy with a piece of turkish toweling and pulling gently during the dam's contractions. Be careful not to squeeze the puppy too hard; merely try to ease it out by moving it gently back and forth. Because even this much delay in delivery may mean the puppy is drowning, do not wait for the bitch to remove the sac. Do it yourself by tearing the sac open to expose the face and head. Then cut the cord anywhere from one-half to three-quarters of

Telstar's Sassy Sister winning the Best 9-12 month Puppy Class at the 1973 Quaker City Futurity show with her handler, Ellen Hoffman. Sassy is owned by Jane Benfield of Alexandria, Virginia.

Damasyn The Commodore with four-year-old Harold Selzle of Long Island, New York. Photograph taken in 1966.

an inch away from the navel. If the cord bleeds excessively, pinch the end of it with your fingers and count five. Repeat if necessary. Then pry open the mouth with your finger and hold the puppy upside-down for a moment to drain any fluids from the lungs. Next, rub the puppy briskly with turkish or paper toweling. You should get it wriggling and whimpering by this time.

If the litter is large, this assistance will help conserve the strength of the bitch and will probably be welcomed by her. However, it is best to allow her to take care of at least the first few herself to preserve the natural instinct and to provide the nutritive values obtained by her consumption of the afterbirths.

DRY BIRTHS

Occasionally the sac will break before the delivery of a puppy and will be expelled while the puppy remains inside, thereby depriving the dam of the necessary lubrication to expel the puppy normally.

Inserting vaseline or mineral oil via your finger will help the puppy pass down the birth canal. This is why it is essential that you be present during the whelping so that you can count puppies and afterbirths and determine when and if assistance is needed.

THE TWENTY-FOUR-HOUR CHECKUP

It is smart to have a veterinarian check the mother and her puppies within 24 hours after the last puppy is born. The vet can check the puppies for cleft palates or umbilical hernia and may wish to give the dam—particularly if she is a show dog—an injection of Pituitin to make sure of the expulsion of all afterbirths and to tighten up the uterus. This can prevent a sagging belly after the puppies are weaned and the bitch is being readied for the show ring.

FALSE PREGNANCY

The disappointment of a false pregnancy is almost as bad for the owner as it is for the bitch. She goes through the gestation period with all the symptoms—swollen stomach, increased appetite, swollen nipples—even makes a nest when the time comes. You may even take an oath that you noticed the ripples on her body from the labor pains. Then, just as suddenly as you made up your mind that she was definitely going to have puppies, you will know that she definitely is not! She may walk around carrying a toy as if it were a puppy for a few days, but she will soon be back to normal and acting just as if nothing happened—and nothing did!

CAESAREAN SECTION

Should the whelping reach the point where there is complication, such as the bitch's not being capable of whelping the puppies herself, the "moment of truth" is upon you and a Caesarean section may be necessary. The bitch may be too small or too immature to expel the puppies herself; or her cervix may fail to dilate enough to allow the young to come down the birth canal; or there may be torsion of the uterus, a dead or monster puppy, a sideways puppy blocking the canal, or perhaps toxemia. A Caesarean section will be the only solution. No matter what the cause, get the bitch to the veterinarian immediately to insure your chances of saving the mother and/or puppies.

The Caesarean section operation (the name derived from the idea that Julius Caesar was delivered by this method) involves the removal of the unborn young from the uterus of the dam by surgical incision into the walls through the abdomen. The operation is performed when it has been determined that for some reason the puppies cannot be delivered normally. While modern surgical methods have made the operation itself reasonably safe, with the dam being perfectly capable of nursing the puppies shortly after the completion of the surgery, the chief danger lies in the ability to spark life into the puppies immediately upon their removal from the womb. If the mother dies, the time element is even more important in saving the young, since the oxygen supply ceases upon the death of the dam, and the difference between life and death is measured in seconds.

After surgery, when the bitch is home in her whelping box with the babies, she will probably nurse the young without distress. You must be sure that the sutures are kept clean and that no redness or swelling or ooze appears in the wound. Healing will take place naturally, and no salves or ointments should be applied unless prescribed by the veterinarian, for fear the puppies will get it into their systems. If there is any doubt, check the bitch for fever, restlessness (other than the natural concern for her young) or a lack of appetite, but do not anticipate trouble.

EPISIOTOMY

Even though large dogs are generally easy whelpers, any number of reasons might occur to cause the bitch to have a difficult birth. Before automatically resorting to Caesarean section, many veterinarians are now trying the technique known as episiotomy.

Used rather frequently in human deliveries, episiotomy (pronounced A-PEASE-E-*OTT*-O-ME) is the cutting of the membrane between the rear opening of the vagina back almost to the opening of the anus. After delivery it is stitched together, and barring complications, heals easily, presenting no problem in future births.

SOCIALIZING YOUR PUPPY

The need for puppies to get out among other animals and people cannot be stressed enough. Kennel-reared dogs are subject to all sorts of idiosyncrasies and seldom make good house dogs or normal members of the world around them when they grow up.

The crucial age, which determines the personality and general behavior patterns which will predominate during the rest of the dog's life, are formed between the ages of three and ten weeks. This is particularly true during the 21st to 28th day. It is essential that the puppy be socialized during this time by bringing him into family life as much as possible. Floor surfaces, indoor and outdoor, should be experienced; handling by all members of the family and visitors is important; preliminary grooming gets him used to a lifelong necessity; light training, such as setting him up on tables and cleaning teeth and ears and cutting nails, etc., has to be started early if he is to become a show dog. The puppy should be exposed to car riding, shopping tours, a leash around its neck, children—your own and others—and in all possible ways develop relationships with humans.

It is up to the breeder, of course, to protect the puppy from harm or injury during this initiation into the outside world. The benefits

Ch. Damasyn The Russian, bred by Harriet Corey and handled by Carol Selzle for owners Fred and Terry Ferrari of Manhasset, New York. The sire was Damasyn Jalli's Jaimie x Valbrook's Pink Champaign.

reaped from proper attention will pay off in the long run with a well-behaved, well-adjusted grown dog capable of becoming an integral part of a happy family.

REARING THE FAMILY

Needless to say, even with a small litter there will be certain considerations which must be adhered to in order to insure successful rearing of the puppies. For instance, the diet for the mother should be appropriately increased as the puppies grow and take more and more nourishment from her. During the first few days of rest while the bitch just looks over her puppies and regains her strength, she should be left pretty much alone. It is during these first days that she begins to put the puppies on a feeding schedule and feels safe enough about them to leave the whelping box long enough to take a little extended exercise.

It is cruel, however, to try and keep the mother away from the puppies any longer than she wants to be because you feel she is being too attentive or to give the neighbors a chance to peek in at the puppies. The mother should not have to worry about harm coming to her puppies for the first few weeks. The veterinary checkup will be enough of an experience for her to have to endure until she is more like herself once again.

Ch. Walire's Roberta and Ch. Walire's Rollo photographed at three years of age. Sire was Ch. Dictator von Glenhugel x Walire's Rebecca. Bred and owned by Walter and Eleanor Brown of Denver, Colorado.

A red bitch in a field of bluebonnets! Richwyn's Candita, C.D.X. was sired by Ch. Bronze von Tannenwald x Ch. Elsa von Tannenwald and whelped in August, 1970. Bred by Pat Gwyn, Candita is owned by Gordon and Lynette Barnes of Canyon, Texas.

Winner of the 1967 Doberman Pinscher Club of America Specialty Show under judge Peggy Adamson was the great American, Mexican and Canadian Ch. Sultana von Marienburg. She later went on to win Best in Show under judge Elsie Sivori at this event held in conjunction with the Del Monte Kennel Club show. She is pictured here with her handler, Rex Vandeventer, on her fourth birthday. She is owned by the Marienburg Kennels, El Cajon, California.

Tavey's Gaston, litter brother to Ch. Tavey's Gridiron. Owners, Blanche and Charles Wileman, Russtun Dobermanns, Hants, England.

As the puppies continue to thrive and grow, you will notice that they take on individual characteristics. If you are going to keep and show one of the puppies, this is the time to start observing them for various outstanding characteristics.

EVALUATING THE LITTER

A show puppy prospect should be outgoing, (probably the first one to fall out of the whelping box!) and all efforts should be made to socialize the puppy which appears to be the most shy. Once the puppies are about three weeks old, they can and should be handled a great deal by friends and members of the family.

During the third week they begin to try to walk instead of crawl, but they are unsteady on their feet. Tails are used for balancing, and they begin to make sounds.

The crucial period in a puppy's life occurs when the puppy is from 21 to 28 days old, so all the time you can devote to them at this time will reap rewards later on in life. This is the age when several other important steps must be taken in a puppy's life. Weaning should start if it hasn't already, and it is the time to check for worms. Do not worm unnecessarily. A veterinarian should advise on worming and appropriate dosage and can also discuss with you at this time the schedule for serum or vaccination, which will depend on the size of the puppies as well as their age.

Exercise and grooming should be started at this time, with special care and consideration given to the diet. You will find that the dam will help you wean the puppies, leaving them alone more and more as she notices that they are eating well on their own. Begin by

Mrs. Jackie Perry "at home" in Kuala Lumpur, Malaysia. Left to right: Malaysian Champion Von Klebongs Dark Heritage, Australian Ch. Delderland Black Hera and Von Klebongs Dark Havoc.

Opposite, above:
Tess Henseler photographed in 1975 with puppies from a Ch. Thorvald Vom Ahrtal x Pennbrook's Senta litter.

Opposite, below:
Ch. David's Dolf Del Oeste winning Best in Show under judge Glen Sommers at the 1975 Beaumont Kennel Club show in Texas. Handled by Mrs. Betty Moore for owner David M. Newcomb of Houston, Texas. Dolf's show record includes three all-breed Bests in Show, four Specialties, 16 Group Firsts, 28 Placements and 77 Bests of Breed. The Newcombs purchased Dolf at six-weeks-of age from Jane P. Robb. Melanie Newcomb put eight points on him including a five-point major and a Specialty Best of Breed from the classes. He was shown to his championship by Norton and Betty Moore. Norton showed him his first time out as a Specialty to a Best in Show.

leaving them with her during the night for comfort and warmth; eventually, when she shows less interest, keep them separated entirely.

By the time the fifth week of their lives arrives you will already be in love with every one of them and desperately searching for reasons to keep them all. They recognize you—which really gets to you!—and they box and chew on each other and try to eat your finger and a million other captivating antics which are special with puppies. Their stomachs seem to be bottomless pits, and their weight will rise. At eight to ten weeks, the puppies will be weaned and ready to go.

SPAYING AND CASTRATING

A wise old philosopher once said, "Timing in life is everything!" No statement could apply more readily to the age-old question which every dog owner is faced with sooner or later. . . to spay or not to spay.

For the one-bitch pet owner, spaying is the most logical answer, for it solves many problems. The pet is usually not of top breeding quality, and therefore there is no great loss to the bloodline; it takes the pressure off the family if the dog runs free with children and certainly eliminates the problem of repeated litters of unwanted puppies or a backyard full of eager males twice a year.

But for the owner or breeder, the extra time and protection which must be afforded a purebred quality bitch can be most worthwhile—even if it is only until a single litter is produced after the first heat. It is then not too late to spay, the progeny can perpetuate the bloodline, the bitch will have been fulfilled—though it is merely an old wives' tale that bitches should have at least one litter to be "normal"—and she may then be retired to her deserved role as family pet once again.

With spaying the problem of staining and unusual behavior around the house is eliminated without the necessity of having to keep her in "pants" or administering pills, sprays, or shots. . . which most veterinarians do not approve of anyway.

In the case of males, castration is seldom contemplated, which to me is highly regrettable. The owner of the male dog merely overlooks the dog's ability to populate an entire neighborhood, since they do not have the responsibility of rearing and disposing of the puppies. But when you take into consideration all the many females the male dog can impregnate it is almost more essential that the males be taken out of circulation than that the female be. The male dog will still be inclined to roam but will be less frantic about leaving the grounds, and you will find that a lot of the wanderlust has left him.

Opposite:
Australian Ch. Ecquen Bengazi with owner Pat Boullivant's children in Melbourne, Australia.

Grand Prize Futurity winner at the first "true" Quaker City Doberman Pinscher Club Specialty Show was Ch. Civetta's Wolf Whistle of Kami, C.D., bred by Kay Martin and Arnold Orlander. Handled by Kay Martin of Brooklyn, New York. Ashbey photo.

Opposite:

Lovely portrait of Lady Springyard of Farlington, sired by the American import Bayard of Tavey. Owners of "Sheba" are Charles and Blanche Wileman, Russtun Dobermanns, Hants, England.

Damasyn The Berman's Blick, C.D., bred by Bernie Berman of South-fields, New York. Blick was a litter brother to Berman Brier, the Grand Victor.

STERILIZING FOR HEALTH

When considering the problem of spaying or castrating, the first consideration after the population explosion should actually be the health of the dog or bitch. Males are frequently subject to urinary diseases, and sometimes castration is a help. Your veterinarian can best advise you on this problem. Another aspect to consider is the kennel dog which is no longer being used at stud. It is unfair to keep him in a kennel with females in heat when there is no chance for him to be used. There are other more personal considerations for both kennel and one-dog owners, but when making the decision remember that it is final. You can always spay or castrate, but once the deed is done there is no return!

Opposite:
Lovely headstudy of The Sundance Kid, owned by the Keiners in Jefferson City, Missouri. The sire was Ch. Damasyn Carly of Jerseystone x Damasyn Tartnsweet.

American and Canadian Ch. Tranell's Maxwell Smart, pictured here winning the Working Group under judge Richard Greathouse at the 1972 Susque-Nango Kennel Club show with his handler, Monroe Stebbins, Jr. Max was an American and Canadian Best in Show winner, a multi-Group winner and a sire of champions. He was among the Top Five Dobermans in the U.S. throughout his career as a Special and was retired in December, 1973 with a Group First win at the prestigious Eastern Dog Club show. Max is owned by Ray Carlisle of Spring Valley, New York.

Opposite, below:
The 1975 W.E.L.K.S. show in England with Mrs. Julia Curnow of Tavey fame judging the Puppy Bitch Class. First in line is the winner, Ariki Arataki, handled by Derek King. "Sammy" is one of the Dobes owned and shown by Margaret and Derek King, Burghfield, Bucks, England.

English Champion Studbriar Chieftain, owned by the Derek Kings, Burghfield, Bucks, England.

Damasyn The Royal Riot photographed at three months of age at Peggy Adamson's Damasyn Kennels in Roslyn Heights, New York.

Opposite:
Ch. Ebonaire's Key Note shown finishing with a third major win, this one at the Catonville Kennel Club show in 1967. The sire was Ch. Egothel's All American x Ebonaire's En Garde. J.M. Stebbins handled for owner Dr. Herbert Freiman.

Six-week-old Barchet Maverick, bred and owned by Patricia D. Edwards, D.V.M. of Snellville, Georgia. The sire was Ch. Gra Lemor Demetrius v d Victor x Ch. Holly Woods Ricochet.

American and Canadian Ch. Hotai Sweet William, bred and owned by the Hotai Kennels of V. Markley in Marion, Ohio.

Another dog from the Damasyn Kennels, Damasyn The Tassi, C.D., owned by Carl Hester.

18. FEEDING AND NUTRITION

FEEDING PUPPIES

There are many diets today for young puppies, including all sorts of products on the market for feeding the newborn, for supplementing the feeding of the young and for adding this or that to diets, depending on what is lacking in the way of a complete diet.

When weaning puppies, it is necessary to put them on four meals a day, even while you are tapering off with the mother's milk. Feeding at six in the morning, noontime, six in the evening and midnight is about the best schedule, since it fits in with most human eating plans. Meals for the puppies can be prepared immediately before or after your own meals, without too much of a change in your own schedule.

6 A.M.

Two meat and two milk meals serve best and should be served alternately, of course. Assuming the 6 A.M. feeding is a milk meal, the contents should be as follows: Goat's milk is the very best milk to feed puppies but is expensive and usually available only a drug stores, unless you live in farm country where it could be readily available fresh and still less expensive. If goat's milk is not available, use evaporated milk (which can be changed to powdered milk later on) diluted two parts evaporated milk and one part water, along with raw egg yoke, honey or Karo syrup, sprinkled with high-protein baby cereal and some wheat germ. As the puppies mature, cottage cheese may be added or, at one of the two milk meals, it can be substituted for the cereal.

NOONTIME

A puppy chow which has been soaked in warm water or beef broth according to the time specified on the wrapper should be mixed with raw or simmered chopped meat in equal proportions with vitamin powder added.

6 P.M.

Repeat the milk meal—perhaps varying the type of cereal from wheat to oats, or corn or rice.

Opposite:
Roanoke Copelier of
Copper Bronze
pictured at three
months of age. She is
owned by Mrs. Logan
Mitchell, Copper
Bronze Kennels,
Leicestershire,
England.

Ch. Alisaton's Intimate Miss (pictured here) was sired by Ch. Damasyn the Troycen x Ch. Arabar's Impertinence. She is owned and bred by Joann and Gwyn Lynn Satalino of Old Westbury, New York. Tia's puppy career included 22 Firsts, six Reserves and a Best of Winners and Best in Sweepstakes at a Connecticut-New York Specialty show. She was the Grand Prize Futurity winner at the 1974 DPCA National Specialty show and Reserve Winners Bitch from the Bred-by-Exhibitor Class. Tia is a Group winner and finished owner-breeder-handled with three majors.

MIDNIGHT

Repeat the meat meal. If raw meat was fed at noon, the evening meal might be simmered.

Please note that specific proportions on this suggested diet are not given. However, it's safe to say that the most important ingredients are the milk and cereal, and the meat and puppy chow which forms the basis of the diet. Your veterinarian can advise on the portion sizes if there is any doubt in your mind as to how much to use.

If you notice that the puppies are cleaning their plates you are perhaps not feeding enough to keep up with their rate of growth. Increase the amount at the next feeding. Observe them closely; puppies should each "have their fill," because growth is very rapid at this age. If they have not satisfied themselves, increase the amount so that they do not have to fight for the last morsel. They will not overeat if they know there is enough food available. Instinct will usually let them eat to suit their normal capacity.

Magnificent headstudy of Walheim's Willowbrook Tessa, C.D., bred by Mr. John Wirtheim. Tessa has points in the championship classes as well. Her sire was Ch. Singendwald's Prince Kuhio x Ch. El Campeon's Tentadora. Owned by Pat Gwyn, Canyon, Texas.

If there is any doubt in your mind as to any ingredient you are feeding, ask yourself, "Would I give it to my own baby?" If the answer is no, then don't give it to your puppies. At this age, the comparison between puppies and human babies can be a good guide.

If there is any doubt in your mind, I repeat: ask your veterinarian to be sure.

Many puppies will regurgitate their food, perhaps a couple of times, before they manage to retain it. If they do bring up their food, allow them to eat it again, rather than clean it away. Sometimes additional saliva is necessary for them to digest it, and you do not want them to skip a meal just because it is an unpleasant sight for you to observe.

This same regurgitation process holds true sometimes with the bitch, who will bring up her own food for her puppies every now and then. This is a natural instinct on her part which stems from the days when dogs were giving birth in the wilds. The only food the mother could provide at weaning time was too rough and indigestible for her puppies. Therefore, she took it upon herself to pre-digest the food until it could be taken and retained by her young. Bitches today will sometimes resort to this, especially bitches which love having litters and have a strong maternal instinct. Some dams will help you wean their litters and even give up feeding entirely once they see you are taking over.

WEANING THE PUPPIES

When weaning the puppies the mother is kept away from the little ones for longer and longer periods of time. This is done over a period of several days. At first she is separated from the puppies for several hours, then all day, leaving her with them only at night for comfort and warmth. This gradual separation aids in helping the mother's milk to dry up gradually, and she suffers less distress after feeding a litter.

If the mother continues to carry a great deal of milk with no signs of its tapering off, consult your veterinarian before she gets too uncomfortable. She may cut the puppies off from her supply of milk too abruptly if she is uncomfortable, before they should be completely on their own.

There are many opinions on the proper age to start weaning puppies. If you plan to start selling them between six and eight weeks, weaning should begin between two and three weeks of age. Here again, each bitch will pose a different situation. The size and weight of the litter should help determine the time, and your veterinarian will have an opinion, as he determines the burden the bitch is carrying by the size of the litter and her general condition. If she is being pulled down by feeding a large litter, he may suggest that you start at two weeks. If she is glorying in her motherhood without any apparent

Ch. Civetta's Black Drongo of Kami, C.D.X. pictured winning the Breed at the 1974 South Jersey Kennel Club show under judge Howard Tyler. Whelped in April, 1972, Drongo was bred and is owned by Arnold Orlander and Kay Martin, pictured handling him. Drongo received 14 of his 15 championship points under Dobe breeder-judges. Drongo has gone Best of Breed at DPCA Chapter Club Specialty Shows and at the end of 1975 is working for his U.D. degree. His owners aim to have Drongo a full-titled champion U.D.T. dog—the complete Doberman!

Opposite:
Ch. Marwood Anubis
de Scudamore, C.D.
and Reikon of
Stocklea. Both dogs
are owned by Mrs.
James G. Skidmore II
of Norwalk,
Connecticut. Anubis,
or Jason as he is
called at home, is
working on his C.D.X.

taxing of her strength, he may suggest three to four weeks. You and he will be the best judges. But remember, there is no substitute that is as perfect as mother's milk—and the longer the puppies benefit from it, the better. Other food yes, but mother's milk first and foremost for the healthiest puppies!

Third in a Class of 15 Stud Dogs at the 1975 Doberman Pinscher Club of America National Specialty in San Diego, was American and Canadian Ch. Hotai Sweet William, pictured here with his sons Hotai Bobalink, Top Puppy at this same show and owned by William Yater of Atlanta, Georgia, and Ch. Domani's Prince William, a Group winner, bred and owned by Dee Chinatella and Philip Cardaro of Folsom, Louisiana.

FEEDING THE ADULT DOG

The puppies' schedule of four meals a day should drop to three by six months and then to two by nine months; by the time the dog reaches one year of age, it is eating one meal a day.

The time when you feed the dog each day can be a matter of the dog's preference or your convenience, so long as once in every 24 hours the dog receives a meal that provides him with a complete, balanced diet. In addition, of course, fresh clean water should be available at all times.

There are many brands of dry food, kibbles and biscuits on the market which are all of good quality. There are also many varieties of canned dog food which are of good quality and provide a balanced diet for your dog. But, for those breeders and exhibitors who show their dogs, additional care is given to providing a few "extras" which enhance the good health and good appearance of show dogs.

A good meal or kibble mixed with water or beef broth and raw meat is perhaps the best ration to provide. In cold weather many breeders add suet or corn oil (or even olive or cooking oil) to the mixture and others make use of the bacon fat after breakfast by pouring it over the dog's food.

Salting a dog's food in the summer helps replace the salt he "pants away" in the heat. Many breeders sprinkle the food with garlic powder to sweeten the dog's breath and prevent gas, especially in

Quicke of Dawn with a litter of seven sired by Ch. Dictator von Glenhugel. Quike's owner and breeder of this litter was R.G. Allen of Vienna, Virginia. Photographed in 1946.

breeds that gulp or wolf their food and swallow a lot of air. I prefer garlic powder; the salt is too weak and the clove is too strong.

There are those, of course, who cook very elaborately for their dogs, which is not necessary if a good meal and meat mixture is provided. Many prefer to add vegetables, rice, tomatoes, etc., in with everything else they feed. As long as the extras do not throw the nutritional balance off, there is little harm, but no one thing should be fed to excess. Occasionally liver is given as a treat at home. Fish, which

Ch. Galaxy's Corry Carina winning one of her 24 Bests in Show (as of the end of 1975). Always handled by Jane Forsyth for co-owners Mrs. Cheever Porter of New York City and F. and E. D'Amico. This Best in Show win at the June, 1974 Middlesex Kennel Club show was preceded by Corry's 61 Working Group Firsts. Photo by Ashbey.

Below:
Elfred's Prim-A-Dona pictured winning Best of Winners and Best of Opposite Sex at the 1972 New Brunswick Kennel Club show under judge Eleanore Evers. Handled by Ellen Hoffman for owner Jane N. Benfield, Telstar Dobermans, Alexandria, Virginia. The sire was Elfred's Telstar x Bremon Bittersweet.

most veterinarians no longer recommend even for cats, is fed to puppies, but should not be given in excess of once a week. Always remember that no one thing should be given as a total diet. Balance is most important; a 100 per cent meat diet can kill a dog.

THE ALL MEAT DIET CONTROVERSY

In March of 1971, the National Research Council investigated a great stir in the dog fancy about the all-meat dog-feeding controversy. It was established that meat and meat by-products constitute a complete balanced diet for dogs only when it is further fortified with vitamins and minerals.

Therefore, a good dog chow or meal mixed with meat provides the perfect combination for a dog's diet. While the dry food is a complete diet in itself, the fresh meat additionally satisfies the dog's anatomically and physiologically meat-oriented appetite. While dogs are actually carnivores, it must be remembered that when they were feeding themselves in the wild they ate almost the entire animal they captured, including its stomach contents. This provided some of the vitamins and minerals we must now add to the diet.

In the United States, the standard for diets which claim to be ''complete and balanced'' is set by the Subcommittee on Canine Nutrition of the National Research Council (NRC) of the National Academy of Sciences. This is the official agency for establishing the nutritional requirements of dog foods. Most foods sold for dogs and cats meet these requirements, and manufactuers are proud to say so on their labels, so look for this when you buy. Pet food labels must be approved by the Association of American Feed Control Officials, Pet Foods Committee. Both the Food and Drug Administration and the Federal Trade Commission of the AAFCO define the word ''balanced'' when referring to dog food as:

''Balanced is a term which may be applied to pet food having all known required nutrients in a proper amount and proportion based upon the recommendations of a recognized authority (The National Research Council is one) in the field of animal nutrition, for a given set of physiological animal requirements.''

With this much care given to your dog's diet, there can be little reason for not having happy well-fed dogs in proper weight and proportions for the show ring.

OBESITY

As we mentioned before, there are many ''perfect'' diets for your dogs on the market today. When fed in proper proportions, they should keep your dogs in ''full bloom.'' However, there are those owners who, more often than not, indulge their own appetites and are inclined to overfeed their dogs as well. A study in Great Britain in the early 1970's found that a major percentage of obese people also had obese dogs. The entire family was overfed and all suffered from the same condition.

Obesity in dogs is a direct result of the animal's being fed more food that he can properly "burn up" over a period of time, so it is stored as fat or fatty tissue in the body. Pet dogs are more inclined to become obese than show dogs or working dogs, but obesity also is a factor to be considered with the older dog, since his exercise is curtailed.

A lack of "tuck up" on a dog, or not being able to feel the ribs, or great folds of fat which hang from the underside of the dog can all be considered as obesity. Genetic factors may enter into the picture, but usually the owner is at fault.

The life span of the obese dog is decreased on several counts. Excess weight puts undue stress on the heart as well as the joints. The dog becomes a poor anesthetic risk and has less resistance to viral or bacterial infections. Treatment is seldom easy or completely effective, so emphasis should be placed on not letting your dog get FAT in the first place!

ORPHANED PUPPIES

The ideal solution to feeding orphaned puppies is to be able to put them with another nursing dam who will take them on as her own. If this is not possible within your own kennel, or a kennel that you know of, it is up to you to care for and feed the puppies. Survival is possible but requires a great deal of time and effort on your part.

Your substitute formula must be precisely prepared, always served heated to body temperature and refrigerated when not being fed. Esbilac, a vacuum-packed powder, with complete feeding instructions on the can, is excellent and about as close to mother's milk as you can get. If you can't get Esbilac, or until you do get Esbilac, there are two alternative formulas that you might use.

Mix one part boiled water with five parts of evaporated milk and add one teaspoonful of di-calcium phosphate per quart of formula. Di-calcium phosphate can be secured at any drug store. If they have it in tablet form only, you can powder the tablets with the back part of a tablespoon. The other formula for newborn puppies is a combination of eight ounces of homogenized milk mixed well with two egg yolks.

You will need baby bottles with three-hole nipples. Sometimes doll bottles can be used for the newborn puppies, which should be fed at six-hour intervals. If they are consuming sufficient amounts, their stomachs should look full, or slightly enlarged, though never distended. The amount of formula to be fed is proportionate to the size, age, growth and weight of the puppy, and is indicated on the can of Esbilac or on the advice of your veterinarian. Many breeders like to keep a baby scale nearby to check the weight of the puppies to be sure they are thriving on the formula.

One of the top-winning Dobermans in this country, Ch. Weichardt's A-Go-Go, C.D., owned by E.S. Barrett of Palos Verdes Estates, California. Mr. Barrett is editor and publisher of *The Doberman Quarterly Magazine.*

At two to three weeks you can start adding Pablum or some other high protein baby cereal to the formula. Also, baby beef can be licked from your finger at this age, or added to the formula. At four weeks the surviving puppies should be taken off the diet of Esbilac and put on a more substantial diet, such as wet puppy meal or chopped beef. However, Esbilac powder can still be mixed in with the food for additional nutrition. The jarred baby foods of pureed meats make for a smooth changeover also, and can be blended into the diet.

HOW TO FEED THE NEWBORN PUPPIES

When the puppy is a newborn, remember that it is vitally important to keep the feeding procedure as close to the natural mother's routine as possible. The newborn puppy should be held in your lap in

Jay-Dee's Silent Shadow with her litter of 11 puppies sired by Ch. Triadel Honey B's Blak Rites. Both Dobermans are owned by Donna Smith of the Shacado Kennels in Alberta, Canada.

10-week-old Roanoke Nayrilla Wild Melody, bred by Mrs. Jean Ryan and owned by Mr. James and Mrs. D.C. Richardson of Essex, England.

your hand in an almost upright position with the bottle at an angle to allow the entire nipple area to be full of the formula. Do not hold the bottle upright so the puppy's head has to reach straight up toward the ceiling. Do not let the puppy nurse too quickly or take in too much air and possibly get the colic. Once in a while, take the bottle away and let him rest a while and swallow several times. Before feeding, test the nipple to see that the fluid does not come out too quickly, or by the same token, too slowly so that the puppy gets tired of feeding before he has had enough to eat.

When the puppy is a little older, you can place him on his stomach on a towel to eat, and even allow him to hold on to the bottle or to "come and get it" on his own. Most puppies enjoy eating and this will be a good indication of how strong an appetite he has and his ability to consume the contents of the bottle.

It will be necessary to "burp" the puppy. Place a towel on your shoulder and hold the puppy on your shoulder as if it were a human baby, patting and rubbing it gently. This will also encourage the puppy to defecate. At this time, you should observe for diarrhea or other intestinal disorders. The puppy should eliminate after each feeding with occasional eliminations between times as well. If the puppies do not eliminate on their own after each meal, massage their stomachs and under their tails gently until they do.

Ch. Marks-Tey Waystar, lovely black daughter of Ch. Marks-Tey Hondo x Ch. Marks-Tey Melanie. She was the youngest puppy ever to win Best of Winners at the DPCA National Specialty Show, at 8½ months. It was also her first show! Gene Hupt handled for owners Keith and Joanna Walker, Marks-Tey Dobermans, Centralia, Illinois.

You must keep the puppies clean. If there is diarrhea or if they bring up a little formula, they should be washed and dried off. Under no circumstances should fecal matter be allowed to collect on their skin or fur.

All this—plus your determination and perseverance—might save an entire litter of puppies that would otherwise have died without their real mother.

GASTRIC TORSION

Gastric torsion, or bloat, sometimes referred to simply as "twisted stomach," has become more and more prevalent. Many dogs that in the past had been thought to die of blockage of the stomach or intestines because they had swallowed toys or other foreign objects are now suspected of having been the victims of gastric torsion and the bloat that followed.

Though life can be saved by immediate surgery to untwist the organ, the rate of fatality is high. Symptoms of gastric torsion are unusual restlessness, excessive salivation, attempts to vomit, rapid respiration, pain and the eventual bloating of the abdominal region.

The cause of gastric torsion can be attributed to overeating, excess gas formation in the stomach, poor function of the stomach or intestine, or general lack of exercise. As the food ferments in the stomach, gases form which may twist the stomach in a clockwise direction so that the gas is unable to escape. Surgery, where the stomach is untwisted counter-clockwise, is the safest and most successful way to correct the situation.

To avoid the threat of gastric torsion, it is wise to keep your dog well exercised to be sure the body is functioning normally. Make sure that food and water are available for the dog at all times, thereby reducing the tendency to overeat. With self-service dry feeding, where the dog is able to eat intermittently during the day, there is not the urge to "stuff" at one time.

If you notice any of the symptoms of gastric torsion, call your veterinarian immediately! Death can result within a matter of hours!

19. GENERAL CARE AND MANAGEMENT

TATTOOING

Ninety per cent success has been reported on the return of stolen or lost dogs that have been tattooed. More and more this simple, painless, inexpensive method of positive identification for dogs is being reported all over the United States. Long popular in Canada, along with nose prints, the idea gained interest in this country when dognapping started to soar as unscrupulous people began stealing dogs for resale to research laboratories. Pet dogs that wander off and lost hunting dogs have always been a problem. The success of tattooing has been significant.

Tattooing can be done by the veterinarian for a minor fee. There are several dog "registries" that will record your dog's number and help you locate it should it be lost or stolen. The number of the dog's American Kennel Club registration is most often used on thoroughbred dogs, or the owner's Social Security number in the case of mixed breeds. The best place for the tattoo is the groin. Some prefer the inside of an ear, and the American Kennel Club has rules that the judges officiating at the AKC dog shows not penalize the dog for the tattoo mark.

The tattoo mark serves not only to identify your dog should it be lost or stolen, but offers positive identification in large kennels where several litters of the same approximate age are on the premises. It is a safety measure against unscrupulous breeders "switching" puppies. Any age is a proper age to tattoo, but for safety's sake, the sooner the better.

The buzz of the needle might cause your dog to be apprehensive, but the pricking of the needle is virtually painless. The risk of infection is negligible when done properly, and the return of your beloved pet may be the reward for taking the time to insure positive identification for your dog. Your local kennel club will know of a dog registry in your area.

Sophie Copper Bronze, owned by Mrs. Logan Mitchell of Leicestershire, England. Eight weeks after producing eight puppies, Sophie won a Reserve C.C. under judge K.V. Franland and another under judge J. Brambley. Sophie has consistently won the A.O.C. Class under both national and international judges; among them, Professor Bodingbauer and Herr Willi Rothfuss of Germany, and Peter Knoop and Peggy Adamson of the United States. Sophie has also won C.C.'s in 1973 at the Crufts and the Manchester shows.

OUTDOOR HOUSEBREAKING

If you are particular about your dog's behavior in the house, where you expect him to be clean and respectful of the carpets and furniture, you should also want him to have proper manners outdoors. Just because the property belongs to you doesn't necessarily mean he should be allowed to empty himself any place he chooses. Before long the entire yard will be fouled and odorous and the dog will be completely irresponsible on other people's property as well. Dogs seldom recognize property lines.

If your dog does not have his own yard fenced in, he should be walked on leash before being allowed to run free and before being penned up in his own yard. He will appreciate his own run being kept clean. You will find that if he has learned his manners outside, his manners inside will be better. Good manners in "toilet training" are especially important with big dogs!

OTHER IMPORTANT OUTDOOR MANNERS

Excessive barking is perhaps the most objectionable habit a dog indulges in out of doors. It annoys neighbors and makes for a noisy dog in the house as well. A sharp jerk on the leash will stop a dog from excessive barking while walking; trees and shrubs around a dog run will cut down on barking if a dog is in his own run. However, it is unfair to block off his view entirely. Give him some view—preferably of his own home—to keep his interest. Needless to say, do not leave a dog that barks excessively out all night.

You will want your dog to bark at strangers, so allow him this privilege. Then after a few "alerting" barks tell the dog to be quiet (with the same word command each time). If he doesn't get the idea, put him on leash and let him greet callers with you at the door until he does get the idea.

Do not let your dog jump on visitors either. Leash training may be necessary to break this habit as well. As the dog jumps in the air, pull back on the lead so that the dog is returned to the floor abruptly. If he attempts to jump up on you, carefully raise your knee and push him away by leaning against his chest.

Ch. Damasyn The Pert Patrice, C.D.X. She was by Meadow Mist Elegy x Ch. Damasyn The Sonnet, C.D. She was also known as the granddam of the famous Warlock.

Do not let your dog roam free in the neighborhood no matter how well he knows his way home. Especially do not let your dog roam free to empty himself on the neighbors' property or gardens!

A positive invitation to danger is to allow your dog to chase cars or bicycles. Throwing tin cans or chains out of car windows at them has been suggested as a cure, but can also be dangerous if they hit the dog instead of the street. Streams of water from a garden hose or water pistol are the least dangerous, but leash control is still the most scientific and most effective.

If neighbors report that your dog barks or howls or runs from window to window while you are away, crate training or room train-

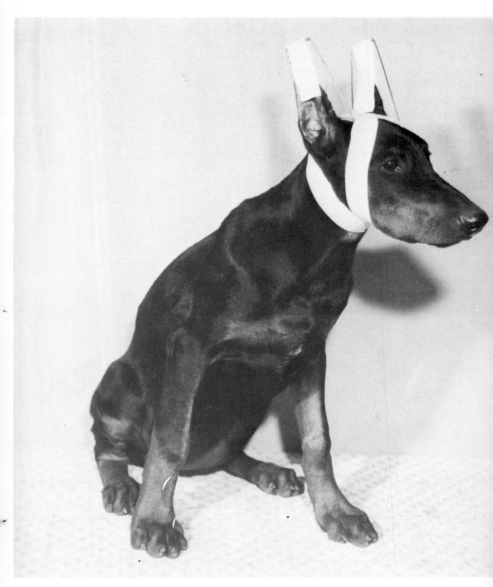

Keep the Doberman's ear rack clean to protect him from possible infections.

Opposite:
Ch. Sultana von Marienburg at six years of age.

ing for short periods of time may be indicated. If you expect to be away for longer periods of time, put the dog in the basement or a single room where he can do the least damage. The best solution of all is to buy him another dog or cat for companionship. Let them enjoy each other while you are away and have them both welcome you home!

GERIATRICS

If you originally purchased good healthy stock and cared for your dog throughout his life, there is no reason why you cannot expect your dog to live to a ripe old age. With research and the remarkable foods produced for dogs, especially this past decade or so, his chances of longevity have increased considerably. If you have cared for him well, your dog will be a sheer delight in his old age, just as he was while in his prime.

We can assume you have fed him properly if he is not too fat. Have you ever noticed how fat people usually have fat dogs because

A typical Frankskirby Doberman pictured at 14 months of age: the famous Tessa, or Frankskirby Red Christel, pictured at the Maidston Open Show in England. Tessa was handled by her owner, Joyce Spaughton, Frankskirby Dobermans, Kent, England.

they indulge their dogs' appetite as they do their own? If there has been no great illness, then you will find that very little additional care and attention are needed to keep him well. Exercise is still essential, as is proper food, booster shots, and tender loving care.

Even if a heart condition develops, there is still no reason to believe your dog cannot live to an old age. A diet may be necessary, along with medication and limited exercise, to keep the condition under control. In the case of deafness, or partial blindness, additional care must be taken to protect the dog, but neither infirmity will in any way shorten his life. Prolonged exposure to temperature variances, overeating, excessive exercise, lack of sleep, or being housed with younger, more active dogs may take an unnecessary toll on the dog's energies and introduce serious trouble. Good judgment, periodic veterinary checkups and individual attention will keep your dog with you for many added years.

When discussing geriatrics, the question of when a dog becomes old or aged usually is asked. We have all heard the old saying that one year of a dog's life is equal to seven years in a human. This theory is strictly a matter of opinion, and must remain so, since so many outside factors enter into how quickly each individual dog "ages." Recently, a new chart was devised which is more realistically equivalent:

DOG	MAN
6 months	10 years
1 year	15 years
2 years	24 years
3 years	28 years
4 years	32 years
5 years	36 years
6 years	40 years
7 years	44 years
8 years	48 years
9 years	52 years
10 years	56 years
15 years	76 years
21 years	100 years

It must be remembered that such things as serious illnesses, poor food and housing, general neglect and poor beginnings as puppies will take their toll on a dog's general health and age him more quickly than a dog that has led a normal, healthy life. Let your veterinarian help you determine an age bracket for your dog in his later years.

While good care should prolong your dog's life, there are several "old age" disorders to be on the lookout for no matter how well he may be doing. The tendency toward obesity is the most common, but constipation is another. Aging teeth and a slowing down of the digestive processes may hinder digestion and cause constipation, just as any major change in diet can bring on diarrhea. There is also the possibility of loss or impairment of hearing or eyesight which will also tend to make the dog wary and distrustful. Other behavioral changes may result as well, such as crankiness, loss of patience and lack of interest; these are the most obvious changes. Other ailments may manifest themselves in the form of rheumatism, arthritis, tumors and warts, heart disease, kidney infections, male prostatism and female disorders. Of course, all of these require a veterinarian's checking the degree of seriousness and proper treatment.

Take care to avoid infectious diseases. When these hit the older dog, they can debilitate him to an alarming degree, leaving him open to more serious complications and a shorter life.

DOG INSURANCE

Much has been said for and against canine insurance, and much more will be said before this kind of protection for a dog becomes universal and/or practical. There has been talk of establishing a Blue Cross-type plan similar to that now existing for humans. However, the best insurance for your dog is *you*! Nothing compensates for tender, loving care. Like the insurance policies for humans, there will be a lot of fine print in the contracts revealing that the dog is not covered after all. These limited conditions usually make the acquisition of dog insurance expensive and virtually worthless.

Blanket coverage policies for kennels or establishments which board or groom dogs can be an advantage, especially in transporting dogs to and from their premises. For the one-dog owner, however, whose dog is a constant companion, the cost for limited coverage is not necessary.

THE HIGH COST OF BURIAL

Pet cemeteries are mushrooming across the nation. Here, as with humans, the sky can be the limit for those who wish to bury their pets ceremoniously. The costs of satin-lined caskets, grave stones, flowers, etc. run the gamut of prices to match the emotions and means of the owner. This is strictly a matter of what the bereaved owner wishes to do.

IN THE EVENT OF YOUR DEATH. . .

This is a morbid thought perhaps, but ask yourself the question, "If death were to strike at this moment, what would become of my beloved dogs?"

Perhaps you are fortunate enough to have a relative, friend or spouse who could take over immediately, if only on a temporary basis. Perhaps you have already left instructions in your last will and testament for your pet's dispensation, as well as a stipend for their perpetual care.

Provide definite instructions before a disaster occurs and your dogs are carted off to the pound, or stolen by commercially minded neighbors with "resale" in mind. It is a simple thing to instruct your lawyer about your wishes in the event of sickness or death. Leave instructions as to feeding, etc., posted on your kennel room or kitchen bulletin board, or wherever your kennel records are kept. Also, tell several people what you are doing and why. If you prefer to keep such instructions private, merely place them in sealed envelopes in a known place with directions that they are to be opened only in the

Ritza, owned by Eleanor Carpenter. Ritza's ears were never cut and remained like this all her life. This photograph was taken by the famous dog photographer Tauskey.

event of your demise. Eliminate the danger of your animals suffering in the event of an emergency that prevents your personal care of them.

KEEPING RECORDS

Whether or not you have one dog, or a kennel full of them, it is wise to keep written records. It takes only a few moments to record dates of inoculations, trips to the vet, tests for worms, etc. It can avoid confusion or mistakes, or having your dog not covered with immunization if too much time elapses between shots because you have to guess at the last shot.

Make the effort to keep all dates in writing rather than trying to commit them to memory. A rabies injection date can be a problem if you have to recall that "Fido had the shot the day Aunt Mary got back from her trip abroad, and, let's see, I guess that was around the end of June."

In an emergency, these records may prove their value if your veterinarian cannot be reached and you have to use another, or if you move and have no case history on your dog for the new veterinarian. In emergencies, you do not always think clearly or accurately, and if dates, and types of serums used, etc., are a matter of record, the veterinarian can act more quickly and with more confidence.

20. SHOWING YOUR DOBERMAN

Let us assume that after a few months of tender loving care, you realize your dog is developing beyond your wildest expectations and that the dog you selected is very definitely a show dog! Of course, every owner is prejudiced. But if you are sincerely interested in going to dog shows with your dog and making a champion of him, now is the time to start casting a critical eye on him from a judge's point of view.

There is no such thing as a perfect dog. Every dog has some faults, perhaps even a few serious ones. The best way to appraise your dog's degree of perfection is to compare him with the Standard for the breed, or before a judge in a show ring.

MATCH SHOWS

For the beginner there are "mock" dog shows, called Match Shows, where you and your dog go through many of the procedures of a regular dog show, but do not gain points toward championship. These shows are usually held by kennel clubs, annually or semiannually, and much ring poise and experience can be gained there. The age limit is reduced to two months at match shows to give puppies four months of training before they compete at the regular shows when they reach six months of age. Classes range from two to four months; four to six months; six to nine months; and nine to twelve months. Puppies compete with others of their own age for comparative purposes. Many breeders evaluate their litters in this manner, choosing which is the most outgoing, which is the most poised, the best showman, etc.

For those seriously interested in showing their dogs to full championship, these match shows provide important experience for both the dog and the owner. Class categories may vary slightly, according to number of entries, but basically include all the classes that are included at a regular point show. There is a nominal entry fee and, of course, ribbons and usually trophies are given for your efforts as well. Unlike the point shows, entries can be made on the day of the show right on the show grounds. They are unbenched and provide an informal, usually congenial atmosphere for the amateur, which helps to make the ordeal of one's first adventures in the show ring a little less nerve-wracking.

THE POINT SHOWS

It is not possible to show a puppy at an American Kennel Club sanctioned point show before the age of six months. When your dog reaches this eligible age, your local kennel club can provide you with the names and addresses of the show-giving superintendents in your area who will be staging the club's dog show for them, and where you must write for an entry form.

Earl von Forell, Vice Champion du Monde at the 1973 Dortmund World Show, a champion in France in 1974 and also a champion in Luxembourg in 1974. He is the sire of another top French Dobe, Vega de la Morliere. Owned by one of France's top breeders and judges, m. m.a. demangeat of Orvault-Nantes, France.

The magnificent American and Canadian Ch. Brandendorf's Periwinkle, the top-winning blue of all time and sire of nearly a dozen champions. Bred, owned and shown by Marilyn Meshirer, Brandendorf Kennels, Long Island, New York.

Ch. Thorvald v Ahrtal, sired by Ch. Cassio v Ahrtal (sire of 38 champions) out of Illissa v Ahrtal (dam of four champions). Bred and owned by Tess Henseler, Ahrtal Kennels, Ottsville, Pennsylvania.

Opposite:

Ch. Tedell Indulto v Ri-Jan's, bred by Janie Garrick and Kathleen Priest, is owned by Theodora S. Linck, Tedell Kennels, Toledo, Ohio. He was whelped in July 1972 and sired by the late Ch. Tedell Eleventh Hour x Ch. Ri-Jan's Seneca Love Call. As of the end of 1975 Indulto had six Group Firsts, several Specialties, and many Bests of Breed and Group Placings. From his first litter out of Ch. Balmoral Bonnet of Norlock, he sired his first champion, Ch. Tedell Nottingham Palace. Many of his offspring are pointed and winning Sweepstakes.

The forms are mailed in a pamphlet called a premium list. This also includes the names of the judges for each breed, a list of the prizes and trophies, the name and address of the show-giving club and where the show will be held, as well as rules and regulations set up by the American Kennel Club which must be abided by if you are to enter.

A booklet containing the complete set of show rules and regulations may be obtained by writing to the American Kennel Club, Inc., 51 Madison Avenue, New York, N.Y., 10010.

When you write to the Dog Show Superintendent, request not only your premium list for this particular show, but ask that your name be added to their mailing list so that you will automatically receive all premium lists in the future. List your breed or breeds and they will see to it that you receive premium lists for Specialty shows as well.

Unlike the match shows where your dog will be judged on ring behavior, at the point shows he will be judged on conformation to the breed Standard. In addition to being at least six months of age (on the

Gemae Bellzebub, Group Second at a recent Taconic Hills Kennel Club show.

day of the show) he must be a purebred for a point show. This means both of his parents and he are registered with the American Kennel Club. There must be no alterations or falsifications regarding his appearance. Females cannot have been spayed and males must have both testicles in evidence. No dyes or powders may be used to enhance the appearance, and any lameness or deformity or major deviation from the Standard for the breed constitutes a disqualification.

With all these things in mind, groom your dog to the best of your ability in the specified area for this purpose in the show hall and walk into the show ring with great pride of ownership and ready for an appraisal of your dog by the judge.

The presiding judge on that day will allow each and every dog a certain amount of time and consideration before making his decisions. It is never permissible to consult the judge regarding either

Ch. Damasyn Liana, owned by Cal Smith of Wilmington, Delaware, pictured winning at the 1964 Trenton Kennel Club show under judge Joseph Quirk; the handler is J. Monroe Stebbins, Jr.

your dog or his decision while you are in the ring. An exhibitor never speaks unless spoken to, and then only to answer such questions as the judge may ask—the age of the dog, the dog's bite, or to ask you to move your dog around the ring once again.

However, before you reach the point where you are actually in the ring awaiting the final decisions of the judge, you will have had to decide in which of the five classes in each sex your dog should compete.

Point Show Classes

The regular classes of the AKC are: Puppy, Novice, Bred-by-Exhibitor, American-Bred, Open; if your dog is undefeated in any of the regular classes (divided by sex) in which it is entered, he or she is *required* to enter the Winners Class. If your dog is placed second in the class to the dog which won Winners Dog or Winners Bitch, hold the dog or bitch in readiness as the judge must consider it for Reserve Winners.

PUPPY CLASSES shall be for dogs which are six months of age and over but under twelve months, which were whelped in the U.S.A. or Canada, and which are not champions. Classes are often divided 6 and (under) 9, and 9 and (under) 12 months. The age of a dog shall be calculated up to and inclusive of the first day of a show. For example, a dog whelped on Jan. 1st is eligible to compete in a puppy class on July 1st, and may continue to compete up to and including Dec. 31st of the same year, but is not eligible to compete Jan. 1st of the following year.

THE NOVICE CLASS shall be for dogs six months of age or over, whelped in the U.S.A. or Canada which have not, prior to the closing of entries, won three first prizes in the Novice Class, a first prize in Bred-by-Exhibitor, American-Bred or Open Class, nor one or more points toward a championship title.

THE BRED-BY-EXHIBITOR CLASS shall be for dogs whelped in the U.S.A. which are six months of age and over, which are not champions, and which are owned wholly or in part by the person or by the spouse of the person who was the breeder or one of the breeders of record. Dogs entered in the BBE Class must be handled by an owner or by a member of the immediate family of an owner, i.e., the husband, wife, father, mother, son, daughter, brother or sister.

THE AMERICAN-BRED CLASS is for all dogs (except champions) six months of age or over, whelped in the U.S.A. by reason of a mating that took place in the U.S.A.

THE OPEN CLASS is for any dog six months of age or over, except in a member specialty club show held for only American-Bred dogs, in which case the class is for American-Bred dogs only.

Ch. Tatjan of Reklaw, owned by Mr. Frihof Wickstrom of Canada. Tatjan is a red son of Dictator.

Best of Breed at the 1953 Detroit Kennel Club show as Ch. Damasyn The Ember, owned by Dr. Wilfred Shute. The sire was Ch. Dictator von Glenhugel x Damasyn The April Rain.

Opposite:

Ch. Damasyn The Kiss, owned by Eldon Pryiborowski of California. She was a red daughter of Dictator and Damasyn The Flaming Sable and is pictured here winning at a show in the early 1950's.

WINNERS DOG and WINNERS BITCH: After the above male classes have been judged, the first-place winners are then *required* to compete in the ring. The dog judged "Winners Dog" is awarded the points toward his championship title.

RESERVE WINNERS are selected immediately after the Winners Dog. In case of a disqualification of a win by the AKC, the Reserve Dog moves up to "Winners" and receives the points. After all male classes are judged, the bitch classes are called.

BEST OF BREED OR BEST OF VARIETY COMPETITION is limited to Champions of Record or dogs (with newly acquired points, for a 90-day period prior to AKC confirmation) which have completed championship requirements, and Winners Dog and Winners Bitch (or the dog awarded Winners if only one Winners prize has been awarded), together with any undefeated dogs which have been shown only in non-regular classes; all compete for Best of Breed or Best of Variety (if the breed is divided by size, color, texture or length of coat hair, etc.).

BEST OF WINNERS: If the WD or WB earns BOB or BOV, it automatically becomes BOW; otherwise they will be judged together for BOW (following BOB or BOV judging).

BEST OF OPPOSITE SEX is selected from the remaining dogs of the opposite sex to Best of Breed or Best of Variety.

OTHER CLASSES may be approved by the AKC: STUD DOGS, BROOD BITCHES, BRACE CLASS, TEAM CLASS; classes consist-

The late Senator Joseph McCarthy and his wife, Jean, pose with their Damasyn Doberman, purchased from Peggy Adamson. They later purchased a second Dobe from Peggy. *Newsweek* photograph by Ed Wergeles.

"Oh dear, what have I done now?" seems to be what this Doberman is saying. This picture was a $500 first prize winner for Tom McNally of Glenview, Illinois, in a Gaines Dog Research Center photo contest back in 1960. Photo courtesy of Gaines.

Damasyn Jalli's Jaimie, sire of the fabulous Ch. Damasyn The Russian. Jaimie is owned by Peggy Adamson. The sire was Ch. Damasyn Carly of Jerseystone x Ch. Jalli-Alli, C.D.

Opposite:
Ch. Retrac's Jody Morgansonne pictured at seven months of age while winning at a show in June, 1967. Her sire was Ch. Ru-Mar's Morgansonne, C.D. x Retrac's Tapadero. Jody is co-owned by Ruth Morgan and Frank McGowan. She was co-bred by Ruth Morgan and Christy Comer. Jody's handler is Ruth Morgan of the Morgansonne Kennels in Carmichael, California.

ing of local dogs and bitches may also be included in a show if approved by the AKC (special rules are included in the AKC Rule Book).

The MISCELLANEOUS CLASS shall be for purebred dogs of such breeds as may be designated by the AKC. No dog shall be eligible for entry in this class unless the owner has been granted an Indefinite Listing Privilege (ILP) and unless the ILP number is given on the entry form. Application for an ILP shall be made on a form provided by the AKC and when submitted must be accompanied by a fee set by the Board of Directors.

All Miscellaneous Breeds shall be shown together in a single class except that the class may be divided by sex if so specified in the premium list. There shall be *no* further competition for dogs entered in this class. Ribbons for 1st, 2nd, 3rd and 4th shall be Rose, Brown, Light Green and Gray, respectively. This class is open to the following Miscellaneous dog breeds: Australian Cattle Dogs, Australian Kelpies, Border Collies, Cavalier King Charles Spaniels, Ibizan Hounds, Miniature Bull Terriers, and Spinoni Italiani.

If Your Dog Wins a Class. . .

Study the classes to make certain your dog is entered in a proper class for his or her qualifications. If your dog wins his class, the rule states: *You are required* to enter classes for Winners, Best of Breed and Best of Winners (no additional entry fees). The rule states, "No eligible dog may be withheld from competition." It is not mandatory that you stay for group judging. *If your dog wins a group*, however, *you must stay for Best-in-Show competition.*

THE PRIZE RIBBONS AND WHAT THEY STAND FOR

No matter how many entries there are in each class at a dog show, if you place first through fourth position you will receive a ribbon. These ribbons commemorate your win and can be impressive when collected and displayed to prospective buyers when and if you have puppies for sale, or if you intend to use your dog at public stud.

All ribbons from the American Kennel Club licensed dog shows will bear the American Kennel Club seal, the name of the show, the date and the placement. In the classes the colors are blue for first, red for second, yellow for third, and white for fourth. Winners Dog or Winners Bitch ribbons are purple, while Reserve Dog and Reserve Bitch ribbons are purple and white. Best of Winners ribbons are blue and white; Best of Breed, purple and gold; and Best of Opposite Sex ribbons are red and white.

In the six groups, first prize is a blue rosette or ribbon, second placement is red, third yellow, and fourth white. The Best In Show rosette is either red, white and blue, or incorporates the colors used in the show-giving club's emblem.

QUALIFYING FOR CHAMPIONSHIP

Championship points are given for Winners Dog and Winners Bitch in accordance with a scale of points established by the American Kennel Club based on the popularity of the breed in entries, and the number of dogs competing in the classes. This scale of points varies in different sections of the country, but the scale is published in the front of each dog show catalog. These points may differ between the dogs and the bitches at the same show. You may, however, win additional points by winning Best of Winners, if there are fewer dogs than bitches entered, or vice versa. Points never exceed five at any one show, and a total of fifteen points must be won to constitute a championship. These fifteen points must be won under at least three different judges, and you must acquire at least two major wins. Anything from a three to five point win is a major, while one and two point wins are minor wins. Two major wins must be won under two different judges to meet championship requirements.

OBEDIENCE TRIALS

Some shows also offer Obedience Trials, which are considered as separate events. They give the dogs a chance to compete and score on performing a prescribed set of exercises intended to display their training in doing useful work.

There are three obedience titles for which they may compete. First, the Companion Dog or C.D. title; second, the Companion Dog Excellent or C.D.X.; and third, the Utility Dog or U.D. Detailed information on these degrees is contained in a booklet entitled Official Obedience Regulations and may be obtained by writing to the American Kennel Club.

JUNIOR SHOWMANSHIP COMPETITION

Junior Showmanship Competition is for boys and girls in different age groups handling their own dogs or one owned by their immediate family. There are four divisions: Novice A, for the ten to 12 year olds; Novice B, for those 13 to 16 years of age, with no previous junior showmanship wins; Open C, for ten to 12 year olds; and Open D, for 13 to 16 year olds who have earned one or more JS awards.

As Junior Showmanship at the dog shows increased in popularity, certain changes and improvements had to be made. As of April 1, 1971, the American Kennel Club issued a new booklet containing the Regulations for Junior Showmanship which may be obtained by writing to the A.K.C. at 51 Madison Avenue, New York, N.Y. 10010.

Sheri, owned by Grace Joffe, Liquorish Dobes, Miami, Florida.

DOG SHOW PHOTOGRAPHERS

Every show has at least one official photographer who will be more than happy to take a photograph of your dog with the judge, ribbons and trophies, along with your or your handler. These make marvelous remembrances of your top show wins and are frequently framed along with the ribbons for display purposes. Photographers can be paged at the show over the public address system, if you wish to obtain this service. Prices vary, but you will probably find it costs little to capture these happy moments, and the photos can always be used in the various dog magazines to advertise your dog's wins.

TWO TYPES OF DOG SHOWS

There are two types of dog shows licensed by the American Kennel Club. One is the all-breed show which includes classes for all the recognized breeds, and groups of breeds; i.e., all terriers, all toys, etc. Then there are the specialty shows for one particular breed which also offer championship points.

Ch. Damasyn The Ruff 'n' Reddy, owned by Dennis Clardy of St. Joseph, Missouri. Reddy is pictured winning at a show in the 1970's. Sire was Ch. Damasyn Carly of Jerseystone x Damasyn The Tartnsweet.

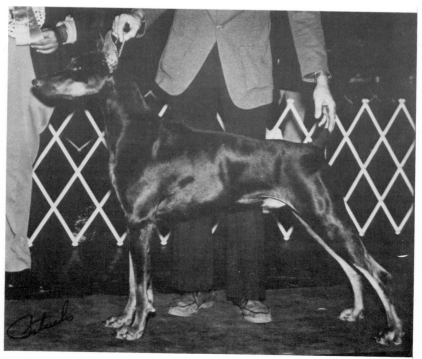

Ch. Belmont's Red Lancer, bred and owned by Mr. and Mrs. J. Schindewolf in the early 1960's. The sire was Ch. Dobe Acres Cinnamon x Ch. Cissi of Jan Har.

BENCHED OR UNBENCHED DOG SHOWS

The show-giving clubs determine, usually on the basis of what facilities are offered by their chosen show site, whether their show will be benched or unbenched. A benched show is one where the dog show superintendent supplies benches (cages for toy dogs). Each bench is numbered and its corresponding number appears on your entry identification slip which is sent to you prior to the show date. The number also appears in the show catalog. Upon entering the show you should take your dog to the bench where he should remain until it is time to groom him before entering the ring to be judged. After judging, he must be returned to the bench until the official time of dismissal from the show. At an unbenched show the club makes no provision whatsoever for your dog other than an enormous tent (if an outdoor show) or an area in a show hall where all crates and grooming equipment must be kept.

Benched or unbenched, the moment you enter the show grounds you are expected to look after your dog and have it under complete control at all times. This means short leads in crowded aisles or getting out of cars. In the case of a benched show, a "bench chain" is needed. It should allow the dog to move around, but not get down off the bench. It is also not considered "cute" to have small tots leading enormous dogs around a dog show where the child might be dragged into the middle of a dog fight.

Well-known Joanna Walker and her Ch. Marks-Tey Shawn, C.D. at her Marks-Tey Kennels in Centralia, Illinois.

Damasyn The Little Red Surrey, bred and owned by Peggy Adamson of Roslyn Heights, New York. The sire was Ch. Agitator of Doberland x Ch. Damasyn The Sultry Sister.

Opposite:
Ch. Tedell Barcarolle photographed at 22 months winning Best of Breed at the 1974 Greenwich Kennel Club at a show judged by Arnold Woolf. Handled by Robert J. Stebbins for owners Mr. and Mrs. Richard Duklis and bred by Theodora Linck.

T OF
ED

PROFESSIONAL HANDLERS

If you are new in the fancy and do not know how to handle your dog to his best advantage, or if you are too nervous or physically unable to show your dog, you can hire a licensed professional handler who will do it for you for a specified fee. The more successful or well-known handlers charge slightly higher rates, but generally speaking there is a pretty uniform charge for this service. As the dog progresses with his wins in the show ring, the fee increases proportionately. Included in this service is professional advice on when and where to show your dog, grooming, a statement of your wins at each show, and all trophies and ribbons that the dog accumulates. Any cash award is kept by the handler as a sort of "bonus."

When engaging a handler, it is advisable to select one that does not take more dogs to a show than he can properly and comfortably handle. You want your dog to receive his individual attention and not

Ch. Marks-Tey's Hanover, top winning red son of Ch. Ebonaire's Gridiron x Marks-Tey's Mischief Maker. The sire of several outstanding get including the top-producing Ch. Marks-Tey Melanie and her sister, Ch. Hanover's Amsel, C.D. Bred and owned by Keith and Joanna Walker of Centralia, Illinois.

Photo By Ritter

Ch. Gra-Lemor Demetrius pictured winning Best of Breed over an entry of 89 Dobermans at the 1970 International Kennel Club of Chicago show under judge A. Peter Knoop. He is a son of Ch. Damasyn Derringer.

be rushed into the ring at the last moment because the handler has been busy with too many other dogs in other rings. Some handlers require that you deliver the dog to their establishment a few days ahead of the show so they have ample time to groom and train him. Others will accept well-behaved and previously trained and groomed dogs at ringside, if they are familiar with the dog and the owner. This should be determined well in advance of the show date. NEVER expect a handler to accept a dog at ringside that is not groomed to perfection!

There are several sources for locating a professional handler. Dog magazines carry their classified advertising; a note or telephone call to the American Kennel Club will put you in touch with several in your area. Usually, you will be billed after the day of the show.

DO YOU REALLY NEED A HANDLER?

The answer to the above question is sometimes yes! However, the answer most exhibitors give is, "But I can't *afford* a professional handler!" or, "I want to show my dog myself. Does that mean my dog will never do any big winning?"

Do you *really* need a handler to win? If you are mishandling a good dog that should be winning and isn't, because it is made to look simply terrible in the ring by its owner, the answer is yes. If you don't know how to handle a dog properly, why make your dog look bad when a handler could show it to its best advantage?

Some owners simply cannot handle a dog well and still wonder why their dogs aren't winning in the ring, no matter how hard they try. Others are nervous and this nervousness travels down the leash to the dog and the dog behaves accordingly. Some people are extroverts by nature, and these are the people who usually make excellent handlers. Of course, the biggest winning dogs at the shows usually have a lot of "show off" in their nature, too, and this helps a great deal.

THE COST OF CAMPAIGNING A DOG WITH A HANDLER

At present many champions are shown an average of 25 times before completing a championship. In entry fees at today's prices, that adds up to about $200. This does not include motel bills, traveling expenses, or food. There have been dog champions finished in fewer shows, say five to ten shows, but this is the exception rather than the rule. When and where to show should be thought out carefully so that you can perhaps save money on entries. Here is one of the services a professional handler provides that can mean a considerable saving. Hiring a handler can save money in the long run if you just wish to make a champion. If your dog has been winning reserves and not taking the points and a handler can finish him in five to ten shows, you would be ahead financially. If your dog is not really top quality, the length of time it takes even a handler to finish it (depending upon competition in the area) could add up to a large amount of money.

Campaigning a show specimen that not only captures the wins in his breed but wins group and Best in Show awards gets up into the big money. To cover the nation's major shows and rack up a record as one of the top dogs in the nation usually costs an owner between ten and fifteen thousand dollars a year. This includes not only the professional handler's fee for taking the dog into the ring, but the cost of conditioning and grooming, board, advertising in the dog magazines, photographs, etc.

There is great satisfaction in winning with your own dog, especially if you have trained and cared for it yourself. With today's enormous entries at the dog shows and so many worthy dogs competing for top wins, many owners who said "I'd rather do it myself!" and meant it became discouraged and eventually hired a handler anyway.

However, if you really are in it just for the sport, you can and should handle your own dog if you want to. You can learn the tricks by attending training classes, and you can learn a lot by carefully observing the more successful professional handlers as they perform in the ring. Model yourself after the ones that command respect as being the leaders in their profession. But, if you find you'd really rather be at ringside looking on, then do get a handler so that your worthy dog gets his deserved recognition in the ring. To own a good dog and win with it is a thrill, so good luck, no matter how you do it.

21. YOUR DOG, YOUR VETERINARIAN, AND YOU

The purpose of this chapter is to explain why you should never attempt to be your own veterinarian. Quite the contrary, we urge emphatically that you establish good liaison with a reputable veterinarian who will help you maintain happy, healthy dogs. Our purpose is to bring you up to date on the discoveries made in modern canine medicine and to help you work with your veterinarian by applying these new developments to your own animals.

The Dobe in action! Midnite's Kaiser Von Cult bounds out of the water after a swim! Owned by Daniel Gehlsen, Kaiser's sire was Ch. Stacy's Taurus of Marks-Tey.

Three Roanoke champion bitches: left to right, Ch. Cadereyta of Roanoke, Ch. Triogen Tuppeny Feast and Ch. Roanoke Bobadilla. All owned and exhibited by Mr. James and Mrs. D.C. Richardson, Essex, England.

We have provided here "thumbnail" histories of many of the most common types of diseases your dog is apt to come in contact with during his lifetime. We feel that if you know a little something about the diseases and how to recognize their symptoms, your chances of catching them in the preliminary stages will help you and your veterinarian effect a cure before a serious condition develops.

Today's dog owner is a realistic, intelligent person who learns more and more about his dog—inside and out—so that he can care for and enjoy the animal to the fullest. He uses technical terms for parts of the anatomy, has a fleeting knowledge of the miracles of surgery and is fully prepared to administer clinical care for his animals at home. This chapter is designed for study and/or reference and we hope you will use it to full advantage.

We repeat, we do *not* advocate your playing "doctor." This includes administering medication without veterinary supervision, or even doing your own inoculations. General knowledge of diseases, their symptoms and side effects will assist you in diagnosing diseases for your veterinarian. He does not expect you to be an expert, but will appreciate your efforts in getting a sick dog to him before it is too late and he cannot save its life.

ASPIRIN: A DANGER

There is a common joke about doctors telling their patients, when they telephone with a complaint, to take an aspirin, go to bed and let him know how things are in the morning! Unfortunately, that is exactly the way it turns out with a lot of dog owners who think aspirins are curealls and give them to their dogs indiscriminately. Then they call the veterinarian when the dog has an unfavorable reaction.

Aspirins are not panaceas for everything—certainly not for every dog. In an experiment, fatalities in cats treated with aspirin in one laboratory alone numbered ten out of 13 within a two-week period. Dogs' tolerance was somewhat better, as far as actual fatalities, but there was considerable evidence of ulceration in varying degrees on the stomach linings when necropsy was performed.

Aspirin has been held in the past to be almost as effective for dogs as for people when given for many of the everyday aches and pains. The fact remains, however, that medication of any kind should be administered only after veterinary consultation and a specific dosage suitable to the condition is recommended.

While aspirin is chiefly effective in reducing fever, relieving minor pains and cutting down on inflammation, the acid has been proven harmful to the stomach when given in strong doses. Only your veterinarian is qualified to determine what the dosage is, or whether it should be administered to your particular dog at all.

WHAT THE THERMOMETER CAN TELL YOU

You will notice in reading this chapter dealing with the diseases of dogs that practically everything a dog might contract in the way of sickness has basically the same set of symptoms. Loss of appetite, diarrhea, dull eyes, dull coat, warm and/or runny nose, and FEVER!

Therefore, it is most advisable to have a thermometer on hand for checking temperature. There are several inexpensive metal rectal-type thermometers that are accurate and safer than the glass variety which can be broken. This may happen either by dropping, or perhaps even breaking off in the dog because of improper insertion or an aggravated condition with the dog that makes him violently resist the injection of the thermometer. Either kind should be lubricated with Vaseline to make the insertion as easy as possible, after it has been sterilized with alcohol.

The normal temperature for a dog is 101.5° Fahrenheit, as compared to the human 98.6°. Excitement as well as illness can cause this to vary a degree or two, but any sudden or extensive rise in body temperature must be considered as cause for alarm. Your first indication will be that your dog feels unduly "warm" and this is the time to take the temperature, not when the dog becomes very ill or manifests additional serious symptoms. With a thermometer on hand, you can check temperatures quickly and perhaps prevent some illness from becoming serious.

COPROPHAGY

Perhaps the most unpleasant of all phases of dog breeding is to come up with a dog that takes to eating stool. This practice, which is referred to politely as coprophagy, is one of the unsolved mysteries in the dog world. There simply is no explanation to why some dogs do it.

However, there are several logical theories, all or any of which may be the cause. Some say nutritional deficiencies; another says that dogs inclined to gulp their food (which passes through them not entirely digested) find it still partially palatable. There is another

A winner in the mid-1950's was Ch. Pinckney Farms Archon, bred and owned by Dr. and Mrs. C.P. Horton of Carmel, New York.

Beautiful headstudy of Ch. Rancho Dobe's Primo, sired by Ch. Alcor of Millsdod x Ch. Rancho Dobe's Kashmir. Owned by the Rancho Dobe Kennels.

theory that the preservatives used in some meat are responsible for an appealing odor that remains through the digestive process. Then again poor quality meat can be so tough and unchewable that dogs swallow it whole and it passes through them in large undigested chunks.

There are others who believe the habit is strictly psychological, the result of a nervous condition or insecurity. Others believe the dog cleans up after itself because it is afraid of being punished as it was when it made a mistake on the carpet as a puppy. Others claim boredom is the reason, or even spite. Others will tell you a dog does not want its personal odor on the premises for fear of attracting other hostile animals to itself or its home.

The most logical of all explanations and the one most veterinarians are inclined to accept is that it is a deficiency of dietary enzymes. Too much dry food can be bad and many veterinarians suggest trying meat tenderizers, monosodium glutamate, or garlic powder which gives the stool a bad odor and discourages the dog. Yeast or certain vitamins or a complete change of diet are even more often suggested. By the time you try each of the above you will probably discover that the dog has outgrown the habit anyway. However, the condition cannot be ignored if you are to enjoy your dog to the fullest.

There is no set length of time that the problem persists, and the only real cure is to walk the dog on leash, morning and night and after every meal. In other words, set up a definite eating and exercising schedule before coprophagy is an established pattern.

MASTURBATION

A source of embarrassment to many dog owners, masturbation can be eliminated with a minimum of training.

The dog which is constantly breeding anything and everything, including the leg of the piano or perhaps the leg of your favorite guest, can be broken of the habit by stopping its cause.

The over-sexed dog—if truly that is what he is—which will never be used for breeding can be castrated. The kennel stud dog can be broken of the habit by removing any furniture from his quarters or keeping him on leash and on verbal command when he is around people, or in the house where he might be tempted to breed pillows, people, etc.

Hormone imbalance may be another cause and your veterinarian may advise injections. Exercise can be of tremendous help. Keeping the dog's mind occupied by physical play when he is around people will also help relieve the situation.

Females might indulge in sexual abnormalities like masturbation during their heat cycle, or again, because of a hormone imbalance. But if they behave this way because of a more serious problem, a hysterectomy may be indicated.

Damasyn The Scarlet Scimitar, a red male sired by Ch. Damasyn The
Solitaire, C.D.X. out of Damasyn The Little Red Surrey. Bred by Mrs.
Bob Adamson and owned by Ray Kramer. Scimitar is a full brother to
the late Senator Joe McCarthy's Doberman. Mrs. Adamson's Damasyn
Kennels are in Roslyn Heights, New York.

Opposite:
Damasyn The Rocca Djil, U.D., a red female owned by Peggy Adamson and Carol Selzle. Djil had earned her U.D. degree before she was
two years of age and was particularly good at tracking, retrieving and
jumping.

Ch. Damasyn The Tartian, a great sire and a great showman from the Damasyn Kennels of Peggy and Bob Adamson, Roslyn Heights, New York. He sired Ch. Damasyn The Pacesetter, Ch. Damasyn The Troycen, Ch. Damasyn The Tadjen and Damasyn The Tartnsweet. His sire was Ch. Steb's Top Skipper x Damasyn The Strawberry Tart, C.D.

A sharp "no!" command when you can anticipate the act, or a sharp "no!" when caught in the act will deter most dogs if you are consistent in your correction. Hitting or other physical abuse will only confuse a dog.

RABIES

The greatest fear in the dog fancy today is still the great fear it has always been—rabies!

What has always held true about this dreadful disease still holds true today. The only way rabies can be contracted is through the saliva of a rabid dog entering the bloodstream of another animal or person. There is, of course, the Pasteur treatment for rabies which is very effective. There was of late the incident of a little boy bitten by a rabid bat having survived the disease. However, the Pasteur treatment is administered immediately if there is any question of exposure. Even more than dogs being found to be rabid, we now know that the biggest carriers are bats, skunks, foxes, rabbits and other warm-blooded animals, which pass it from one to another, since they do not have the benefit of inoculation. Dogs that run free should be inoculated for protection against these animals. For city or house dogs that never leave their owner's side, it may not be as necessary.

Ch. Damasyn Dia, a red Derringer daughter, winning Best of Breed from the Classes over 45 Specials under judge George Schroth. This was the fourth Best of Breed from the classes for Dia, who went on to Third in the Group at this 1969 Packerland Kennel Club Show.

For many years, Great Britain, because it is an island and because of the country's strictly enforced six-month quarantine, was entirely free of rabies. But in 1969, a British officer brought back his dog from foreign duty and the dog was found to have the disease soon after being released from quarantine. There was a great uproar about it, with Britain killing off wild and domestic animals in a great scare campaign, but the quarantine is once again down to six months and things seem to have returned to a normal, sensible attitude.

Health departments in rural towns usually provide rabies inoculations free of charge. If your dog is outdoors a great deal, or exposed to other animals that are, you might wish to call the town hall and get information on the program in your area. One cannot be too cautious about this dread disease. While the number of cases diminishes each year, there are still thousands being reported and there is still the constant threat of an outbreak where animals roam free. And never forget, there is no cure.

Rabies is caused by a neurotropic virus which can be found in the saliva, brain and sometimes the blood of the warm-blooded animal afflicted. The incubation period is usually two weeks or as long as six months, which means you can be exposed to it without any visible symptoms. As we have said, while there is still no known cure, it can be controlled. It is up to every individual to help effect this control by reporting animal bites, educating the public to the dangers and symptoms and prevention of it, so that we may reduce the fatalities.

There are two kinds of rabies; one form is called "furious," and the other is referred to as "dumb." The mad dog goes through several stages of the disease. His disposition and behavior change radically and suddenly; he becomes irritable and vicious; the eating habits alter, and he rejects food for things like stones and sticks; he be-

Australian Ch. Walamara Brite 'N' Bronze pictured with his owner, Ian Alexander of Melbourne, Australia.

Duke of Lombardy, owned by Joseph Rapisarda of Hillside, New Jersey. Unfortunately, Duke broke a leg and couldn't be shown, though he is obviously of the highest show quality. His sire was Ch. Damasyn The Solitaire, C.D.X.

comes exhausted and drools saliva out of his mouth almost constantly. He may hide in corners, look glassy eyed and suspicious, bite at the air as he races around snarling and attacking with his tongue hanging out. At this point paralysis sets in, starting at the throat so that he can no longer drink water though he desires it desperately; hence, the term hydrophobia is given. He begins to stagger and eventually convulse and death is imminent.

In "dumb" rabies paralysis is swift; the dog seeks dark, sheltered places and is abnormally quiet. Paralysis starts with the jaws, spreads down the body and death is quick. Contact by humans or other animals with the drool from either of these types of rabies on open skin can produce the fatal disease, so extreme haste and proper diagnosis is essential. In other words, you do not have to be bitten by a rabid dog to have the virus enter your system. An open wound or cut that comes in touch with the saliva is all that is needed.

The incubation and degree of infection can vary. You usually contract the disease faster if the wound is near the head, since the virus travels to the brain through the spinal cord. The deeper the wound, the more saliva is injected into the body, the more serious the infection. So, if bitten by a dog under any circumstances—or any warm-blooded animal for that matter—immediately wash out the wound with soap and water, bleed it profusely, and see your doctor as soon as possible.

Also, be sure to keep track of the animal that bit, if at all possible. When rabies is suspected the public health officer will need to send the animal's head away to be analyzed. If it is found to be rabies free, you will not need to undergo treatment. Otherwise, your doctor may advise that you have the Pasteur treatment, which is extremely painful. It is rather simple, however, to have the veterinarian examine a dog for rabies without having the dog sent away for positive diagnosis of the disease. A ten-day quarantine is usually all that is necessary for everyone's peace of mind.

Rabies is no respecter of age, sex or geographical location. It is found all over the world from North Pole to South Pole, and has nothing to do with the old wives' tale of dogs going mad in the hot summer months. True, there is an increase in reported cases during summer, but only because that is the time of the year for animals to roam free in good weather and during the mating season when the battle of the sexes is taking place. Inoculation and a keen eye for symptoms and bites on our dogs and other pets will help control the disease until the cure is found.

VACCINATIONS

If you are to raise a puppy, or a litter of puppies, successfully, you must adhere to a realistic and strict schedule of vaccination. Many puppyhood diseases can be fatal—all of them are debilitating.

Damasyn The Timkin, C.D., foundation bitch of the Arabar Kennels of Barbara Kirfel, Middle Island, New York. Timkin was sired by Robies Colonel, a Top Skipper son, out of Damasyn The Lil Red Lambchop. Timkin lived to be 14 years of age, much loved and much missed by all who knew her.

Tevrac's Typhoon, just under 10 months of age, pictured winning Best Puppy in Show under judge Peggy Adamson at a California Doberman Pinscher Specialty Show in the 1960's. She is a sister to Tsushima who was Best of Breed at the same show.

Ch. Damasyn Carly of Jerseystone, a singleton sired by Ch. Damasyn Derringer x Toledobe's Misty Moonlight. Shown to his championship by Patrick and Judy Doniere for Peggy Adamson, Carly now lives with the Donieres and has sired 17 champions.

According to the latest statistics, 98 per cent of all puppies are being inoculated after 12 weeks of age against the dread distemper, hepatitis and leptospirosis and manage to escape these horrible infections. Orphaned puppies should be vaccinated every two weeks until the age of 12 weeks. Distemper and hepatitis live-virus vaccine should be used, since they are not protected with the colostrum normally supplied to them through the mother's milk. Puppies weaned at six to seven weeks should also be inoculated repeatedly because they will no longer be receiving mother's milk. While not all will receive protection from the serum at this early age, it should be given and they should be vaccinated once again at both nine and 12 weeks of age.

Leptospirosis vaccination should be given at four months of age with thought given to booster shots if the disease is known in the area, or in the case of show dogs which are exposed on a regular basis to many dogs from far and wide. While annual boosters are in order for distemper and hepatitis, every two or three years is sufficient for leptospirosis, unless there is an outbreak in your immediate area. The one exception should be the pregnant bitch since there is reason to believe that inoculation might cause damage to the fetus.

Strict observance of such a vaccination schedule will not only keep your dog free of these debilitating diseases, but will prevent an epidemic in your kennel, or in your locality, or to the dogs which are competing at the shows.

SNAKEBITE

As field trials and hunts and the like become more and more popular with dog enthusiasts, the incident of snakebite becomes more of a likelihood. Dogs that are kept outdoors in runs or dogs that work the fields and roam on large estates are also likely victims.

Most veterinarians carry snakebite serum, and snakebite kits are sold to dog owners for just such purpose. To catch a snakebite in time might mean the difference between life and death, and whether your area is populated with snakes or not, it behooves you to know what to do in case it happens to you or your dog.

Your primary concern should be to get to a doctor or veterinarian immediately. The victim should be kept as quiet as possible (excitement or activity spreads the venom through the body more quickly) and if possible the wound should be bled enough to clean it out before applying a tourniquet, if the bite is severe.

First of all, it must be determined if the bite is from a poisonous or non-poisonous snake. If the bite carries two horseshoe shaped pinpoints of a double row of teeth, the bite can be assumed to be non-poisonous. If the bite leaves two punctures or holes—the result of the two fangs carrying venom—the bite is very definitely poisonous and time is of the essence.

Recently, physicians have come up with an added help in the case of snakebite. A first aid treatment referred to as hypothermia, which is the application of ice to the wound to lower body temperature to a point where the venom spreads less quickly, minimizes swelling, helps prevent infection and has some influence on numbing the pain. If ice is not readily available, the bite may be soaked in ice-cold water. But even more urgent is the need to get the victim to a hospital or a veterinarian for additional treatment.

EMERGENCIES

No matter how well you run your kennel or keep an eye on an individual dog, there will almost invariably be some emergency at some time that will require quick treatment until you get the animal to the veterinarian. The first and most important thing to remember is to keep calm! You will think more clearly and your animal will need to know he can depend on you to take care of him. However, he will be frightened and you must beware of fear biting. Therefore, do not shower him with kisses and endearments at this time, no matter how

English judge Joyce Spaughton with her Nina van Frankskirby pictured at 10 years of age. From pure European stock, Nina was sired by German import Bowesmoor's Fax vom Gerkeraherwinkle (red) x Triogen Test Run (black and tan). Bernard and Joyce Spaughton's Frankskirby Dobermans are located in Kent, England.

sympathetic you feel. Comfort him reassuringly, but keep your wits about you. Before getting him to the veterinarian try to alleviate the pain and shock.

If you can take even a minor step in this direction it will be a help toward the final cure. Listed here are a few of the emergencies which might occur and what you can do AFTER you have called the vet and told him your are coming.

BURNS

If you have been so foolish as not to turn your pot handles toward the back of the stove—for your children's sake as well as your dog's—and the dog is burned, apply ice or ice cold water and treat for shock. Electrical or chemical burns are treated the same; but with an acid or alkali burn, use, respectively, a bicarbonate of soda or vinegar solution. Check the advisability of covering the burn when you call the veterinarian.

DROWNING

Most animals love the water, but sometimes get in "over their heads." Should your dog take in too much water, hold him upside down and open his mouth so that water can empty from the lungs, then apply artificial respiration, or mouth-to-mouth resuscitation. Then treat for shock by covering him with a blanket, administering a stimulant such as coffee with sugar, and soothing him with voice and hand.

FITS AND CONVULSIONS

Prevent the dog from thrashing about and injuring himself, cover with a blanket and hold down until you can get him to the veterinarian.

FROSTBITE

There is no excuse for an animal getting frostbite if you are on your toes and care for the animal. However, should frostbite set in, thaw out the affected area slowly with a circulatory motion and stimulation. Use vaseline to help keep the skin from peeling off and/or drying out.

HEART ATTACK

Be sure the animal keeps breathing by applying artificial respiration. A mild stimulant may be used and give him plenty of air. Treat for shock as well, and get to the veterinarian quickly.

Saber Jet of Hunterlane, one of the first Dobes owned by Mrs. Charles La Plant of the Storm Sun Kennels, Shortsville, New York. Photo taken in March, 1974.

SUFFOCATION

Artificial respiration and treat for shock with plenty of air.

SUN STROKE

Cooling the dog off immediately is essential. Ice packs, submersion in ice water, and plenty of cool air are needed.

WOUNDS

Open wounds or cuts which produce bleeding must be treated with hydrogen peroxide and tourniquets should be used if bleeding is excessive. Also, shock treatment must be given, and the animal must be kept warm.

THE FIRST AID KIT

It would be sheer folly to try to operate a kennel or to keep a dog without providing for certain emergencies that are bound to crop up when there are active dogs around. Just as you would provide a first aid kit for people you should also provide a first aid kit for the animals on the premises.

The first aid kit should contain the following items:

BFI or other medicated powder
jar of Vaseline
Q-tips
bandage—1 inch gauze
adhesive tape
Band-Aids
cotton
boric acid powder

Taimar The Black Talisman, whelped in November, 1970 and owned by Levi Randall of Mississippi. The sire was Damasyn Bo-Tai of Ardon x Damasyn Flippant.

High Halos Calypso, one of the first fawns to be shown and a Reserve Winner at a Mississippi Valley Kennel Club show.

A trip to your veterinarian is always safest, but there are certain preliminaries for cuts and bruises of a minor nature that you can care for yourself.

Cuts, for instance, should be washed out and medicated powder or Vaseline applied with a bandage. The lighter the bandage the better so that the most air possible can reach the wound. Q-tips can be used for removing debris from the eyes after which a mild solution of boric acid wash can be applied. As for sores, use dry powder on wet sores, and Vaseline on dry sores. Use cotton for washing out wounds and drying them.

A particular caution must be given here on bandaging. Make sure that the bandage is not too tight to hamper the dog's circulation. Also, make sure the bandage is made correctly so that the dog does not bite at it trying to get it off. A great deal of damage can be done to a wound by a dog tearing at a bandage to get it off. If you notice the dog is starting to bite at it, do it over or put something on the bandage that smells and tastes bad to him. Make sure, however, that the solution does not soak through the bandage and enter the wound. Sometimes, if it is a leg wound, a sock or stocking slipped on the dog's leg will cover the bandage edges and will also keep it clean.

HOW NOT TO POISON YOUR DOG

Ever since the appearance of Rachel Carson's book *Silent Spring,* people have been asking, "Just how dangerous are chemicals?" In the animal world where disinfectants, room deodorants, parasitic sprays, solutions and aerosols are so widely used, the question has taken on even more meaning. Veterinarians are beginning to ask, "What kind of disinfectant do you use?" or "Have you any fruit trees that have been sprayed recently?" When animals are brought in to their offices in a toxic condition, or for unexplained death, or when entire litters of puppies die mysteriously, there is good reason to ask such questions.

The popular practice of protecting animals against parasites has given way to their being exposed to an alarming number of commercial products, some of which are dangerous to their very lives. Even flea collars can be dangerous, especially if they get wet or somehow touch the genital regions or eyes. While some products are a great deal more poisonous than others, great care must be taken that they be applied in proportion to the size of the dog and the area to be covered. Many a dog has been taken to the vet with an unusual skin problem that was a direct result of having been bathed with a detergent rather than a proper shampoo. Certain products that are safe for dogs can be fatal for cats. Extreme care must be taken to read all ingredients and instructions carefully before use on any animal.

The same caution must be given to outdoor chemicals. Dog owners must question the use of fertilizers on their lawns. Lime, for in-

Damasyn The Egan pictured with her handler, J. Monroe Stebbins, Jr., winning at a show several years ago. She was sired by Ch. Damasyn Derringer out of Jerry Runs Boo Sprite. Bred and owned by Peggy Adamson.

stance, can be harmful to a dog's feet. The unleashed dog that covers the neighborhood on his daily rounds is open to all sorts of tree and lawn sprays and insecticides that may prove harmful to him, if not as a poison, as a producer of an allergy. Many puppy fatalities are reported when they consume mothballs.

There are various products found around the house which can be lethal, such as rat poison, boric acid, hand soap, detergents, and insecticides. The garage too may provide dangers: antifreeze for the car, lawn, garden and tree sprays, paints, etc., are all available for tipping over and consuming. All poisons should be placed on high shelves for the sake of your children as well as your animals.

Perhaps the most readily available of all household poisons are plants. Household plants are almost all poisonous, even if taken in small quantities. Some of the most dangerous are the elephant ear, the narcissus bulb, any kind of ivy leaves, burning bush leaves, the jimson weed, the dumb cane weed, mock orange fruit, castor beans, Scotch broom seeds, the root or seed of the plant called four o'clock, cyclamen, pimpernel, lily of the valley, the stem of the sweet pea, rhododendrons of any kind, spider lily bulbs, bayonet root, foxglove leaves, tulip bulbs, monkshood roots, azalea, wisteria, poinsettia leaves, mistletoe, hemlock, locoweed and arrowglove. In all, there are over 500 poisonous plants in the United States. Peach, elderberry and cherry trees can cause cyanide poisoning if the bark is consumed. Rhubarb leaves either raw or cooked can cause death or violent convulsions. Check out your closets, fields and grounds around your home to see what might be of danger to your pets.

Ch. Liquorish The Ron Rico pictured finishing for his championship with a Best in Show under judge Peter Knoop. The three and one-half year old Rico was handled by Jeffrey L. Brucker for his owner, Grace Joffe, Liquorish Dobes, Miami, Florida.

SYMPTOMS OF POISONING

Be on the lookout for vomiting, hard or labored breathing, whimpering, stomach cramps, and trembling as a prelude to the convulsions. Any delay in a visit to your veterinarian can mean death. Take along the bottle or package or a sample of the plant you suspect to be the cause to help the veterinarian determine the correct antidote.

The most common type of poisoning, which accounts for nearly one-fourth of all animal victims, is staphylococcic-infected food. Salmonella ranks third. These can be avoided by serving fresh food and not letting it lie around in hot weather.

There are also many insect poisonings caused by animals eating cockroaches, spiders, flies, butterflies, etc. Toads and some frogs give off a fluid which can make a dog foam at the mouth—and even kill him—if he bites just a little too hard!

Some misguided dog owners think it is "cute" to let their dogs enjoy a cocktail with them before dinner. There can be serious effects resulting from encouraging a dog to drink—sneezing fits, injuries as

Ch. Dow's Dame, photographed at 10 years of age. Dame was the dam of 16 champions, making her one of the breed's most highly prized brood bitches. This Dictator daughter out of Ch. Dow's Dodie was owned by Eleanor Brown.

Ch. Arabar's Rhapsody, bred by Barbara Kirfel of Middle Island, New York. The sire was Ch. Damasyn Bo-Tairic of Ardon x Damasyn Polonaise of Arabar, C.D.

a result of intoxication, and heart stoppage are just a few. Whiskey for medicinal purposes, or beer for brood bitches should be administered only on the advice of your veterinarian.

There have been cases of severe damage and death when dogs emptied ash trays and consumed cigarettes, resulting in nicotine poisoning. Leaving a dog alone all day in a house where there are cigarettes available on a coffee table is asking for trouble. Needless to

The blue Ch. Zenodobe's Arius with Nancy Woods handling, and the blue Selthanie Happy Hour, C.D., with Leslie F. Lloyd handling.

say, the same applies to marijuana. The narcotic addict who takes his dog along with him on "a trip" does not deserve to have a dog. All the ghastly side effects are as possible for the dog as for the addict, and for a person to submit an animal to this indignity is indeed despicable. Don't think it doesn't happen. Ask the veterinarians that practice near some of your major hippie havens! Unfortunately, in all our major cities the practice is becoming more and more a problem for the veterinarian.

Be on the alert and remember that in the case of any type of poisoning, the best treatment is prevention.

THE CURSE OF ALLERGY

The heartbreak of a child being forced to give up a beloved pet because he is suddenly found to be allergic to it is a sad but true story. Many families claim to be unable to have dogs at all; others seem to be able only to enjoy them on a restricted basis. Many children know animals only through occasional visits to a friend's house or the zoo.

While modern veterinary science has produced some brilliant allergists, such as Dr. Edward Baker of New Jersey, the field is still working on a solution for those who suffer from exposure to their pets. There is no permanent cure as yet.

Over the last quarter of a century there have been many attempts at a permanent cure, but none has proven successful, because the treatment was needed too frequently, or was too expensive to maintain over extended periods of time.

Shanzu Vitu and Odin Black Silhouette, C.D. practice their "long sits" at training class in Australia along with two classmates.

However, we find that most people who are allergic to their animals are also allergic to a variety of other things as well. By eliminating the other irritants, and by taking medication given for the control of allergies in general, many are able to keep pets on a restricted basis. This may necessitate the dog's living outside the house, being groomed at a professional grooming parlor instead of by the owner, or merely being kept out of the bedroom at night. A discussion of this "balance" factor with your medical and veterinary doctors may give new hope to those willing to try.

A paper presented by Mathilde M. Gould, M.D., a New York allergist, before the American Academy of Allergists in the 1960's, and reported in the September-October 1964 issue of the *National Humane Review* magazine, offered new hope to those who are allergic by a method referred to as hyposensitization. You may wish to write to the magazine and request the article for discussion with your medical and veterinary doctors on your individual problem.

Winner of the 1975 (and 1973) Doberman Pinscher Club of America Specialty Show in California was Ch. Brown's B-Brien, owned by Eleanor Brown and handled by Marge Anagnost. Judge Peggy Adamson's selection at this 50th Anniversary Show retired all the trophies, since it was a third triumph for the Brown's Kennels.

DO ALL DOGS CHEW?

All young dogs chew! Chewing is the best possible method of cutting teeth and exercising gums. Every puppy goes through this teething process. True, it can be destructive if not watched carefully, and it is really the responsibility of every owner to prevent the damage before it occurs.

When you see a puppy pick up an object to chew, immediately remove it from his mouth with a sharp "No!" and replace the object with a Nylon or rawhide bone which should be provided for him to do his serious chewing. Puppies take anything and everything into their mouths so they should be provided with proper toys which they cannot chew up and swallow.

BONES

There are many opinions on the kind of bones a dog should have. Anyone who has lost a puppy or dog because of a bone chip puncturing the stomach or intestinal wall will say "no bones" except for the

Nylon or rawhide kind you buy in pet shops. There are those who say shank or knuckle bones are permissible. Use your own judgment, but when there are adequate processed bones which you know to be safe, why risk a valuable animal? Cooked bones, soft enough to be pulverized and put in the food can be fed if they are reduced almost to a powder. If you have the patience for this sort of thing, okay. Otherwise, stick to the commercial products.

As for dogs and puppies chewing furniture, shoes, etc., replace the object with something allowable and safe and put yourself on record as remembering to close closet doors. Keep the puppy in the same room with you so you can stand guard over the furniture.

Electrical cords and sockets, or wires of any kind, present a dangerous threat to chewers. Glass dishes which can be broken are hazardous if not picked up right after feeding.

Chewing can also be a form of frustration or nervousness. Dogs sometimes chew for spite, if owners leave them alone too long or too often. Bitches will sometimes chew if their puppies are taken away from them too soon; insecure puppies often chew thinking they're nursing. Puppies which chew wool or blankets or carpet corners or certain types of materials may have a nutritional deficiency or something lacking in their diet, such as craving the starch that might be left in material after washing. Perhaps the articles have been near something that tastes good and they retain the odor.

The act of chewing has no connection with particular breeds or ages, any more than there is a logical reason for dogs to dig holes outdoors or dig on wooden floors indoors.

So we repeat, it is up to you to be on guard at all times until the need—or habit—passes.

HIP DYSPLASIA

Hip dysplasia, or HD, is one of the most widely discussed of all animal afflictions, since it has appeared in varying degrees in just about every breed of dog. True, the larger breeds seem most susceptible, but it has hit the small breeds and is beginning to be recognized in cats as well.

While HD in man has been recorded as far back as 370 B.C., HD in dogs was more than likely referred to as rheumatism until veterinary research came into the picture. In 1935, Dr. Otto Schales, at Angell Memorial Hospital in Boston, wrote a paper on hip dysplasia and classified the four degrees of dysplasia of the hip joint as follows:

Grade 1—slight (poor fit between ball and socket)

Grade 2—moderate (moderate but obvious shallowness of the socket)

Grade 3—severe (socket quite flat)

Grade 4—very severe (complete displacement of head of femur at early age)

HD is an incurable, hereditary, though not congenital disease of the hip sockets. It is transmitted as a dominant trait with irregular manifestations. Puppies appear normal at birth but the constant wearing away of the socket means the animal moves more and more on muscle, thereby presenting a lameness, a difficulty in getting up and severe pain in advanced cases.

The degree of severity can be determined around six months of age, but its presence can be noticed from two months of age. The problem is determined by X-ray, and if pain is present it can be relieved temporarily by medication. Exercise should be avoided since motion encourages the wearing away of the bone surfaces.

Dogs with HD should not be shown or bred, if quality in the breed is to be maintained. It is essential to check a pedigree for dogs known to be dysplastic before breeding, since this disease can be dormant for many generations.

ELBOW DYSPLASIA

The same condition can also affect the elbow joints and is known as elbow dysplasia. This also causes lameness, and dogs so affected should not be used for breeding.

PATELLAR DYSPLASIA

Some of the smaller breeds of dogs also suffer from patella dysplasia, or dislocation of the knee. This can be treated surgically, but the surgery by no means abolishes the hereditary factor. Therefore, these dogs should not be used for breeding.

All dogs—in any breed—should be X-rayed before being used for breeding. The X-ray should be read by a competent veterinarian, and the dog declared free and clear.

HD PROGRAM IN GREAT BRITAIN

The British Veterinary Association (BVA) has made an attempt to control the spread of HD by appointing a panel of members of their profession who have made a special study of the disease to read X-rays. Dogs over one year of age may be X-rayed and certified as free. Forms are completed in triplicate to verify the tests. One copy remains with the panel, one copy is for the owner's veterinarian, and one for the owner. A record is also sent to the British Kennel Club for those wishing to check on a particular dog for breeding purposes.

THE UNITED STATES REGISTRY

In the United States we have a central Hip Dysplasia Foundation, known as the OFA (Orthopedic Foundation for Animals). This HD control registry was formed in 1966. X-rays are sent for expert evaluation by qualified radiologists.

All you need do for complete information on getting an X-ray for your dog is to write to the Orthopedic Foundation for Animals at 817 Virginia Ave., Columbia, Mo., 65201, and request their dysplasia packet. There is no charge for this kit. It contains an envelope large enough to hold your X-ray film (which you will have taken by your own veterinarian), and a drawing showing how to position the dog properly for X-ray. There is also an application card for proper identification of the dog. Then, hopefully, your dog will be certified "normal." You will be given a registry number which you can put on his pedigree, use in your advertising, and rest assured your breeding program is in good order.

All X-rays should be sent to the address above. Any other information you might wish to have may be requested from Mrs. Robert Bower, OFA, Route 1, Constantine, Mo., 49042.

We cannot urge strongly enough the importance of doing this. While it involves time and effort, the reward in the long run will more than pay for your trouble. To see the heartbreak of parents and children when their beloved dog has to be put to sleep because of severe hip dysplasia as the result of bad breeding is a sad experience. Don't let this happen to your or to those who will purchase your puppies!

Additionally, we should mention that there is a method of palpation to determine the extent of affliction. This can be painful if the animal is not properly prepared for the examination. There have also been attempts to replace the animal's femur and socket. This is not only expensive, but the percentage of success is small.

For those who refuse to put their dog down, there is a new surgical technique which can relieve pain, but in no way constitutes a cure. This technique involves the severing of the pectinius muscle which for some unknown reason brings relief from pain over a period of many months—even up to two years. Two veterinary colleges in the United States are performing this operation at the present time. However, the owner must also give permission to "de-sex" the dogs at the time of the muscle severance. This is a safety measure to help stamp out hip dysplasia, since obviously the condition itself remains and can be passed on.

Impressive headstudy of Ch. Damasyn Carly of Jerseystone, sire of 17 champions.

22. THE BLIGHT OF PARASITES

Anyone who has ever spent countless hours peering down intently at his dog's warm, pink stomach waiting for a flea to appear will readily understand why we call this chapter the "blight of parasites." For it is that dreaded onslaught of the pesky flea that heralds the subsequent arrival of worms.

If you have seen even one flea scoot across that vulnerable expanse of skin you can be sure there are more fleas lurking on other favorite areas of your dog. They seldom travel alone. So it is now an established fact that *la puce*, as the French would say when referring to the flea, has set up housekeeping on your dog and it is going to demand a great deal of your time before you manage to evict them completely, and probably just temporarily, no matter which species your dog is harboring.

Fleas are not always choosy about their host, but chances are your dog has what is commonly known as *Ctenocephalides canis*, the dog flea. If you are a lover of cats also, your dog might even be playing host to a few *Ctenocephalides felis*, the cat flea, or vice versa! The only thing you can be really sure of is that your dog is supporting an entire community of them, all hungry and all sexually oriented, and you are going to have to be persistent in your campaign to get rid of them.

One of the chief reasons they are so difficult to catch is that what they lack in beauty and eyesight (they are blind at birth, throughout infancy and see very poorly or are blind during adulthood,) they make up for in their fantastic ability to jump and scurry about.

While this remarkable ability to jump—some say 150 times the length of their bodies—stands them in good stead with circus entrepeneurs and has given them claim to fame as chariot pullers and acrobats in side show attractions, the dog owner can be reduced to tears at the very thought of the onset of fleas.

Modern research has provided a remedy in the form of flea sprays, dips, collars and tags which can be successful in varying degrees. But there are those who swear by the good old-fashioned methods of removing them by hand, which can be a challenge to your sanity as well as your dexterity.

Damasyn The Syndahr pictured winning a recent Working Group; owned by Bob Chappell of Des Moines, Iowa. Syndahr was sired by Ch. Damasyn The Boatswain x Damasyn The Blackberry Muffin, C.D.

Opposite:
Beautiful headstudy of Damasyn Polonaise of Arabar, C,D. Bred, owned and trained for the obedience ring by Barbara Kirfel, Arabar Kennels, Middle Island, New York.

Since the fleas' conformation (they are built like envelopes, long and flat) with their spiny skeletal system on the outside of their bodies is specifically provided for slithering through hair forests, they are given a distinct advantage to start with. Two antennae on the head select the best spot for digging and then two mandibles penetrate the skin and hit a blood vessel. It is also at this moment that the flea brings into play his spiny contours to prop himself against a few surrounding hairs which prevent him from being scratched off as he puts the bite on your dog. A small tubular tongue is then lowered into the hole to draw out blood and another tube is injected into the hole to pump the saliva of the flea into the wound which prevents the blood from clotting. This allows the flea to drink freely. Simultaneously your dog jumps into the air and gets one of those back legs into action scratching endlessly and in vain.

Now while you may catch an itinerant flea as he mistakenly shortcuts across your dog's stomach, the best hunting grounds are usually in the deep fur down along the dog's back from neck to the base of the tail. However, the flea like every other creature on earth must have water, so several times during its residency it will make its way to the moister areas of your dog, such as the corners of the mouth, the eyes or the genital areas. This is when the flea collars and tags are useful. The fumes from them prevent the fleas from passing the neck to get to the head of your dog.

Your dog can usually support several generations of fleas if he doesn't scratch himself to death or go out of his mind with the itching in the interim. The population of the flea is insured by the strong mating instinct and the wise personal decision of the female flea as to the best time to deposit her eggs. She has the useful capacity to store semen until the time is right to lay the eggs after some previous brief encounter with a passing member of the opposite sex.

When that time comes for her to lay the eggs, she does so without so much as a backward glance and moves on. The dog, during a normal day's wandering, shakes the eggs off along his way, and there the eggs remain until hatched and the baby fleas are ready to jump back on a dog. If any of the eggs remain on the dog, chances are your dog will help them emerge from their shells with his scratching when some adult flea passes in the vicinity.

Larval fleas look like very small and slender maggots; they begin their lives feasting off their own egg shells until your dog comes along and offers the return to the world of adult fleas, whose excrement provides the predigested blood pellets they must have to thrive. They cannot survive on fresh blood, nor are they capable at this tender age of digging for it themselves. We are certain that the expression "two can eat as cheaply as one" originated after some curious scientist made a detailed study of the life cycle of the flea.

After a couple of weeks of this free loading, the baby flea makes his own cocoon and becomes a pupa. This stage lasts long enough for

Another winner from the 1950's was Ch. Jet von der Ravensburg, owned by Walter and May Denker of Long Island, New York. Jet was twice the winner of Best of Breed awards at the Doberman Pinscher Club of America Specialty shows.

Ch. Walire's Rupert, owned by Melba Stafford of Colorado.

the larval flea to grow legs, mandibles, and sharp spines and to flatten out and in general get to be identifiable as the commonly known and obnoxious *Ctenocephalides canis*. The process can take several weeks or several months, depending on weather conditions, heat, moisture, etc., but generally three weeks is all that is required to enable it to start chomping on your dog in its own right.

And so the life of the flea is renewed and begun again, and if you don't have plans to stem the tide, you will certainly see a population explosion that will make the human one resemble an endangered species. Getting rid of fleas can be accomplished by the aforementioned spraying of the dog, or the flea collars and tags, but air, sunshine and a good shaking out of beds, bedding, carpets, cushions, etc., certainly must be undertaken to get rid of the eggs or larvae lying around the premises.

However, if you love the thrill of the chase, and have the stomach for it, you can still try to catch them on safari across your dog's stomach. Your dog will love the attention, that is, if you don't keep pinching a bit of skin instead of that little blackish critter. Chances are

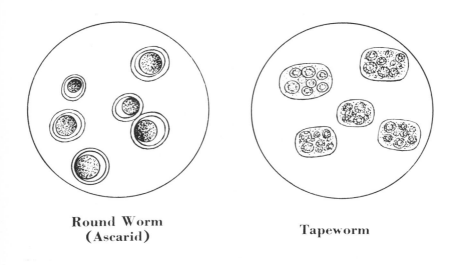

**Round Worm
(Ascarid)**

Tapeworm

Hookworm

Whipworm

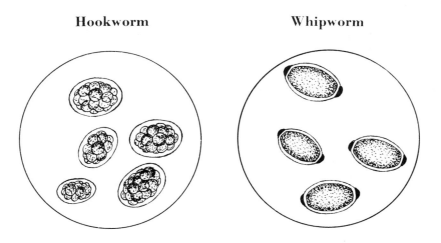

Eggs of certain parasites commonly seen in dogs.

Dr. Howard Cohen handled his Highquest Faith to Best of Breed and Group First at the 1971 Taconic Hills Kennel Club show. Undefeated as a puppy, Faith is now retired.

great you will come up with skin rather than the flea and your dog will lose interest and patience.

Should you be lucky enough to get hold of one, you must either squeeze it to death (which isn't likely) or break it in two with a sharp, strong fingernail (which also isn't likely) or you must release it *underwater* in the toilet bowl and flush immediately. This prospect is only slightly more likely. We strongly suggest that you shape up, clean up, shake out and spray—on a regular basis.

There are those people, however, who are much more philosophical about the flea, since, like the cockroach, it has been around since the beginning of the world. For instance, that old-time philosopher, David Harum, who has been much quoted with his remark, "A reasonable amount of fleas is good for a dog. They keep him from broodin' on bein' a dog." We would rather agree with John Donne who in his *Devotions* reveals that, "The flea, though he kill none, he does all the harm he can." This is especially true if your dog is a show dog! If the scratching doesn't ruin the coat, the inevitable infestations of the parasites the fleas will leave with your dog will!

So we readily see that dogs can be afflicted by both internal and external parasites. The external parasites are known as the aforementioned fleas, plus ticks and lice; while all of these are bothersome, they can be treated. However, the internal parasites, or worms of various kinds, are usually well-infested before discovery and require more substantial means of ridding the dog of them completely.

493

INTERNAL PARASITES

The most common worms are the round worms. These, like many other worms, are carried and spread by the flea and go through a cycle within the dog host. They are excreted in egg or larval form and passed on to other dogs in this manner.

Worm medicine should be prescribed by a veterinarian, and dogs should be checked for worms at least twice a year, or every three months if there is a known epidemic in your area, and during the summer months when fleas are plentiful.

Major types of worms are hookworms, whipworms, tapeworms (the only non-round worm in this list), ascarids (the "typical" round worms), heartworms, kidney and lung worms. Each can be peculiar to a part of the country or may be carried by a dog from one area to another. Kidney and lung worms are quite rare, fortunately. The others are not. Symptoms for worms might be vomiting intermittently, eating grass, lack of pep, bloated stomach, rubbing their tail along the ground, loss of weight, dull coat, anemia and pale gums, eye discharge, or unexplained nervousness and irritability. A dog with worms will usually eat twice as much as he normally would also.

Never worm a sick dog, or a pregnant bitch after the first two weeks she has been bred, and never worm a constipated dog. . . it will retain the strong medicine within the body for too long a time. The best, safest way to determine the presence of worms is to test for them before they do excessive damage.

HOW TO TEST FOR WORMS

Worms can kill your dog if the infestation is severe enough. Even light infestations of worms can debilitate a dog to the point where he is more susceptible to other serious diseases that can kill, if the worms do not.

Today's medication for worming is relatively safe and mild, and worming is no longer the traumatic experience for either dog or owner that it used to be. Great care must be given, however, to the proper administration of the drugs. Correct dosage is a "must" and clean quarters are essential to rid your kennel of these parasites. It is almost impossible to find an animal that is completely free of parasites, so we must consider worming as a necessary evil.

However mild today's medicines may be, it is inadvisable to worm a dog unnecessarily. There are simple tests to determine the presence of worms and this chapter is designed to help you learn how to make these tests yourself. Veterinarians charge a nominal fee for this service, if it is not part of their regular office visit examination. It is a simple matter to prepare fecal slides that you can read yourself on a periodic basis. Over the years it will save you much time and money, especially if you have more than one dog or a large kennel.

All that is needed by way of equipment is a microscope with 100x power. These can be purchased in the toy department in a department or regular toy store for a few dollars, depending on what else you want to get with it, but the basic, least expensive sets come with the necessary glass slides and attachments.

After the dog has defecated, take an applicator stick, or a toothpick with a flat end, or even an old-fashioned wooden matchstick, and gouge off a piece of the stool about the size of a small pea. Have one of the glass slides ready with a large drop of water on it. Mix the two together until you have a cloudy film over a large area of the slide. This smear should be covered with another slide, or a cover slip—though it is possible to obtain readings with just the one open slide. Place your slide under the microscope and prepare to focus in on it. To read the slide you will find that your eye should follow a certain pattern. Start at the top and read from left to right, then right back to the left side and then left over to the right side once again until you have looked at every portion of the slide from the top left to the bottom right side, as illustrated here:

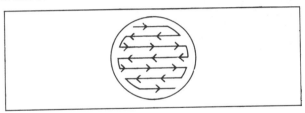

Make sure that your smear is not too thick or watery or the reading will be too dark and confused to make proper identification. Included in this chapter are drawings which will show you what to look for when reading the slides to identify the four most common varieties of worms. If you decide you would rather not make your own fecal examinations, but would prefer to have the veterinarian do it, the proper way to present a segment of the stool for him to examine is as follows:

After the dog has defecated, a portion of the stool, say a square inch from different sections of it, should be placed in a glass jar or plastic container, and labeled with the dog's name and address of the owner. If the sample cannot be examined within three to four hours after passage, it should be refrigerated. Your opinion as to what variety of worms you suspect is sometimes helpful to the veterinarian and may be noted on the label of the jar you submit to him for the examination.

Checking for worms on a regular basis is advisable not only for the welfare of the dog but for the protection of your family, since most worms are transmissible, under certain circumstances, to humans.

A 1956 Gaines Dog Photograph Contest Winner entitled "Eyes right, Baron." The photographer was Gilbert Barrera. This photograph appeared in *Popular Dogs* magazine when the author was its editor and uncovered it in an old dusty file.

23. DICTIONARY OF DOG DISEASES

AN AID TO DIAGNOSIS
—A—

ABORTION—The premature expulsion of embryos from the uterus. If part of a fetus is left in the uterus, serious infection may occur. The first indication of this will be high fever, dry nose and lethargy. The immediate services of a veterinarian are necessary.

ABSCESS—A skin eruption characterized by a localized collection of pus formed as a result of disintegrating tissues of the body. Abscesses may be acute or chronic. An acute abscess forms rapidly and will more than likely burst within a week. It is accompanied by pain, redness, heat and swelling, and may cause a rise in temperature. An abscess is usually the result of infection of a bacterial nature. Treatment consists of medication in the form of antibiotics and salves, ointments, powders or a poultice designed to bring it to a head. A chronic abscess is a slow-developing headless lump surrounded by gathering tissue. This infection is usually of internal origin, and painless unless found in a sensitive area of the body. The same antibiotics and medications are used. Because abscesses of this nature are slow in developing, they are generally slow in dissolving.

ACARUS—One of the parasitic mites which cause mange.

ACHONDROPLASIA—A disease which results in the stunting of growth, or dwarfing of the limbs before birth.

ADENOMA—A non-inflammatory growth or benign tumor found in a prominent gland; most commonly found in the mammary gland of the bitch.

AGALACTIA—A contagious, viral disease resulting in lowered or no production of milk by a nursing bitch. It usually appears in warm weather, and is accompanied by fever and loss of appetite. Abscesses may also form. In chronic cases the mammary gland itself may atrophy.

ALARIASIS—An infection caused by flukes (*Alaria arisaemoides*), which are ingested by the dog. They pass on to the bronchial tract and into the small intestine where they grow to maturity and feed on intestinal contents.

497

Rancho Dobe's Primo winning Best of Breed under the late judge William McInearney his first time shown several years ago. This future champion was also the sire of the great Ch. Rancho Dobe's Storm.

ALLERGY—Dogs can be allergic as well as people to outdoor or indoor surroundings, such as carpet fuzz, pillow stuffings, food, pollen, etc. Recent experiments in hyposensitization have proved effective in many cases when injections are given with follow-up "boosters." Sneezing, coughing, nasal discharges, runny, watery eyes, etc., are all symptomatic.

ALOPECIA—A bare spot, or lack of full growth of hair on a portion of the body; another name for baldness and can be the end result of a skin condition.

AMAUROSIS—Sometimes called "glass eye." A condition that may occur during a case of distemper if the nervous system has been affected, or head injuries sustained. It is characterized by the animal bumping into things or by a lack of coordination. The condition is incurable and sooner or later the optic nerve becomes completely paralyzed.

ANALGESIA—Loss of ability to feel pain with the loss of consciousness or the power to move a part of the body. The condition may be induced by drugs which act on the brain or central nervous system.

ANAL SAC OBSTRUCTION—The sacs on either side of the rectum, just inside the anus, at times may become clogged. If the condition persists, it is necessary for the animal to be assisted in their opening, so that they do not become infected and/or abscess. Pressure is applied by the veterinarian and the glands release a thick, horrible-smelling excretion. Antibiotics or a "flushing" of the glands if infected is the usual treatment, but at the first sign of discomfort in the dog's eliminating, or a "sliding along" the floor, it is wise to check for clogged anal glands.

ANASARCA—Dropsy of the connective tissues of the skin. It is occasionally encountered in fetuses and makes whelping difficult.

ANEMIA—A decrease of red blood cells which are the cells that carry oxygen to the body tissues. Causes are usually severe infestation of parasites, bad diet, or blood disease. Transfusions and medications can be given to replace red blood cells, but the disease is sometimes fatal.

ANEURYSM—A rupture or dilation of a major blood vessel, causing a bulge or swelling of the affected part. Blood gathers in the tissues forming a swelling. It may be caused by strain, injury, or when arteries are weakened by debilitating disease or old age. Surgery is needed to remove the clot.

ANESTROUS—When a female does not come into heat.

ANTIPERISTALSIS—A term given to the reverse action of the normal procedures of the stomach or intestine, which brings their contents closer to the mouth.

ANTIPYRETICS—Drugs or methods used to reduce temperature during fevers. These may take the form of cold baths, purgatives, etc.

ANTISPASMODICS—Medications which reduce spasms of the muscular tissues and soothe the nerves and muscles involved.

ANTISIALICS—Term applied to substances used to reduce excessive salivation.

ARSENIC POISONING—Dogs are particularly susceptible to this type of poisoning. There is nausea, vomiting, stomach pains and convulsions, even death in severe cases. An emetic may save the animal in some cases. Salt or dry mustard (1 tablespoon mixed with 1 teaspoonful of water) can be effective in causing vomiting until the veterinarian is reached.

Damasyn Julie, owned by Marily Cheowsky of Port Washington, New York. The sire was Ch. Damasyn Bo-Tairic of Ardon x Damasyn Jalli's Jancy.

The red Solitaire son, Ch. Damasyn The Davvok, C.D., owned by Tony Jaworawski of Chicago, Illinois.

Ch. Ebonaire's Arundel, litter brother to Ch. Ebonaire's His Excellancy, taking points at Bryn Mawr Kennel Club in June, 1969.

ARTHRITIS—A painful condition of the joints which results in irritation and inflammation. A disease that pretty much confines itself to older dogs, especially in the larger breeds. Limping, irritability and pain are symptomatic. Anti-inflammatory drugs are effective after X-ray determines the severity. Heat and rest are helpful.

ASCITES—A collection of serous fluid in the abdominal cavity, causing swelling. It may be a result of heavy parasitic infestation or a symptom of liver, kidney, tuberculosis or heart diseases.

ASPERGILLOSIS—A disease contracted from poultry and often mistaken for tuberculosis since symptoms are quite similar. It attacks the nervous system and sometimes has disastrous effects on the respiratory system. This fungus growth in the body tissue spreads quickly and is accompanied by convulsions. The dog rubs his nose and there is a bloody discharge.

ASTHMA—Acute distress in breathing. Attacks may occur suddenly at irregular intervals and last as long as half an hour. The condition may be hereditary or due to allergy or heart condition. Antihistamines are effective in minor attacks.

ATAXIA—Muscular incoordination or lack of movement causing an inhibited gait, although the necessary organs and muscle power are coherent. The dog may have a tendency to stagger.

ATOPY—Manifestations of atopy in the dog are a persistent scratching of the eyes and nose. Onsets are usually seasonal—the dog allergic to, say, ragweed will develop the condition when ragweed is in season, or say, house dust all year round. Most dogs afflicted with atopy are multi-sensitive and are affected by something several months out of the year. Treatment is by antihistamines or systemic corticosteroids, or both.

An important Group win under judge Louis Murr for the magnificent Ch. Galaxy's Corry Carina at the 1973 Albany Kennel Club show. Handled exclusively by Jane Forsyth for co-owners Mrs. Cheever Porter of New York City and Frank and Eleanor D'Amico. Shafer photograph.

—B—

BABESIA GIBSONI (or Babesiosis)—A parasitic disease of the tropics, reasonably rare in the U.S.A. to date. Blood tests can reveal its presence and like other parasitic infections the symptoms are loss of appetite, no pep, anemia and elevations in temperature as the disease advances, and enlarged spleen and liver are sometimes evident.

BALANITIS—The medical term for a constant discharge of pus from the penis which causes spotting of clothing or quarters or causes the dog to clean himself constantly. When bacteria gather at the end of the sheath, it causes irritations in the tissue and pus. If the condition becomes serious, the dog may be cauterized or ointment applied.

BLASTOMYCOSIS—A rare infectious disease involving the kidneys and liver. The animal loses its appetite and vomits. Laboratory examination is necessary to determine presence.

BRADYCARDIA—Abnormal slowness of the heartbeat and pulse.

BRONCHITIS—Inflammation of the mucus lining in the respiratory tract, the windpipe or trachea, and lungs. Dampness and cold are usually responsible and the symptoms usually follow a chill, or may be present with cases of pneumonia or distemper. Symptoms are a nagging dry cough, fever, quickened pulse rate, runny nose, perhaps vomiting, and congested nasal passages which must be kept open. Old dogs are particularly affected. It is a highly transmissible disease and isolation from other animals is important. Antibiotics are given.

BRUCELLA CANIS—An infectious disease associated with abortion in bitches in the last quarter of gestation, sterility or stillbirths. A comparable is testicle trouble in male dogs. It is highly contagious and can be diagnosed through blood tests and animals having the infection should be isolated.

—C—

CANCER (tumors, neoplasia, etc.)—A growth of cells which serve no purpose is referred to as a cancer. The growth may be malignant or benign. Malignancy is the spreading type growth and may invade the entire body. Treatment, if the condition is diagnosed and caught in time, may be successful by surgical methods, drugs, or radioactive therapy. Haste in consulting your veterinarian cannot be urged too strongly.

CANKER (Otitis)—A bacterial infection of the ear where the ear may drain, have a dreadful odor, and ooze a dark brown substance all the way out to the ear flap. Cause of canker can be from mites, dirt, excessive hair growth in the ear canal, wax, etc. A daily cleaning and administering of antifungal ointment or powder are in order until the condition is cured. Symptoms are the dog shaking his head, scratching his ear and holding the head to the side.

CARIES—A pathologic change causing destruction of the enamel on teeth and subsequent invasion of the dentine; in other words, a cavity in a tooth. This may result in bad breath, toothache, digestive disorders, etc., depending upon the severity. Cavities in dogs are rare, though we hear more and more of false teeth being made for dogs and occasionally even root canal work for show dogs.

CASTRATION—Surgical removal of the male gonads or sex organs. An anesthesia is necessary and the animal must be watched for at least a week to see that hemorrhage does not occur. It is best performed at an early age—anywhere from three to nine months. Older dogs suffering from a hormonal imbalance or cancer of the gonads are castrated.

CATARACT—An opaque growth covering the lens of the eye. Surgical removal is the only treatment. Cataract may be a result of an injury to the eye or in some cases may be an inherited trait.

CELLULITIS—Inflammation of the loose subcutaneous tissue of the body. A condition which can be symptomatic of several other diseases.

CHEILITIS—Inflammation of the lips.

CHOLECYSTITIS—A condition affecting the gall bladder. The onset is usually during the time an animal is suffering from infectious canine hepatitis. Removal of the gall bladder, which thickens and becomes highly vascular, can effect a complete cure.

CHOREA—Brain damage as a result of distemper which has been severe is characterized by convulsive movements of the legs. It is progressive and if it affects the facial muscles, salivating or difficulty in eating or moving the jaws may be evident. Sedatives may bring relief, but the disease is incurable.

CHOROIDITIS—Inflammation of the choroid coat of the eye which is to be regarded as serious. Immediate veterinary inspection is required.

COCCIDIOSIS—An intestinal disease of parasitic nature and origin. Microscopic organisms reproduce on the walls of the intestinal tract and destroy tissue. Bloody diarrhea, loss of weight and appetite and general lethargy result. Presence of parasites is determined by fecal examination. Sulfur drugs are administered and a complete clean up of the premises is in order since the parasite is passed from one to to another through floor surfaces or eating utensils.

COLOSTRUM—A secretion of the mammary glands for the first day or so after the bitch gives birth. It acts as a purgative for the young, and contains antibodies against distemper, hepatitis and other bacteria.

CONJUNCTIVITIS—Inflammation of the conjunctiva of the eye.

CONVULSIONS—A fit, or violent involuntary contractions of groups of muscles, accompanied by unconsciousness. They are in themselves a symptom of another disease, especially traceable to one affecting the brain; i.e., rabies, or an attack of encephalitis or distemper. It may also be the result of a heavy infestation of parasites or toxic poisonings. Care must be taken that the animal does not injure itself and a veterinarian must be consulted to determine and eliminate the cause.

Ch. Ebonaire's Honor Count winning Best of Breed under judge Mrs. August Riggs at a National Capital Kennel Club show. Bred by Ed and Judy Weiss, Honor is owned by Anita Ortiz of Brooklyn, New York. Honor was also Best of Breed at the 1962 Westminster Kennel Club show under judge Fleitmann. Her sire was Ch. Stebs Top Skipper x Ebonaire's Colonel's Lady.

Opposite:
The magnificent Ch. Damasyn The Russian, bred by Harriet Corey and owned by the Fred Ferraris of Manhassett, New York. The Russian is shown in the ring by Carol Selzle, and he was sired by Damasyn Jalli's Jaimie x Valbrook's Pink Champagne.

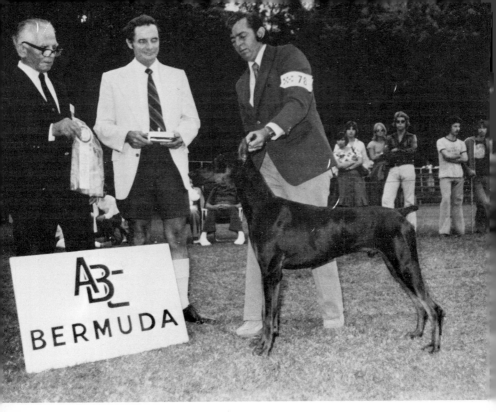

Civetta's Windfall of Kami, owned by Harry Mello, is pictured winning Best Puppy in Show at the November, 1975 Bermuda Kennel Club show under judge Louis Murr. Bred by Arnold Orlander and Kay Martin and whelped in December, 1974. Windfall is by Ch. Rosevale's Dark Temptation, American and Canadian C.D. x Lisitza's Lollipop, C.D.

CRYPTORCHID—A male animal in which neither testicle is present or descended. This condition automatically bars a dog from the show ring.

CYANOSIS—A definite blueness seen in and around the mucous membranes of the face; i.e. tongue, lips and eyes. It is usually synonymous with a circulatory obstruction or heart condition.

CYSTITIS—A disease of the urinary tract which is characterized by inflammation and/or infection in the bladder. Symptoms are straining, frequent urination with little results or with traces of blood, and perhaps a fever. Antibiotics, usually in the sulfur category, as well as antiseptics are administered. This is a condition which is of great discomfort to the animal and is of lengthy duration. Relief must be given by a veterinarian, who will empty bladder by means of catheter or medication to relax the bladder so that the urine may be passed.

—D—

DEMODECTIC MANGE—A skin condition caused by a parasitic mite, *Demodex*, living in hair follicles. This is a difficult condition to get rid of and is treated internally as well as externally. It requires diligent care to free the animal of it entirely.

DERMATITIS—There are many forms of skin irritations and eruptions but perhaps the most common is "contact dermatitis." Redness and itching are present. The irritation is due to something the animal has been exposed to and to which it is allergic. The irritant must be identified and removed. Antihistamines and anti-inflammatory drugs are administered, and in severe cases sedatives or tranquilizers are prescribed to lessen the dog's scratching.

DIABETES (Insipidus)—A deficiency of antidiuretic hormone produced by the posterior pituitary gland. It occurs in older animals and is characterized by the animal's drinking excessive amounts of water and voiding frequently. Treatment is by periodic injection of an antidiuretic drug for the rest of the animal's life.

DIABETES (Mellitus)—Sometimes referred to as sugar diabetes, this is a disorder of the metabolism of carbohydrates caused by lack of insulin production by the cells of the pancreas. Symptoms are the same as in the insipidus type, and in severe cases loss of weight, vomiting or coma may occur. Blood and urine analysis confirm its presence. It is treated by low carbohydrate diet, oral medication and/or insulin injections.

The great Dictator and his owner-handler Peggy Adamson winning the Working Group under the late Lt. Colonel Quirk at the Westminster Show, February 13, 1945.

DIGITOXIN—A medication given to a dog with congestive heart failure. Dosage is, of course, adjusted to severeness of condition and size of the individual animal.

DISC ABNORMALITIES (Intervertebral)—Between each bone in the spine is a connecting structure called an intervertebral disc. When the disc between two vertebrae becomes irritated and protrudes into the spinal canal it forms lesions and is painful. (This is a disease which particularly affects the Dachshund because of its long back in comparison to length of legs.) Paralysis of the legs, reluctance to move, and loss of control of body functions may be symptoms. X-ray and physical examination will determine extent of the condition. Massage helps circulation and pain relievers may be prescribed. Surgery is sometimes successful and portable two-wheel carts which support the hindquarters help.

DISTEMPER—Highly transmissible disease of viral origin which spreads through secretions of nose, eyes or direct oral contact. May be fatal in puppies under 12 weeks. Symptoms of this disease are alternately high and low fevers, runny eyes and nose, loss of appetite and general lassitude, diarrhea and loss of weight. This disease sometimes goes into pneumonia or convulsions if the virus reaches the brain. Chorea may remain if infection has been severe or neglected. Antibiotics are administered and fluids and sedation may be advised by your veterinarian. If the dog has been inoculated, the disease may remain a light case, BUT it is not to be treated lightly. Warmth and rest are also indicated.

DROPSY—Abnormal accumulation of fluid in the tissues or body cavities. Also referred to as edema when accumulations manifest themselves below the skin. In the stomach region it is called ascites. Lack of exercise or poor circulation, particularly in older dogs, may be the cause. While the swellings are painless, excess accumulations in the stomach can cause digestive distress or heart disturbances, and may be associated with diabetes. Occasional diarrhea, lack of appetite, loss of weight, exhaustion, emaciation and death may occur if the condition is not treated.

DYSGERMINOMA—A malignant ovarian tumor. Symptoms are fever, vaginal discharge, vomiting and diarrhea. Tumors vary in size, though more commonly are of the large size and from reports to date, the right ovary is more commonly affected. Radiotherapy may be successful; if not, surgery is required.

—E—

EAR MANGE—Otodectic mange, or parasitic otitis externa. Ear mites suck lymph fluids through the walls of the ear canal. Infections are high when mites are present and a brownish, horrible smelling ooze is present deep down in the canal all the way out to the flap where the secretion has a granular texture. The dog shakes his head, rubs and scrapes. In extreme cases convulsions

Australian Ch. Walamara Alluring Lusta, winner of over 40 challenges including the PAL International in 1974.

or brain damage may result. The ear must be cleaned daily and drugs of an antibiotic and anti-inflammatory nature must be given.

ECLAMPSIA—A toxemia of pregnancy. Shortly before the time a bitch whelps her puppies, her milk may go bad. She will pant as a result of high fever, and go into convulsions. The puppies must be taken away from the mother immediately. This is usually the result of an extreme lack of calcium during pregnancy. Also known as milk fever.

ECTROPION—All breeders of dogs with drooping eyelids or exaggerated haws will be familiar with this condition, where the lower eyelid turns out. It can be a result of an injury, as well as hereditary in some breeds, but can be corrected surgically.

ECZEMA—Eczema is another form of skin irritation which may confine itself to redness and itching, or go all the way to a scaly skin surface or open wet sores. This is sometimes referred to as "hot spots." A hormone imbalance or actual diet deficiency may prevail. Find the cause and remove it. Medicinal baths and ointments usually provide a cure, but cure is a lengthy process and the condition frequently recurs.

Ch. Damasyn The Flame, a red bitch sired by Dictator out of Damasyn The Flaming Sable. Co-breeders were Peggy Adamson and Eldon P. Prziborowski. The Flame was whelped in March of 1949. Owner, Mr. Prziborowski of San Bruno, California.

EDEMA—Abnormal collections of fluids in the tissues of the body.

ELBOW DYSPLASIA—Term applies to a developmental abnormality of the elbow joints. It is hereditary.

EMPHYSEMA—Labored breathing caused by distended or ruptured lungs. May be acute or chronic and is not uncommon.

EMPYEMA—Accumulation of pus or purulent fluid, in a body cavity resembling an abscess. Another term for pleurisy.

ENCEPHALITIS—Brain fever associated with meningitis. An inflammation of the brain caused by a virus, rabies or perhaps tuberculosis. It may also be caused by poisonous plants, bad food or lead poisoning. Dogs go "wild," running in circles, falling over, etc. Paralysis and death frequently result. Cure depends on extent of infection and speed with which it is diagnosed and treated.

ENDOCARDITIS—Inflammation and bacterial infection of the smooth membrane that lines the inside of the heart.

ENTERITIS—Intestinal inflammation of serious import. It can be massive or confine itself to one spot. Symptoms are diarrhea, bloody at times, vomiting, and general discomfort. Antibiotics are prescribed and fluids, if the diarrhea and vomiting have been excessive. Causes are varied; may follow distemper or other infections or bacterial infection through intestinal worms.

Ch. Devil Tree's Black Shaft wins the Working Group under judge Heywood Hartley and the 1975 Bucks County Kennel Club show. Jeffrey Brucker handled for owners George and Sheila West of Pound Ridge, New York.

Sundance R'Leziah, bred and owned by Faith and Charles Keiner of Jefferson City, Missouri. The sire was Ch. Damasyn Bo-Tairic x Benbridge's Castanet.

American and Canadian Ch. Brandendorg's Bold Venture winning at a show on the way to his championship. Bred, owned and handled by Marilyn Meshirer, Brandendorf Kennels, Long Island, New York.

ENTROPION—A turning in of the margin of the eyelids. As a result, the eyelashes rub on the eyeball and cause irritation resulting in a discharge from the eye. Here again it is a condition peculiar to certain breeds—particularly Chow Chows—or may be the result of an injury which failed to heal properly. Infection may result as the dog will rub his eyes and cause a swelling. It is painful, but can be cured surgically.

ENTEROTOXEMIA—A result of toxins and gases in the intestine. As bacteria increase in the intestine, intermittent diarrhea and/or constipation results from maldigestion. If the infection reaches the kidney through the circulatory system, nephritis results. The digestive system must be cleaned out by use of castor oil or colonic irrigation, and outwardly by antibiotics.

Ch. Marwood Anubis de Scudamore, C.D., multiple Best of Breed and Group winner, owned by Mrs. James Skidmore, II of the Scudamore Kennels in Norwalk, Connecticut. Jason is a red and rust dog, 27½ inches square, and is working for his C.D.X. degree.

Frankskirby Firestamm (Ch. Iceberg of Tavey x Nina van Frankskirby), owned by H. Barnett, Esquire, England. Firestamm is pictured here at one year and four months of age. This all black and tan "F" litter included: Firewald, Fireberg, Firestroll, Fire Patrol, Fire Brigade, Fire Parade and Firedobe.

One of the Top Working Dogs for three years in a row—Ch. Andelane's Indigo Rock, owned by Robert Bishop of Inkster, Michigan. Rock's offspring are following in his footsteps.

EOSINOPHILIC MYOSITIS—Inflammation of the muscles dogs use for chewing. Persistent attacks usually lasting one or more weeks. They come and go over long periods of time, coming closer and closer together. Difficulty in swallowing, swelling of the face, or even the dog holding his mouth open will indicate the onset of an attack. Anti-inflammatory drugs are the only known treatment. Cause unknown, outlook grave.

EPILEPSY—The brain is the area affected and fits and/or convulsions may occur early or late in life. It cannot be cured; however, it can be controlled with medication. Said to be hereditary. Convulsions may be of short duration or the dog may just appear to be dazed. It is rarely fatal. Care must be taken to see that the dog does not injure itself during an attack.

EPIPHORA—A constant tearing which stains the face and fur of dogs. It is a bothersome condition which is not easily remedied either with outside medication or by surgical tear duct removal. There has been some success in certain cases reported from a liquid medication given with the food and prescribed by veterinarians. This condition may be caused by any one or more of a number of corneal irritations, such as nasal malfunction or the presence of foreign matter in the superficial gland of the third eyelid. After complete examination as to the specific cause, a veterinarian can decide whether surgery is indicated.

ESOPHAGEAL DIVERTICULUM—Inflammation or sac-like protrusions on the walls of the esophagus resembling small hernias. It is uncommon in dogs, but operable, and characterized by gagging, listlessness, temperature and vomiting in some cases.

—F—

FALSE PREGNANCY (or pseudopregnancy)—All the signs of the real thing are present in this heart-breaking and frustrating condition. The bitch may even go into false labor near the end of the 63-day cycle and build a nest for her hoped-for puppies. It may be confirmed by X-ray or a gentle feeling for them through the stomach area. Hormones can be injected to relieve the symptoms.

FROSTBITE—Dead tissue as a result of extreme cold. The tissues become red, swollen and painful, and may peel away later, causing open lesions. Ointments and protective coverings should be administered until irritation is alleviated.

FUSOSPIROCHETAL DISEASE—Bad breath is the first and most formidable symptom of this disease of the mouth affecting the gums. Bloody saliva and gingivitis or ulcers in the mouth may also be present, and the dog may be listless due to lack of desire to eat. Cleaning the teeth and gums daily with hydrogen peroxide in prescribed dosage by the veterinarian is required. Further diagnosis of the disease can be confirmed by microscopic examination of smears, though these fusiform bacteria might be present in the mouth of a dog which never becomes infected. Attempts to culture these anaerobes have been unsuccessful.

—G—

GASTRIC DILATION—This is an abnormal swelling of the abdomen due to gas or overeating. Consumption of large amounts of food especially if dry foods are eaten, and then large quantities of water make the dog "swell." The stomach twists so that both ends are locked off. Vomiting is impossible, breathing is hampered and the dog suffers pain until the food is expelled. Dogs that gulp their food and swallow air with it are most susceptible. Immediate surgery may be required to prevent the stomach from bursting. Commonly known as bloat.

GASTRITIS—Inflammation of the stomach caused by many things—spoiled food which tends to turn to gas, overeating, eating foreign bodies, chemicals or even worms. Vomiting is usually the first symptom though the animal will usually drink great quantities of water which more often than not it throws back up. A 24-hour fast which eliminates the cause is the first step toward cure. If vomiting persists chunks of ice cubes put down the throat may help. Hopefully the dog will lick them himself. Keep the dog on a liquid diet for another 24 hours before resuming his regular meals.

GASTRO-ENTERITIS—Inflammation of the stomach and intestines. There is bleeding and ulceration in the stomach and this serious condition calls for immediate veterinary help.

GASTRODUODENITIS—Inflammation of the stomach and duodenum.

GINGIVITIS or gum infection—Badly tartared teeth are usually the cause of this gum infection characterized by swelling, redness at the gum line, bleeding and bloody saliva. Bad breath also. Improper diet may be a cause of it. Feeding of only soft foods as a steady diet allows the tartar to form and to irritate the gums. To effect a cure, clean the teeth and perhaps the veterinarian will also recommend antibiotics.

Ch. Kilburn
Escort, C.D.
By Ch. Emperor
x Illena of
Marienland.

GLAUCOMA—Pressure inside the eyeball builds up, the eyeball becomes hard and bulgy and a cloudiness of the entire corneal area occurs. The pupil is dilated and the eye is extremely sensitive. Blindness is inevitable unless treatment is prompt at the onset of the disease. Cold applications as well as medical prescriptions are required with also the possibility of surgery, though with no guarantee of success.

GLOSSITIS—Inflammation of the tongue.

GOITER—Enlargement of the thyroid gland, sometimes requiring surgery. In minor cases, medication—usually containing iodine— is administered.

Ch. Berman Brier, the first Doberman to win the Grand Victor award in America (in 1957 at the Chicagoland Show). This magnificent red son of Ch. Damasyn The Solitaire, C.D.X., out of Berman Aramina was owned by Bernie Berman of Monroe, New York.

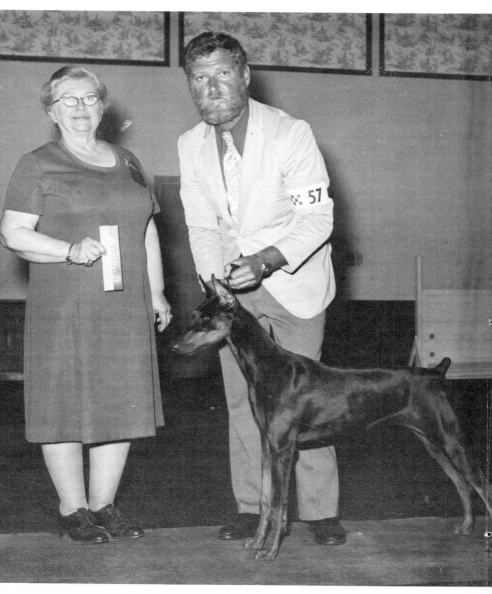

Liquorish Alfaro's Kahlua pictured winning Reserve Bitch at the 1975 Tampa Florida Specialty Show under the well-known and highly respected breeder-judge Marge Kilburn. Jeff Joffe handled for owners Charlie and Hedie Steadman of Hialeah, Florida. The sire was Ch. Liquorish The Ron Rico.

HARELIP—A malformation of the upper lip characterized by a cleft palate. Difficulty in nursing in exaggerated cases can result in starvation or puny development. Operations can be performed late in life.

HEART DISEASE—Heart failure is rare in young dogs, but older dogs which show an unusual heavy breathing after exercise or are easily tired may be victims of heart trouble, and an examination is in order. As it grows worse, wheezing, coughing or gasping may be noticed. Other symptoms indicating faulty circulation may manifest themselves as the animal retains more body fluids as the circulation slows down. Rest, less exercise, and non-fattening diets are advised and medication to remove excess fluids from the body are prescribed. In many cases, doses of digitalis may be recommended.

HEARTWORM (*Dirofilaria immitis*)—This condition does not necessarily debilitate a working dog or a dog that is extremely active. It is diagnosed by a blood test and a microscopic examination to determine the extent of the microfilariae. If positive, further differentials are made for comparison with other microfilariae. Treatment consists of considerable attention to the state of nutrition, and liver and kidney functions are watched closely in older dogs. Medication is usually treatment other than surgery and consists of dithiazine iodine therapy over a period of two weeks. Anorexia and/or fever may occur and supplemental vitamins and minerals may be indicated. Dogs with heavy infestations are observed for possible foreign protein reaction from dying and decomposing worms, and are watched for at least three months.

HEATSTROKE—Rapid breathing, dazed condition, vomiting, temperature, and collapse in hot weather indicate heatstroke. It seems to strike older dogs especially if they are overweight or have indulged in excessive activity. Reduce body temperature immediately by submerging dog in cold water, apply ice packs, cold enemas, etc. Keep dog cool and quiet for at least 24 hours.

HEMATOMA—A pocket of blood that may collect in the ear as a result of an injury or the dog's scratching. Surgery is required to remove the fluid and return skin to cartilage by stitching.

HEMOPHILIA—Excessive bleeding on the slightest provocation. Only male subjects are susceptible and it is a hereditary disease passed on by females. Blood coagulants are now successfully used in certain cases.

HEPATITIS, Infectious canine—This disease of viral nature enters the body through the mouth and attacks primarily the liver. Puppies are the most susceptible to this disease and run a fever and drink excessive amounts of water. Runny eyes, nose, vomiting, and general discomfort are symptoms. In some cases blood builders or even blood transfusions are administered since the virus has a tendency to thin the blood. This depletion of the blood often leaves the dog open to other types of infection and complete recovery is a lengthy process. Antibiotics are usually given and supplemental diet and blood builders are a help. Vaccination for young puppies is essential.

HERNIA (diaphragmatic)—An injury is usually responsible for this separation or break in the wall of the diaphragm. Symptoms depend on severity; breathing may become difficult, there is some general discomfort or vomiting. X-rays can determine the extent of damage and the only cure is surgery.

HERNIA (umbilical)—Caused by a portion of the abdominal viscera protruding through a weak spot near the navel. Tendency toward hernia is said to be largely hereditary.

Best of Breed at the 1972 Doberman Pinscher Club of America Specialty was Ch. Lu Jac's Stinger, bred and owned by Jack and Louise Strutt of Ohio. The sire was Ch. Highland Satan's Image x Highbriar Willow's Wand.

HIP DYSPLASIA—or HD is a wearing away of the ball and socket of the hip joint. It is a hereditary disease. The symptoms of this bone abnormality are a limp and an awkwardness in raising or lowering the body. X-ray will establish severity and it is wise in buying or selling a dog of any breed to insist on a radiograph to prove the animal is HD clear. The condition can be detected as early as three months and if proven the dog should have as little exercise as possible. There is no cure for this condition. Only pain relievers can be given for the more severe cases. No animal with HD should be used for breeding.

HOOKWORM—Hookworms lodge in the small intestines and suck blood from the intestinal wall. Anemia results from loss of blood. Loss of weight, pale gums, and general weakness are symptoms. Microscopic examination of the feces will determine presence.

Emphasis on diet improvement and supplements to build up the blood is necessary and, of course, medication for the eradication of the hookworms. This can be either oral or by veterinary injection.

HYDROCEPHALUS—A condition also known as "water head" since a large amount of fluid collects in the brain cavity, usually before birth. This may result in a difficult birth and the young are usually born dead or die shortly thereafter. Euthanasia is recommended on those that do survive since intelligence is absent and violence to themselves or to others is liable to occur.

HYDRONEPHROSIS—Due to a cystic obstruction the kidney collects urine which cannot be passed through the ureter into the bladder, causing the kidney to swell (sometimes to five times its normal size) and giving pain in the lumbar region. The kidney may atrophy, if the condition goes untreated.

—I—

ICHTHYOSIS—A skin condition over elbows and hocks. Scaliness and cracked skin cover the area particularly that which comes in contact with hard surfaces. Lubricating oils well rubbed into the skin and keeping the animal on soft surfaces are solutions.

IMPETIGO—Skin disease seen in puppies infested by worms, distemper, or teething problems. Little soft pimples cover the surface of the skin. Sulfur ointments and ridding the puppy of the worms are usually sufficient cure as well.

INTERDIGITAL CYSTS—Growths usually found in the legs. They are painful and cause the dog to favor the paw or not walk on it at all. Surgery is the only cure and antibiotic ointments to keep dirt and infection out are necessary.

INTESTINAL OBSTRUCTIONS—When a foreign object becomes lodged in the intestines and prevents passage of stool constipation results from the blockage. Hernia is another cause of obstruction or stoppage. Pain, vomiting, loss of appetite are symptoms. Fluids, laxatives or enemas should be given to remove blockage. Surgery may be necessary after X-ray determines cause. Action must be taken since death may result from long delay or stoppage.

IRITIS—Inflammation of the iris or colored part of the eye. May be caused by the invasion of foreign bodies or other irritants.

—J—

JAUNDICE—A yellow discoloration of the skin. Liver malfunction causes damage by bile seeping into the circulatory system and being dispensed into the body tissue, causing discoloration of the skin. It may be caused by round worms, liver flukes or gall stones. It may be either acute or chronic and the animal loses ambition, convulses or vomits, sometimes to excess. It may be cured once the cause has been eliminated. Neglect can lead to death.

Three-year-old Gayamon the Brandy Alexandra, C.D.X., owned by Grace Joffe of Miami, Florida. Brandy is a Dolph von Tannenwald daughter and the dam of the Joffe's Ch. Liquorish the Ron Rico.

—K—

KERATITIS—Infection of the cornea of the eye. Distemper or hepatitis may be a cause. Sensitivity to light, watery discharge and pain are symptomatic. Treatment depends on whether the lesion is surface irritation or a puncture of the cornea. Warm compresses may help until the veterinarian prescribes the final treatment. Sedatives or tranquilizers may be prescribed to aid in preventing the dog from rubbing the eye.

KIDNEY WORM—The giant worm that attacks the kidney and kidney tissue. It can reach a yard in length. The eggs of this rare species of worm are passed in the dog's urine rather than the feces. These worms are found in raw fish. It is almost impossible to detect them until at least one of the kidneys is completely destroyed or an autopsy reveals its presence. There is no known cure at this point and, therefore, the only alternative is not to feed raw fish.

—L—

LEAD POISONING—Ingestion of lead-based paints or products such as linoleum containing lead is serious. Symptoms are vomiting, behavior changes and/or hysteria or even convulsions in severe cases. It can be cured by medication if caught early enough. Serious damage can be done to the central nervous system. Blood samples are usually taken to determine amount in the blood. Emetics may be required if heavy intake is determined.

LEPTOSPIROSIS—This viral infection is dangerous and bothersome because it affects many organs of the body before lodging itself in the kidneys. Incubation is about two weeks after exposure to the urine of another affected dog. Temperature, or subtemperature, pain and stiffness in the hindquarters are not uncommon, nor is vomiting. Booster shots after proper vaccination at a young age are usually preventative, but once afflicted, antibiotics are essential to cure.

LOCKJAW (tetanus)—Death rate is very high in this bacterial disease. Puncture wounds may frequently develop into lockjaw. Symptoms are severe. As the disease progresses high fever and stiffness in the limbs becomes serious though the dog does not lose consciousness. Sedatives must be given to help relax the muscles and dispel the spasms. When the stiffness affects the muscles of the face, intravenous feeding must be provided. If a cure is effected, it is a long drawn out affair. Lockjaw bacteria are found in soil and in the feces of animals and humans.

LYMPHOMA (Hodgkins disease)—Malignant lymphoma most frequently is found in dogs under four years of age, affects the lymph glands, liver and spleen. Anorexia and noticeable loss of weight are apparent as well as diarrhea. Depending on area and organ, discharge may be present. The actual neoplasm or tumorous growth may be surrounded by nodules or neoplastic tissue which should be surgically removed under anesthesia.

—M—

MAMMARY NEOPLASMS—25 per cent of all canine tumors are of mammary origin. About half of all reported cases are benign. They are highly recurrent and, when cancerous, fatalities are high. Age or number of litters has nothing to do with the condition itself or the seriousness.

MANGE—The loss of a patch of hair usually signals the onset of mange, which is caused by any number of types of microscopic mites. The veterinarian will usually take scrapings to determine which of the types it is. Medicated baths and dips plus internal and external medication is essential as it spreads rapidly and with care can be confined to one part of the body. Antibiotics are prescribed.

MASTITIS (mammary gland infection)—After the birth of her young, a bitch may be beset by an infection causing inflammation of the mammary glands which produce milk for the puppies. Soreness and swelling make it painful for her when the puppies nurse. Abscess may form and she will usually run a fever. Hot compresses and antibiotics are necessary and in some instances hormone therapy.

MENINGITIS—Inflammation affecting the membranes covering the brain and/or spinal cord. It is a serious complication which may result from a serious case of distemper, tuberculosis, hardpad, head injury, etc. Symptoms are delirium, restlessness, high temperature, and dilated pupils in the eyes. Paralysis and death are almost certain.

METRITIS—This infection, or inflammation of the uterus, causes the dog to exude a bloody discharge. Vomiting and a general lassitude are symptoms. Metritis can occur during the time the bitch is in season or right after giving birth. Antibiotics are used, or in severe cases hysterectomy.

MONORCHIDISM—Having only one testicle.

MOTION SICKNESS—On land, on sea, or in the air, your dog may be susceptible to motion sickness. Yawning, or excessive salivation, may signal the onset, and there is eventual vomiting. One or all of the symptoms may be present and recovery is miraculously fast once the motion ceases. Antinauseant drugs are available for animals which do not outgrow this condition.

MYELOMA—Tumor of the bone marrow. Lameness and evidence of pain are symptoms as well as weight loss, depression and palpable tumor masses. Anemia or unnatural tendency to bleed in severe cases may be observed. The tumors may be detected radiographically, but no treatment has yet been reported for the condition.

—N—

NEONATAL K-9 HERPESVIRUS INFECTION—Though K-9 herpesvirus infection, or CHV, has been thought to be a disease of the respiratory system in adult dogs, the acute necrotizing and hemorrhagic disease occurs only in infant puppies. The virus multiplies in the respiratory system and female genital tracts of older dogs. Puppies may be affected in the vaginal canal. Unfortunately the symptoms resemble other neonatal infections, even hepatitis, and only after autopsy can it be detected.

NEPHROTIC SYNDROME—Symptoms may be moist or suppurative dermatitis, edema or hypercholesteremia. It is a disease of the liver and may be the result of another disease. Laboratory data and biopsies may be necessary to determine the actual cause if it is other than renal disease. This is a relatively uncommon thing in dogs, and liver and urinal function tests are made to determine its presence.

Gayamon the Brandy Alexandra, C.D.X. "cat-napping." This Ch. Dolph von Tannenwald daughter out of Ch. Arjean's The Fortune is owned by Grace Joffe of Miami, Florida.

NEURITIS—Painful inflammation of a nerve.

NOSEBLEED (epistaxis)—A blow or other injury which causes injury to the nasal tissues is usually the cause. Tumors, parasites, foreign bodies, such as thorns or burs or quills, may also be responsible. Ice packs will help stem the tide of blood, though coagulants may also be necessary. Transfusions in severe cases may be indicated.

—O—

ORCHITIS—Inflammation of the testes.

OSTEOGENESIS IMPERFECTA—Or "brittle bones" is a condition that can be said to be both hereditary and dietary. It may be due to lack of calcium or phosphorus or both. Radiographs show "thin" bones with deformities throughout the skeleton. Treatment depends on cause.

OSTEOMYELITIS (enostosis)—Bone infection may develop after a bacterial contamination of the bone, such as from a compound fracture. Pain and swelling denote the infection and wet sores may accompany it. Lack of appetite, fever and general inactivity can be expected. Antibiotics are advised after X-ray determines severity. Surgery eliminates dead tissue or bone splinters to hasten healing.

OTITIS—Inflammation of the ear.

—P—

PANCREATITIS—It is difficult to palpate for the pancreas unless it is enlarged, which it usually is if this disease is present. Symptoms

Alfaro's Liquorish Cutty Sark pictured winning the 9-12 Puppy Class at a 1975 DPCA show under judge Frank D'Amico. Cutty Sark was sired by Ch. Liquorish the Ron Rico x Dagmar von Davar. Owned by Grace Joffe, Liquorish Dobes, Miami, Florida.

to note are as in other gastronomic complaints such as vomiting, loss of appetite, anorexia, stomach pains and general listlessness. This is a disease of older dogs though it has been diagnosed in young dogs as well. Blood, urine and stool examination and observation of the endocrine functions of the dog are in order. Clinical diseases that may result from a serious case of pancreatitis are acute pancreatitis which involves a complete degeneration of the pancreas, atrophy, fibrous and/or neoplasia, cholecystitis. Diabetes mellitus is also a possibility.

PATELLAR LUXATION—"Trick knees" are frequent in breeds that have been "bred down" from Standard to Toy size, and is a condition where the knee bone slips out of position. It is an off again, on again condition that can happen as a result of a jump or excessive exercise. It if is persistent, anti-inflammatory drugs may be given or in some cases surgery can correct it.

PERITONITIS—Severe pain accompanies this infection or inflammation of the lining of the abdominal cavity. Extreme sensitivity to touch, loss of appetite and vomiting occur. Dehydration and weight loss is rapid and anemia is a possibility. Antibiotics should

Damasyn Tartika, C.D. was owned and trained to her obedience title by Carol Selzle of Long Island, New York. Tartika was a litter sister of American and Canadian Ch. Damasyn The Tartian and grandmother of Ch. Damasyn The Forecast.

Opposite:
Ch. Damasyn The Troycen, bred by Peggy Adamson and owned by Russ Meyer. The sire was Ch. Damasyn The Tartian x Damasyn Bo-Tassi of Ardon. He is pictured here winning the Working Group at the Bronx County Kennel Club show in 1971. He is the sire of ten champions to date with many more pointed.

kill the infection and a liquid diet for several days is advised. Pain-killers may be necessary or drainage tubes in severe cases.

PHLEBITIS—Inflammation of a vein.

PLACENTA—The afterbirth which accompanies and has been used to nourish the fetus. It is composed of three parts; the chorion, amnion, and allantois.

POLYCYTHEMIA VERA—A disease of the blood causing an elevation of hemoglobin concentration. Blood-letting has been effective. The convulsions that typify the presence can be likened to epileptic fits and last for several minutes. The limbs are stiff and the body feels hot. Mucous membranes are congested, the dog may shiver, and the skin has a ruddy discoloration. Blood samples must be taken and analyzed periodically. If medication to reduce the production of red blood cells is given, it usually means the dog will survive.

PROCTITIS—Inflammation of the rectum.

PROSTATITIS—Inflammation of the prostate gland.

PSITTACOSIS—This disease which affects birds and people has been diagnosed in rare instances in dogs. A soft, persistent cough indicates the dog has been exposed, and a radiograph will show a cloudy portion on the affected areas of the lung. Antibiotics such as aureomycin have been successful in the known cases and cure has been effected in two to three weeks' time. This is a highly contagious disease, to the point where it can be contracted during a post mortem.

PYOMETRA—This uterine infection presents a discharge of pus from the uterus. High fever may turn to below normal as the infection persists. Lack of appetite with a desire for fluids and frequent urination are evidenced. Antibiotics and hormones are known cures. In severe cases, hysterectomy is performed.

—R—

RABIES (hydrophobia)—The most deadly of all dog diseases. The Pasteur treatment is the only known cure for humans. One of the viral diseases that affects the nervous system and damages the brain. It is contracted by the intake, through a bite or cut, of saliva from an infected animal. It takes days or even months for the symptoms to appear, so it is sometimes difficult to locate, or isolate, the source. There are two reactions in a dog to this disease. In the paralytic type of rabies the dog can't swallow and salivates from a drooping jaw, and progressive paralysis eventually overcomes the entire body. The animal goes into coma and eventually dies. In the furious type of rabies the dog turns vicious, eats strange objects, in spite of a difficulty in swallowing, foams at the mouth, and searches out animals or people to attack—hence the expression "mad dog." Vaccination is available for dogs that run loose.

Examination of the brain is necessary to determine actual diagnosis.

RECTAL PROLAPSE—Diarrhea, straining from constipation or heavy infestations of parasites are the most common cause of prolapse which is the expulsion of a part of the rectum through the anal opening. It is cylindrical in shape, and must be replaced within the body as soon as possible to prevent damage. Change in diet, medication to eliminate the cause, etc. will effect a cure.

RETINAL ATROPHY—A disease of the eye that is highly hereditary and may be revealed under ophthalmoscopic examination. Eventual blindness inevitably results. Dogs with retinal atrophy should not be used for breeding. Particularly prominent in certain breeds where current breeding trends have tended to change the shape of the head.

RHINITIS—Acute or chronic inflammation of the mucous membranes of the nasal passages. It is quite common in both dogs and cats. It is seldom fatal, but requires endless "nursing" on the part of the owner for survival, since the nose passages must be kept open so the animal will eat. Dry leather on the nose though there is excessive discharge, high fever, sneezing, etc., are symptoms. Nose discharge may be bloody and the animal will refuse to eat, making it listless. The attacks may be recurrent and medication must be administered.

RICKETS—The technical name for rickets is osteomalacia and is due to not enough calcium in the body. The bones soften and the legs become bowed or deformed. Rickets can be cured if caught in early stages by improvement in diet.

RINGWORM—The dread of the dog and cat world! This is a fungus disease where the hair falls out in circular patches. It spreads rapidly and is most difficult to get rid of entirely. Drugs must be administered "inside and out!" The cure takes many weeks and much patience. Ultraviolet lights will show hairs green in color so it is wise to have your animal, or new puppy, checked out by the veterinarian for this disease before introducing him to the household. It is contracted by humans.

ROOT CANAL THERAPY—Injury to a tooth may be treated by prompt dental root canal therapy which involves removal of damaged or necrotic pulp and placing of opaque filling material in the root canal and pulp chamber.

—S—

SALIVARY CYST—Surgery is necessary when the salivary gland becomes clogged or non-functional, causing constant salivation. A swelling becomes evident under the ear or tongue. Surgery will release the accumulation of saliva in the duct of the salivary gland, though it is at times necessary to remove the salivary gland in its

Two Marks-Tey winners at the Doberman Pinscher Club of Indiana Show were Marks-Tey Larkspur, Best in Sweepstakes, and Ch. Marks-Tey The Maverick, Winners Dog for a five-point major. Both owned by their breeder Keith Walkers, Marks-Tey Dobermans, Centralia, Illinois.

entirety. Zygomatic salivary cysts are usually a result of obstructions in the four main pairs of salivary glands in the mouth. Infection is more prevalent in the parotid of the zygomatic glands located at the rear of the mouth, lateral to the last upper molars. Visual symptoms may be protruding eyeballs, pain when moving the jaw, or a swelling in the roof of the mouth. If surgery is necessary, it is done under general anesthesia and the obstruction removed by dissection. Occasionally, the zygomatic salivary gland is removed as well. Stitches or drainage tubes may be necessary or dilation of the affected salivary gland. Oral or internal antibiotics may be administered.

SCABIES—Infection from a skin disease caused by a sarcoptic mange mite.

SCURF (dandruff)—A scaly condition of the body in areas covered with hair. Dead cells combined with dried sweat and sebaceous oil gland materials.

SEBORRHEA—A skin condition also referred to as "stud tail," though studding has nothing to do with the condition. The sebaceous or oil-forming glands are responsible. Accumulation of dry skin, or scurf, is formed by excessive oily deposits while the hair becomes dry or falls out altogether.

SEPTICEMIA—When septic organisms invade the bloodstream, it is called septicemia. Severe cases are fatal as the organisms in the blood infiltrate the tissues of the body and all the body organs are affected. Septicemia is the result of serious wounds, especially joints and bones. Abscess may form. High temperature and/or shivering may herald the onset, and death occurs shortly thereafter since the organisms reproduce and spread rapidly. Close watch on all wounds, antibiotics and sulfur drugs are usually prescribed.

SHOCK (circulatory collapse)—The symptoms and severity of shock vary with the cause and nervous system of the individual dog. Severe accident, loss of blood, and heart failure are the most common cause. Keep the dog warm, quiet and get him to a veterinarian right away. Symptoms are vomiting, rapid pulse, thirst, diarrhea, "cold, clammy feeling" and then eventually physical collapse. The veterinarian might prescribe plasma transfusion, fluids, perhaps oxygen, if pulse continues to be too rapid. Tranquilizers and sedatives are sometimes used as well as antibiotics and steroids. Relapse is not uncommon, so the animal must be observed carefully for several days after initial shock.

SINUSITIS—Inflammation of a sinus gland that inhibits breathing.

SNAKEBITE—The fact must be established as to whether the bite was poisonous or non-poisonous. A horse-shoe shaped double row of toothmarks is a non-poisonous bite. A double, or two-hole puncture, is a poisonous snake bite. Many veterinarians now carry anti-venom serum and this must be injected intramuscularly almost immediately. The veterinarian will probably inject a tranquilizer and other antibiotics as well. It is usually a four-day wait before the dog is normal once again, and the swelling completely gone. During this time the dog should be kept on medication.

SPIROCHETOSIS—Diarrhea which cannot be checked through normal anti-diarrhea medication within a few days may indicate spirochetosis; while spirochetes are believed by some authorities to be present and normal to gastrointestinal tracts, unexplainable diarrhea may indicate its presence in great numbers. Large quantities could precipitate diarrhea by upsetting the normal balance of the organ, though it is possible for some dogs which are infected to have no diarrhea at all.

SPONDYLITIS—Inflammation and loosening of the vertebrae.

STOMATITIS—Mouth infection. Bleeding or swollen gums or excessive salivation may indicate this infection. Dirty teeth are usually the cause. Antibiotics and vitamin therapy are indicated; and, of course, scraping the teeth to eliminate the original cause. See also GINGIVITIS.

STRONGYLIDOSIS—Disease caused by strongyle worms that enter the body through the skin and lodge in the wall of the small intestine. Bloody diarrhea, stunted growth, and thinness are general symptoms, as well as shallow breathing. Heavy infestation or neglect leads to death. Isolation of an affected animal and medication will help eliminate the problem, but the premises must also be cleaned thoroughly since the eggs are passed through the feces.

SUPPOSITORY—A capsule comprised of fat or glycerine introduced into the rectum to encourage defecation. A paper match with the ignitible sulfur end torn off may also be used. Medicated suppositories are also used to treat inflammation of the intestine.

—T—

TACHYCARDIA—An abnormal acceleration of the heartbeat. A rapid pulse signaling a disruption in the heart action. Contact a veterinarian at once.

TAPEWORM—There are many types of tapeworms, the most common being the variety passed along by the flea. It is a white, segmented worm which lives off the wall of the dog's intestine and keeps growing by segments. Some of these are passed and can be

Lovely head studies of Mrs. Dorothy Parker's Ch. Tavey's Stormy Medallion and Ch. Hensel Midnight Max. Mrs. Parker's kennel is in Norfolk, England.

seen in the stool or adhering to the hairs on the rear areas of the dog or even in his bedding. It is a difficult worm to get rid of since, even if medication eliminates segments, the head may remain in the intestinal wall to grow again. Symptoms are virtually the same as for other worms: debilitation, loss of weight, occasional diarrhea, and general listlessness. Medication and treatment should be under the supervision of a veterinarian.

TETANUS (lockjaw)—A telarius bacillus enters the body through an open wound and spreads where the air does not touch the wound. A toxin is produced and affects the nervous system, particularly the brain or spine. The animal exhibits a stiffness, slows down considerably and the legs may be extended out beyond the body even when the animal is in a standing position. The lips have a twisted appearance. Recovery is rare. Tetanus is not common in dogs, but it can result from a bad job of tail docking or ear cropping, as well as from wounds received by stepping on rusty nails.

THALLOTOXICOSIS or thallium poisoning—Thallium sulfate is a cellular-toxic metal used as a pesticide or rodenticide and a ready cause of poisoning in dogs. Thallium can be detected in the urine by a thallium spot test or by spectrographic analysis by the veterinarian. Gastrointestinal disturbances signal the onset with vomiting, diarrhea, anorexia and stomach cramps. Sometimes a cough or difficulty in breathing occurs. Other intestinal disorders may also manifest themselves as well as convulsions. In mild cases the disease may be simply a skin eruption, depending upon the damage to the kidneys. Enlarged spleens, edema or nephrosis can develop. Antibiotics and a medication called dimercaprol are helpful, but the mortality rate is over 50 per cent.

THROMBUS—A clot in the blood vessel or the heart.

TICK PARALYSIS— Seasonal tick attacks or heavy infestations of ticks can result in a dangerous paralysis. Death is a distinct reality at this point and immediate steps must be taken to prevent total paralysis. The onset is observed usually in the hindquarters. Lack of coordination, a reluctance to walk, and difficulty in getting up can be observed. Complete paralysis kills when infection reaches the respiratory system. The paralysis is the result of the saliva of the tick excreted as it feeds.

TOAD POISONING—Some species of toads secrete a potent toxin. If while chasing a toad your dog takes it in his mouth, more than likely the toad will release the toxin from its parotid glands which will coat the mucous membranes of the dog's throat. The dog will salivate excessively, suffer prostration, cardiac arrhythmia. Some tropical and highly toxic species cause convulsions that result in death. Caught in time, there are certain drugs that can be used to counteract the dire effects. Try washing the dog's mouth with large amounts of water and get him to a veterinarian quickly.

TONSILLECTOMY—Removal of the tonsils. A solution called epine-phrine, injected at the time of surgery, makes excessive bleeding almost a thing of the past in this otherwise routine operation.

TOXEMIA—The presence of toxins in the bloodstream, which nor-mally should be eliminated by the excretory organs.

TRICHIASIS—A disease condition of the eyelids, the result of neglect of earlier infection or inflammation.

—U—

UREMIA—When poisonous materials remain in the body, because they are not eliminated through the kidneys, and are recirculated in the bloodstream. A nearly always fatal disease—sometimes within hours—preceded by convulsions and unconsciousness. Vet-erinary care and treatment are urgent and imperative.

URINARY BLADDER RUPTURE—Injury or pelvic fractures are the most common causes of a rupture in this area. Anuria usually occurs in a few days when urine backs up into the stomach area. Stomach pains are characteristic and a radiograph will determine the seriousness. Bladder is flushed with saline solution and sur-gery is usually required. Quiet and little exercise is recommended during recovery.

—V—

VENTRICULOCORDECTOMY—Devocalization of dogs, also known as aphonia. In diseases of the larynx this operation may be used. Portions of the vocal cords are removed by manual means or by electrocautery. Food is withheld for a day prior to surgery and premedication is administered. Food is again provided 24 hours after the operation. At the end of three or four months, scar tissue develops and the dog is able to bark in a subdued manner. Compli-cations from surgery are few, but the psychological effects on the animal are to be reckoned with. Suppression of the barking varies from complete to merely muted, depending on the veterinarian's ability and each individual dog's anatomy.

—W—

WHIPWORMS—Parasites that inhabit the large intestine and the ce-cum. Two to three inches in length, they appear "whip-like" and symptoms are diarrhea, loss of weight, anemia, restlessness or even pain, if the infestation is heavy enough. Medication is best prescribed by a veterinarian. Cleaning of the kennel is essential, since infestation takes place through the mouth. Whipworms reach maturity within thirty days after intake.

24. PURSUING A CAREER IN DOGS

One of the biggest joys for those of us who love dogs is to see someone we know or someone in our family grow up in the fancy and go on to enjoy the sport of dogs in later life. Many dog lovers, in addition to leaving codicils in their wills, are providing in other ways for veterinary scholarships for deserving youngsters who wish to make their association with dogs their profession.

Unfortunately, many children who have this earnest desire are not always able to afford the expense of an education that will take them through veterinary school, and they are not eligible for scholarships. In recent years, however, we have had a great innovation in this field—a college course for those interested in earning an Animal Science degree, which costs less than half of what it costs to complete veterinary courses. These students have been a boon to the veterinrians, and a number of colleges are now offering the program.

With each passing year, the waiting rooms of veterinarians have become more crowded, and the demands on the doctors' time for research, consultation, surgery and treatment have consumed more and more of the working hours over and above his regular office hours. The tremendous increase in the number of dogs and cats and other domestic animals, both in cities and in the suburbs, has resulted in an almost overwhelming consumption of veterinarians' time.

Until recently most veterinary help consisted of kennel men or women who were restricted to services more properly classified as office maintenance rather than actual veterinary assistance. Needless to say, their part in the operation of a veterinary office is both essential and appreciated, as are the endless details and volumes of paperwork capably handled by office secretaries and receptionists. However, still more of a veterinarian's duties could be handled by properly trained semiprofessionals.

With exactly this additional service in mind, many colleges are now conducting two-year courses in animal science for the training of such semiprofessionals, thereby opening a new field for animal technologists. The time saved by the assistance of these trained semiprofessionals will relieve veterinarians of the more mechanical chores

Ch. Ebonaire's Gridiron, bred by Judy Weiss of Levittown, New York. He is pictured here after going Winners Dog at the 1960 Monmouth Country Kennel Club show.

The 1963 Bundessieger Argus v Neroberg, SchH III, owned by Germany's most famous breeder and judge, Willi Rothfuss.

Joywalk's Blackfoot Brave, C.D., pictured at five months of age. The sire was American and Canadian Ch. Doberlyn's Kaiser v Kraysing x Joywalk's Ebony Heidi, C.D. Owners are Joyce and Wallace Leach, Cheshire, Connecticut.

and will allow them more time for diagnosing and general servicing of their clients.

"Delhi Tech," the State University Agricultural and Technical College at Delhi, New York, has recently graduated several classes of these technologists, and many other institutions of learning are offering comparable two-year courses at the college level. Entry requirements are usually that each applicant must be a graduate of an approved high school or have taken the State University admissions examination. In addition, each applicant for the Animal Science Technology program must have some previous credits in mathematics and science, with chemistry an important part of the science background.

The program at Delhi was a new educational venture dedicated to the training of competent technicians for employment in the biochemical field and has been generously supported by a five-year grant, designated as a "Pilot Development Program in Animal Science." This grant provided both personal and scientific equipment with such obvious good results when it was done originally pursuant to a contract with the United States Department of Health, Education, and Welfare. Delhi is a unit of the State University of New York and is accredited by the Middle States Association of Colleges and Secondary Schools. The campus provides offices, laboratories and animal quarters and is equipped with modern instruments to train technicians in laboratory animal care, physiology, pathology, microbiology, anesthesia, X-ray and germ-free techniques. Sizable animal colonies are maintained in air-conditioned quarters: animals housed include mice, rats, hamsters, guinea-pigs, gerbils and rabbits, as well as dogs and cats.

First-year students are given such courses as livestock production, dairy food science, general, organic and biological chemistry, mammalian anatomy, histology and physiology, pathogenic microbiology and quantitative and instrumental analysis, to name a few. Second year students matriculate in general pathology, animal parasitology, animal care and anesthesia, introductory psychology, animal breeding, animal nutrition, hematology and urinalysis, radiology, genetics, food sanitation and meat inspection, histological techniques, animal laboratory practices and axenic techniques. These, of course, may be supplemented by electives that prepare the student for contact with the public in the administration of these duties. Such recommended electives include public speaking, botany, animal reproduction and other related subjects.

In addition to Delhi and the colleges which got in early on the presentation of these courses, more and more universities are offering training for animal technologists. Students at the State University of Maine, for instance, receive part of their practical training at the Animal Medical Center in New York City, and after this actual experience can perform professionally immediately upon entering a veterinarian's employ.

Ch. Tara's Aventina, a lovely red owned by Frank D'Amico of Long Island, New York, pictured winning under judge Sadie Edmiston. William Gilbert photograph.

Under direct veterinary supervision they are able to perform all of the following procedures as a semi-professional:

*Recording of vital information relative to a case. This would include such information as the client's name, address, telephone number and other facts pertinent to the visit. The case history would include the breed, age of the animal, its sex, temperature, etc.

*Preparation of the animal for surgery

*Preparation of equipment and medicaments to be used in surgery.

*Preparation of medicaments for dispensing to clients on prescription of the attending veterinarian.

*Administration and application of certain medicines.

*Administration of colonic irrigations.

*Application or changing of wound dressings.

*Cleaning of kennels, exercise runs and kitchen utensils.

*Preparation of food and the feeding of patients.

*Explanation to clients on the handling and restraint of their pets, including needs for exercise, house training and elementary obedience training.

*First-aid treatment for hemorrhage, including the proper use of tourniquets

*Preservation of blood, urine and pathologic material for the purpose of laboratory examination

*General care and supervision of the hospital or clinic patients to insure their comfort.

*Nail trimming and grooming of patients.

High school graduates with a sincere affection and regard for animals and a desire to work with veterinarians and perform such clinical duties as mentioned above will find they fit in especially well. Women particularly will be useful since, over and beyond the strong maternal instinct that goes so far in the care and the recovery phase when dealing with animals, women will find the majority of the positions will be in the small animal field, their dexterity will also fit in well. Students having financial restrictions that preclude their education and licensing as full-fledged veterinarians can in this way pursue careers in an area close to their actual desire. Their assistance in the pharmaceutical field, where drug concerns deal with laboratory animals, covers another wide area for trained assistance. The career opportunities are varied and reach into job opportunities in medical centers, research institutions and government health agencies; at present, the demand for graduates far exceeds the current supply of trained personnel.

As far as the financial remunerations, yearly salaries are estimated at an average of $5,000.00 for a starting point. As for the estimate of basic college education expenses, they range from $1800.00 to $2200.00 per year for out-of-state residents, and include tuition, room and board, college fees, essential textbooks and limited personal expenses. These personal expenses, of course, will vary with individual students, as well as the other expenses, but we present an average. It is obvious that the costs are about half of the costs involved in becoming a full-fledged veterinarian, however.

Damasyn The King of Trumps was owned by Dorothy Bowden of New York City. His sire was Ch. Damasyn The Solitaire, C.D.X., and the dam was Eldorado Rowana.

Ch. Von Mac's Manoc pictured winning at a 1971 show with handler Betty Moore. Manoc is owned by J. Clifford Beardsmore of Houston, Texas.

PART TIME KENNEL WORK

Youngsters who do not wish to go on to become veterinarians or animal technicians can get valuable experience and extra money by working part-time after school and weekends, or full-time during summer vacations, in a veterinarian's office. The exposure to animals and office procedure will be time well spent.

Another great help to veterinarians has been the housewife who loves animals and wishes to put in some time at a job away from the house, especially if her children are grown or away at college. If she can clean up in her own kennel she can certainly clean up in a veterinarian's office, and she will learn much about handling and caring for her own animals while she is making money.

Kennel help is also an area that is wide open for retired men. They are able to help out in many areas where they can learn and stay active, and most of the work allows them to set their own pace.

The gentility that age and experience brings is also beneficial to the animals they will deal with; for their part, the men find great reward in their contribution to animals and will be keeping their hand in the business world as well.

PROFESSIONAL HANDLERS

For those who wish to participate in the sport of dogs and whose interests or abilities do not center around the clinical aspects of the fancy, there is yet another avenue of involvement.

For those who excel in the show ring, who enjoy being in the limelight and putting their dogs through their paces, a career in professional handling may be the answer. Handling may include a weekend of showing a few dogs for special clients, or it may be a full-time career which can also include boarding, training, conditioning, breeding and showing of dogs for several clients.

Depending on how deeply your interest runs, the issue can be solved by a lot of preliminary consideration before it becomes necessary to make a decision. The first move would to to have a long, serious talk with a successful professional handler to learn the pros and cons of such a profession. Watching handlers in action from ringside as they perform their duties can be revealing. A visit to their kennels for

Ch. Talacon Daisy Upsula winning Best in Show at the 1975 Newton Kennel Club Show. Daisy was the winner of Best of Breed at the Independant Specialty Show of the Quaker City Doberman Pinscher Club, and is owned by Joseph and Barbara Micallef.

Ch. Lauritz vom Ahrtal is pictured winning Best of Opposite Sex and Best of Winners at a 1974 show under judge Frank D'Amico. Owner-breeder-handler is Tess Henseler, Ahrtal Kennels, Ottsville, Pennsylvania. Lauritz was seven years old at the time of this win. His sire was Ch. Felix vom Ahrtal x Cristel vom Ahrtal.

Ch. Beth v Glenhugel, litter sister in the famous "B" litter including champions Bengal, Binchin and Berta von Glenhugel (all reds), and the famous Ch. Domossi of Marienland.

Ch. Domani's Prince William is pictured winning on the way to his championship at a recent show. Handling for owners Dee Chiantella and Phil Cardaro is Jeffrey Lynn Brucker. The sire was American and Canadian Ch. Hotai Sweet William x Ch. Housecarl Helene of Diversha.

Opposite:

The magnificent Ch. Rancho Dobe's Storm, twice winner of the coveted Best in Show award at the Westminster Kennel Club Show in Madison Square Garden in New York City. Stormie's back-to-back wins in 1952 and 1953 were testimony to this great dog's elegance and style. Always handled by Peter Knoop for owner Len Carey of Greenwich, Connecticut.

an on-the-spot revelation of the behind-the-scenes responsibilities is essential! And working for them full or part time would be the best way of all to resolve any doubt you might have!

Professional handling is not all glamour in the show ring. There is plenty of "dirty work" behind the scenes 24 hours of every day. You must have the necessary ability and patience for this work, as well as the ability and patience to deal with CLIENTS—the dog owners who value their animals above almost anything else and would expect a great deal from you in the way of care and handling. The big question you must ask yourself first of all is: do you *really* love dogs enough to handle it. . .

DOG TRAINING

Like the professional handler, the professional dog trainer has a most responsible job! You not only need to be thoroughly familiar with the correct and successful methods of training a dog but also

Ch. Ebonaire's Fine n' Dandy wins the Best of Breed ribbon at a Suffolk County Kennel Club show under judge Cassavoy. The sire was Ch. Ebonaire's Entertainer x Carla v Westerwald.

Ch. The Sundance Kid, sired by Ch. Damasyn Carly of Jerseystone x Damasyn The Tartnsweet. Sundance finished with four majors before he was two years of age.

must have the ability to communicate with dogs. True, it is very rewarding work, but training for the show ring, obedience, or guard dog work must be done exactly right for successful results to maintain a business reputation.

Training schools are quite the vogue nowadays, with all of them claiming success. But careful investigation should be made before enrolling a dog. . . and even more careful investigation should be made of their methods and of their actual successes before becoming associated with them.

GROOMING PARLORS

If you do not wish the 24-hour a day job which is required by a professional handler or professional trainer, but still love working with and caring for dogs, there is always the very profitable grooming business. Poodles started the ball rolling for the swanky, plush grooming establishments which sprang up like mushrooms all over the major cities, many of which seem to be doing very well. Here again, handling dogs and the public is necessary for a successful operation, as well as skill in the actual grooming of the dogs, and of all breeds.

While shops flourish in the cities, some of the suburban areas are now featuring mobile units which by appointment will visit your home with a completely equipped shop on wheels and will groom your dog right in your own driveway!

THE PET SHOP

Part-time or full-time work in a pet shop can help you make up your mind rather quickly as to whether or not you would like to have a shop of your own. For those who love animals and are concerned with their care and feeding, the pet shop can be a profitable and satisfying association. Supplies which are available for sale in these shops are almost limitless, and a nice living can be garnered from pet supplies if the location and population of the city you choose warrant it.

DOG JUDGING

There are also those whose professions or age or health prevent them from owning or breeding or showing dogs, and who turn to judging at dog shows after their active years in the show ring are no longer possible. Breeder-judges make a valuable contribution to the fancy by judging in accordance with their years of experience in the fancy, and the assignments are enjoyable. Judging requires experience, a good eye for dogs and an appreciation of a good animal.

MISCELLANEOUS

If you find all of the aforementioned too demanding or not within your abilities, there are still other aspects of the sport for you to enjoy and participate in at will. Writing for the various dog magazines, books or club newsletters, dog photography, portrait painting, club activities, making dog coats, or needlework featuring dogs, typing pedigrees or perhaps dog walking. All, in their own way, contribute to the sport of dogs and give great satisfaction. Perhaps, where Samoyeds are concerned, you may wish to learn to train for racing, or sled hauling, or you might even wish to learn the making of the sleds!

25. GLOSSARY OF DOG TERMS

ACHILLES HEEL—The major tendon attaching the muscle of the calf from the thigh to the hock

AKC—The American Kennel Club. Address: 51 Madison Avenue, N.Y., N.Y. 10010

ALBINO—Pigment deficiency, usually a congenital fault, which renders skin, hair and eyes pink

AMERICAN KENNEL CLUB—Registering body for canine world in the United States. Headquarters for the stud book, dog registrations, and federation of kennel clubs. They also create and enforce the rules and regulations governing dog shows in the U.S.A.

ALMOND EYE—The shape of the eye opening, rather than the eye itself, which slants upwards at the outer edge, hence giving it an almond shape

ANUS—Anterior opening found under the tail for purposes of alimentary canal elimination

ANGULATION—The angles formed by the meeting of the bones

APPLE-HEAD—An irregular roundedness of topskull. A domed skull

APRON—On long-coated dogs, the longer hair that frills outward from the neck and chest

BABBLER—Hunting dog that barks or howls while out on scent

BALANCED—A symmetrical, correctly proportioned animal; one with correct balance with one part in regard to another

BARREL—Rounded rib section; thorax; chest

BAT EAR—An erect ear, broad at base, rounded or semicircular at top, with opening directly in front

BAY—The howl or bark of the hunting dog

BEARD—Profuse whisker growth

BEAUTY SPOT—Usually roundish colored hair on a blaze of another color. Found mostly between the ears

BEEFY—Overdevelopment or overweight in a dog, particularly hindquarters

BELTON—A color designation particularly familiar to Setters. An intermingling of colored and white hairs

BITCH—The female dog

Best in Show winner at the 1976 San Paolo, Brazil show was Alisaton's Infra Red, owned by Professor Strenger of San Paolo. The judge was the German Doberman fancier Hans Wilberhauser. The sire was Damasyn The Troycen x a Bo-Tairic daughter, Ch. Arabar's Impertinence.

Opposite:

Ch. Egothel's All-American, a typy prepotent sire of champions that has passed on the quality and showmanship of his forebearers. "Bruno" has the same substance and temperament attributed to Top Skipper, Storm, Dictator, and Delegate, all of which can be found in his illustrious pedigree. His contribution to the breed is an important one. Owned by Bernard J. Gallagher, Philadelphia, Pennsylvania.

BLAZE—A type of marking. White strip running up the center of the face between the eyes

BLOCKY—Square head

BLOOM—Dogs in top condition are said to be "in full bloom"

BLUE MERLE—A color designation. Blue and gray mixed with black. Marbled-like appearance

BOSSY—Overdevelopment of the shoulder muscles

BRACE—Two dogs which move as a pair in unison

BREECHING—Tan-colored hair on inside of the thighs

Elfred's Telstar going Best of Winners at the 1963 Black Mountain Kennel Club show. Bred by Ellen Hoffman, Telstar's sire was Ch. Elfred's Spark Plug x Elfred's Joy. The owner is Jane N. Benfield of Alexandria, Virginia. Telstar was the foundation stud for her breeding program.

BRINDLE—Even mixture of black hairs with brown, tan or gray

BRISKET—The forepart of the body below the chest

BROKEN COLOR—A color broken by white or another color

BROKEN-HAIRED—A wiry coat

BROKEN-UP FACE—Receding nose together with deep stop, wrinkle, and undershot jaw

BROOD BITCH—A female used for breeding

BRUSH—A bushy tail

BURR—Inside part of the ear which is visible to the eye

BUTTERFLY NOSE—Parti-colored nose or entirely flesh color

BUTTON EAR—The edge of the ear which folds to cover the opening of the ear

CANINE—Animals of the family Canidae which includes not only dogs but foxes, wolves, and jackals

CANINES—The four large teeth in the front of the mouth often referred to as fangs

CASTRATE—The surgical removal of the testicles on the male dog

CAT-FOOT—Round, tight, high-arched feet said to resemble those of a cat

CHARACTER—The general appearance or expression said to be typical of the breed

CHEEKY—Fat cheeks or protruding cheeks

CHEST—Forepart of the body between the shoulder blades and above the brisket

CHINA EYE—A clear blue wall eye

CHISELED—A clean cut head, especially when chiseled out below the eye

CHOPS—Jowls or pendulous lips

CLIP—Method of trimming coats according to individual breed standards

CLODDY—Thick set or plodding dog

CLOSE-COUPLED—A dog short in loins; comparatively short from withers to hipbones

COBBY—Short-bodied; compact

COLLAR—Usually a white marking, resembling a collar, around the neck

CONDITION—General appearance of a dog showing good health, grooming and care

CONFORMATION—The form and structure of the bone or framework of the dog in comparison with requirements of the Standard for the breed

CORKY—Active and alert dog

COUPLE—Two dogs

COUPLING—Leash or collar-ring for a brace of dogs

COUPLINGS—Body between withers and the hipbones indicating either short or long coupling

COW HOCKED—when the hocks turn toward each other and sometimes touch

CRANK TAIL—Tail carried down

CREST—Arched portion of the back of the neck

CROPPING—Cutting or trimming of the ear leather to get ears to stand erect

CROSSBRED—A dog whose sire and dam are of two different breeds

CROUP—The back part of the back above the hind legs. Area from hips to tail

CROWN—The highest part of the head; the topskull

CRYPTORCHID—Male dog with neither testicle visible

CULOTTE—The long hair on the back of the thighs

CUSHION—Fullness of upper lips

DAPPLED—Mottled marking of different colors with none predominating

DEADGRASS—Dull tan color

DENTITION—Arrangement of the teeth

DEWCLAWS—Extra claws, or functionless digits on the inside of the four legs; usually removed at about three days of age

DEWLAP—Loose, pendulous skin under the throat

DISH-FACED—When nasal bone is so formed that nose is higher at the end than in the middle or at the stop

DISQUALIFICATION—A dog which has a fault making it ineligible to compete in dog show competition

DISTEMPER TEETH—Discolored or pitted teeth as a result of having had distemper

DOCK—To shorten the tail by cutting

DOG—A male dog, though used freely to indicate either sex

1973 Best of Breed at the Doberman Pinscher Club of America Specialty Show was Ch. Brown's B-Brien under judge Robert Wills. This was a win he repeated at the 1975 show under judge Peggy Adamson. Owned by Eleanor Brown.

DOMED—Evenly rounded in topskull; not flat but curved upward

DOWN-FACED—When nasal bone inclines toward the tip of the nose

DOWN IN PASTERN—Weak or faulty pastern joints; a let-down foot

DROP EAR—The leather pendant which is longer than the leather of the button ear

DRY NECK—Taut skin

DUDLEY NOSE—Flesh-colored or light brown pigmentation in the nose

ELBOW—The joint between the upper arm and the forearm

ELBOWS OUT—Turning out or off the body and not held close to the sides

EWE NECK—Curvature of the top of neck

EXPRESSION—Color, size and placement of the eyes which give the dog the typical expression associated with his breed

FAKING—Changing the appearance of a dog by artificial means to make it more closely resemble the Standard. White chalk to whiten fur, etc.

FALL—Hair which hangs over the face

FEATHERING—Long hair fringe on ears, legs, tail, or body

FEET EAST AND WEST—Toes turned out

FEMUR—The large heavy bone of the thigh

FIDDLE FRONT—Forelegs out at elbows, pasterns close, and feet turned out

FLAG—A long-haired tail

FLANK—The side of the body between the last rib and the hip

FLARE—A blaze that widens as it approaches the topskull

FLAT BONE—When girth of the leg bones is correctly elliptical rather than round

FLAT-SIDED—Ribs insufficiently rounded as they meet the breastbone

FLEWS—Upper lips, particularly at inner corners

FOREARM—Bone of the foreleg between the elbow and the pastern

FOREFACE—Front part of the head, before the eyes; muzzle

FROGFACE—Usually overshot jaw where nose is extended by the receding jaw

FRINGES—Same as feathering

FRONT—Forepart of the body as viewed head-on

FURROW—Slight indentation or median line down center of the skull to the top

GAY TAIL—Tail carried above the top line

GESTATION—The period during which the bitch carries her young; 63 days in the dog

GOOSE RUMP—Too steep or sloping a croup

GRIZZLE—Bluish-gray color

GUN-SHY—When a dog fears gun shots

GUARD HAIRS—The longer stiffer hairs which protrude through the undercoat

HARD-MOUTHED—The dog that bites or leaves tooth marks on the game he retrieves

HARE-FOOT—A narrow foot

HARLEQUIN—A color pattern, patched or pied coloration, predominantly black and white

HAW—A third eyelid or membrane at the inside corner of the eye

HEEL—The same as the hock

HEIGHT—Vertical measurement from the withers to the ground, or shoulder to the ground

HOCK—The tarsus bones of the hind leg which form the joint between the second thigh and the metatarsals.

HOCKS WELL LET DOWN—When distance from hock to the ground is close to the ground

HOUND—Dog commonly used for hunting by scent

HOUND-MARKED—Three-color dogs; white, tan and black, predominating color mentioned first

HUCKLEBONES—The top of the hipbones

HUMERUS—The bone of the upper arm

Ch. Brigum of Jan Har, owned by Jane MacDonald and photographed in the 1950's.

INBREEDING—The mating of closely related dogs of the same standard, usually brother to sister

INCISORS—The cutting teeth found between the fangs in the front of the mouth

ISABELLA—Fawn or light bay color

KINK TAIL—A tail which is abruptly bent, appearing to be broken

KNUCKLING-OVER—An insecurely knit pastern joint often causes irregular motion while dog is standing still

LAYBACK—Well placed shoulders

LAYBACK—Receding nose accompanied by an undershot jaw

LEATHER—The flap of the ear

LEVEL BITE—The front or incisor teeth of the upper and lower jaws meet exactly

Tedell Nottingham Palace, whelped in July, 1973 was sired by Ch. Tedell Indulto x Ch. Balmoral Bonnet of Norlock. At the end of 1975 his record was two Specialty Shows, plus several other Bests of Breed and Group Placings. He is a fifth generation descendant from Theodora Linck's Ch. Highbriar Blackbird, C.D.

LINE BREEDING—The mating of related dogs of the same breed to a common ancestor. Controlled inbreeding. Usually grandmother to grandson, or grandfather to granddaughter.

LIPPY—Lips that do not meet perfectly

LOADED SHOULDERS—When shoulder blades are out of alignment due to overweight or overdevelopment on this particular part of the body

LOIN—The region of the body on either side of the vertebral column between the last ribs and the hindquarters

LOWER THIGH—Same as second thigh

LUMBER—Excess fat on a dog

LUMBERING—Awkward gait on a dog

MANE—Profuse hair on the upper portion of neck

MANTLE—Dark-shaded portion of the coat or shoulders, back and sides

MASK—Shading on the foreface

MEDIAN LINE—Same as furrow

MOLARS—Rear teeth used for actual chewing

MOLERA—Abnormal ossification of the skull

MONGREL—Puppy or dog whose parents are of two different breeds

MONORCHID—A male dog with only one testicle apparent

MUZZLE—The head in front of the eyes—this includes nose, nostrils and jaws as well as the foreface

The start of something good. . . Ch. Alisaton's Kinderwicke got herself talked about at the 1973 Doberman Pinscher Club of America National Specialty Show when she jumped into the arms of her 17-year-old owner-breeder-handler, Gwyn Lynn Satalino, after winning Best of Winners from the Bred by Exhibitor Class. This marvelous trick has gotten Kinderwicke talked about at all the shows when she does her famous jump every time she wins!

Ch. Castle Lane Querida Miranda pictured winning the Grand Futurity Stakes at the 1972 DPCA Specialty Show under judge Charles A.T. O'Neill over an entry of 172 dogs. Judy Doniere handled and is co-owner of Miranda with Doris Booher. Breeder was Shirley Clardy. Eleanor Brown presents the trophy. Miranda's sire was Ch. Damasyn Carly of Jerseystone x Damasyn Tartnsweet.

MUZZLE-BAND—White markings on the muzzle

NICTITATING EYELID—The thin membrane at the inside corner of the eye which is drawn across the eyeball. Sometimes referred to as the third eyelid

NOSE—Scenting ability

OCCIPUT—The upper crest or point at the top of the skull

OCCIPITAL PROTUBERANCE—The raised occiput itself

OCCLUSION—The meeting or bringing together of the upper and lower teeth.

OLFACTORY—Pertaining to the sense of smell

OTTER TAIL—A tail that is thick at the base, with hair parted on under side

OUT AT SHOULDER—The shoulder blades are set in such a manner that the joints are too wide, hence jut out from the body

OUTCROSSING—The mating of unrelated individuals of the same breed

OVERHANG—A very pronounced eyebrow

OVERSHOT—The front incisor teeth on top overlap the front teeth of the lower jaw. Also called pig jaw.

PACK—Several hounds kept together in one kennel

PADDLING—Moving with the forefeet wide, to encourage a body roll motion

PADS—The underside, or soles, of the feet

Ch. Alcor von Millsdod photographed at 17½ months of age. Alcor was one of the greats of yesteryear.

Telstar's Sassy Sister winning Best in Match at a Potomac Valley Doberman Pinscher Club of Northern Virginia Match Show. The sire was Ch. Elfred's Golden Nugget x Elfred's Prim-A-Dona. Owner-handler, Jane N. Benfield, Telstar Dobermans, Alexandria, Virginia.

PARTI-COLORED—Variegated in patches of two or more colors
PASTERN—The collection of bones forming the joint between the radius and ulna and the metacarpals
PEAK—Same as occiput
PENCILING—Black lines dividing the tan colored hair on the toes
PIED—Comparatively large patches of two or more colors. Also called parti-colored or piebald
PIGEON-BREAST—A protruding breastbone
PIG JAW—Jaw with overshot bite
PILE—The soft hair in the undercoat
PINCER BITE—A bite where the incisor teeth meet exactly
PLUME—A feathered tail which is carried over the back
POINTS—Color on face, ears, legs and tail in contrast to the rest of the body color
POMPON—Rounded tuft of hair left on the end of the tail after clipping
PRICK EAR—Carried erect and pointed at tip

PUPPY—Dog under one year of age

QUALITY—Refinement, fineness

QUARTERS—Hind legs as a pair

RACY—Tall, of comparatively slight build

RAT TAIL—The root thick and covered with soft curls—tip devoid of
hair or having the appearance of having been clipped

RINGER—A substitute for close resemblance

RING TAIL—Carried up and around and almost in a circle

ROACH BACK—Convex curvature of back

Ch. Brown's Gi Gi photographed at 11 years of age, a result of a brother-sister breeding (sired by Ch. Brown's Dion out of Ch. Brown's Bridget). Owned by Eleanor Brown of St. Charles, Missouri.

ROAN—A mixture of colored hairs with white hairs. Blue roan, orange roan, etc.

ROMAN NOSE—A nose whose bridge has a convex line from forehead to nose tip. Ram's nose

ROSE EAR—Drop ear which folds over and back revealing the burr

ROUNDING—Cutting or trimming the ends of the ear leather

RUFF—The longer hair growth around the neck

SABLE—A lacing of black hair in or over a lighter ground color

SADDLE—A marking over the back, like a saddle

SCAPULA—The shoulder blade

SCREW TAIL—Naturally short tail twisted in spiral formation

Ch. Ebonaire's Mr. Esquire (bred by Judy and Ed Weiss) wins Best in Show at the 1966 Newton Kennel Club show under judge Marie Meyer. The owner is Harry Wagner; the sire was Ch. Ebonaire's Entertainer x Ebonaire's Joyeuse Noel.

SCISSORS BITE—A bite in which the upper teeth just barely overlap the lower teeth

SELF COLOR—One color with lighter shadings

SEMIPRICK EARS—Carried erect with just the tips folding forward

SEPTUM—The line extending vertically between the nostrils

SHELLY—A narrow body which lacks the necessary size required by the Breed Standard

SICKLE TAIL—Carried out and up in a semicircle

SLAB SIDES—Insufficient spring of ribs

SLOPING SHOULDER—The shoulder blade which is set obliquely or "laid back"

SNIPEY—A pointed nose

SNOWSHOE FOOT—Slightly webbed between the toes

SOUNDNESS—The general good health and appearance of a dog in its entirety

SPAYED—A female whose ovaries have been removed surgically

SPECIALTY CLUB—An organization to sponsor and promote an individual breed

SPECIALTY SHOW—A dog show devoted to the promotion of a single breed

SPECTACLES—Shading or dark markings around the eyes or from eyes to ears

SPLASHED—Irregularly patched color on white or vice versa

SPLAY FOOT—A flat or open-toed foot

SPREAD—The width between the front legs

SPRING OF RIBS—The degree of rib roundness

SQUIRREL TAIL—Carried up and curving slightly forward

STANCE—Manner of standing

STARING COAT—Dry harsh hair, sometimes curling at the tips

STATION—Comparative height of a dog from the ground—either high or low

STERN—Tail of a sporting dog or hound

STERNUM—Breastbone

STIFLE—Joint of hind leg between thigh and second thigh. Sometimes called the ham

STILTED—Choppy, up-and-down gait of straight-hocked dog

STOP—The step-up from nose to skull between the eyes

STRAIGHT-HOCKED—Without angulation; straight behind

SUBSTANCE—Good bone. Or in good weight, or well muscled dog

SUPERCILIARY ARCHES—The prominence of the frontal bone of the skull over the eye

Marks-Tey Black Gold taking the Winners Bitch award at the 1975 Blackhawk Kennel Club show in Amboy, Illinois, under judge Mabel M. Sheppard. She is by Ch. Marks-Tey Shawn, C.D., x Ch. Marks-Tey Vale. Owner is Sue Shumway of Rockford, Illinois.

Ch. Tedell Black Chiffon is pictured winning at a Battle Creek Kennel Club show. She was sired by Ch. Ru-Mars Morgansonne, C.D. x Highbriar Ionia, a litter sister to Ch. Highbriar Valencia. Owned by Theodora Linck, Tedell Kennels, Toledo, Ohio.

SWAYBACK—Concave curvature of the back between the withers and the hipbones

TEAM—Four dogs usually working in unison

THIGH—The hindquarter from hip joint to stifle

THROATINESS—Excessive loose skin under the throat

THUMB-MARKS—Black spots in the tan markings on the pasterns

TICKED—Small isolated areas of black or colored hairs on a white background

TIMBER—Bone, especially of the legs

TOPKNOT—Tuft of hair on the top of head

TRIANGULAR EYE—The eye set in surrounding tissue of triangular shape. A three-cornered eye

TRI-COLOR—Three colors on a dog, white, black and tan

TRUMPET—Depression or hollow on either side of the skull just behind the eye socket; comparable to the temple area in man

TUCK-UP—Body depth at the loin

TULIP EAR—Ear carried erect with slight forward curvature along the sides

TURN-UP—Uptilted jaw

TYPE—The distinguishing characteristics of a dog to measure its worth against the Standard for the breed

UNDERSHOT—The front teeth of the lower jaw overlapping or projecting beyond the front teeth of the upper jaw

UPPER-ARM—The humerus bone of the foreleg between the shoulder blade and forearm

VENT—Tan-colored hair under the tail

WALLEYE—A blue eye also referred to as a fish or pearl eye

WEAVING—When the dog is in motion, the forefeet or hind feet cross

WEEDY—A dog too light of bone

WHEATEN—Pale yellow or fawn color

WHEEL-BACK—Back line arched over the loin; roach back

WHELPS—Unweaned puppies

WHIP TAIL—Carried out stiffly straight and pointed

WIRE-HAIRED—A hard wiry coat

WITHERS—The peak of the first dorsal vertebra; highest part of the body just behind the neck

WRINKLE—Loose, folding skin on forehead and/or foreface

INDEX